THE LOEB CLASSICAL LIBRARY

FOUNDED BY JAMES LOEB

EDITED BY

G. P. GOOLD

GREEK ELEGIAC POETRY

LCL 258

GREEK ELEGIAC POETRY

FROM THE SEVENTH TO THE FIFTH CENTURIES BC

EDITED AND TRANSLATED BY

DOUGLAS E. GERBER

HARVARD UNIVERSITY PRESS
CAMBRIDGE, MASSACHUSETTS
LONDON, ENGLAND
1999

Library of Congress Cataloging-in-Publication Data

Greek elegiac poetry : from the seventh to the fifth centuries BC
/ edited and translated by Douglas E. Gerber.
p.   cm.—(The Loeb classical library ; 258)
Includes bibliographical references
ISBN 0-674-99582-1
1. Elegiac poetry, Greek—Translations into English.
I. Gerber, Douglas E.
II. Series.
PA3623.E44G75   1999
881′.0108—dc21
98-26152

CONTENTS

CONTENTS

PREFACE

This volume aims at providing a text and translation of the elegiac poets contained in the second edition of M. L. West's two volumes, *Iambi et Elegi Graeci* (Oxford 1989 and 1992). For various reasons, however, a number of poets have been omitted. West includes four of the Seven Sages (Bias, Chilon, Periander, Pittacus) who are reported to have composed elegies, but nothing has survived. Several of the poets in Campbell's Loeb *Greek Lyric* also composed elegies and these are included in his volumes. The poets involved and the location of their elegies in his five volumes are as follows: Anacreon (ii.146-49), Aristotle (v.218-19), Clonas (ii.330-33 s.v. Polymnestus), Echembrotus (iii.200-201), Ion (iv.360-67), Melanippides (v.14-15), Olympus (ii.272-73), Polymnestus (ii.330-31), Sacadas (iii.202-205), Sappho (i.2-7), Simonides (iii.506-19), Sophocles (iv.330-33), Timocreon (iv.94-97). Some minor poets were not included because of space limitations. Finally, Antimachus has been omitted, since it would be more appropriate to include his elegiac fragments in a translation of his entire remains.

I have not attempted to include all the testimonia, but only those that are significant. Similarly, the apparatus criticus is reduced to what I have judged most important. In some instances a fragment is cited or referred to in several sources, but only the most important are given. The reader can find the others in the editions of West or Gentili-Prato. The numbering of the fragments follows West, that of the testimonia is my own. In my translations I have attempted to provide an English rendering which represents the Greek as closely as possible without being stilted or ambiguous.

It remains to express my deep gratitude to Professors Christopher Brown, Leslie Murison, William Race, Robert Renehan, and Emmet Robbins, who read and commented on substantial portions. Their generosity and expertise are much appreciated.

University of Western Ontario   Douglas E. Gerber

For Joan
uxori singulari

INTRODUCTION

In English the word 'elegy' has strong threnodic over-tones, but that clearly is not true of most of the poems in this volume.[1] Almost any topic, apart from the scurrilous or obscene, was considered suitable for archaic elegy and in this period it is therefore more appropriate to define elegy as simply a poem composed in elegiac couplets.[2] Most of the poems in this volume were presumably composed for performance at symposia and therefore would seldom have exceeded 100 verses, but there is also evidence for elegies of much greater length, poems dealing with the history of a particular state,[3] although none of these has survived intact. In all likelihood these were delivered at public festivals, perhaps for competition. We have an in-

[1] The discussion that follows reproduces much that is in my section on elegy in D. E. Gerber (ed.), *A Companion to the Greek Lyric Poets* (Leiden 1997) 91-132. In addition to the bibliography cited there see K. Bartol, *Greek Elegy and Iambus. Studies in Ancient Literary Sources* (Poznan 1993).

[2] For a succinct account of its metrical characteristics see M. L. West, *Greek Metre* (Oxford 1982) 44-46.

[3] Mimnermus' *Smyrneis* (see frr. 13, 13a and test. 10) may be an example. See also Tyrtaeus test. 1 with n. 3. Simonides' elegiac poem on the battle of Plataea (frr. 10-17 *IEG*[2]) may well be of considerable length.

scription commemorating the victory in the Pythian games of 586 won by Echembrotus of Arcadia, "singing songs and elegies" (ἀείδων μέλεα καὶ ἐλέγους),[4] but we are not told of the content of these elegies.

In the passage just cited we have the earliest example of the word ἔλεγος (*elegos*). It next appears in Euripides and Aristophanes where the meaning is similar to that of its English derivative, namely, a poem or song of lamentation. This, however, is probably a later development, prompted perhaps by the regular practice in the fifth century of composing epigrams on the dead in elegiac couplets. In the inscription of Echembrotus there is nothing to indicate the contents of his elegies. The contrast with μέλεα (songs) may point to a difference in musical accompaniment, the former accompanied by a stringed instrument and the latter by a wind instrument, but it is also possible that *elegos* is here essentially a metrical term. Such is clearly the meaning in one of the earliest occurrences of ἐλεγεῖον (*elegeion*), since Critias (see fr. 4) states that Alcibiades' name cannot be accommodated ἐλεγείῳ, i.e., either to the elegiac couplet as a whole or more specifically to the pentameter. In the fourth century we meet the form ἐλεγεία (*elegeia*), as in the introduction to Solon frr. 4a and 4b, and here too it is a metrical term. In fact, *elegeion* and *elegeia* are essentially synonyms, denoting a poem or, in the plural, a collection of poems in elegiac couplets.

The etymology of *elegos* is unclear. The ancient lexicographers postulated a variety of derivations, and others have been proposed by modern scholars, the likeliest being a

[4] For the full text and a translation see Gerber, *Companion* p. 94, or Campbell's Loeb *Greek Lyric* iii.200 f.

derivation from Armenian *elegn*, reed. A reed instrument, the *aulos* (pipe or oboe),[5] was certainly used to accompany elegies at times and, although the evidence is somewhat problematic, I agree with those who argue that it provided the regular accompaniment.

Callinus

Callinus was a native of Ephesus in Ionia and can be dated to the middle of the 7th century. Strabo (test. 1) claims that he is older than Archilochus because the latter referred to the destruction of the Magnesians, whereas Callinus mentions their prosperity; but only a short period may have elapsed between the two references. All the meagre remains of Callinus are concerned with warfare, especially the fighting against the Cimmerians who came down from the eastern area of the Black Sea into Phrygia and Lydia and succeeded in burning the temple of Artemis in Ephesus.

The one substantial fragment of Callinus is an attempt to rouse his countrymen from their inactivity and to display the utmost courage in battle. It is a fine example of martial poetry, superior to that of Tyrtaeus on the same topic.

Tyrtaeus

A number of our sources (testt. 1-8) state that when the Spartans were embroiled in the Second Messenian War

---

[5] On the *aulos* see M. L. West, *Ancient Greek Music* (Oxford 1992) 81-109.

(latter part of the 7th century) they received an oracle from Delphi to obtain an adviser from Athens, and the Athenians sent them Tyrtaeus, a lame schoolmaster. Whatever truth there is in all this, what has survived of his poetry is concerned primarily with two issues: exhortations to the Spartans to fight with the utmost bravery and support for the government of the state, probably as a result of civil strife arising from setbacks in the war.

The three longest fragments (10-12) describe the ideal soldier and the disgrace that attends those who are cowardly. Their poetic quality, however, is uneven. Although there is some striking imagery, there are also awkward transitions, repetition, and padding. Like Callinus' verses, there is indebtedness to epic language, but unlike Callinus, Tyrtaeus is not averse to following closely a lengthy Homeric passage, as a comparison between *Iliad* 22.66-76 and fr. 8.19-30 illustrates.

It is sometimes said that Tyrtaeus' poetry is representative of the only kind of literature that was accepted in Sparta in his time, but in fact in contrast to two centuries later there is ample evidence that the visual arts were flourishing and that several poets and musicians visited Sparta. In addition, we must remember that Alcman, also Spartan, was roughly contemporary with Tyrtaeus, and his poetry is very different.

Mimnermus

The *Suda* (test. 1) assigns the poet's *floruit* to 632-29 and this seems to be substantially correct. In fr. 14 Mimnermus states that he learned from his elders of the

4

exploits of a hero who routed the Lydian cavalry and if this refers to the defeat of Gyges by the Smyrnaeans in the 660s, Mimnermus will have been born not long before. Mimnermus seems to be urging the citizens to emulate this hero and the occasion may be the attack of Alyattes, the fourth king of Lydia, who succeeded in razing Smyrna about 600.

In test. 1 the *Suda* gives Mimnermus' homeland as either Colophon or Smyrna, and in several sources he is referred to as simply a Colophonian. Fr. 9, however, and the fact that he composed a *Smyrneis* (fr. 13a) strongly suggest that he was from Smyrna. The error may have arisen from his having frequently mentioned Colophon. Also, in contrast to Smyrna "Colophon had a continuous tradition down to Hellenistic times" (West, *Studies* 72) and was the homeland of such famous poets as Xenophanes and Antimachus.

According to test. 9 Mimnermus' poems were collected in two books, but he is never cited from a specific book. Instead, we have six fragments (4, 5, 8, 10, 12, 24) assigned to a work entitled *Nanno* and one (13a) to a *Smyrneis*. Since the former embrace a wide range of topics, it is probable that the title *Nanno* was given to a collection of poems. The fact that the *Smyrneis* contained a proem in which the double genealogy of the Muses was given (fr. 13) suggests that it was of substantial length. If we are to believe testt. 3 and 4, Nanno was a pipe-player loved by Mimnermus.

Horace and Propertius (testt. 11-12) speak of Mimnermus as a love poet, but only fr. 1 has much to say on this topic and even here the emphasis is on the brevity of youth and the horrors of old age (as in frr. 2-5). Regardless of the subject matter, however, Mimnermus is a consummate poet and it is not surprising that he made such an impression on Hellenistic and Roman poets.

Solon

In the year 594/93 Solon was made archon in Athens and he lived until shortly after Pisistratus became tyrant in 560. Much of his surviving poetry falls into clearly defined periods: before his archonship, afterwards when he defends his reforms, and in his last years when he warns the Athenians against supporting Pisistratus. A ten-year period after his archonship was spent in travel, to Egypt and Cyprus (frr. 19 and 28).

Solon is not to be included among poets of the highest rank, but he also does not deserve the low esteem in which he is sometimes held. Fr. 4, for example, with its effective use of personification, imagery, anaphora, and chiasmus, reveals a high level of poetic skill. Fr. 13, however, the longest elegy we have from the archaic period and perhaps a complete poem, is of poorer quality. Because of its lack of cohesiveness it has generated a considerable bibliography, as critics attempt to explain the train of thought and central theme. But for all its imperfections it shows us a more reflective and philosophical Solon than we find in most of his other verses and thereby fills out our picture of the man.

Some of Solon's fragments are in iambic trimeters and trochaic tetrameters, but their contents do not differ from many in elegiac meter, an indication that the distinction usually found between elegy and iambus in Archilochus no longer applies.

Theognis

Under the name Theognis is a collection of poems which most would agree represents an anthology containing genuine works of Theognis, selections from other elegists (e.g., Tyrtaeus, Mimnermus, Solon), and anonymous poems, together with numerous verses repeated throughout the corpus, usually with some slight variation. Disagreement arises, however, concerning how and when the anthology was formed and what segments should be assigned to Theognis.[6]

Almost nothing is known about Theognis the man, except that he was an aristocrat living in Megara during a period of political turmoil when class distinctions were breaking down. There is some evidence that he went into exile. The *Suda* (test. 1) dates his floruit to 544/41 and this may be substantially correct, but our uncertainty about the authorship of certain segments makes his dating highly problematic.

Many of the poems are addressed to a boy Cyrnus, who is also called by his patronymic Polypaïdes, and in most instances these contain admonitions to abide by aristocratic ideals. Some critics treat the presence of Cyrnus' name as proof of authenticity, but the name could easily have been added by someone who wished to pass off his verses as the work of Theognis.

The collection as we have it begins with four short invocations, followed by a very controversial segment (vv. 19

[6] On the formation of the anthology see the sensible remarks of E. Bowie in G. W. Most (ed.), *Collecting Fragments: Fragmente sammeln* (Göttingen 1997) 61-66.

ff.) in which the poet mentions a seal that is to be placed on his verses. This has the appearance of a prologue and in vv. 237-54 we seem to have an epilogue. The intervening verses are more cohesive than those which follow and 19-254 may represent in large part the earliest collection of his poetry. Finally, at some stage the pederastic segments were gathered together to form Book II.

Except for Homer, Hesiod, and the Homeric Hymns, the elegies of Theognis represent the earliest poems to have been preserved in manuscripts of their own. Since these elegies are clearly not all the work of Theognis, it would be more accurate to refer to them as *Theognidea*, but I have used the term Theognis throughout.

Xenophanes

Xenophanes is better known as a pre-Socratic philosopher, but only the elegiac fragments will be considered here. Born in Colophon about 565, he left when the Medes overran his city in the late 540s and spent the rest of his life in various places in Magna Graecia (see test. 1 and fr. 8). He died about 470.

In addition to the poems in hexameters, most of which are concerned with the nature of deity and with explanations of natural phenomena (wind, rain, celestial bodies), we are told that he also composed iambic poetry. None of this has survived, but we do have one fragment (see n. 5 on test. 1) consisting of an iambic trimeter followed by a dactylic hexameter, and hexameters interspersed with trimeters may have been more common, especially when the poem had the character of a lampoon (see n. 1 on test. 2).

The three major elegiac fragments have as their subject

matter the ideal symposium, criticism of the excessive esteem in which athletes are held, and a denunciation of the soft life led by Colophonian aristocrats. One thread which runs throughout all three is the emphasis on usefulness.

Minor Poets

Little can be said about the remaining poets that is not obvious from the testimonia or fragments. Some are very shadowy figures and the chronological order in which they are placed is extremely tentative. The Adespota contain two fragments (61 and 62) which might be the work of Archilochus.

BIBLIOGRAPHY

The following list contains works cited either by author's name alone or by author together with a short title. Other works referred to are cited in sufficient detail as they appear in the notes. Journal citations employ the abbreviations listed in *L'Année Philologique*. For further bibliography see D. E. Gerber, "Early Greek Elegy and Iambus 1921-1989," *Lustrum* 33 (1991) 7-225 and 401-409.

Allen = A. Allen, *The Fragments of Mimnermus. Text and Commentary* (Stuttgart 1993)

Carrière = J. Carrière, *Théognis, Poèmes Élégiaques. Texte établi, traduit et commenté.* Nouvelle édition (Paris 1975)

Garzya = A. Garzya, *Teognide, Elegie. Testo critico, introduzione, traduzione e note con un scelta di testimonianze antiche e un lessico* (Florence 1958)

Gentili-Prato = B. Gentili and C. Prato (edd.), *Poetae Elegiaci. Testimonia et Fragmenta.* Pars prior (Leipzig 1979, 1988²), Pars altera (Leipzig 1985)

Hudson-Williams = T. Hudson-Williams, *The Elegies of Theognis and other Elegies included in the Theognidean Sylloge. A Revised Text ... with Introduction, Commentary and Appendices* (London 1910)

BIBLIOGRAPHY

IEG = M.L. West, *Iambi et Elegi Graeci* (Oxford 1989, 1992)

Mosshammer = A. A. Mosshammer, *The Chronicle of Eusebius and Greek Chronographic Tradition* (Lewisburg 1979)

Van Groningen = B. A. van Groningen, *Théognis. Le premier livre, édité avec un commentaire* (Amsterdam 1966)

Vetta = M. Vetta, *Teognide, Libro Secondo. Introduzione, testo critico, traduzione e commento* (Rome 1980)

West, *Studies* = M. L. West, *Studies in Greek Elegy and Iambus* (Berlin 1974)

Young = D. Young (ed.), *Theognis* (Leipzig 1969, 1971[2])

GREEK ELEGIAC POETRY

CALLINUS

TESTIMONIA

1 Strabo 14.1.40 (= fr. 3 West)

καὶ τὸ παλαιὸν δὲ συνέβη τοῖς Μάγνησιν ὑπὸ Τρη-
ρῶν ἄρδην ἀναιρεθῆναι, Κιμμερικοῦ ἔθνους, εὐτυχή-
σαντας πολὺν χρόνον, τῷ δ᾽ ἑξῆς ἔτει Μιλησίους
κατασχεῖν τὸν τόπον. Καλλῖνος μὲν οὖν ὡς εὐτυχούν-
των ἔτι τῶν Μαγνήτων μέμνηται καὶ κατορθούντων ἐν
τῷ πρὸς τοὺς Ἐφεσίους πολέμῳ, Ἀρχίλοχος δὲ (fr. 20)
ἤδη φαίνεται γνωρίζων τὴν γενομένην αὐτοῖς συμ-
φοράν, κλαίειν ⟨φάσκων τὰ⟩ (add. West) Θασίων οὐ τὰ
Μαγνήτων κακά. ἐξ οὗ καὶ αὐτὸν νεώτερον εἶναι τοῦ
Καλλίνου τεκμαίρεσθαι πάρεστιν. Quae sequuntur v.
ad fr. 5.

2 Orion *etym.* s.v. ἔλεγος (col. 58.8 Sturz)

εὑρετὴ⟨ν⟩ δὲ τοῦ ἐλεγείου οἱ μὲν τὸν Ἀρχίλοχον, οἱ δὲ
Μίμνερμον, οἱ δὲ Καλλῖνον παλαιότερον.

---

[1] For similar claims that Callinus invented the elegiac couplet
see *Gramm. Lat.* vi.107, 376, 639 Keil. Photius (v.158 Henry), on

CALLINUS

TESTIMONIA

1 Strabo, *Geography*

And in ancient times it happened that the Magnesians, who had long been prosperous, were utterly destroyed at the hands of the Treres, a Cimmerian tribe, and that in the following year the Milesians took possession of the place. Now Callinus mentions the Magnesians as still prosperous and as successful in their war with the Ephesians, but Archilochus is clearly already aware of the disaster that befell them, ⟨since he says that⟩ he bewails the woes of the Thasians, not those of the Magnesians. As a result one may infer that he is later than Callinus.[1]

---

[1] For the same chronology see Arch. test. 8. Athenaeus 12.525c cites both Callinus and Archilochus as sources for the destruction of the Magnesians at the hands of the Ephesians.

2 Orion, *Lexicon*

Some say that the elegiac couplet originated with Archilochus, others with Mimnermus, and others with Callinus at an earlier time.[1]

the authority of Proclus, names Callinus and Mimnermus as being among the best elegiac poets.

3 Paus. 9.9.5 (= fr. 6 West)

ἐποιήθη δὲ ἐς τὸν πόλεμον τοῦτον καὶ ἔπη Θηβαΐς
(Θηβαίοις codd., corr. Hemsterhuys)· τὰ δὲ ἔπη ταῦτα
Καλλῖνος (Καλαῖνος codd., corr. Sylburg), ἀφικόμενος
αὐτῶν ἐς μνήμην, ἔφησεν Ὅμηρον τὸν ποιήσαντα
εἶναι, Καλλίνῳ (Καλαίνῳ codd., corr. Sylburg) δὲ
πολλοί τε καὶ ἄξιοι λόγου κατὰ ταὐτὰ ἔγνωσαν.

4 Strabo 13.1.48 (= fr. 7 West)

συνοικειοῦσι δὲ καὶ τὴν ἱστορίαν εἴτε μῦθον τούτῳ τῷ
τόπῳ (sc. Χρύσῃ) τὴν περὶ τῶν μυῶν. τοῖς γὰρ ἐκ τῆς
Κρήτης ἀφιγμένοις Τεύκροις, οὓς πρῶτος παρέδωκε
Καλλῖνος ὁ τῆς ἐλεγείας ποιητής, ἠκολούθησαν δὲ
πολλοί, χρησμὸς ἦν αὐτόθι ποιήσασθαι τὴν μονήν,
ὅπου ἂν οἱ γηγενεῖς αὐτοῖς ἐπιθῶνται· συμβῆναι δὲ
τοῦτο αὐτοῖς φασι περὶ Ἀμαξιτόν· νύκτωρ γὰρ πολὺ
πλῆθος ἀρουραίων μυῶν ἐξανθῆσαν διαφαγεῖν ὅσα
σκύτινα τῶν τε ὅπλων καὶ τῶν χρηστηρίων· τοὺς δὲ
αὐτόθι μεῖναι. τούτους δὲ καὶ τὴν Ἴδην ἀπὸ τῆς ἐν
Κρήτῃ προσονομάσαι.

5 Strabo 13.4.8

φησὶ δὲ Καλλισθένης (FGrHist 124 F 29) ἁλῶναι τὰς
Σάρδεις ὑπὸ Κιμμερίων πρῶτον, εἶθ᾽ ὑπὸ Τρηρῶν καὶ
Λυκίων, ὅπερ καὶ Καλλῖνον δηλοῦν τὸν τῆς ἐλεγείας
ποιητήν, ὕστατα δὲ τὴν ἐπὶ Κύρου καὶ Κροίσου
γενέσθαι ἅλωσιν. λέγοντος δὲ τοῦ Καλλίνου τὴν

3 Pausanias, *Description of Greece*

And on this war there was composed the epic poem *Thebais*. When Callinus had occasion to mention this poem he said that Homer was its author,[1] and many good authorities have shared the judgement of Callinus.

[1] On this see J. A. Davison, *From Archilochus to Pindar* (London 1968) 81-82.

4 Strabo, *Geography*

And they also associate the history or myth about the mice with this place (Chrysa). When the Teucrians arrived from Crete—Callinus the elegiac poet was the first to hand down an account of them and many have followed him—they had an oracle which told them to stay wherever the earth-born attacked them. And they say that this happened to them round Hamaxitus,[1] for by night a great horde of field mice burst forth and devoured all the leather on their arms and utensils, and there they stayed. And it was they who gave the name Ida (to the mountain) after the Ida in Crete.

[1] South of Troy near cape Lectum.

5 Strabo, *Geography*

Callisthenes says that Sardis was captured first by the Cimmerians,[1] then by the Treres and the Lycians, as the elegiac poet Callinus reveals, and that the final capture was in the time of Cyrus and Croesus. But when Callinus

ELEGIAC POETRY

ἔφοδον τῶν Κιμμερίων ἐπὶ τοὺς Ἡσιονῆας γεγονέναι,
καθ᾿ ἣν Σάρδεις ἑάλωσαν, εἰκάζουσιν οἱ περὶ τὸν
Σκήψιον (Demetr. Sceps. fr. 41 Gaede) Ἰαστὶ λέγεσθαι
Ἡσιονεῖς τοὺς Ἀσιονεῖς· τάχα γὰρ ἡ Μῃονία, φησίν,
Ἀσία ἐλέγετο.

FRAGMENTS

1 Stob. 4.10.12

Καλλίνου·

μέχρις τέο κατάκεισθε; κότ᾿ ἄλκιμον ἕξετε θυμόν,
ὦ νέοι; οὐδ᾿ αἰδεῖσθ᾿ ἀμφιπερικτίονας
ὧδε λίην μεθιέντες; ἐν εἰρήνῃ δὲ δοκεῖτε
ἧσθαι, ἀτὰρ πόλεμος γαῖαν ἅπασαν ἔχει

. . . .

5   καί τις ἀποθνῄσκων ὕστατ᾿ ἀκοντισάτω.
τιμῆέν τε γάρ ἐστι καὶ ἀγλαὸν ἀνδρὶ μάχεσθαι
γῆς πέρι καὶ παίδων κουριδίης τ᾿ ἀλόχου
δυσμενέσιν· θάνατος δὲ τότ᾿ ἔσσεται, ὁππότε κεν δὴ
Μοῖραι ἐπικλώσωσ᾿. ἀλλά τις ἰθὺς ἴτω
10   ἔγχος ἀνασχόμενος καὶ ὑπ᾿ ἀσπίδος ἄλκιμον ἦτορ
ἔλσας, τὸ πρῶτον μειγνυμένου πολέμου.
οὐ γάρ κως θάνατόν γε φυγεῖν εἱμαρμένον ἐστὶν
ἄνδρ᾿, οὐδ᾿ εἰ προγόνων ᾖ γένος ἀθανάτων.
πολλάκι δηϊοτῆτα φυγὼν καὶ δοῦπον ἀκόντων
15   ἔρχεται, ἐν δ᾿ οἴκῳ μοῖρα κίχεν θανάτου.

18

CALLINUS

says that the invasion of the Cimmerians was against the
Esioneis, at which time Sardis was captured, the Scepsian
and his followers conjecture that the Asioneis were called
Esioneis in the Ionic dialect: for perhaps Maeonia, he says,
used to be called Asia.

[1] See Strabo on fr. 5.

FRAGMENTS

1 Stobaeus, *Anthology*

From Callinus:

How long are you going to lie idle? Young men,
when will you have a courageous spirit? Don't those
who live round about make you feel ashamed of be-
ing so utterly passive? You think that you are sitting
in a state of peace, but all the land is in the grip of
war[1] . . .[2] even as one is dying let him make a final
cast of his javelin. For it is a splendid honour for a
man to fight on behalf of his land, children, and
wedded wife against the foe. Death will occur only
when the Fates have spun it out. Come, let a man
charge straight ahead, brandishing his spear and
mustering a stout heart behind his shield, as soon as
war is engaged. For it is in no way fated that a man
escape death, not even if he has immortal ancestors
in his lineage. Often one who has escaped from the
strife of battle and the thud of javelins and has re-
turned home meets with his allotted death in his

19

ἀλλ᾽ ὁ μὲν οὐκ ἔμπης δήμῳ φίλος οὐδὲ ποθεινός,
  τὸν δ᾽ ὀλίγος στενάχει καὶ μέγας, ἤν τι πάθῃ·
λαῷ γὰρ σύμπαντι πόθος κρατερόφρονος ἀνδρὸς
  θνήσκοντος, ζώων δ᾽ ἄξιος ἡμιθέων·
20 ὥσπερ γάρ μιν πύργον ἐν ὀφθαλμοῖσιν ὁρῶσιν·
  ἔρδει γὰρ πολλῶν ἄξια μοῦνος ἐών.

1 τεῦ codd., corr. Fick   8 ὀκκότε Bach   11 μιγν-
codd., corr. Bucherer

2 Strabo 14.1.4

αὗται μὲν δώδεκα Ἰωνικαὶ πόλεις, προσελήφθη δὲ
ὕστερον καὶ Σμύρνα εἰς τὸ Ἰωνικόν, ἐναγαγόντων
Ἐφεσίων· ἦσαν γὰρ αὐτοῖς σύνοικοι τὸ παλαιόν,
ἡνίκα καὶ Σμύρνα ἐκαλεῖτο ἡ Ἔφεσος· καὶ Καλλῖνός
που οὕτως ὠνόμακεν αὐτήν, Σμυρναίους τοὺς Ἐφε-
σίους καλῶν ἐν τῷ πρὸς τὸν Δία λόγῳ·

  Σμυρναίους δ᾽ ἐλέησον,

2a Pergit Strabo

καὶ πάλιν·

  μνῆσαι δ᾽, εἴ κοτέ τοι μηρία καλὰ βοῶν
  ⟨Σμυρναῖοι κατέκηαν⟩.

Quae sequuntur v. ad Hippon. fr. 50.

2a 2 suppl. Casaubon

house. But he is not in any case loved or missed by
the people, whereas the other, if he suffer some mis-
hap, is mourned by the humble and the mighty. All
the people miss a stout-hearted man when he dies
and while he lives he is the equal of demigods. For
in the eyes of the people he is like a tower, since
single-handed he does the deeds of many.

[1] Probably with the Cimmerians (cf. fr. 5).　　[2] The meter
shows that at least one verse is missing, probably more.

2 Strabo, *Geography*

These are the twelve Ionian cities, but at a later time
Smyrna was also added, having been brought into the
Ionian league by the Ephesians. For of old the Ephesians
were fellow inhabitants of the Smyrnaeans, when Ephesus
was also called Smyrna. And Callinus somewhere has so
named it, when he calls the Ephesians Smyrnaeans in his
address to Zeus:

　　have mercy on the Smyrnaeans,

2a and again:

　　remember, if ever (the Smyrnaeans burned) fine
　　thigh bones of oxen for you

21

3 = test. 1

4 St. Byz. (p. 634.3 Meineke)

Τρῆρος χωρίον Θρᾴκης, καὶ Τρῆρες Θρᾴκιον ἔθνος. λέγεται καὶ τρισυλλάβως παρὰ Καλλίνῳ τῷ ποιητῇ·

Τρήερας ἄνδρας ἄγων.

Θεόπομπος (*FGrHist* 115 F 378) Τρᾶρας αὐτοὺς καλεῖ.

Τρήερας West, Τρήρεας codd.

5 Strabo 14.1.40 (quae praecedunt v. ad test. 1)

ἄλλης δέ τινος ἐφόδου τῶν Κιμμερίων μέμνηται πρεσβυτέρας ὁ Καλλῖνος, ἐπὰν φῇ·

νῦν δ᾽ ἐπὶ Κιμμερίων στρατὸς ἔρχεται
ὀβριμοεργῶν,

ἐν ᾗ τὴν Σάρδεων ἅλωσιν δηλοῖ.

ὄβριμος ἔργων codd., corr. Xylander

6 = test. 3

7 = test. 4

4 Stephanus of Byzantium, *Lexicon of Place-names*

Treros is a place in Thrace and the Treres are a Thracian tribe. The word has three syllables in the poet Callinus:

bringing Trerian men

Theopompus calls them Trares.

5 Strabo, *Geography*

And Callinus mentions another, earlier invasion of the Cimmerians when he says:

now the horde of Cimmerians, with their acts of violence, is advancing,

by which he is clearly referring to the capture of Sardis.[1]

[1] Cf. test. 5.

TYRTAEUS

TESTIMONIA

1 *Suda* (iv.610.5 Adler)

Τυρταῖος, Ἀρχεμβρότου, Λάκων ἢ Μιλήσιος, ἐλεγειο-
ποιὸς καὶ αὐλητής· ὃν λόγος τοῖς μέλεσι χρησάμενον
παροτρῦναι Λακεδαιμονίους πολεμοῦντας Μεσσηνίοις
καὶ ταύτῃ ἐπικρατεστέρους ποιῆσαι. ἔστι δὲ παλαίτα-
τος, σύγχρονος τοῖς ἑπτὰ κληθεῖσι σοφοῖς, ἢ καὶ
παλαίτερος. ἤκμαζε γοῦν κατὰ τὴν λε΄ ὀλυμπιάδα.
ἔγραψε πολιτείαν Λακεδαιμονίοις, καὶ ὑποθήκας δι᾽
ἐλεγείας, καὶ μέλη πολεμιστήρια, βιβλία ε΄.

Τυρταῖος· ὅτι οἱ Λακεδαιμόνιοι ὤμοσαν ἢ Μεσ-
σήνην αἱρήσειν ἢ αὐτοὶ τεθνήξεσθαι. χρήσαντος δὲ
τοῦ θεοῦ στρατηγὸν παρὰ Ἀθηναίων λαβεῖν, λαμ-
βάνουσι Τυρταῖον τὸν ποιητήν, χωλὸν ἄνδρα· ὃς ἐπ᾽
ἀρετὴν αὐτοὺς παρακαλῶν εἷλε τῷ κ΄ ἔτει τὴν Μεσσή-
νην· καὶ ταύτην κατέσκαψαν καὶ τοὺς αἰχμαλώτους ἐν
τοῖς Εἴλωσι κατέταξαν.

---

[1] Presumably a conjecture based on the difficulty of imagining
a Spartan poet composing in Ionic.   [2] The date may be a little
early (see n. on fr. 5). Jerome (p. 96b Helm) dates him to 633-632.

24

TYRTAEUS

TESTIMONIA

1 *Suda*

Tyrtaeus, son of Archembrotus, a Laconian or Milesian[1] elegiac poet and pipe-player. It is said that by means of his songs he urged on the Lacedaemonians in their war with the Messenians and in this way enabled them to get the upper hand. He is very ancient, contemporary with those called the Seven Sages, or even earlier. He flourished in the 35th Olympiad (640-637).[2] He wrote a constitution[3] for the Lacedaemonians, precepts[4] in elegiac verse, and war songs,[5] in five books.[6]

Tyrtaeus. The Lacedaemonians swore that they would either capture Messene or die, and when the god gave them an oracle to take a general from the Athenians, they took the poet Tyrtaeus, a man who was lame.[7] By exhorting them to valour he captured Messene in the 20th year.[8] They razed it and grouped the prisoners among the helots.

---

[3] Perhaps a reference to the *Eunomia* (see frr. 1-2).   [4] Frr. 10-12 and 18-23a may be included in this category.   [5] None of these has survived, since those ascribed to Tyrtaeus (frr. 856-57 *PMG*) are considered spurious.   [6] No source cites from a specific book.   [7] See testt. 3 and 7.   [8] A confusion arising from fr. 5.7. Tyrtaeus lived during the Second, not the First, Messenian War.

ELEGIAC POETRY

Athenian Origin

2 Pl. *Leges* 1.629a-b

προστησώμεθα γοῦν Τυρταῖον, τὸν φύσει μὲν Ἀθη-
ναῖον, τῶνδε δὲ πολίτην γενόμενον, ὃς δὴ μάλιστα
ἀνθρώπων περὶ ταῦτα ἐσπούδακεν, εἰπὼν ὅτι "οὔτ᾽ ἂν
μνησαίμην οὔτ᾽ ἐν λόγῳ ἄνδρα τιθείμην" οὔτ᾽ εἴ τις
πλουσιώτατος ἀνθρώπων εἴη, φησίν, οὔτ᾽ εἰ πολλὰ
ἀγαθὰ κεκτημένος, εἰπὼν σχεδὸν ἅπαντα, ὃς μὴ περὶ
τὸν πόλεμον ἄριστος γίγνοιτ᾽ ἀεί. ταῦτα γὰρ ἀκήκοάς
που καὶ σὺ τὰ ποιήματα.

3 Schol. ad loc. (p. 301 Greene)

ὁ Τυρταῖος οὗτος Ἀθηναῖος ἐγένετο, εὐτελὴς τὴν
τύχην· γραμματιστὴς γὰρ ἦν καὶ χωλὸς τὸ σῶμα,
καταφρονούμενος ἐν Ἀθήναις. τοῦτον Λακεδαιμονίοις
ἔχρησεν ὁ Ἀπόλλων μεταπέμψασθαι, ὅτε πρὸς Μεσ-
σηνίους εἶχον τὴν μάχην καὶ ἐν ἀπορίᾳ κατέστησαν
πολλῇ, ὡς δὴ ἱκανοῦ αὐτοῖς ἐσομένου πρὸς τὸ συν-
ιδεῖν τὸ λυσιτελές· αὐτῷ γὰρ ἐπέτρεψε χρήσασθαι
συμβούλῳ. Quae sequuntur v. ad fr. 5.3.

4 Lycurg. *in Leocr.* 106

τίς γὰρ οὐκ οἶδε τῶν Ἑλλήνων ὅτι Τυρταῖον στρατη-
γὸν ἔλαβον παρὰ τῆς πόλεως, μεθ᾽ οὗ καὶ τῶν πολε-

TYRTAEUS

Athenian Origin

2 Plato, *Laws*

Let us cite in support Tyrtaeus, who was an Athenian by birth but became a citizen of the Lacedaemonians;[1] he beyond all others had a keen interest in these matters, saying "I would not mention or take account of a man,"[2] though he were the richest of men or possessed many good things—he mentions almost all of them—, if he were not always the best in war. Presumably you too have heard these poems.

[1] The Athenian origin of Tyrtaeus is cited, and elaborated on, by a large number of sources. It is generally treated as an example of Athenian propaganda, in spite of the fact that Plato, our earliest authority, was an admirer of Sparta.   [2] Fr. 12.1. See n. ad loc.

3 Scholiast on the passage

This Tyrtaeus was an Athenian, one whose station in life was lowly; for he was a schoolmaster, lame, and looked down upon at Athens. Apollo gave the Lacedaemonians an oracle to send for him, when they were fighting the Messenians and were in great difficulty, since he would suffice for them to see what was to their advantage. Apollo ordered them to use him as an adviser.

4 Lycurgus, *Against Leocrates*

Who of the Greeks does not know that the Lacedaemonians took Tyrtaeus from our city (i.e., Athens) as their gen-

μίων ἐκράτησαν καὶ τὴν περὶ τοὺς νέους ἐπιμέλειαν
συνετάξαντο, οὐ μόνον εἰς τὸν παρόντα κίνδυνον ἀλλ'
εἰς ἅπαντα τὸν αἰῶνα βουλευσάμενοι καλῶς· κατέλιπε
γὰρ αὐτοῖς ἐλεγεῖα ποιήσας, ὧν ἀκούοντες παιδεύ-
ονται πρὸς ἀνδρείαν. Quae sequuntur v. ad fr. 10.

5 Philod. *de mus.* 17 (p. 28 Kemke)

]· περὶ μὲν τοῦ Λακε[δαιμονίο]υς, ὅταν μαχησόμ[ενοι
ἐν]διδῶσιν, αὐλοῖ[ς χ]ρῆσθα[ι καὶ] λύραις, οὐθὲν ἔτι
δεῖ λέγ[ειν]. τὸ δὲ Τυρταῖον αὐτοὺς [ἀνει]ληφέναι καὶ
προτετιμ[ηκέ]ναι διὰ μουσικὴν ἀνιστ[όρη]τον ἔοικεν
εἶναι, πάντων μὲν σχεδὸν ὁμολογούν[των] κατὰ χρη-
σμὸν αὐτὸν ἐξ Ἀ[θη]νῶν μεταπεπέμφθαι, π[λείσ]των
δὲ γινωσκόντων ὅ[τι] ποιητὴς ἦν καὶ διὰ ποη[μά]των
γενναίας διανοί[ας πε]ριεχόντων [

6 Diod. Sic. 8.27.1-2

οἱ Σπαρτιᾶται ὑπὸ Μεσσηνίων ἡττηθέντες εἰς Δελ-
φοὺς πέμψαντες ἠρώτων περὶ πολέμου. ἔχρησε
δὲ αὐτοῖς παρὰ Ἀθηναίων λαβεῖν ἡγεμόνα. οἱ Λακε-
δαιμόνιοι προτραπέντες ὑπὸ Τυρταίου οὕτω προθύμως
εἶχον πρὸς παράταξιν, ὥστε μέλλοντες παρατάτ-
τεσθαι τὰ ὀνόματα σφῶν αὐτῶν ἐγράψαντο εἰς
σκυταλίδα καὶ ἐξῆψαν ἐκ τῆς χειρός, ἵνα τελευτῶντες

eral and with him prevailed over their enemies and established their system of training for the young, planning well not only for the present danger but for all time? For Tyrtaeus composed and left them elegiac poems and by listening to them they are taught to be brave.

5 Philodemus, *On Music*[1]

With regard to the Lacedaemonians' use of pipes and lyres whenever they struck up a tune at the onset of battle, there is no need to say anything more. But that they took Tyrtaeus and honoured him above others because of his music does not seem to be recorded, since almost everyone agrees that he had been sent for from Athens in accordance with an oracle and most people know that he was a poet and that by means of poems which contained noble thoughts . . .

[1] I have printed the text as it will appear in D. Dellatre's edition. For this text and an analysis of the passage see E. Puglia, "Tirteo nei papiri ercolanesi," *Miscellanea Papyrologica* I (Florence 1990) 27-35. He also discusses a citation of fr. 10.15-16 in these papyri and its relevance for the debate whether fr. 10 represents one poem or two.

6 Diodorus Siculus, *World History*

When the Spartans suffered defeat at the hands of the Messenians they sent to Delphi and asked about the war. The god advised them in an oracle to procure a leader from the Athenians. The Lacedaemonians, urged on by Tyrtaeus, were so eager for battle that when they were about to be drawn up in battle order they wrote their names on a small stick and tied it on their arms, in order

μὴ ἀγνοῶνται ὑπὸ τῶν οἰκείων. οὕτω παρέστησαν
ταῖς ψυχαῖς ἔτοιμοι πρὸς τὸ τῆς νίκης ἀποτυγ-
χάνοντες ἑτοίμως ἐπιδέχεσθαι τὸν ἔντιμον θάνατον.

7 Paus. 4.15.6

ἐγένετο δὲ καὶ Λακεδαιμονίοις μάντευμα ἐκ Δελφῶν
τὸν Ἀθηναῖον ἐπάγεσθαι σύμβουλον. ἀποστέλλουσιν
οὖν παρὰ τοὺς Ἀθηναίους τόν τε χρησμὸν ἀπαγ-
γελοῦντας καὶ ἄνδρα αἰτοῦντας παραινέσοντα ἃ χρή
σφισιν. Ἀθηναῖοι δὲ οὐδέτερα θέλοντες, οὔτε Λακε-
δαιμονίους ἄνευ μεγάλων κινδύνων προσλαβεῖν μοῖ-
ραν τῶν ἐν Πελοποννήσῳ τὴν ἀρίστην οὔτε αὐτοὶ
παρακοῦσαι τοῦ θεοῦ, πρὸς ταῦτα ἐξευρίσκουσι καὶ—
ἦν γὰρ Τυρταῖος διδάσκαλος γραμμάτων νοῦν τε
ἥκιστα ἔχειν δοκῶν καὶ τὸν ἕτερον τῶν ποδῶν
χωλός—τοῦτον ἀποστέλλουσιν ἐς Σπάρτην. ὁ δὲ ἀφ-
ικόμενος ἰδίᾳ τε τοῖς ἐν τέλει καὶ συνάγων ὁπόσους
τύχοι καὶ τὰ ἐλεγεῖα καὶ τὰ ἔπη σφίσι τὰ ἀνάπαιστα
ᾖδεν.

8 Plut. apophth. Lac. 230d

πυνθανομένου δέ τινος, διὰ τί Τυρταῖον τὸν ποιητὴν
ἐποιήσαντο πολίτην, "ὅπως" ἔφη (sc. Παυσανίας)

that if they died they might be recognized by their kins-men.[1] So ready were they in spirit to accept willingly an honourable death, should they fail to achieve victory.

[1] This detail is also recorded by Polyaenus 1.17 and Justin 3.5. In 15.66.3 Diodorus again mentions Tyrtaeus' Athenian origin.

7 Pausanias, *Description of Greece*

The Lacedaemonians received an oracle from Delphi to procure the Athenian as counsellor. They therefore des-patched messengers to the Athenians to announce the ora-cle and asked for a man to advise them what they should do. The Athenians, unwilling either that the Lacedaemon-ians should annex the best part of the Peloponnese without great risk or that they themselves should take no heed of the god, devised accordingly. There was a schoolmaster, Tyrtaeus, who seemed to have little sense[1] and who was lame in one foot,[2] and they sent him to Sparta.[3] Upon his arrival he sang his elegiac and anapaestic verses, both pri-vately to those in office and to as many as he could gather together.

[1] Diogenes Laertius 2.43 reports that the Athenians spoke of Tyrtaeus as 'deranged' (παρακόπτειν). [2] Porphyr. in Hor. *A.P.* 402 (p. 176 Holder) adds that he was also 'one-eyed' (*luscum*). [3] That the Athenians sent Tyrtaeus as an insult to the Spartans is recorded by Ampelius 14 (*per ludibrium*), Justin 3.5 (*in con-temptum*), and ps.-Acron in Hor. *A.P.* 402 (*in contumeliam*).

8 Plutarch, *Sayings of Spartans*

When someone asked why they had made the poet Tyrtaeus a citizen, Pausanias said: "so that a foreigner

"μηδέποτε ξένος φαίνηται ἡμῶν ἡγεμών."

Miscellaneous

9 Peek, *Griechische Vers-Inschriften* 749 (Acarnaniae)

τὸμ Μούσαις, ὦ ξεῖνε, τετιμένον ἐνθάδε κρύπτει
Τιμόκριτογ κόλπωι κυδιάνειρα κόνις.
Αἰτωλῶν γὰρ παισὶ πάτρας ὕπερ εἰς ἔριν ἐλθὼν
ὠγαθὸς ἢ νικᾶν ἤθελε‹ν› ἢ τεθνάναι·
5   πίπτει δ᾽ ἔμ προμάχοισι λιπὼμ πατρὶ μύριον
ἄλγος,
ἀλλὰ τὰ παιδείας οὐκ ἀπέκρυπτε καλά·
Τυρταίου δὲ Λάκαιναν ἐνὶ στέρνοισι φυλάσσων
ῥῆσιν τὰν ἀρετὰν εἵλετο πρόσθε βίου.

10 Ath. 14.630f

πολεμικοὶ δ᾽ εἰσὶν οἱ Λάκωνες, ὧν καὶ οἱ υἱοὶ τὰ
ἐμβατήρια μέλη ἀναλαμβάνουσιν, ἅπερ καὶ ἐνόπλια
καλεῖται. καὶ αὐτοὶ δ᾽ οἱ Λάκωνες ἐν τοῖς πολέμοις
τὰ Τυρταίου ποιήματα ἀπομνημονεύοντες ἔρρυθμον
κίνησιν ποιοῦνται. Φιλόχορος δέ (*FGrHist* 328 F 216)
φησιν κρατήσαντας Λακεδαιμονίους Μεσσηνίων διὰ

might never seem to be our leader."[1]

1 For other references to Tyrtaeus' non-Spartan origin see Strabo ad fr. 2.12-15, Aelian *V.H.* 12.50 (= Terp. test. 7 Campbell), Themist. *or.* 15.197c, and Orosius *adv. pag.* 1.21.7.

Miscellaneous

9 Inscription (3rd c. B.C.)

Stranger, the dust that brings glory to men conceals here in its bosom Timocritus, honoured by the Muses. For when the brave man came into conflict with the sons of the Aetolians on behalf of his homeland, it was his desire either to be victorious or to die. He fell among the front ranks and left his father with pain beyond measure, but he did not lose sight of his noble upbringing. Taking to heart the Spartan declaration of Tyrtaeus, he chose valour ahead of life.[1]

1 P. Friedländer, *AJP* 63 (1942) 78-82, argues that the author is Damagetus, several of whose epigrams are included in the *Anthologia Graeca*. Whoever the author is, he is clearly echoing passages in Tyrtaeus.

10 Athenaeus, *Scholars at Dinner*

The Spartans are warlike and their sons adopt the marching songs which are called *enoplia*.[1] And the Spartans themselves in their wars march in time to the poems of Tyrtaeus which they recite from memory. Philochorus says that after the Lacedaemonians prevailed over the Messen-

τὴν Τυρταίου στρατηγίαν ἐν ταῖς στρατείαις ἔθος
ποιήσασθαι, ἂν δειπνοποιήσωνται καὶ παιωνίσωσιν,
ᾄδειν καθ᾽ ἕνα ‹τὰ› (add. Kaibel) Τυρταίου· κρίνειν δὲ
τὸν πολέμαρχον καὶ ἆθλον διδόναι τῷ νικῶντι κρέας.

11 Plut. *Cleom.* 2.3

Λεωνίδαν μὲν γὰρ τὸν παλαιὸν λέγουσιν ἐπερωτη-
θέντα, ποῖός τις αὐτῷ φαίνεται ποιητὴς γεγονέναι
Τυρταῖος, εἰπεῖν "ἀγαθὸς νέων ψυχὰς κακκανήν." ἐμ-
πιπλάμενοι γὰρ ὑπὸ τῶν ποιημάτων ἐνθουσιασμοῦ
παρὰ τὰς μάχας ἠφείδουν ἑαυτῶν.

12 Hor. *A.P.* 401-403

post hos insignis Homerus / Tyrtaeusque mares animos in
Martia bella / versibus exacuit.

13 Pollux 4.107

τριχορίαν δὲ Τυρταῖος ἔστησε, τρεῖς Λακώνων χο-
ρούς, καθ᾽ ἡλικίαν ἑκάστην, παῖδας ἄνδρας γέροντας.

14 Schol. Dionys. Thrac. (*Gramm. Gr.* i(3).168.8 Hilgard)

ποιητὴς δὲ κεκόσμηται τοῖς τέσσαρσι τούτοις, μέτρῳ,
μύθῳ, ἱστορίᾳ καὶ ποιᾷ λέξει, καὶ πᾶν ποίημα μὴ

ians because of the generalship of Tyrtaeus, they established the custom in their campaigns that, after dinner and the hymn of thanksgiving, each sing in turn the poems of Tyrtaeus; their military commander acts as judge and gives a prize of meat to the winner.

1 Literally, songs 'under arms.'

11 Plutarch, *Life of Cleomenes*

They say that Leonidas of old, when asked what sort of poet he thought Tyrtaeus was, replied: "a good one to incite the hearts of the young."[1] For filled with inspiration by his poems they were unsparing of their lives in battle.

1 Similarly Plut. *de sollert. anim.* 1.959a and *apophth. Lac.* 235e.

12 Horace, *Art of Poetry*

After these (sc. Orpheus and Amphion) Homer achieved his fame and Tyrtaeus with his verses sharpened manly hearts for the wars of Mars.[1]

1 For Tyrtaeus in association with Homer see also Quintilian 10.1.56 and 12.11.27.

13 Pollux, *Vocabulary*

Tyrtaeus established three choruses of Spartans on the basis of age: boys, men, and old men.

14 Scholiast on Dionysius of Thrace

A poet is equipped with these four things, meter, myth, narrative, and diction of a particular kind, and any poem

μετέχον τῶν τεσσάρσων τούτων οὐκ ἔστι ποίημα·
ἀμέλει τὸν Ἐμπεδοκλέα καὶ τὸν Τυρταῖον καὶ τοὺς
περὶ ἀστρολογίας εἰπόντας οὐ καλοῦμεν ποιητάς, εἰ
καὶ μέτρῳ ἐχρήσαντο, διὰ τὸ μὴ χρήσασθαι αὐτοὺς
τοῖς τῶν ποιητῶν χαρακτηριστικοῖς.

Τυρταῖον ‹τὸν Πύθιον› Gigante, Ἄρατον Cataudella

FRAGMENTS

1 Arist. *Pol.* 5.6.1306b36

ἔτι ὅταν οἱ μὲν ἀπορῶσι λίαν, οἱ δὲ εὐπορῶσι (γίνον
ται αἱ στάσεις). καὶ μάλιστα ἐν τοῖς πολέμοις τοῦτο
γίνεται· συνέβη δὲ καὶ τοῦτο ἐν Λακεδαίμονι, ὑπὸ τὸν
Μεσσηνιακὸν πόλεμον· δῆλον δὲ {καὶ τοῦτο} (del.
Verrall) ἐκ τῆς Τυρταίου ποιήσεως τῆς καλουμένης
Εὐνομίας· θλιβόμενοι γάρ τινες διὰ τὸν πόλεμον
ἠξίουν ἀνάδαστον ποιεῖν τὴν χώραν.

2 P. Oxy. xxxviii.2824, ed. Turner

```
              ]..ε θεοπρο[π
                ]..φ..ενακ[
              ].μαντειασαν[
5              ]τειδεταθή.[
              ]πάντ᾽ εἰδεν.[
              ἄ]νδρας ἀνιστ[αμεν
              ]ι[.]ηγαλα[
```

that does not partake of these four is not a poem. For instance, we do not give the name of poet to Empedocles and Tyrtaeus and those who talk about astronomy, even if they employed meter, because they did not make use of what characterizes a poet.[1]

[1] The last sentence also appears in *Anecd. Gr.* ii.734.14 Bekker.

FRAGMENTS

1 Aristotle, *Politics*

Furthermore, factions arise whenever some (aristocrats) are extremely poor and others are well off. And this happens especially during wars; it happened too in Sparta in the course of the Messenian War, as is clear from the poem of Tyrtaeus called *Eunomia*.[1] For some, hard pressed because of the war, demanded a redistribution of the land.

[1] Perhaps 'Law and Order' is an adequate rendering of the word. As A. Andrewes, "Eunomia," *CQ* 32 (1938) 89-102, explains, the word describes "a condition of the state in which citizens obey the law, not a condition of the state in which the laws are good" (p. 89).

2 Oxyrhynchus papyrus (late 1st or early 2nd cent. A.D.)

. . .[1] dear to the gods . . . let us obey (the kings since

]θ̣εοῖσι φί[λ
10]ῳ πει̣θ̣ώμε̣θα κ[
]α̣ν̣ ἐγγύτεροι γέν[εος·
αὐτὸς γὰρ Κρονίων] καλλιστεφάνου ⌊πόσις
Ἥρης
Ζεὺς Ἡρακλείδαις] ἄστυ δέδωκε τό⌊δε,
15 οἷσιν ἅμα προλιπ⌋όντες Ἐρινεὸν ⌊ἠνεμόεντα
εὐρεῖαν Πέλοπ⌋ο⌊ς⌋ νῆσον ἀφικόμ⌊εθα
]γλαυκώπ[ι]δος[

13 τήνδε δέδωκε πόλιν Strabo (τηνδεδωκε palimps., δε supra
lin. sec. Lasserre), ἄστυ ἔδωκε? West

Strabo 8.4.10 (quae praecedunt v. ad fr. 8)

καὶ γὰρ εἶναί φησιν ἐκεῖθεν ἐν τῇ ἐλεγείᾳ ἣν ἐπι-
γράφουσιν Εὐνομίαν· "αὐτὸς—ἀφικόμεθα." ὥστ᾽ ἢ
ταῦτα ἀκυρωτέον (ἠκύρωται codd., corr. Porson) τὰ
ἐλεγεῖα, ἢ Φιλοχόρῳ (FGrHist 328 F 215) ἀπιστητέον
τῷ φήσαντι Ἀθηναῖόν τε καὶ Ἀφιδναῖον καὶ Καλλισ-
θένει (124 F 24) καὶ ἄλλοις πλείοσι τοῖς εἰποῦσιν
ἐξ Ἀθηνῶν ἀφικέσθαι, δεηθέντων Λακεδαιμονίων
κατὰ χρησμὸν ὃς ἐπέταττε παρ᾽ Ἀθηναίων λαβεῖν
ἡγεμόνα.

38

they are?) nearer to the race (of the gods?). For Zeus himself, the son of Cronus and husband of fair-crowned Hera, has given this state to the descendants of Heracles.[2] With them we left windy Erineus[3] and came to the wide island of Pelops[4] . . . of the grey-eyed[5] . . .

Strabo, *Geography*

For Tyrtaeus says that he came from there[6] in the elegy entitled *Eunomia* (vv. 12-15). Consequently we must either deny the validity of these elegiac verses or we must disbelieve Philochorus, who said that Tyrtaeus was an Athenian and Aphidnean,[7] and Callisthenes and a great many others who said that he came from Athens when the Spartans asked for him in accordance with an oracle which instructed them to obtain a leader from Athens.

[1] In what precedes v. 9 there are references to consultation of the Delphic oracle and to men standing up, presumably to speak. [2] On this myth and its significance see I. Malkin, *Myth and Territory in the Spartan Mediterranean* (Cambridge 1994) 15-45. See also n. 2 on fr. 19.   [3] In Doris in central Greece. Thucydides (1.107) calls Doris the "mother city of the Lacedaemonians" and names Erineus as one of three towns in it.   [4] Although the Peloponnese (lit. 'island of Pelops') is not strictly an island, it was so defined because of the narrow isthmus.   [5] Athena. [6] Generally taken to mean 'from Lacedaemon,' but some understand 'from Erineus.'   [7] No doubt here the deme Aphidnae in Athens, but there was also a place of the same name in Laconia.

4

    Φοίβου ἀκούσαντες Πυθωνόθεν οἴκαδ᾽ ἔνεικαν
      μαντείας τε θεοῦ καὶ τελέεντ᾽ ἔπεα·
    ἄρχειν μὲν βουλῆς θεοτιμήτους βασιλῆας,
      οἷσι μέλει Σπάρτης ἱμερόεσσα πόλις,
5   πρεσβυγενέας τε γέροντας· ἔπειτα δὲ δημότας
      ἄνδρας
    εὐθείαις ῥήτραις ἀνταπαμειβομένους
    μυθεῖσθαί τε τὰ καλὰ καὶ ἔρδειν πάντα δίκαια,
      μηδέ τι βουλεύειν τῇδε πόλει ⟨σκολιόν⟩·
    δήμου τε πλήθει νίκην καὶ κάρτος ἕπεσθαι.
10   Φοῖβος γὰρ περὶ τῶν ὧδ᾽ ἀνέφηνε πόλει.

    1 οἱ τάδε νικᾶν Plut., corr. Amyot   3 βουλη cod.
excerpti (V)   4 Σπάρτας Plut.   5 πρεσβυγενεῖς δὲ V
(-έας Bergk), πρεσβύτας τε Plut.   6 εὐθείην ῥήτρας V
7 δὲ V, corr. Dindorf   8 μηδέ τι ἐπιβουλεύειν V, corr. Bach:
μηδ᾽ ἐπιβουλεύειν Dindorf σκολιόν add. Bach

Plut. *Lyc.* 6

οὕτω δὲ περὶ ταύτην ἐσπούδασε τὴν ἀρχὴν ὁ Λυ-
κοῦργος ὥστε μαντείαν ἐκ Δελφῶν κομίσαι περὶ
αὑτῆς, ἣν ῥήτραν καλοῦσιν. ἔχει δὲ οὕτως·

    Διὸς Συλλανίου καὶ Ἀθανᾶς Συλλανίας ἱερὸν
    ἱδρυσάμενον, φυλὰς φυλάξαντα καὶ ὠβὰς
    ὠβάξαντα, τριάκοντα γερουσίαν σὺν ἀρχαγέταις
    καταστήσαντα, ὥρας ἐξ ὥρας ἀπελλάζειν μεταξὺ

TYRTAEUS

4

After listening to Phoebus they brought home from
Pytho the god's oracles and sure predictions. The
divinely honoured kings, in whose care is Sparta's
lovely city, and the aged elders are to initiate coun-
sel; and then the men of the people, responding
with straight utterances, are to speak fair words, act
justly in everything, and not give the city (crooked)
counsel. Victory and power are to accompany the
mass of the people. For so was Phoebus' revelation
about this to the city.[1]

[1] The text is a combination from Plutarch and Diodorus, but
there are many who argue that vv. 7-10 should not be assigned to
Tyrtaeus and a few who print the first two verses from Plutarch
followed by the entire text of Diodorus. The Spartan *rhetra* (liter-
ally 'utterance') and the rider are highly controversial and it must
suffice to refer to H. T. Wade-Gery, *CQ* 37 (1943) 62-72, 38 (1944)
1-9, 115-26 = *Essays in Greek History* (Oxford 1958) 37-85, and
D. Ogden, *JHS* 114 (1994) 85-102. My translation below of Plu-
tarch is deliberately literal; consult Wade-Gery and Ogden for in-
terpretations, textual problems, and bibliography. See also West,
Studies 184-86, and D. Musti, *RFIC* 124 (1996) 257-81.

Plutarch, *Life of Lycurgus*

Lycurgus laid such stress on this office that he obtained an
oracle about it from Delphi; they call it a *rhetra* and it runs
as follows:

After founding a temple of Zeus Syllanios and
Athene Syllania, tribing the tribes and obing the
obes, establishing thirty as a council of elders along
with the kings, hold apellae season after season be-

ELEGIAC POETRY

Βαβύκας τε καὶ Κνακιῶνος, οὕτως εἰσφέρειν τε
καὶ ἀφίστασθαι, δάμω δὲ ἀν‹τα›γορίαν ἤμην καὶ
κράτος.

. . . ὕστερον μέντοι, τῶν πολλῶν ἀφαιρέσει καὶ
προσθέσει τὰς γνώμας διαστρεφόντων καὶ παραβια-
ζομένων, Πολύδωρος καὶ Θεόπομπος οἱ βασιλεῖς
τάδε τῇ ῥήτρᾳ παρενέγραψαν·

αἱ δὲ σκολιὰν ὁ δᾶμος ἔροιτο, τοὺς
πρεσβυγενέας καὶ ἀρχαγέτας ἀποστατῆρας
εἶμεν.

. . . ἔπεισαν δὲ καὶ αὐτοὶ τὴν πόλιν ὡς τοῦ θεοῦ ταῦτα
προστάσσοντος, ὥς που Τυρταῖος ἐπιμέμνηται διὰ
τούτων· "Φοίβου—ἀνταπαμειβομένους."

Excerpta e Diodoro (7.12.5-6)

ὅτι ὁ αὐτὸς Λυκοῦργος ἤνεγκε χρησμὸν ἐκ Δελφῶν
περὶ τῆς φιλαργυρίας τὸν ἐν παροιμίας μέρει μνη-
μονευόμενον·

ἁ φιλοχρηματία Σπάρταν ὀλεῖ, ἄλλο δὲ οὐδέν.

(ἡ Πυθία ἔχρησε τῷ Λυκούργῳ περὶ τῶν πολιτικῶν
οὕτως marg.)

‹ὧ›δε γὰρ ἀργυρότοξος ἄναξ ἑκάεργος
    Ἀπόλλων
χρυσοκόμης ἔχρη πίονος ἐξ ἀδότου·
ἄρχειν—πόλει.

42

tween Babyca and Cnacion, thus bring in and set
aside (proposals), but the right to speak in opposi-
tion and the power are to belong to the people.

... Afterwards, however, when the multitude distorted and
perverted proposals by subtraction and addition, the kings
Polydorus and Theopompus subjoined the following:

If the people should speak crookedly, the elders and
kings are to be setters-aside.

... And they actually persuaded the city that the god
ordered this, as Tyrtaeus mentions in these verses (1-6).[2]

2 The rider is not in fact mentioned in the verses cited by
Plutarch.

Excerpts from Didorus Siculus, *World History*

That the same Lycurgus brought an oracle from Delphi
concerning love of money and its memory is preserved in
the form of a proverb:

Love of money and nothing else will destroy Sparta.[3]

The Pythia gave Lycurgus the following oracle about the
constitution (marginal comment).

For thus Apollo who works from afar, the golden-
haired lord of the silver bow, prophesied from his
rich shrine:
(vv. 3-10)

3 Bergk inserted this in his fr. 3, but there is no reason to assign
it to Tyrtaeus, hence the omission of fr. 3 in West's edition.

ELEGIAC POETRY

5

ἡμετέρῳ βασιλῆϊ, θεοῖσι φίλῳ Θεοπόμπῳ,
    ὃν διὰ Μεσσήνην εἵλομεν εὐρύχορον,
Μεσσήνην ἀγαθὸν μὲν ἀροῦν, ἀγαθὸν δὲ
    φυτεύειν·
    ἀμφ᾿ αὐτὴν δ᾿ ἐμάχοντ᾿ ἐννέα καὶ δέκ᾿ ἔτη
5 νωλεμέως αἰεὶ ταλασίφρονα θυμὸν ἔχοντες
    αἰχμηταὶ πατέρων ἡμετέρων πατέρες·
εἰκοστῷ δ᾿ οἱ μὲν κατὰ πίονα ἔργα λιπόντες
    φεῦγον Ἰθωμαίων ἐκ μεγάλων ὀρέων.

3 ἀγαθὴν bis Buttmann   φυτεῦσαι Olympiodorus
4 ἄμφω τῷδε Strabo, ἀμφ᾿ αὐτὴν Paus.

Paus. 4.6.5

οὗτος δὲ ὁ Θεόπομπος ἦν καὶ ὁ πέρας ἐπιθεὶς τῷ
πολέμῳ· μαρτυρεῖ δέ μοι καὶ τὰ ἐλεγεῖα τῶν Τυρταίου
λέγοντα "ἡμετέρῳ—εὐρύχορον."

Schol. Plat. *Leg.* 629a (p. 301 Greene). Quae praecedunt
v. ad test. 3.

ἀφικόμενος δὲ οὗτος (sc. Τυρταῖος) εἰς Λακεδαίμονα
καὶ ἐπίπνους γενόμενος συνεβούλευσεν αὐτοῖς ἀν-
ελέσθαι τὸν πρὸς Μεσσηνίους πόλεμον, προτρέπων
παντοίως· ἐν οἷς καὶ τὸ φερόμενον εἰπεῖν ἔπος,
"Μεσσήνην—φυτεύειν."

cf. Olympiod. in *Alc.* I p. 103 Westerink (= schol. p. 100
Greene), Strab. 8.5.6

44

5

. . . to(?) our king Theopompus dear to the gods,
through whom we captured spacious Messene,
Messene good to plough and good to plant. For
nineteen years the spearmen fathers of our fathers
fought ever unceasingly over it, displaying steadfast
courage in their hearts, and in the twentieth year
the enemy fled from the high mountain range of
Ithome, abandoning their rich farmlands.[1]

[1] No source cites these as consecutive verses and many pre-
fer to print three separate fragments. The first sentence is incom-
plete and so the force of the initial dative cannot be determined.
Pausanias (4.13.7) dates the end of the war to 724, but V. Parker,
"The Dates of the Messenian Wars," *Chiron* 21 (1991) 25-47,
makes a good case for dating the First War to c. 690-670 and con-
sequently the Second to the latter part of the 7th century. See also
Mosshammer 204-209.

Pausanias, *Description of Greece*

It was this Theopompus who put an end to the war and
my evidence is the elegiac verses of Tyrtaeus which say (vv.
1-2).

Scholiast on Plato, *Laws*

Upon arriving in Lacedaemon and becoming inspired
Tyrtaeus advised them to wage war against the Messen-
ians, urging them on by every means possible, including
the famous verse (v. 3).

Strabo 6.3.3

Μεσσήνη δὲ ἑάλω πολεμηθεῖσα ἐννεακαίδεκα ἔτη,
καθάπερ καὶ Τυρταῖός φησι· "ἀμφ'—ὀρέων."

cf. Strab. 8.4.10 (v. fr. 8), Paus. 4.15.2 (vv. 4-6), 4.13.6 (vv. 7-8)

6 Paus. 4.14.4-5

τὰ δὲ ἐς αὐτοὺς Μεσσηνίους παρὰ Λακεδαιμονίων
ἔσχεν οὕτως. πρῶτον μὲν αὐτοῖς ἐπάγουσιν ὅρκον
μήτε ἀποστῆναί ποτε ἀπ' αὐτῶν μήτε ἄλλο ἐρ-
γάσασθαι νεώτερον μηδέν· δεύτερα δὲ φόρον μὲν
οὐδένα ἐπέταξαν εἰρημένον, οἱ δὲ τῶν γεωργουμένων
τροφῶν σφισιν ἀπέφερον ἐς Σπάρτην πάντων τὰ
ἡμίσεα. προείρητο δὲ καὶ ἐπὶ τὰς ἐκφορὰς τῶν
βασιλέων καὶ ἄλλων τῶν ἐν τέλει καὶ ἄνδρας ἐκ τῆς
Μεσσηνίας καὶ τὰς γυναῖκας ἐν ἐσθῆτι ἥκειν μελαίνῃ,
καὶ τοῖς παραβᾶσιν ἐπέκειτο ποινή. ‹ἐς τὰς› τιμωρίας
δὲ ἃς ὕβριζον ἐς τοὺς Μεσσηνίους Τυρταίῳ πεποιη-
μένα ἐστιν·

ὥσπερ ὄνοι μεγάλοις ἄχθεσι τειρόμενοι,
δεσποσύνοισι φέροντες ἀναγκαίης ὕπο λυγρῆς
ἥμισυ παντὸς ὅσον καρπὸν ἄρουρα φέρει.

3 πάνθ' ὅσ(σ)ων Paus. (ret. West), παντὸς ὅσον Ahrens, alia
alii

TYRTAEUS

Strabo, *Geography*

Messene was captured after a war of nineteen years, as Tyrtaeus says (vv. 4-8).

6 Pausanias, *Description of Greece*

As for the Messenians themselves they received the following treatment from the Lacedaemonians. First they exacted from them an oath never to revolt or to engage in any other act of rebellion. Second, they imposed no fixed tribute on them, but they brought to Sparta half of all their farm produce. And there was also a proclamation that the men come from Messenia with their wives dressed in black to the funerals of the kings and of other officials, and punishment was imposed on the transgressors. As for the penalties with which they mistreated the Messenians, there are the verses composed by Tyrtaeus:

> like asses worn out by heavy burdens, bringing to their masters out of grievous necessity half of all the produce that the land brings forth.

7 Pergit Paus.

ὅτι δὲ καὶ συμπενθεῖν ἔκειτο αὐτοῖς ἀνάγκη δεδή-
λωκεν ἐν τῷδε·

δεσπότας οἰμώζοντες, ὁμῶς ἄλοχοί τε καὶ αὐτοί,
εὖτέ τιν' οὐλομένη μοῖρα κίχοι θανάτου.

8 Strabo 8.4.10

πλεονάκις δὲ ἐπολέμησαν διὰ τὰς ἀποστάσεις τῶν
Μεσσηνίων. τὴν μὲν οὖν πρώτην κατάκτησιν αὐτῶν
φησι Τυρταῖος ἐν τοῖς ποιήμασι κατὰ τοὺς τῶν
πατέρων πατέρας γενέσθαι (fr. 5.6)· τὴν δὲ δευτέραν,
καθ' ἢν ἑλόμενοι συμμάχους Ἀργείους τε καὶ
†Ἠλείους (Ἀρκάδας Kramer) καὶ Πισάτας ἀπέστησαν,
Ἀρκάδων μὲν Ἀριστοκράτην τὸν Ὀρχομενοῦ βασιλέα
παρεχομένων στρατηγόν, Πισατῶν δὲ Πανταλέοντα
τὸν Ὀμφαλίωνος, ἡνίκα φησὶν αὐτὸς στρατηγῆσαι
τὸν πόλεμον τοῖς Λακεδαιμονίοις. Quae sequuntur v. ad
fr. 2.12-15.

9 Arist. *Eth. Nic.* 3.8.5.1116a36

καὶ οἱ προτάττοντες (v.l. προστάττοντες), κἂν ἀνα-
χωρῶσι τύπτοντες, τὸ αὐτὸ δρῶσι· καὶ οἱ πρὸ τῶν
τάφρων καὶ τῶν τοιούτων παρατάττοντες· πάντες γὰρ
ἀναγκάζουσι· δεῖ δὲ οὐ δι' ἀνάγκην ἀνδρεῖον εἶναι,
ἀλλ' ὅτι καλόν.

7 Pausanias continues

And that they were forced to share in their mourning Tyrtaeus has shown as follows:

> wailing for their masters, they and their wives alike,
> whenever the baneful lot of death came upon any.

8 Strabo, *Geography*

On more than one occasion they went to war because of the revolts of the Messenians. Tyrtaeus says in his poems that the first conquest of them took place at the time of the fathers' fathers, the second at the time when the Messenians chose Argives, Arcadians(?),[1] and Pisatans as allies and revolted, the Arcadians providing Aristocrates, king of Orchomenus, as general, and the Pisatans providing Pantaleon the son of Omphalion, at which time Tyrtaeus says that he himself served as general in the war for the Lacedaemonians.

[1] See n. 3 on fr. 23a.

9 Aristotle, *Nicomachean Ethics*

And those who draw up troops in front of them and beat them if they give ground are doing the same thing, as well as those who draw them up in battle order in front of trenches[1] and such things, since they are all using compulsion. A man ought to be brave not because he is compelled to be, but because it is noble.

Eustrat. ad loc. (*Comm. in Arist. Graeca* xx.165.1)

τοῦτο περὶ Λακεδαιμονίων λέγοι ἄν· τοιαύτην γάρ
τινα μάχην ὅτε πρὸς Μεσσηνίους ἐπολέμουν ἐμαχέ-
σαντο, ἧς καὶ Τυρταῖος μνημονεύει.

10 Lycurg. *in Leocr.* 107. Quae praecedunt v. ad test. 4.

καὶ περὶ τοὺς ἄλλους ποιητὰς οὐδένα λόγον ἔχοντες,
περὶ τούτου οὕτω σφόδρα ἐσπουδάκασιν ὥστε νόμον
ἔθεντο, ὅταν ἐν τοῖς ὅπλοις ἐξεστρατευμένοι (ἐκστρ.
codd., corr. van Es) ὦσι (εἰσὶν codd., corr. Becker),
καλεῖν ἐπὶ τὴν τοῦ βασιλέως σκηνὴν ἀκουσομένους
τῶν Τυρταίου ποιημάτων ἅπαντας, νομίζοντες οὕτως
ἂν αὐτοὺς μάλιστα πρὸ τῆς πατρίδος ἐθέλειν ἀπο-
θνήσκειν. χρήσιμον δ᾽ ἐστὶ καὶ τούτων ἀκοῦσαι τῶν
ἐλεγείων, ἵν᾽ ἐπίστησθε οἷα ποιοῦντες εὐδοκίμουν
παρ᾽ ἐκείνοις·

> τεθνάμεναι γὰρ καλὸν ἐνὶ προμάχοισι πεσόντα
> ἄνδρ᾽ ἀγαθὸν περὶ ᾗ πατρίδι μαρνάμενον,
> τὴν δ᾽ αὑτοῦ προλιπόντα πόλιν καὶ πίονας ἀγροὺς
> πτωχεύειν πάντων ἔστ᾽ ἀνιηρότατον,
> 5   πλαζόμενον σὺν μητρὶ φίλῃ καὶ πατρὶ γέροντι
> παισί τε σὺν μικροῖς κουριδίῃ τ᾽ ἀλόχῳ.
> ἐχθρὸς μὲν γὰρ τοῖσι μετέσσεται οὕς κεν ἵκηται,
> χρησμοσύνῃ τ᾽ εἴκων καὶ στυγερῇ πενίῃ,
> αἰσχύνει τε γένος, κατὰ δ᾽ ἀγλαὸν εἶδος ἐλέγχει,
> 10   πᾶσα δ᾽ ἀτιμίη καὶ κακότης ἕπεται.

Eustratius on the passage

One could say this about the Lacedaemonians; for when they waged war against the Messenians, such was their manner of fighting, as Tyrtaeus mentions.

1 It may be significant that a trench seems to be mentioned in fr. 23a.19.

10 Lycurgus, *Against Leocrates*

And although they took no account of other poets, they placed such high value on him that they passed a law that whenever they took to the field under arms they should all be called to the king's tent to listen to the poems of Tyrtaeus, judging that by so doing they would be especially willing to die for their homeland. And it is useful for you to listen to these elegiac verses, so that you may know by what kind of deeds they won esteem in their eyes:

> It is a fine thing for a brave man to die when he has fallen among the front ranks while fighting for his homeland, and it is the most painful thing of all to leave one's city and rich fields for a beggar's life, wandering about with his dear mother and aged father, with small children and wedded wife. For giving way to need and hateful poverty, he will be treated with hostility by whomever he meets, he brings disgrace on his line, belies his splendid form, and every indignity and evil attend him. If then

εἰ δ᾽ οὕτως ἀνδρός τοι ἀλωμένου οὐδεμί᾽ ὤρη
γίνεται οὔτ᾽ αἰδώς, οὐδ᾽ ὀπίσω γένεος,
θυμῷ γῆς πέρι τῆσδε μαχώμεθα καὶ περὶ παίδων
θνήσκωμεν ψυχέων μηκέτι φειδόμενοι.
15 ὦ νέοι, ἀλλὰ μάχεσθε παρ᾽ ἀλλήλοισι μένοντες,
μηδὲ φυγῆς αἰσχρῆς ἄρχετε μηδὲ φόβου,
ἀλλὰ μέγαν ποιεῖσθε καὶ ἄλκιμον ἐν φρεσὶ θυμόν,
μηδὲ φιλοψυχεῖτ᾽ ἀνδράσι μαρνάμενοι·
τοὺς δὲ παλαιοτέρους, ὧν οὐκέτι γούνατ᾽ ἐλαφρά,
20 μὴ καταλείποντες φεύγετε, τοὺς γεραιούς.
αἰσχρὸν γὰρ δὴ τοῦτο, μετὰ προμάχοισι πεσόντα
κεῖσθαι πρόσθε νέων ἄνδρα παλαιότερον,
ἤδη λευκὸν ἔχοντα κάρη πολιόν τε γένειον,
θυμὸν ἀποπνείοντ᾽ ἄλκιμον ἐν κονίῃ,
25 αἱματόεντ᾽ αἰδοῖα φίλαις ἐν χερσὶν ἔχοντα—
αἰσχρὰ τά γ᾽ ὀφθαλμοῖς καὶ νεμεσητὸν
ἰδεῖν—
καὶ χρόα γυμνωθέντα· νέοισι δὲ πάντ᾽ ἐπέοικεν,
ὄφρ᾽ ἐρατῆς ἥβης ἀγλαὸν ἄνθος ἔχῃ,
ἀνδράσι μὲν θηητὸς ἰδεῖν, ἐρατὸς δὲ γυναιξὶ
30 ζωὸς ἐών, καλὸς δ᾽ ἐν προμάχοισι πεσών.
ἀλλά τις εὖ διαβὰς μενέτω ποσὶν ἀμφοτέροισι
στηριχθεὶς ἐπὶ γῆς, χεῖλος ὀδοῦσι δακών.

1 ἐπὶ codd., corr. Francke   11 εἶθ᾽ οὕτως codd., corr.
Francke   12 οὔτ᾽ . . . οὔτ᾽ codd. NA, οὐδ᾽ . . . οὔτ᾽ recc., οὐδ᾽
. . . οὐδ᾽ Wilamowitz, οὔτ᾽ . . . οὐδ᾽ Gentili-Prato   τέλος codd.,
γένεος Ahrens, οὔτ᾽ ὄπις οὔτ᾽ ἔλεος Bergk   16 αἰσχρᾶς
codd., corr. Sauppe   29 θνητοῖσιν codd., θηητὸς Reiske

there is no regard or respect for a man who wanders
thus, nor yet for his family after him, let us fight with
spirit for this land and let us die for our children, no
longer sparing our lives. Come, you young men,
stand fast at one another's side and fight, and do not
start shameful flight or panic, but make the spirit in
your heart strong and valiant, and do not be in love
of life when you are fighting men. Do not abandon
and run away from elders, whose knees are no lon-
ger nimble, men revered. For this brings shame,
when an older man lies fallen among the front ranks
with the young behind him, his head already white
and his beard grey, breathing out his valiant spirit in
the dust, clutching in his hands his bloodied geni-
tals—this is a shameful sight and brings indignation
to behold—his body naked. But for the young ev-
erything is seemly, as long as he has the splendid
prime of lovely youth; while alive, men marvel at the
sight of him and women feel desire, and when he has
fallen among the front ranks, he is fair. Come, let ev-
eryone stand fast, with legs set well apart and both
feet fixed firmly on the ground, biting his lip with his
teeth.[1]

[1] Critics are divided whether we have one poem or two, the
second beginning at v. 15 (see n. 1 on test. 5). In spite of the initial
γάρ, some treat the poem as complete.

11 Stob. 4.9.16

Τυρταίου·

ἀλλ', Ἡρακλῆος γὰρ ἀνικήτου γένος ἐστέ,
θαρσεῖτ'·—οὔπω Ζεὺς αὐχένα λοξὸν ἔχει—
μηδ' ἀνδρῶν πληθὺν δειμαίνετε, μηδὲ φοβεῖσθε,
ἰθὺς δ' ἐς προμάχους ἀσπίδ' ἀνὴρ ἐχέτω,
5   ἐχθρὴν μὲν ψυχὴν θέμενος, θανάτου δὲ μελαίνας
κῆρας ⟨ὁμῶς⟩ αὐγαῖς ἠελίοιο φίλας.
ἴστε γὰρ ὡς Ἄρεος πολυδακρύου ἔργ' ἀΐδηλα,
εὖ δ' ὀργὴν ἐδάητ' ἀργαλέου πολέμου,
καὶ μετὰ φευγόντων τε διωκόντων τ' ἐγένεσθε,
10   ὦ νέοι, ἀμφοτέρων δ' ἐς κόρον ἠλάσατε.
οἳ μὲν γὰρ τολμῶσι παρ' ἀλλήλοισι μένοντες
ἔς τ' αὐτοσχεδίην καὶ προμάχους ἰέναι,
παυρότεροι θνήσκουσι, σαοῦσι δὲ λαὸν ὀπίσσω·
τρεσσάντων δ' ἀνδρῶν πᾶσ' ἀπόλωλ' ἀρετή.
15   οὐδεὶς ἄν ποτε ταῦτα λέγων ἀνύσειεν ἕκαστα,
ὅσσ', ἢν αἰσχρὰ πάθῃ, γίνεται ἀνδρὶ κακά·
ἀργαλέον γὰρ ὄπισθε μετάφρενόν ἐστι δαΐζειν
ἀνδρὸς φεύγοντος δηΐῳ ἐν πολέμῳ·
αἰσχρὸς δ' ἐστὶ νέκυς κατακείμενος ἐν κονίῃσι
20   νῶτον ὄπισθ' αἰχμῇ δουρὸς ἐληλάμενος.
ἀλλά τις εὖ διαβὰς μενέτω ποσὶν ἀμφοτέροισι
στηριχθεὶς ἐπὶ γῆς, χεῖλος ὀδοῦσι δακών,
μηρούς τε κνήμας τε κάτω καὶ στέρνα καὶ ὤμους
ἀσπίδος εὐρείης γαστρὶ καλυψάμενος·

11 Stobaeus, *Anthology*

From Tyrtaeus:

Come, take courage, for your stock is from uncon-
quered Heracles[1]—not yet does Zeus hold his neck
aslant[2]—and do not fear throngs of men or run in
flight, but let a man hold his shield straight toward
the front ranks, despising life and loving the black
death-spirits no less than the rays of the sun. You
know how destructive the deeds of woeful Ares are,
you have learned well the nature of grim war, you
have been with the pursuers and the pursued, you
young men, and you have had more than your fill of
both. Those who dare to stand fast at one another's
side and to advance towards the front ranks in hand-
to-hand conflict, they die in fewer numbers and they
keep safe the troops behind them;[3] but when men
run away, all esteem[4] is lost. No one could sum up in
words each and every evil that befalls a man, if he
suffers disgrace. For to pierce a man behind the
shoulder blades as he flees in deadly combat is grue-
some,[5] and a corpse lying in the dust, with the point
of a spear driven through his back from behind, is a
shameful sight. Come, let everyone stand fast, with
legs set well apart and both feet fixed firmly on the
ground, biting his lip with his teeth, and covering
thighs, shins below, chest, and shoulders with the
belly of his broad shield;[6] in his right hand let him

25   δεξιτερῇ δ᾽ ἐν χειρὶ τινασσέτω ὄβριμον ἔγχος,
        κινείτω δὲ λόφον δεινὸν ὑπὲρ κεφαλῆς·
        ἔρδων δ᾽ ὄβριμα ἔργα διδασκέσθω πολεμίζειν,
        μηδ᾽ ἐκτὸς βελέων ἑστάτω ἀσπίδ᾽ ἔχων,
        ἀλλά τις ἐγγὺς ἰὼν αὐτοσχεδὸν ἔγχεϊ μακρῷ
30   ἢ ξίφει οὐτάζων δήϊον ἄνδρ᾽ ἑλέτω,
        καὶ πόδα πὰρ ποδὶ θεὶς καὶ ἐπ᾽ ἀσπίδος ἀσπίδ᾽
        ἐρείσας,
        ἐν δὲ λόφον τε λόφῳ καὶ κυνέην κυνέῃ
        καὶ στέρνον στέρνῳ πεπληγμένος ἀνδρὶ μαχέσθω,
        ἢ ξίφεος κώπην ἢ δόρυ μακρὸν ἑλών.
35   ὑμεῖς δ᾽, ὦ γυμνῆτες, ὑπ᾽ ἀσπίδος ἄλλοθεν ἄλλος
        πτώσσοντες μεγάλοις βάλλετε χερμαδίοις
        δούρασί τε ξεστοῖσιν ἀκοντίζοντες ἐς αὐτούς,
        τοῖσι πανόπλοισιν πλησίον ἱστάμενοι.

4 εἰς codd., corr. Camerarius   5 ἐχθρὰν codd., corr. Bergk
6 ὁμῶς suppl. Grotius   13 σάουσι codd., corr. Buttmann
16 ἂν codd., corr. Valckenaer   μάθῃ West   17 ἁρπαλέον
Ahrens   33 πεπαλημένος codd., corr. Brunck
34 ἔχων West   38 πανοπλίοισι(ν) codd., corr. Dindorf

12 Stob. 4.10.1 (vv. 1-14) + 6 (vv. 15-44)

Τυρταίου·

        οὔτ᾽ ἂν μνησαίμην οὔτ᾽ ἐν λόγῳ ἄνδρα τιθείμην
        οὔτε ποδῶν ἀρετῆς οὔτε παλαιμοσύνης,

56

brandish a mighty spear and let him shake the plumed crest above his head in a fearsome manner. By doing mighty deeds let him learn how to fight and let him not stand—he has a shield—outside the range of missiles, but coming to close quarters let him strike the enemy, hitting him with long spear or sword; and also, with foot placed alongside foot and shield pressed against shield, let everyone draw near, crest to crest, helmet to helmet, and breast to breast, and fight against a man, seizing the hilt of his sword or his long spear. You light-armed men, as you crouch beneath a shield on either side, let fly with huge rocks and hurl your smooth javelins at them, standing close to those in full armour.

[1] Cf. frr. 2.13 and 19.8.   [2] Precise significance uncertain, but the phrase seems to mean that Zeus has not yet turned his face away; he is still on the side of the Spartans and so there is no reason to despair.   [3] Or less probably, "the future populace." [4] A somewhat free rendering of $\dot{a}\rho\epsilon\tau\dot{\eta}$, a word which here encompasses the qualities of excellence deemed necessary for one to be an ideal soldier.   [5] Ahrens' $\dot{a}\rho\pi a\lambda\acute{\epsilon}o\nu$ 'desirable' has been adopted by some, but Tyrtaeus may be showing an aversion both to killing from behind and to being killed from behind.
[6] For the problems presented by Tyrtaeus' description of armour and battle tactics see H. L. Lorimer, *ABSA* 42 (1947) 76-138, esp. 121-28, A. M. Snodgrass, *Early Greek Armour and Weapons* (Edinburgh 1964) 181-82, and P. Cartledge, *JHS* 97 (1977) 11-27.

12 Stobaeus, *Anthology*[1]

From Tyrtaeus:

I would not mention or take account of a man for his prowess in running or in wrestling, not even if

οὐδ᾽ εἰ Κυκλώπων μὲν ἔχοι μέγεθός τε βίην τε,
    νικῴη δὲ θέων Θρηΐκιον Βορέην,
5 οὐδ᾽ εἰ Τιθωνοῖο φυὴν χαριέστερος εἴη,
    πλουτοίη δὲ Μίδεω καὶ Κινύρεω μάλιον,
οὐδ᾽ εἰ Τανταλίδεω Πέλοπος βασιλεύτερος εἴη,
    γλῶσσαν δ᾽ Ἀδρήστου μειλιχόγηρυν ἔχοι,
οὐδ᾽ εἰ πᾶσαν ἔχοι δόξαν πλὴν θούριδος ἀλκῆς·
10   οὐ γὰρ ἀνὴρ ἀγαθὸς γίνεται ἐν πολέμῳ
εἰ μὴ τετλαίη μὲν ὁρῶν φόνον αἱματόεντα,
    καὶ δηΐων ὀρέγοιτ᾽ ἐγγύθεν ἱστάμενος.
ἥδ᾽ ἀρετή, τόδ᾽ ἄεθλον ἐν ἀνθρώποισιν ἄριστον
    κάλλιστόν τε φέρειν γίνεται ἀνδρὶ νέῳ.
15 ξυνὸν δ᾽ ἐσθλὸν τοῦτο πόληΐ τε παντί τε δήμῳ,
    ὅστις ἀνὴρ διαβὰς ἐν προμάχοισι μένῃ
νωλεμέως, αἰσχρῆς δὲ φυγῆς ἐπὶ πάγχυ λάθηται,
    ψυχὴν καὶ θυμὸν τλήμονα παρθέμενος,
θαρσύνῃ δ᾽ ἔπεσιν τὸν πλησίον ἄνδρα παρεστώς·
20   οὗτος ἀνὴρ ἀγαθὸς γίνεται ἐν πολέμῳ.
αἶψα δὲ δυσμενέων ἀνδρῶν ἔτρεψε φάλαγγας
    τρηχείας, σπουδῇ δ᾽ ἔσχεθε κῦμα μάχης.
αὐτὸς δ᾽ ἐν προμάχοισι πεσὼν φίλον ὤλεσε θυμόν,
    ἄστυ τε καὶ λαοὺς καὶ πατέρ᾽ εὐκλεΐσας,
25 πολλὰ διὰ στέρνοιο καὶ ἀσπίδος ὀμφαλοέσσης
    καὶ διὰ θώρηκος πρόσθεν ἐληλαμένος.
τὸν δ᾽ ὀλοφύρονται μὲν ὁμῶς νέοι ἠδὲ γέροντες,
    ἀργαλέῳ δὲ πόθῳ πᾶσα κέκηδε πόλις,
καὶ τύμβος καὶ παῖδες ἐν ἀνθρώποις ἀρίσημοι
30   καὶ παίδων παῖδες καὶ γένος ἐξοπίσω·

he had the size and strength of the Cyclopes and outstripped Thracian Boreas[2] in the race, nor if he were more handsome than Tithonus[3] in form and richer than Midas[4] and Cinyras,[5] nor if he were more kingly than Pelops,[6] son of Tantalus, and had a tongue that spoke as winningly as Adrastus',[7] nor if he had a reputation for everything save furious valour. For no man is good in war unless he can endure the sight of bloody slaughter and, standing close, can lunge at the enemy. This is excellence, this the best human prize and the fairest for a young man to win. This is a common benefit for the state and all the people, whenever a man with firm stance among the front ranks never ceases to hold his ground, is utterly unmindful of shameful flight, risking his life and displaying a steadfast spirit, and standing by the man next to him speaks encouragingly. This man is good in war. He quickly routs the bristling ranks of the enemy and by his zeal stems the tide of battle. And if he falls among the front ranks, pierced many times through his breast and bossed shield[8] and corselet from the front, he loses his own dear life but brings glory to his city, to his people, and to his father. Young and old alike mourn him, all the city is distressed by the painful loss, and his tomb and children are pointed out among the people, and his children's children and his line after

οὐδέ ποτε κλέος ἐσθλὸν ἀπόλλυται οὐδ' ὄνομ'
   αὐτοῦ,
ἀλλ' ὑπὸ γῆς περ ἐὼν γίνεται ἀθάνατος,
ὅντιν' ἀριστεύοντα μένοντά τε μαρνάμενόν τε
   γῆς πέρι καὶ παίδων θοῦρος Ἄρης ὀλέσῃ.
35 εἰ δὲ φύγῃ μὲν κῆρα τανηλεγέος θανάτοιο,
   νικήσας δ' αἰχμῆς ἀγλαὸν εὖχος ἕλῃ,
πάντες μιν τιμῶσιν, ὁμῶς νέοι ἠδὲ παλαιοί,
   πολλὰ δὲ τερπνὰ παθὼν ἔρχεται εἰς Ἀΐδην,
γηράσκων δ' ἀστοῖσι μεταπρέπει, οὐδέ τις αὐτὸν
40   βλάπτειν οὔτ' αἰδοῦς οὔτε δίκης ἐθέλει,
πάντες δ' ἐν θώκοισιν ὁμῶς νέοι οἵ τε κατ' αὐτὸν
   εἴκουσ' ἐκ χώρης οἵ τε παλαιότεροι.
ταύτης νῦν τις ἀνὴρ ἀρετῆς εἰς ἄκρον ἱκέσθαι
   πειράσθω θυμῷ μὴ μεθιεὶς πολέμου.

1 τιθείμην Plato bis, τιθείην Stob.   2 παλαισμοσύνης
cod. M   6 κινυρέοιο μᾶλλον codd., corr. M. Schmidt
11 ὁρᾶν Plato 629e   17 αἰσχρᾶς SM (-ὸς A), corr. Bergk
44 πόλεμον codd., corr. Camerarius

13 Galen. *de plac. Hippocr. et Plat.* 3.309 sq. (p. 190 De
   Lacy) = *SVF* ii.255 von Arnim

ὥσπερ γὰρ ἐξ Ὁμήρου καὶ Ἡσιόδου βραχέα παρ-
εθέμην ὀλίγῳ πρόσθεν ὧν ὁ Χρύσιππος ἔγραψεν,

them. Never do his name and good fame perish, but
even though he is beneath the earth he is immortal,
whoever it is that furious Ares slays as he displays his
prowess by standing fast and fighting for land and
children. And if he escapes the doom of death that
brings long sorrow and by his victory makes good his
spear's splendid boast, he is honoured by all, young
and old alike, many are the joys he experiences be-
fore he goes to Hades, and in his old age he stands
out among the townsmen; no one seeks to deprive
him of respect and his just rights, but all men at the
benches yield their place to him, the young, those of
his own age, and the elders. Let everyone strive now
with all his heart to reach the pinnacle of this excel-
lence, with no slackening in war.

[1] Plato, *Laws* 1.629a-630b (see test. 2), quotes vv. 1 and, with
slight changes, most of 11-12 and paraphrases the contents of 1-
20; in 660e-661a he again quotes v. 1 and paraphrases 1-12. We
also have 13-16 in Theognis 1003-1006 (with σοφῷ in place of
νέῳ) and much of 37-42 is repeated in Theognis 935-38.
[2] The North Wind. [3] A Trojan youth, brother of Priam, with
whom the goddess Eos fell in love. [4] A Phrygian king whose
touch was said to turn everything to gold. [5] A king of Cy-
prus (cf. *Iliad* 11.20 ff.). [6] The Peloponnese was named af-
ter him (see fr. 2.15). For a lengthy account of the main myth asso-
ciated with him see Pindar, *Olympian* 1. [7] A king of Argos,
the only one of the Seven against Thebes to survive. [8] See
n. 6 on fr. 11.

13 Galen, *On the Doctrines of Hippocrates and Plato*

For just as a short time ago I cited as evidence a few pas-
sages which Chrysippus took from Homer and Hesiod,

οὕτως ἐξ Ὀρφέως καὶ Ἐμπεδοκλέους καὶ Τυρταίου
καὶ Στησιχόρου καὶ Εὐριπίδου καὶ ἑτέρων ποιητῶν
ἐπῶν μνημονεύει παμπόλ‹λ›ων ὁμοίαν ἐχόντων ἀτο-
πίαν, οἷον καὶ ὅταν εἴπῃ Τυρταῖον λέγοντα

αἴθωνος δὲ λέοντος ἔχων ἐν στήθεσι θυμόν.

ὅτι μὲν γὰρ ἔχει ὁ λέων θυμόν, ἀκριβῶς ἅπαντες
ἄνθρωποι καὶ πρὶν ἀκοῦσαι Τυρταίου γιγνώσκομεν,
οὐ μὴν Χρυσίππῳ γ' ἔπρεπε παραθέσθαι τὸ ἔπος
ἀφαιρουμένῳ τοὺς λέοντας τὸν θυμόν. . . . Τυρταῖος δέ
γε, καθάπερ οὖν καὶ Ὅμηρος καὶ Ἡσίοδος καὶ ἁπλῶς
εἰπεῖν ἅπαντες οἱ ποιηταί, σφοδρότατον ἔχειν φησὶ
τοὺς λέοντας τὸν θυμόν, ὥστε καὶ τῶν ἀνθρώπων
ὅστις ἂν ᾖ θυμοειδέστατος, εἰκάζουσι λέοντι.

14 Plut. de Stoic. repugn. 14.1039e (= SVF iii.39 von
Arnim)

καὶ μὴν οὐχ ἕτερα δεῖ βιβλία διειλῆσαι τοῦ Χρυ-
σίππου τὴν πρὸς αὑτὸν ἐνδεικνυμένους μάχην, ἀλλ' ἐν
αὐτοῖς τούτοις ποτὲ μὲν ‹τὸ› τοῦ Ἀντισθένους (fr. 67
Caizzi) ἐπαινῶν προφέρεται, τὸ δεῖν κτᾶσθαι νοῦν ἢ
βρόχον, καὶ τοῦ Τυρταίου τὸ

πρὶν ἀρετῆς πελάσαι τέρμασιν ἢ θανάτου.

15-16 = 856-857 PMG

so he mentions a great many verses from Orpheus, Empedocles, Tyrtaeus, Stesichorus, Euripides, and other poets which are similarly inept, such as when he speaks of Tyrtaeus as saying

> with a tawny lion's spirit in his (your) breast.

For we all know very well that a lion has spirit, even before listening to Tyrtaeus, and it was quite inappropriate for Chrysippus to cite the verse since he denies spirit to lions. . . . But Tyrtaeus, like Homer and Hesiod and in short all poets, says that lions have the most violent spirit, and as a result they compare to a lion anyone who is extremely spirited.

14 Plutarch, *On Stoic Self-Contradictions*

And it is not necessary to unroll other books as a display of Chrysippus in conflict with himself, since in these books themselves he now cites with approval the saying of Antisthenes that there is need to acquire intelligence or the noose and that of Tyrtaeus:

> before one draws near to the culmination of excellence or dies

17 Choerob. in Hephaest. (p. 196.6 Consbruch)

εὑρίσκεται δὲ ἁπλῶς ἐν μέσῳ λέξεως κοινὴ καὶ ἐν
παλιμβακχείῳ, ὡς καὶ παρὰ Τυρταίῳ

–⏑⏑ ἥρῶες –⏑⏑ –⏑⏑ –⏑⏑ – –

οὕτω γὰρ ἔλαβε τὸν δεύτερον πόδα τοῦ στίχου.

18-23 P. Berol. 11675, ed. Wilamowitz

18 P. Berol. 11675 fr. A col. i

$$\qquad\quad ἀ]γαλλομένη$$
$$\qquad\quad]α καὶ κροκόεντα$$
$$\qquad\text{desunt versus tres}$$
6 $$\qquad\quad]πυ[..(.)].[.]ν$$
$$\qquad\quad τερ]άεσσι Διός$$

19 P. Berol. 11675 fr. A col. ii

$$\qquad\qquad].οσ[$$
$$\qquad -τ]ηράς τε λίθων κα[ὶ$$
$$\qquad\quad]ν ἔθνεσιν εἰδομ[ένους$$
$$\qquad βρ]οτολοιγὸς Ἄρης ακ[$$
5 $$\qquad\quad]ιθείῃ, τοὺς δ' ὑπερα[$$
$$\qquad\quad]ν ἐοικότες η[$$
$$\qquad]αι κοίλης ἀσπίσι φραξάμ[ενοι,$$
χωρὶς Πάμφυλοί τε καὶ Ὑλλεῖς ἠδ[ὲ Δυμᾶνες,
ἀνδροφόνους μελίας χερσὶν ἀν[ασχόμενοι.
10 ....]δ' ἀθανάτοισι θεοῖς ἐπὶ πάντ[α τρέποντες

17 Choeroboscus on Hephaestion

A common syllable[1] is generally found in the middle of a word and in a palimbacchius ($--\cup$), as in Tyrtaeus

> heroes

since this is how he scanned the second foot of the line.

[1] I.e., one capable of being either long or short.

18-23 Berlin papyrus (3rd c. B.C.)[1]

[1] It seems likely that more than one poem is represented by the fragments. Unless otherwise indicated, the supplements are those of Wilamowitz.

18 Same papyrus

> . . . she exulting . . . and saffron-coloured (dress?) . . . portents of Zeus

19 Same papyrus

> . . . hurlers(?) of stones and . . . like hordes of wasps(?) . . . Ares, the bane of men, . . . like . . . making a fence with hollow shields,[1] Pamphyloi, Hylleis, and (Dymanes)[2] separately, brandishing in their (your?) hands murderous spears of ash. . . . (entrusting) everything to the immortal gods . . . we will

.....]ατερμ...ιηι πεισόμεθ᾽ ἡγεμ[ό
ἀλλ᾽ εὐθὺς σύμπαντες ἀλοιησέο[μεν
ἀ]νδράσιν αἰχμηταῖς ἐγγύθεν ἱσ[τάμενοι.
δεινὸς δ᾽ ἀμφοτέρων ἔσται κτύπος[
15   ἀσπίδας εὐκύκλους ἀσπίσι τυπτ[
        ]ήσουσιν ἐπ᾽ ἀλλήλοισι π[εσόντες·
θώρηκε]ς δ᾽ ἀνδρῶν στήθεσιν ἀμ[φι
λοιγὸ]ν ἐρωήσουσιν ἐρεικόμενο[ι
        αἱ δ᾽ ὑπὸ] χερμαδίων βαλλόμεναι μ[εγάλων
20   χάλκεια]ι κ[όρυ]θες καναχὴν ἔξου[σι

2 βλητ]ῆρας Snell   fin. τοξότας ἄνδρας West
3 σφηκῶ]ν Sitzler   5 ἰθείη vel]ι θείη   8 Ὑλλέες Snell
10 οὕτω] Wil., οὔπω] West   11 ὄκνου] ἄτερ μονίη . . .
ἡγεμ[όνων Wil.   12 αλοιησεν[pap., corr. West
15 τυπτ[ομένων Wil.   16 fin. Lobel   18 λοιγὸ]ν West

20 P. Berol. 11675 fr. B col. i

Διωνύσο]ιο τιθήνηι
      -κό]μου Σεμέλης
          ]ωεμψ.[...]σει
                    ]
5   ].[   ]
              ]μενη[   ]
              ]εικελον[   ]
        ]α φέρειν
      ἀ]εθλοφ[ό]ροι περὶ νίκης
10   τέ]ρμ᾽ ἐπιδερκόμενοι

66

obey the . . . of our leader(s). But all together at once
we will crush . . ., standing close to the spearmen.[3]
The din will be terrible . . . as both sides dash(?)
round shields against shields (and?) falling upon
each other they will . . .; and (corselets) on men's
breasts, though rent . . ., will ward off (destruction)
(and the bronze) helmets, struck (by huge) stones,
will ring out . . .

[1] See n. 6 on fr. 11.   [2] The three Dorian tribes, said to
be descended from Hyllus, son of Heracles, and the two sons
of Aegimius, whose father was Dorus, eponym of the Dorians.
See n. 2 on fr. 2.   [3] Probably the enemy rather than fellow
Spartans.

20 Same papyrus

. . . nurse of Dionysus[1] . . . of (fair)-haired Semele[2]
. . .(like?) prize-winning (horses?)[3] . . . with our eyes
on the goal (we will vie?) for victory . . . conveying a

καλ]λίτροχον ἅρμα φέροντες
]όμενοι
]εύοντας ὄπισθεν
]χαίτας ὑπὲρ κεφαλῆς
15   ]συνοίσομεν ὀξὺν ἄρηα
].θεσιν.[.].[   ]
ο]ὐδὲ λογήσει
]σέχων

1 τιθήνηι vel -ην vel -ης   2 καλλικό]μου Wil.
11 καλ]λίτροχον West   13 ν]εύοντας vel χ]εύοντας West

21-22 P. Berol. 11675 fr. B col. ii, fr. C col. i

23 P. Berol. 11675 fr. C col. ii

ο.[..]στευο[
ἐξείης πα[
  τεῖχος α.[.]οστη[
οισ.μπαλλομε[
5   κλῆρος καὶ ταφ[
Μεσσηνίων[
  τεῖχος τερυ[
οἱ μὲν γὰρ β[
  ἀντίοι ἱστ[α
10 οἱ δ' ἐκτὸς [βελέων
  ἐν δὲ μέσοις ἡμεῖς σ.[
πύργου δυ[
  λείψουσ' ἰλη[δὸν

well-wheeled chariot . . . behind . . . hair above the
head[4] . . . we will engage in keenly contested war . . .
and (he?) will take no account of . . .

[1] Perhaps Mt. Nyssa (cf. Terpander fr. 9 Campbell).
[2] Mother of Dionysus.   [3] Perhaps a simile resembling that of
Iliad 22.162 ff.   [4] Presumably either the mane above the
horse's head or the helmet plumes above a soldier's head.

21-22 Same papyrus

Fr. 21 consists of only the first few letters of 17 verses. There is
a reference to fighting and vv. 5 and 7 begin with ἀργεσ[τ "clear-
ing," an epithet of the south wind in *Il*. 11.306 and of the west wind
in Hes. *Theog*. 379. The repetition suggests a simile, perhaps com-
paring the scattering of the enemy to the clearing effects of the
wind. Fr. 22 contains only five letters.

23 Same papyrus

. . . one after another . . . wall . . . allotment of land
and (grave?) . . . of the Messenians . . . wall . . . for
some . . . stand(ing) face to face . . . and others out-
side (the range of missiles) . . . and in the middle we
. . . of a tower . . . they will leave in throngs . . . and as

οἱ δ᾽ ὡς ἐκ πο[

15   κυ[ ]αδ[

τοῖς ἴκελοι μ[

    Ἥρης αἰδοίης [

εὖτ᾽ ἂν Τυνδαρί[δαι

5 τάφ[ος West, τάφ[ρος Wilamowitz   10 suppl. West (coll. fr. 11.28)

23a P. Oxy. xlvii.3316, ed. Haslam

10   .]...[.].ενων[..].χει βέλε᾽ ἄγρ[ια

γλαυκῶπις θυ[γ]άτηρ αἰγιόχ[οιο Διός.

πολλοὶ δὲ ξυστοῖσιν ἀκοντισσ[

    α]ἰχμῆις ὀξείηις ἄνδρες ἐπισ[

γ]υμνομάχοι προθέ[ο]ντες ὑπ[

15   .]καδες Ἀργείωννγελ[...]χ[

...].ιμεν παρὰ τεῖχ[ος

....]θιηισιν· ὕδωρ ..[

....]παρ᾽ Ἀθηναίης γ[λαυκώπιδος

...]ιψαντ.[.] τάφρο.[

20   πάντ]ας μὲν κτενέουσ[ι

Σπα]ρτιητέων ὁπόσου[ς

ἐξ]οπίσω φεύγοντας α[

10 ἴ]σχει West   fin. Παλλὰς Ἀθήνη Gentili-Prato
15 Ἀρ]κάδες Haslam   Ἀργείω(ι) νῦν? Haslam

24 = test. 9.7-8

70

those from . . . like them . . . of august Hera . . . whenever the Tyndaridae[1] . . .

[1] Castor and Pollux.

23a Oxyrhynchus papyrus (early 3rd c. A.D.)[1]

. . . the grey-eyed daughter of aegis-bearing Zeus (checks?) the savage missiles. Many (will?) let fly with javelins . . . sharp points[2] . . . the light-armed men running forward . . . Arcadians(?) . . . of the Argives(?)[3] . . . along the wall . . . water . . . from (grey-eyed) Athena . . . trench[4] . . . they will kill all . . . of the Spartans as many as . . . fleeing in retreat. . .

[1] I have omitted the first nine verses, which are too mutilated to be translated.   [2] It is not clear whether these are spear points or the sharp points of the javelins.   [3] The Argives and apparently the Arcadians are mentioned in fr. 8 as allies of the Messenians, but the historicity of an Argive alliance has been questioned by K. Tausend, *Tyche* 8 (1993) 197-201.   [4] Cf. fr. 9.

MIMNERMUS

TESTIMONIA

1 *Suda* (iii.397.20 Adler)

Μίμνερμος Λιγυρτυάδου, Κολοφώνιος ἢ Σμυρναῖος ἢ
Ἀστυπαλαιεύς, ἐλεγειοποιός. γέγονε δ᾽ ἐπὶ τῆς λζ´
ὀλυμπιάδος, ὡς προτερεύειν τῶν ζ´ σοφῶν· τινὲς δὲ
αὐτοῖς καὶ συγχρονεῖν λέγουσιν. ἐκαλεῖτο δὲ καὶ Λι-
γυαστάδης διὰ τὸ ἐμμελὲς καὶ λιγύ. ἔγραψε βιβλία
†ταῦτα πολλά.

2 Strabo 14.1.28

ἄνδρες δ᾽ ἐγένοντο Κολοφώνιοι τῶν μνημονευομένων
Μίμνερμος, αὐλητὴς ἅμα καὶ ποιητὴς ἐλεγείας, καὶ
Ξενοφάνης ὁ φυσικὸς . . .

---

[1] See n. 1 on test. 1. Several other sources also refer to
Mimnermus as a Colophonian (testt. 6, 18, 19 Gent.-Pr. and test.
10 below).

MIMNERMUS

TESTIMONIA

1 *Suda*

Mimnermus, son of Ligyrtyades, from Colophon or Smyrna or Astypalaea,[1] an elegiac poet. He flourished in the 37th Olympiad (632-29) and so is earlier than the Seven Sages, although some say that he was their contemporary. He was also called Ligyaistades[2] because of his harmonious clarity. He wrote . . . books.[3]

[1] An island in the southern Aegean and clearly an error (see Allen 13 n. 17). Fr. 9 strongly suggests that he was from Smyrna and the mention of both Colophon and Smyrna in that fragment may have contributed to the confusion.   [2] Probably derived from Solon fr. 20.3.   [3] For possible restorations of the corruption (lit. "these many books") see Allen 23 n. 9. Perhaps the text originally said something like "He wrote two books containing many poems."

2 Strabo, *Geography*

Among the Colophonians[1] who are remembered there were Mimnermus, who was both a pipe-player and an elegiac poet, and Xenophanes the natural philosopher . . .

3 Ath. 13.597a

παρέλιπον δὲ καὶ τὴν Μιμνέρμου αὐλητρίδα Ναννὼ
καὶ τὴν Ἑρμησιάνακτος τοῦ Κολοφωνίου Λεόντιον.

4 Hermesian. fr. 7.35-40 Powell ap. Ath. 13.597f

35 Μίμνερμος δέ, τὸν ἡδὺν ὃς εὕρετο πολλὸν
        ἀνατλὰς
      ἦχον καὶ μαλακοῦ πνεῦμ᾽ ἀπὸ πενταμέτρου,
    καίετο μὲν Ναννοῦς, πολιῷ δ᾽ ἐπὶ πολλάκι λωτῷ
      κνημωθεὶς κώμους εἶχε σὺν Ἐξαμύῃ·
    †ἠδ᾽ ἤχθεε† δ᾽ Ἑρμόβιον τὸν ἀεὶ βαρὺν ἠδὲ
        Φερεκλῆν
40 ἐχθρόν, μισήσας οἷ᾽ ἀνέπεμψεν ἔπη.

5 *Anth. Pal.* 12.168.1-2 = *HE* 3086-87 (Ποσιδίππου)

Ναννοῦς καὶ Λύδης ἐπίχει δύο, καὶ †φερεκάστου
  Μιμνέρμου καὶ τοῦ σώφρονος Ἀντιμάχου.

1 φιλεράστου Jacobs, φιλέρωτος Allen

74

3 Athenaeus, *Scholars at Dinner*

I have also omitted Mimnermus' pipe-player Nanno and
the Leontion of Hermesianax[1] of Colophon.

[1] A Hellenistic poet who wrote three books of elegies on his
mistress Leontion, including a catalogue of the love affairs of
poets and philosophers (see test. 4 below).

4 Hermesianax

And Mimnermus, who after much suffering[1] discov-
ered the sweet sound and breath given off by the
soft pentameter, was on fire for Nanno, and often
with his lips encircled(?) on the grey lotus-pipe he
would hold revel with Examyes. But he . . . the ever
grievous Hermobius and hostile Pherecles,[2] hating
the kind of verses he (Pherecles?) sent forth.

[1] If correctly translated, this implies that he took up poetry as
a result of unhappy love affairs, but perhaps the meaning is "af-
ter much perseverence."   [2] Possibly Hermobius resisted
Mimnermus' advances, but responded to the love poetry of
Pherecles. For attempts to restore the introductory verb see Al-
len 19.

5 *Palatine Anthology* (Posidippus)

Pour in two (ladles) of Nanno and Lyde, two of
amorous(?) Mimnermus and the temperate Anti-
machus.[1]

[1] Antimachus of Colophon (5th-4th c. B.C.) composed an ele-
giac poem celebrating his love for Lyde.

6 Alex. Aet. fr. 5.4-5 Powell ap. Ath. 15.699b

Μιμνέρμου δ᾽ εἰς ἔπος ἄκρον ἰὼν
παιδομανεῖ σὺν ἔρωτι †πότην ἴσον†·

5 παιδομανὴς ἐν ἔρωτι Schweighäuser   ποτ᾽ ἦν idem

7 Ps.-Plut. *de musica* 8.1133f = Hipponax fr. 153 W.

καὶ ἄλλος δ᾽ ἐστὶν ἀρχαῖος νόμος καλούμενος Κρα-
δίας, ὅν φησιν Ἱππῶναξ Μίμνερμον αὐλῆσαι. ἐν ἀρ-
χῇ γὰρ ἐλεγεῖα μεμελοποιημένα οἱ αὐλῳδοὶ ᾖδον.

8 Ath. 14.620c

Χαμαιλέων δὲ ἐν τῷ περὶ Στησιχόρου (fr. 28 Wehrli)
καὶ μελῳδηθῆναί φησιν οὐ μόνον τὰ Ὁμήρου ἀλλὰ
καὶ τὰ Ἡσιόδου καὶ Ἀρχιλόχου, ἔτι δὲ Μιμνέρμου καὶ
Φωκυλίδου.

9 Porph. in Hor. *epist.* 2.2.101 (p. 399 Holder)

Mimnermus duos libros †luculentibus† scripsit.

    luculenti‹s versi›bus Garzya

6 Alexander Aetolus

And following Mimnermus' verses to the full with
his mad love for boys he[1] . . .

[1] The subject is Boeotus, a Sicilian writer of parodies. In spite
of the textual uncertainties the passage alludes clearly to peder-
astic verse in Mimnermus' poetry (cf. fr. 1.9).

7 Pseudo-Plutarch, *On Music*

And there is also another ancient melody called Cradias,[1]
which Hipponax says Mimnermus performed on the pipe.
For in the beginning those who sang to the pipe sang ele-
gies set to music.

[1] Literally 'melody of the fig branch.' Hesychius s.v. explains it
as "a melody they pipe over those escorted out as scapegoats,
whipped with fig branches and fig leaves."

8 Athenaeus, *Scholars at Dinner*

Chamaeleon in his work *On Stesichorus* says that not only
Homer's verses were set to music but also those of
Hesiod and Archilochus and in addition Mimnermus and
Phocylides.

9 Porphyrio on Horace, *Epistles*

Mimnermus wrote two books[1] of splendid verses(?).

[1] Our only source for the number of Mimnermus' books in the
Alexandrian edition.

10 Callim. *Aetia* fr. 1.11-12 Pf.

τοῖν δὲ] δυοῖν Μίμνερμος ὅτι γλυκύς, αἱ κατὰ
λεπτὸν
......] ἡ μεγάλη δ᾽ οὐκ ἐδίδαξε γυνή.

12 ῥήσιες suppl. Rostagni, κῶραί γ᾽ Allen

Schol. Flor. ad loc.

παρα]τίθεταί τε ἐν σ(υγ)κρίσει τὰ ὀλίγων στί[χ(ων)
ὄν]τα ποιήματα Μιμνέρμου τοῦ Κο[λοφω]νίου καὶ
Φιλίτα τοῦ Κῴου βελτίονα [τ(ῶν) πολ]υστίχων αὐ-
τ(ῶν) φάσκων εἶναι [...

11 Hor. *epist.* 1.6.65-66

si, Mimnermus uti censet, sine amore iocisque
nil est iucundum, vivas in amore iocisque.

Porph. ad loc. (p. 235 Holder)

Mimnermus elegiarum scriptor fuit. amores plus incom-
modi quam gaudia habere demonstrat.

12 Prop. 1.9.11-12

plus in amore valet Mimnermi versus Homero:
carmina mansuetus lenia quaerit Amor.

10 Callimachus, *Aetia*

Of the two (types of poetry) it was his slender (verses?), not the big lady, that revealed Mimnermus' sweetness.

Florentine scholia on the passage

He places in comparison the poems of a few lines of Mimnermus the Colophonian and of Philetas the Coan, declaring that they are better than their own poems of many lines.[1]

[1] The two verses of Callimachus (together with the surrounding verses omitted here) and the remarks of the scholiast have been the subject of much controversy, which is conveniently summarized by Allen 146-56. I have adopted his conclusions, namely, that 'the big lady' is the *Smyrneis* (cf. fr. 13A) and 'the slender verses' the short poems making up the *Nanno*.

11 Horace, *Epistles*

If, as Mimnermus believes, there is no joy without love and jests,[1] may you live amid love and jests.

Porphyrio on the passage

Mimnermus was a writer of elegies. He shows that love affairs involve more trouble than joy.

[1] Cf. fr. 1.1.

12 Propertius

In love the verses of Mimnermus prevail over those of Homer. Gentle love calls for soft songs.

See also Callinus test. 2.

FRAGMENTS

1 Stob. 4.20.16

Μιμνέρμου·

τίς δὲ βίος, τί δὲ τερπνὸν ἄτερ χρυσέης
    Ἀφροδίτης;
τεθναίην, ὅτε μοι μηκέτι ταῦτα μέλοι,
κρυπταδίη φιλότης καὶ μείλιχα δῶρα καὶ εὐνή,
    οἷ᾽ ἥβης ἄνθεα γίνεται ἁρπαλέα
5   ἀνδράσιν ἠδὲ γυναιξίν· ἐπεὶ δ᾽ ὀδυνηρὸν ἐπέλθῃ
    γῆρας, ὅ τ᾽ αἰσχρὸν ὅμως καὶ καλὸν ἄνδρα
    τιθεῖ,
αἰεί μιν φρένας ἀμφὶ κακαὶ τείρουσι μέριμναι,
    οὐδ᾽ αὐγὰς προσορέων τέρπεται ἠελίου,
ἀλλ᾽ ἐχθρὸς μὲν παισίν, ἀτίμαστος δὲ γυναιξίν·
10   οὕτως ἀργαλέον γῆρας ἔθηκε θεός.

Plut. *de virt. mor.* 6.445f

ἀκολάστων μὲν γὰρ αἵδε φωναί· "τίς . . . μέλοι."

1 χάρις pro βίος Plut.   ἄνευ Plut.   χρυσῆς codd., corr.
Brunck   2 μέλει Plut.   4 οἱ M, εἰ A: οἷ᾽ Bergk, οἷ᾽ Ahrens
5 τ᾽ codd., corr. Gesner   6 ὅμως καὶ κακὸν Hermann
7 μὲν codd., corr. Bergk   8 προσορῶν codd., corr. dub.
West

FRAGMENTS

1 Stobaeus, *Anthology*

From Mimnermus:

> What life is there, what pleasure without golden
> Aphrodite? May I die when I no longer care about
> secret intrigues, persuasive gifts, and the bed,[1] those
> blossoms of youth that men and women find al-
> luring. But when painful old age comes on, which
> makes even a handsome man ugly, grievous cares
> wear away his heart and he derives no joy from
> looking upon the sunlight; he is hateful to boys and
> women hold him in no honour. So harsh has the god[2]
> made old age.

Plutarch, *On Moral Virtue*

These are the utterances of intemperate people (vv. 1-2).

[1] On v. 3 see C. M. Dawson, *YCS* 19 (1966) 49.   [2] Pre-
sumably Zeus in view of fr. 2.16.

2 Stob. 4.34.12

Μιμνέρμου·

ἡμεῖς δ', οἷά τε φύλλα φύει πολυάνθεμος ὥρη
ἔαρος, ὅτ' αἶψ' αὐγῆς αὔξεται ἠελίου,
τοῖς ἴκελοι πήχυιον ἐπὶ χρόνον ἄνθεσιν ἥβης
τερπόμεθα, πρὸς θεῶν εἰδότες οὔτε κακὸν
5   οὔτ' ἀγαθόν· Κῆρες δὲ παρεστήκασι μέλαιναι,
ἡ μὲν ἔχουσα τέλος γήραος ἀργαλέου,
ἡ δ' ἑτέρη θανάτοιο· μίνυνθα δὲ γίνεται ἥβης
καρπός, ὅσον τ' ἐπὶ γῆν κίδναται ἠέλιος.
αὐτὰρ ἐπὴν δὴ τοῦτο τέλος παραμείψεται ὥρης,
10   αὐτίκα δὴ τεθνάναι βέλτιον ἢ βίοτος·
πολλὰ γὰρ ἐν θυμῷ κακὰ γίνεται· ἄλλοτε οἶκος
τρυχοῦται, πενίης δ' ἔργ' ὀδυνηρὰ πέλει·
ἄλλος δ' αὖ παίδων ἐπιδεύεται, ὧν τε μάλιστα
ἱμείρων κατὰ γῆς ἔρχεται εἰς Ἀΐδην·
15   ἄλλος νοῦσον ἔχει θυμοφθόρον· οὐδέ τίς ἐστιν
ἀνθρώπων ᾧ Ζεὺς μὴ κακὰ πολλὰ διδοῖ.

1 πολυανθέος ὥρῃ (-άνθεος A) Bergk   2 αὐγὴ codd.,
corr. Schneidewin   10 αὐτίκα τεθνάμεναι Bach, prob.
Gent.-Pr.   βέλτερον Friis Johansen et Allen

3 Stob. 4.50.32

Μιμνέρμου SM (Μενάνδρου A)·

τὸ πρὶν ἐὼν κάλλιστος, ἐπὴν παραμείψεται ὥρη,
οὐδὲ πατὴρ παισὶν τίμιος οὔτε φίλος.

2 Stobaeus, *Anthology*

From Mimnermus:

> We are like the leaves which the flowery season of
> spring brings forth, when they quickly grow beneath
> the rays of the sun; like them we delight in the
> flowers of youth for an arm's length of time, knowing
> neither the bad nor the good that comes from the
> gods.[1] But the dark spirits of doom stand beside us,
> one holding grievous old age as the outcome, the
> other death. Youth's fruit is short-lived, lasting as
> long as the sunlight spreads over the earth.[2] And
> when the end of this season passes by, straightway
> death is better than life. For many are the miseries
> that beset one's heart. Sometimes a man's estate
> wastes away and a painful life of poverty is his; an-
> other in turn lacks sons and longing for them most of
> all he goes beneath the earth to Hades; another has
> soul-destroying illness. There is no one to whom
> Zeus does not give a multitude of ills.

[1] Precise meaning debated, but perhaps a reference to life's changing fortunes, which cannot be known in advance.
[2] I.e., for a day.

3 Stobaeus, *Anthology*

From Mimnermus:

> When his season (of youth) passes, not even a father
> who was once most handsome is honoured or loved
> by his sons.

4 Stob. 4.50.68

Μιμνέρμου Ναννοῦς·

Τιθωνῷ μὲν ἔδωκεν ἔχειν κακὸν ἄφθιτον ⟨ ⟩
  γῆρας, ὃ καὶ θανάτου ῥίγιον ἀργαλέου.

1 σχεῖν codd., corr. Gesner   fin. ὁ Ζεὺς suppl. Gesner, αἰεὶ
Schneidewin

5 Stob. 4.50.69

Μιμνέρμου Ναννοῦς·

  ἀλλ᾽ ὀλιγοχρόνιον γίνεται ὥσπερ ὄναρ
  ἥβη τιμήεσσα· τὸ δ᾽ ἀργαλέον καί ἄμορφον
    γῆρας ὑπὲρ κεφαλῆς αὐτίχ᾽ ὑπερκρέμεται,
  ἐχθρὸν ὁμῶς καὶ ἄτιμον, ὅ τ᾽ ἄγνωστον τιθεῖ
    ἄνδρα,
5 βλάπτει δ᾽ ὀφθαλμοὺς καὶ νόον ἀμφιχυθέν.

2 οὐλόμενον pro ἀργαλέον Theognis   3 αὐτίχ᾽ ὑπὲρ
κεφαλῆς γῆρας Theognis

6 Diog. Laert. 1.60

φασὶ δὲ αὐτὸν (sc. Σόλωνα) καὶ Μιμνέρμου γράψαντος

  αἲ γὰρ ἄτερ νούσων τε καὶ ἀργαλέων
    μελεδωνέων
  ἑξηκονταέτη μοῖρα κίχοι θανάτου,

ἐπιτιμῶντα αὐτῷ εἰπεῖν· (Sol. fr. 20).

1 μελεδώνων codd., corr. Cobet

4 Stobaeus, *Anthology*

From Mimnermus' *Nanno*:

> He[1] gave Tithonus[2] an everlasting evil, old age,
> which is more terrible than even woeful death.

[1] No doubt Zeus.　　[2] Brother of Priam and loved by Eos, who asked Zeus to make him immortal, but neglected to ask for eternal youth as well.

5 Stobaeus, *Anthology*[1]

From Mimnermus' *Nanno*

> But precious youth is like a fleeting dream; in no
> time grievous and hideous old age, hateful as well as
> dishonoured, hangs over one's head. It makes a man
> unrecognisable and hampers eyes and mind when it
> is poured round.

[1] Vv. 1-3 also appear as Theognis 1020-22 and some, including West, assign the three preceding verses in Theognis to Mimnermus. Gentili-Prato combine frr. 4 and 5, with a lacuna after fr. 4. For opposition to both views see Allen 59-61.

6 Diogenes Laertius, *Lives of the Philosophers*

They say that when Mimnermus wrote

> Would that my fated death might come at sixty, unattended by sickness and grievous cares,

Solon rebuked him, saying (fr. 20).

ELEGIAC POETRY

7 *Anth. Pal.* 9.50 (Μιμνέρμου. παραίνεσις εἰς τὸ ἀνέτως
ζῆν) = Theognis 795-96

σὴν αὐτοῦ φρένα τέρπε· δυσηλεγέων δὲ πολιτέων
ἄλλος τίς σε κακῶς, ἄλλος ἄμεινον ἐρεῖ.

1 τὴν σαυτοῦ . . . πολιτῶν codd., corr. Renner   2 τοισε,
τοῖσδε codd. Theogn.   ἀμείνον' *Anth. Pal.*, ἀμείνον v.l. Theogn.

8 Stob. 3.11.2

Μιμνέρμου (Μενάνδρου codd., corr. Gaisford) Ναννοῦς

ἀληθείη δὲ παρέστω
σοὶ καὶ ἐμοί, πάντων χρῆμα δικαιότατον.

9 Strabo 14.1.4

ὕστερον δὲ ὑπὸ Αἰολέων ἐκπεσόντες κατέφυγον εἰς
Κολοφῶνα καὶ μετὰ τῶν ἐνθένδε ἐπιόντες τὴν σφετέ-
ραν ἀπέλαβον, καθάπερ καὶ Μίμνερμος ἐν τῇ Ναννοῖ
φράζει, μνησθεὶς τῆς Σμύρνης ὅτι περιμάχητος ἀεί·

†αἰπύτε† Πύλον Νηλήϊον ἄστυ λιπόντες
ἱμερτὴν Ἀσίην νηυσὶν ἀφικόμεθα,
ἐς δ' ἐρατὴν Κολοφῶνα βίην ὑπέροπλον ἔχοντες
ἑζόμεθ', ἀργαλέης ὕβριος ἡγεμόνες·

7 *Palatine Anthology*

From Mimnermus. An exhortation to live intemperately.

> Enjoy yourself. Some of the harsh citizens will speak
> ill of you, some better.[1]

[1] All will be critical, differing only in the degree of criticism.

8 Stobaeus, *Anthology*

From Mimnermus' *Nanno*

> Let there be truth between you and me; of all pos-
> sessions it is the most just.[1]

[1] 'Justice' or fairness in an erotic relationship signifies recipro-
cal affection, and truth is an essential requirement for this to take
place.

9 Strabo, *Geography*

Later, upon being expelled by the Aeolians, they (the
Smyrnaeans) fled to Colophon and upon attacking their
own land with the Colophonians they regained it, as
Mimnermus states in his *Nanno*, after mentioning that
Smyrna was always an object of contention:

> . . .[1] leaving Pylos, the city of Neleus, we came on
> our ships to longed-for Asia and with overwhelm-
> ing force we settled in lovely Colophon, the instiga-
> tors of harsh aggression; and setting out from there,

5   κεῖθεν †διαστήεντος† ἀπορνύμενοι ποταμοῖο
      θεῶν βουλῇ Σμύρνην εἴλομεν Αἰολίδα.

1 αἰπύτε vel ἐπεί τε codd., αἰπείάν τε Hiller, Αἰπὺ < > τε West,
αἶψα δ᾿ ἔπειτα Allen, alii alia   Πύλου Bergk, prob. Allen
3 δ᾿ ἄρα τὴν codd., corr. Wyttenbach   5 δ᾿ Ἀλήεντος
Brunck, prob. Allen, δ᾿ αὖτε Μέλητος Cook, alii alia
6 εἴδομεν codd., corr. Brunck

10 Strabo 14.1.3

Κολοφῶνα δὲ Ἀνδραίμων Πύλιος (κτίζει), ὥς φησι καὶ
Μίμνερμος ἐν τῇ Ναννοῖ.

11 Strabo 1.2.40

εἰ δὲ ὥσπερ ὁ Σκήψιός φησι (fr. 50 Gaede) παραλαβὼν
μάρτυρα Μίμνερμον, ὃς ἐν τῷ ὠκεανῷ ποιήσας τὴν
οἴκησιν τοῦ Αἰήτου πρὸς ταῖς ἀνατολαῖς ἐκτὸς
πεμφθῆναί φησιν ὑπὸ τοῦ Πελίου τὸν Ἰάσονα καὶ
κομίσαι τὸ δέρος, οὔτ᾿ ἂν ἡ ἐπὶ τὸ δέρος ἐκεῖσε πομπὴ
πιθανῶς λέγοιτο εἰς ἀγνῶτας καὶ ἀφανεῖς τόπους, οὔθ᾿
ὁ δι᾿ ἐρήμων καὶ ἀοίκων καὶ καθ᾿ ἡμᾶς τοσοῦτον
ἐκτετοπισμένων πλοῦς οὔτ᾿ ἔνδοξος οὔτε πασιμέλων.

    οὐδέ κοτ᾿ ἂν μέγα κῶας ἀνήγαγεν αὐτὸς Ἰήσων
      ἐξ Αἴης τελέσας ἀλγινόεσσαν ὁδόν,

from the river . . .,[2] by the will of the gods we cap-
tured Aeolian Smyrna.

[1] Some see here a mention of Αἰπύ, a town in Messenia. This is
defended by C. Brillante in *Scritti . . . Gentili* I (Rome 1993) 267-
78 who however locates both Aipy and Pylos in Triphylia, north-
west of Messenia. For a full discussion of both textual and his-
torical problems in the fragment see Allen 75-85.   [2] The
corruption must conceal the name of the river. The two can-
didates, Meles and Ales, both present problems. The Meles is
near Smyrna, not Colophon, and the Ales is south of Colophon,
whereas Smyrna lies to the north.

10 Strabo, *Geography*

Andraemon of Pylos[1] founded Colophon, as Mimnermus
says in his *Nanno*.

[1] Presumably the leader of the colonizing expedition men-
tioned in fr. 9.1.

11 Strabo, *Geography*

But if it is as Demetrius of Scepsis states, calling upon
the authority of Mimnermus who places the dwelling of
Aeetes in Oceanus far out at the rising of the sun and says
that Jason was sent by Pelias and brought back the fleece,
the expedition for it there, to unknown and obscure re-
gions, would not sound plausible, and a voyage through
desolate, uninhabited territory so far removed from us
would be neither famous nor of interest to everyone.

Jason would never have brought back the great
fleece from Aea[1] on his own[2] at the end of a painful

ὑβριστῇ Πελίῃ τελέων χαλεπῆρες ἄεθλον,
οὐδ' ἂν ἐπ' Ὠκεανοῦ καλὸν ἵκοντο ῥόον.

1 οὐδ' ὁκόταν codd., corr. Porson   μετὰ codd., corr.
Brunck

11a Pergit Strabo

καὶ ὑποβάς·

Αἰήταο πόλιν, τόθι τ' ὠκέος Ἠελίοιο
   ἀκτῖνες χρυσέῳ κεῖαται ἐν θαλάμῳ
Ὠκεανοῦ παρὰ χεῖλος, ἵν' ᾤχετο θεῖος Ἰήσων.

3 χείλεσιν codd. (χείλεσ' ἵν' ed. Ald.), corr. Bergk

12 Ath. 11.470a

Μίμνερμος δὲ Ναννοῖ ἐν εὐνῇ φησι χρυσῇ κατεσκευ-
ασμένῃ πρὸς τὴν χρείαν ταύτην ὑπὸ Ἡφαίστου τὸν
Ἥλιον καθεύδοντα περαιοῦσθαι πρὸς τὰς ἀνατολάς,
αἰνισσόμενος τὸ κοῖλον τοῦ ποτηρίου. λέγει δὲ οὕτως·

Ἠέλιος μὲν γὰρ ἔλαχεν πόνον ἤματα πάντα,
   οὐδέ ποτ' ἄμπαυσις γίνεται οὐδεμία
ἵπποισίν τε καὶ αὐτῷ, ἐπὴν ῥοδοδάκτυλος Ἠὼς
   Ὠκεανὸν προλιποῦσ' οὐρανὸν εἰσαναβῇ.
5 τὸν μὲν γὰρ διὰ κῦμα φέρει πολυήρατος εὐνή,
   κοίλη, Ἡφαίστου χερσὶν ἐληλαμένη,

journey, completing for the insolent Pelias an ordeal
fraught with difficulty, nor would they have reached
the fair stream of Oceanus.[3]

[1] Apparently identified here with Colchis, the traditional
home of Aeetes at the eastern end of the Black Sea. Homer uses
the adjectival equivalent (Αἰαίη) of Circe's island (*Od.* 10.135,
12.3) and Circe was the sister of Aeetes.   [2] Probably an allu-
sion to Hera's aid rather than to Medea's or Aphrodite's, since the
latter two had nothing to do with the arrival at Oceanus (v. 4).
[3] Chronological order is inverted in order to give prominence to
recovery of the fleece.

11a Strabo continues

And further on:

Aeetes' city, where the rays of the swift Sun[1] lie in a
golden storeroom at the edge of Oceanus, where
god-like Jason went.

[1] The Sun was Aeetes' father.

12 Athenaeus, *Scholars at Dinner*

In *Nanno* Mimnermus says that the Sun is conveyed to
the place of his rising while he sleeps in a golden bed
constructed for this purpose by Hephaestus. Mimnermus
hints at the hollow shape of the cup, speaking as follows:

For the Sun's lot is toil every day and there is never
any respite for him and his horses, from the moment
rose-fingered Dawn leaves Oceanus and goes up
into the sky. A lovely bed, hollow, forged by the
hands of Hephaestus, of precious gold and winged,

χρυσοῦ τιμήεντος, ὑπόπτερος, ἄκρον ἐφ᾽ ὕδωρ
εὕδονθ᾽ ἁρπαλέως χώρου ἀφ᾽ Ἑσπερίδων
γαῖαν ἐς Αἰθιόπων, ἵνα δὴ θοὸν ἅρμα καὶ ἵπποι
10   ἑστᾶσ᾽, ὄφρ᾽ Ἠὼς ἠριγένεια μόλῃ·
ἔνθ᾽ ἐπέβη ἑτέρων ὀχέων Ὑπερίονος υἱός.

Philod. de pietate (P. Hercul. 1088 fr. 2 ii + 433 fr. 2 i; I.
Boserup, ZPE 8 (1971) 110; A. Schober, Cronache Erco-
lanesi 18 (1988) 93) = fr. 23 W.

[. . . καὶ τὸν] Ἥλιον [καὶ ἄλλους] τινὰς [θεοὺς
πολυ]μόχθο[υς πεποιή]κασι . . . Μί]μνερ[μος] μ[ὲν οὐ
δι]αφωνεῖν δ[οκ]εῖ, [κα]θ᾽ ἑ{σ}κάστ[η]ν [νύκ]τα καθ-
εύ[δειν αὐ]τὸν λέγων.

1 λέλαχεν Hoffmann, πόνον ἔλλαχεν Hermann   2 κοτ᾽
Bach   6 κοίλη codd., corr. Meineke: ποικίλη Kaibel, prob.
West   7 ὑπόπτερον A, corr. Heyne   8 εὕδονθ᾽ ὅθ᾽ A,
corr. Musurus   χοροῦ A, corr. Musurus   9 ἵν᾽ ἀληθοον
A, corr. Meineke   11 σφετέρων Bergk, ἐπεβήσεθ᾽ ἑῶν
Schneidewin, prob. Gent.-Pr.

13 Paus. 9.29.4

Μίμνερμος δὲ ἐλεγεῖα ἐς τὴν μάχην ποιήσας τὴν
Σμυρναίων πρὸς Γύγην τε καὶ Λυδούς, φησὶν ἐν τῷ
προοιμίῳ θυγατέρας Οὐρανοῦ τὰς ἀρχαιοτέρας Μού-
σας, τούτων δὲ ἄλλας νεωτέρας εἶναι Διὸς παῖδας.

carries him, as he sleeps soundly, over the waves on the water's surface from the place of the Hesperides[1] to the land of the Ethiopians,[2] where his swift chariot and horses stand[3] until early-born Dawn comes. There the son of Hyperion mounts his other vehicle.[4]

Philodemus, *On Piety*

. . . they have represented the Sun and some other gods as enduring much toil . . . Mimnermus does not seem to disagree, since he says that the Sun sleeps every night.

[1] Daughters of Night (Hes. *Theog.* 213) who guarded golden apples in the far west. [2] Here a mythical race located in the far east. [3] It is unclear whether Mimnermus assumes that the Sun had a new chariot and horses every day or that they somehow got back to the east while the Sun slept. The poet does not suggest that they were also in the 'bed.' [4] I.e., other than his bed, if the text is sound.

13 Pausanias, *Description of Greece*

Mimnermus, who composed elegiac verses on the battle of the Smyrnaeans with Gyges and the Lydians, says in the preface that the more ancient Muses are daughters of Ouranos (Sky)[1] and that the other, younger Muses are children of Zeus.

Comm. in Alcman., P. Oxy. 2390 fr. 2 col. ii 28-29 (5 fr. 2 *PMGF*, 81 Calame)

Γῆς [μὲν] Μούσα[ς] θυγατέρας ὡς Μίμνερμ[ος]τας ἐγε[νεαλόγησε.

13a Comm. in Antim., P. Univ. Mediol. 17 col. ii 26 (p. 276 Matthews), ed. Vogliano

"σ[υνάγε]ιν (suppl. West) δμω[ῆ]ισ᾿ ἐνδέξεται" (Antim. fr. 105 Matthews)· ἀντὶ τοῦ ἐπ[ιτ]άξῃ<ι>. Μίμνερμ[ος] δ᾿ [ἐν] τῆι Σμυρν[η]ΐδι·

   ὡς οἱ πὰρ βασιλῆος, ἐπε[ί ῥ᾿] ἐ[ν]εδέξατο
      μῦθο[ν],
   ἤ[ΐξ]αν κοίληι[ς ἀ]σπίσι φραξάμενοι.

1 ῥ᾿ vel τ᾿ suppl. Maas   2 Vogliano

14 Stob. 3.7.11

Μιμνέρμου·

   οὐ μὲν δὴ κείνου γε μένος καὶ ἀγήνορα θυμὸν
      τοῖον ἐμέο προτέρων πεύθομαι, οἵ μιν ἴδον
   Λυδῶν ἱππομάχων πυκινὰς κλονέοντα φάλαγγας
      Ἕρμιον ἂμ πεδίον, φῶτα φερεμμελίην·
5   τοῦ μὲν ἄρ᾿ οὔ ποτε πάμπαν ἐμέμψατο Παλλὰς
      Ἀθήνη
   δριμὺ μένος κραδίης, εὖθ᾿ ὅ γ᾿ ἀνὰ προμάχους

Oxyrhynchus papyrus commentary on Alcman (2nd c. A.D.)

In the genealogy given by Mimnermus, the Muses are daughters of Ge (Earth).

[1] The same genealogy is attributed to Mimnermus and Alcman by schol. 16b on Pind. *Nem.* 3 (iii.43.19 Dr.). Cf. also Diod. Sic. 4.7.1.

13a Milan papyrus commentary on Antimachus

"(so that?) he (she) might order the servant women to bring together," with $\dot{\epsilon}\nu\delta\dot{\epsilon}\xi\epsilon\tau\alpha\iota$ instead of $\dot{\epsilon}\pi\iota\tau\dot{\alpha}\xi\eta$ 'order.' Compare Mimnermus in *Smyrneis*:

> So the king's[1] men charged, when he gave the word of command, making a fence with their hollow shields.[2]

[1] Probably Gyges.   [2] Cf. Tyrt. fr. 19.7.

14 Stobaeus, *Anthology*

From Mimnermus:

> That man's[1] strength and heroic spirit were not such (as yours), as I learn from my elders who saw him, ash spear in hand, routing the thick ranks of the Lydian cavalry on the plain of Hermus.[2] At no time whatsoever did Pallas Athena[3] find fault with his heart's fierce strength, when he sped among the

σεύαιθ' αἱματόεν‹τος ἐν› ὑσμίνῃ πολέμοιο,
πικρὰ βιαζόμενος δυσμενέων βέλεα·
οὐ γάρ τις κείνου δηίων ἔτ' ἀμεινότερος φὼς
ἔσκεν ἐποίχεσθαι φυλόπιδος κρατερῆς
ἔργον, ὅτ' αὐγῇσιν φέρετ' ὠκέος ἠελίοιο

10

2 ἐμεῦ codd., corr. West   5 κοτε Bach   6 ἔσθ' ὅτ'
M, εὐθ' ὅτ' A, corr. Schneidewin   7 σεῦ ἦθ' M, σεύηθ' A,
corr. Schneidewin   ‹τος ἐν› suppl. Gesner
8 βιαζομένου codd., βιαζόμενος ed. Schowiana   9 ληῶν
Bergk   11 αὐγαῖσι‹ν› codd., corr. Bergk   12 ‹εἴκελα
χαλκείοις τεύχεσι λαμπόμενος› suppl., e.g., West

15 Et. Gen. (p. 20 Calame) et Sym. (p. 19 Berger) = Et.
Mag. 187.45

βάξις· σημαίνει δὲ τὴν φήμην καὶ τὴν ῥῆσιν. Μίμνερ-
μος·

καί μιν ἐπ' ἀνθρώπους βάξις ἔχει χαλεπή.

16 Ibidem

ἀργαλέης αἰεὶ βάξιος ἱέμενοι,

παρὰ τὸ βάζω, βάξω, βάξις.

fore-fighters in the combat of bloody war, defying
the enemies' bitter shafts. For none of his foes
remained better than he in going about the task of
strenuous war, when he rushed (with his bronze
armour gleaming like?)[4] the rays of the swift sun.

[1] Identity unknown, but apparently one whose heroism is con-
trasted with the feebleness of the poet's contemporaries. Per-
haps he fought against the Lydian Gyges in the 660s.   [2] The
river Hermus rises in Phrygia and flows into the Aegean north
of Smyrna.   [3] There was a prominent temple of Athena in
7th-cent. Smyrna.   [4] It is difficult to explain v. 11 without
emending or assuming something in the lost pentameter to
govern the dative 'rays.'

15 *Etymologicum Genuinum* and *Symeonis*

βάξις means 'report' or 'speech.' Cf. Mimnermus:

and he has a harsh report among men

16 Same sources

ever eager for grievous report,[1]

βάξις from βάζω ('speak'), βάξω.

[1] Apparently of those who always wish to hear something bad
said of others. The second passage follows directly on the first and
presumably also belongs to Mimnermus.

17 Schol. T in Hom. *Il.* 16.287 (iv.230 Erbse), "ὃς Παίο-
νας ἱπποκορυστάς"

Μίμνερμος·

Παίονας ἄνδρας ἄγων, ἵνα τε κλειτὸν γένος
ἵππων.

παιᾶνας cod., corr. Bekker

18 Ath. 4.174a

ὁ δὲ αὐτὸς ἱστορεῖ κἀν τῷ τετάρτῳ καὶ εἰκοστῷ τῆς
αὐτῆς πραγματείας (Demetr. Sceps. fr. 14 Gaede) Δαί-
την ἥρωα τιμώμενον παρὰ τοῖς Τρωσίν, οὗ μνημο-
νεύει‹ν› Μίμνερμον.

19 Ael. *V.H.* 12.36

ἐοίκασιν οἱ ἀρχαῖοι ὑπὲρ τοῦ ἀριθμοῦ τῶν τῆς Νιόβης
παίδων μὴ συνᾴδειν ἀλλήλοις. Ὅμηρος (*Il.* 24.603)
μὲν ἓξ λέγει ‹ἄρρενας› καὶ τοσαύτας κόρας, Λᾶσος
(fr. 706 *PMG*) δὲ δὶς ἑπτὰ λέγει . . . Μίμνερμος εἴκοσι,
καὶ Πίνδαρος (fr. 52n S.-M.) τοσούτους.

20 Plut. *de facie lun.* 19.931e

εἰ δὲ μή, Θέων ἡμῖν οὗτος τὸν Μίμνερμον ἐπάξει καὶ
τὸν Κυδίαν (fr. 715 *PMG*) καὶ τὸν Ἀρχίλοχον (fr. 112
W.), πρὸς δὲ τούτοις τὸν Στησίχορον (fr. 271 *PMGF*)

MIMNERMUS

17 Scholiast on Homer, *Iliad*

Cf. Mimnermus:

> bringing men from Paeonia,[1] where (there is) a famous race of horses

[1] The Paeonians were Thracian allies of Troy in Homer, led first by Pyraechmes (*Il.* 2.848, 16.287 f.) and later by Asteropaeus (*Il.* 21.155).

18 Athenaeus, *Scholars at Dinner*

The same author in the 24th book of the same work[1] records that Daites[2] was honoured as a hero by the Trojans and that Mimnermus mentions him.

[1] Demetrius of Scepsis (born c. 214 B.C.) wrote a lengthy work on the Trojan catalogue in *Iliad* 2.   [2] Not mentioned by our Homer.

19 Aelian, *Historical Miscellany*

The ancients seem to disagree with one another on the number of Niobe's children. Homer speaks of six males and as many girls, Lasus of fourteen . . ., Mimnermus of twenty, and Pindar of the same number.[1]

[1] For the myth of Niobe and the variant number of her children see Allen 129-31. Allen also points out that Mt. Sipylus, the petrified Niobe in myth, was not far from Smyrna.

20 Plutarch, *The Face in the Moon*

If you do not (remember the recent eclipse of the sun), Theon here will adduce for us Mimnermus,[1] Cydias, and Archilochus and in addition to them Stesichorus and

ELEGIAC POETRY

καὶ τὸν Πίνδαρον (Pae. 9.2-5 S.-M.) ἐν ταῖς ἐκλείψεσιν
ὀλοφυρομένους, "ἄστρον φανερώτατον κλεπτόμενον"
καὶ "μέσῳ ἄματι νύκτα γινομέναν" καὶ τὴν ἀκτῖνα τοῦ
ἡλίου "σκότους ἀτραπὸν ‹ἐσσυμέναν›" φάσκοντας.

21 Sallust. Argum. ii in Soph. *Ant.*

στασιάζεται δὲ τὰ περὶ τὴν ἡρωίδα ἱστορούμενα καὶ
τὴν ἀδελφὴν αὐτῆς Ἰσμήνην. ὁ μὲν γὰρ Ἴων ἐν τοῖς
διθυράμβοις (fr. 740 PMG) καταπρησθῆναί φησιν
ἀμφοτέρας ἐν τῷ ἱερῷ τῆς Ἥρας ὑπὸ Λαοδάμαντος
(Λαομέδοντος codd., corr. Brunck) τοῦ Ἐτεοκλέους·
Μίμνερμος δέ φησι τὴν μὲν Ἰσμήνην προσομιλοῦσαν
Περικλυμένῳ (Θεοκλυμένῳ codd., corr. Robert) ὑπὸ
Τυδέως κατὰ Ἀθηνᾶς ἐγκέλευσιν τελευτῆσαι. ταῦτα
μὲν οὖν ἐστιν τὰ ξένως περὶ τῶν ἡρωίδων ἱστορού-
μενα.

21a Cod. Athen. 1083, ed. S. Kugéas, *Sitz.-Ber. bay.
Akad.* 1910 (4) (= *Corp. Paroem. suppl.*, 1961, V), p.
15

"ἄριστα χωλὸς οἰφεῖ." φησὶν ὅτι αἱ Ἀμαζόνες τοὺς
γιγνομένους ἄρσενας ἐπήρουν, ἢ σκέλος ἢ χεῖρα
περιελόμεναι· πολεμοῦντες δὲ πρὸς αὐτὰς οἱ Σκύθαι
καὶ βουλόμενοι πρὸς αὐτὰς σπείσασθαι ἔλεγον ὅτι
συνέσονται τοῖς Σκύθαις εἰς γάμον ἀπηρώτοις καὶ οὐ
λελωβημένοις· ἀποκριναμένη δὲ πρὸς αὐτοὺς ἡ

Pindar, who bewail during eclipses and speak of "the most conspicuous star being stolen away" and "night occurring in mid-day" and the sun's ray "speeding along a path of darkness."[2]

1 There was a total eclipse at Smyrna on April 6, 648, but Mimnermus need not have referred to an eclipse in his own lifetime.   2 The first and third quotations are garbled versions of passages in Pindar's *Paean* 9 and the second is usually assigned to Stesichorus.

21 Sallustius' preface to Sophocles, *Antigone*

There is disagreement in the stories told of the heroine (Antigone) and her sister Ismene. Ion in his dithyrambs says that both were burned to death in Hera's temple by Laodamas, the son of Eteocles. But Mimnermus says that Ismene was killed by Tydeus at the command of Athena when she was making love to Periclymenus.[1] These then are the strange stories told about the heroines.

1 For pictorial representations see Allen 133 f.

21a Manuscript on proverbs

"A lame man makes the best lover." It is said that the Amazons maimed their male children by removing a leg or a hand. When the Scythians were at war with them and wanted to make a truce, they assured the Amazons that they would not be married to maimed or mutilated

ELEGIAC POETRY

Ἀντιάνειρα ἡγεμὼν τῶν Ἀμαζόνων εἶπεν· "ἄριστα χωλὸς οἰφεῖ." μέμνηται τῆς παροιμίας Μίμ‹ν›ερμος.

Dubia et Spuria

22 Schol. Lyc. 610 (p. 206.28 Scheer)

ἡ Ἀφροδίτη, καθά φησι Μίμνερμος, ὑπὸ Διομήδους τρωθεῖσα παρεσκεύασε τὴν Αἰγιάλειαν πολλοῖς μὲν μοιχοῖς συγκοιμηθῆναι, ἐρασθῆναι δὲ καὶ ὑπὸ (Ἱππολύτου vel ‑τῳ schol., corr. Scheer) Κομήτου τοῦ Σθενέλου υἱοῦ. τοῦ δὲ Διομήδους παραγενομένου εἰς τὸ Ἄργος ἐπιβουλεῦσαι αὐτῷ· τὸν δὲ καταφυγόντα εἰς τὸν βωμὸν τῆς Ἥρας διὰ νυκτὸς φυγεῖν σὺν τοῖς ἑταίροις καὶ ἐλθεῖν εἰς Ἰταλίαν πρὸς Δαῦνον βασιλέα, ὅστις αὐτὸν ‹δόλῳ› (suppl. Scheer) ἀνεῖλεν.

23 Philod. de pietate, v. ad fr. 12

24 Stob. 4.38.3

κατὰ ἰατρῶν Μιμνέρμου Ναννοῦ·

‹ › οἷα δὴ φιλοῦσιν {οἱ} ἰατροὶ λέγειν

102

Scythians. But Antianeira, the leader of the Amazons, replied to them: "a lame man makes the best lover." Mimnermus recalls the proverb.[1]

---

[1] As it stands, the proverb is iambic, but there is no evidence that Mimnermus composed in this meter. It is possible, however, that he adapted it to the elegiac meter or simply alluded to it in a more general way. Other sources cite the proverb without mentioning Mimnermus. According to Strabo 14.1.4 Smyrna was named after an homonymous Amazon.

Doubtful and Spurious Works

22 Scholiast on Lycophron

According to Mimnermus, because Aphrodite had been wounded by Diomedes she caused (his wife) Aegialeia to go to bed with many lovers and to be loved by Cometes, the son of Sthenelus. And when Diomedes arrived in Argos she plotted against him. He took refuge at the altar of Hera but fled during the night with his companions and went to Italy to king Daunus, who killed him by a trick.

24 Stobaeus, *Anthology*

From Mimnermus' *Nanno*, against physicians:

As physicians are wont to say, that minor conditions

τὰ φαῦλα μείζω καὶ τὰ δείν᾽ ὑπὲρ φόβον,
πυργοῦντες αὑτούς.

25 Stob. 4.57.11

Μιμνέρμου·

<   > ἐκ Νεοπτολέμου·
δεινοὶ γὰρ ἀνδρὶ πάντες ἐσμὲν εὐκλεεῖ
ζῶντι φθονῆσαι, κατθανόντα δ᾽ αἰνέσαι.

26 *Epimer. in Hom.* (p. 224.68 Dyck)

γύναι· κατὰ ἀποκοπὴν τοῦ ξ. τὸ δὲ παρὰ Μιμνέρμῳ
(μιμηέρμνω cod., corr. Cramer: Μενάνδρῳ Meineke)·

ὦ Ζεῦ πολυτίμητ᾽, ὡς καλαὶ νῶν αἱ γυναῖ.

are worse and serious conditions are beyond fear, magnifying themselves.[1]

[1] The verses, because of meter and dialect, cannot be assigned to Mimnermus. Presumably there is a lacuna containing the name of their author as well as the citation from Mimnermus.

25 Stobaeus, *Anthology*

From Mimnermus:

〈   〉 from *Neoptolemus*. For we are all wonderfully prone to envy a famous man when he's alive and to praise him when he's dead.[1]

[1] As in fr. 24, a lacuna is to be assumed. This section in Stobaeus is entitled "That one should not speak insultingly of the dead" and the lost verses of Mimnermus must have been on that topic. The words "from Neoptolemus" (omitted in MS S) suggest the title of a tragedy, with the author's name in the preceding lacuna.

26 *Homeric Parsings*

γύναι, with removal of the letter ξ. It occurs in Mimnermus:

O much-honoured Zeus, how beautiful are the wives we two have[1]

[1] M. Fileni, *QUCC* 26 (1977) 83-86, has made a strong case, on metrical and lexical grounds, for assigning the verse to Menander. Menander is an error for Mimnermus in Stobaeus' citation of frr. 3 and 8.

SOLON

TESTIMONIUM

1 *Suda* (iv.396.29 Adler)

Σόλων, Ἐξηκεστίδου, Ἀθηναῖος, φιλόσοφος, νομοθέ-
της καὶ δημαγωγός. γέγονε δὲ ἐπὶ τῆς μζ′ Ὀλυμπιά-
δος, οἱ δὲ νϛ′. ἐπιβουλευθεὶς δ᾽ ὑπὸ Πεισιστράτου
τοῦ τυράννου ἀπεδήμησεν ἐν Κιλικίᾳ καὶ ἔκτισε
πόλιν, ἣν Σόλους ἐκάλεσεν ἐξ αὑτοῦ. οἱ δὲ καὶ τοὺς ἐν
Κύπρῳ Σόλους ἐξ αὐτοῦ φασι καὶ τελευτῆσαι αὐτὸν ἐν
Κύπρῳ. ἔγραψε νόμους Ἀθηναίοις, οἵ τινες ἄξονες
ὠνομάσθησαν διὰ τὸ γραφῆναι αὐτοὺς ἐν ξυλίνοις
ἄξοσιν Ἀθήνησι· ποίημα δι᾽ ἐλεγείων, ὃ Σαλαμὶς
ἐπιγράφεται· ὑποθήκας δι᾽ ἐλεγείας· καὶ ἄλλα. ἔστι δὲ

SOLON

TESTIMONIUM

Much of our information about Solon can be found in Aristotle's *Constitution of Athens,* Plutarch's *Life of Solon,* and Diogenes Laertius 1.45-67, all available in Loeb editions. Herodotus 1.29-33 gives an account of Solon's visit to Croesus, king of Lydia, but this is improbable on chronological grounds, since Croesus became ruler c. 560 and Solon died about a year later (see n. 2 below). For a full list of testimonia see A. Martina, *Solon. Testimonia veterum* (Rome 1968), and for Solon's laws see E. Ruschenbusch, Σόλωνος νόμοι. *Die Fragmente des solonischen Gesetzeswerkes mit einer Text- und Überlieferungsgeschichte* (Wiesbaden 1966).

1 *Suda*

Solon, son of Execestides,[1] an Athenian philosopher, lawgiver and leader of the people. He flourished in the 47th Olympiad (592/89), according to others in the 56th (556/3).[2] When the tyrant Pisistratus plotted against him, he spent time abroad in Cilicia and founded a city which he called Soloi after himself.[3] Others say that also Soloi in Cyprus was named after him and that he died in Cyprus.[4] He wrote laws for the Athenians which were given the name *axones*[5] because they were written on wooden axles in Athens. He wrote an elegiac poem entitled *Salamis*,[6] elegiac exhortations, and others.[7] He is also one of the Seven

ELEGIAC POETRY

καὶ οὗτος εἷς τῶν ζ΄ ὀνομαζομένων σοφῶν. καὶ φέρεται αὐτοῦ ἀπόφθεγμα τόδε, μηδὲν ἄγαν, ἢ τό, γνῶθι σαυτόν.

FRAGMENTS

1-3. Σαλαμίς

1 Plut. *Sol.* 8.1-3

ἐπεὶ δὲ μακρόν τινα καὶ δυσχερῆ πόλεμον οἱ ἐν ἄστει περὶ τῆς Σαλαμινίων νήσου Μεγαρεῦσι πολεμοῦντες ἐξέκαμον, καὶ νόμον ἔθεντο μήτε γράψαι τινὰ μήτ᾽ εἰπεῖν αὖθις ὡς χρὴ τὴν πόλιν ἀντιποιεῖσθαι τῆς Σαλαμῖνος, ἢ θανάτῳ ζημιοῦσθαι, βαρέως φέρων τὴν ἀδοξίαν ὁ Σόλων καὶ τῶν νέων ὁρῶν πολλοὺς δεομένους ἀρχῆς ἐπὶ τὸν πόλεμον, αὐτοὺς δὲ μὴ θαρροῦντας ἄρξασθαι διὰ τὸν νόμον, ἐσκήψατο μὲν ἔκστασιν τῶν λογισμῶν, καὶ λόγος εἰς τὴν πόλιν ἐκ τῆς οἰκίας διεδόθη παρακινητικῶς ἔχειν αὐτόν· ἐλεγεῖα δὲ κρύφα συνθεὶς καὶ μελετήσας ὥστε λέγειν

108

Sages, as they are called. The maxims "Nothing in excess" and "Know yourself" are said to be his.

1 See introduction to fr. 22a.   2 The first date is close to that commonly assigned to his archonship (594/3), the latter close to the probable year of his death. According to Phaenias (fr. 21 Wehrli), as reported by Plutarch (*Solon* 32.3), Solon lived less than two years after Pisistratus became tyrant (560/59).
3 A few other sources also mention this (e.g., Diog. Laert. 1.51).
4 On Soloi in Cyprus see fr. 19. Diog. Laert. 1.62 claims that Solon died in Cyprus at the age of 80.   5 See P. J. Rhodes, *A Commentary on the Aristotelian* Athenaion Politeia (Oxford 1981) 131-35, for a thorough discussion of the word.   6 Frr. 1-3.
7 Diog. Laert. 1.61 states that Solon's elegies contained 5000 lines and he adds that Solon also composed iambic poems and epodes. No mention is made elsewhere of the latter.

FRAGMENTS

1-3. *Salamis*

1 Plutarch, *Life of Solon*

When the Athenians grew tired of waging a long and difficult war with Megara over the island Salamis, they passed a law that in future no one, on pain of death, was to propose in writing or orally that the city should lay claim to Salamis. Solon found the disgrace hard to bear and when he saw that many of the young men wanted to renew the war, but lacked the courage to do so themselves because of the law, he pretended to be out of his mind and word was passed from his household to the city that he showed signs of madness. He secretly composed elegiac verses and after practising so as to recite them from memory, he suddenly

ἀπὸ στόματος, ἐξεπήδησεν εἰς τὴν ἀγορὰν ἄφνω,
πιλίδιον περιθέμενος, ὄχλου δὲ πολλοῦ συνδραμόντος
ἀναβὰς ἐπὶ τὸν τοῦ κήρυκος λίθον ἐν ᾠδῇ διεξῆλθε
τὴν ἐλεγείαν, ἧς ἐστιν ἀρχή·

> αὐτὸς κῆρυξ ἦλθον ἀφ᾽ ἱμερτῆς Σαλαμῖνος,
>   κόσμον ἐπέων ᾠδὴν ἀντ᾽ ἀγορῆς θέμενος.

τοῦτο τὸ ποίημα Σαλαμὶς ἐπιγέγραπται, καὶ στίχων
ἑκατόν ἐστι, χαριέντως πάνυ πεποιημένον.

2 ᾠδὴν glossema censet West

2 Diog. Laert. 1.47

ἦν δὲ τὰ ἐλεγεῖα τὰ μάλιστα καθαψάμενα τῶν Ἀθη-
ναίων τάδε·

> εἴην δὴ τότ᾽ ἐγὼ Φολεγάνδριος ἢ Σικινήτης
>   ἀντί γ᾽ Ἀθηναίου πατρίδ᾽ ἀμειψάμενος·
> αἶψα γὰρ ἂν φάτις ἥδε μετ᾽ ἀνθρώποισι γένοιτο·
>   "Ἀττικὸς οὗτος ἀνήρ, τῶν Σαλαμιναφετέων."

Plut. praec. gerendae reip. 17.813f (Φολεγάνδριος—
ἀμειψάμενος)

1 Σικινίτης v.l.   4 Σαλαμίναφετων cod. B, Σαλαμῖν᾽
ἀφέντων F,P p.c.; Σαλαμιναφετῶν Vossius (-τέων Renner)

rushed into the marketplace, wearing a little felt cap. When a large crowd had assembled, he mounted the herald's stone and recited the elegy which begins:

> I have come in person as a herald from lovely Salamis, composing song, an adornment of words, instead of speech.

This poem was entitled *Salamis* and contains a hundred lines, a very fine composition.[1]

[1] Plutarch goes on to state that the poem had the desired effect. The law was repealed, Solon was placed in command, and Salamis was captured. For other similar accounts of Solon's role see Demosthenes 19.252, Polyaenus 1.20.1, Diogenes Laertius 1.46 et al.

2 Diogenes Laertius, *Lives of the Philosophers*

The elegiac verses which especially appealed to the Athenians were the following:

> In that case may I change my country and be a Pholegandrian or Sikinite[1] instead of an Athenian. For this report would quickly be spread among men: "This man is an Athenian, one of the Salamisceders."

[1] Pholegandros and Sikinos are two very small islands in the southern Cyclades.

3 Pergit Diogenes

εἶτα·

ἴομεν ἐς Σαλαμῖνα μαχησόμενοι περὶ νήσου
ἱμερτῆς χαλεπόν τ' αἶσχος ἀπωσόμενοι.

Schol. Dem. (ii.81.11 Dilts)

2 ἀπωσάμενοι schol. Dem.

4 Dem. 19.254-56

λέγε δή μοι λαβὼν καὶ τὰ τοῦ Σόλωνος ἐλεγεῖα ταυτί,
ἵν' εἰδῇθ' ὅτι καὶ Σόλων ἐμίσει τοὺς οἵους οὗτος
ἀνθρώπους . . . λέγε σύ·

ἡμετέρη δὲ πόλις κατὰ μὲν Διὸς οὔποτ' ὀλεῖται
αἶσαν καὶ μακάρων θεῶν φρένας ἀθανάτων·
τοίη γὰρ μεγάθυμος ἐπίσκοπος ὀβριμοπάτρη
Παλλὰς Ἀθηναίη χεῖρας ὕπερθεν ἔχει·
5   αὐτοὶ δὲ φθείρειν μεγάλην πόλιν ἀφραδίῃσιν
ἀστοὶ βούλονται χρήμασι πειθόμενοι,
δήμου θ' ἡγεμόνων ἄδικος νόος, οἷσιν ἕτοιμον
ὕβριος ἐκ μεγάλης ἄλγεα πολλὰ παθεῖν·
οὐ γὰρ ἐπίστανται κατέχειν κόρον οὐδὲ
παρούσας
10   εὐφροσύνας κοσμεῖν δαιτὸς ἐν ἡσυχίῃ
. . . .
πλουτέουσιν δ' ἀδίκοις ἔργμασι πειθόμενοι
. . . .

112

3 Diogenes continues

And then:

> Let us go to Salamis to fight for a lovely island and
> clear away bitter disgrace.

4 Demosthenes, *On the Embassy*

Please take and read these elegiac verses of Solon, so that
you (the jury) may know that Solon too hated such men (as
the defendant) . . . Now read:

> Our state will never perish through the dispensa-
> tion of Zeus or the intentions of the blessed immor-
> tal gods; for such a stout-hearted guardian, Pallas
> Athena, born of a mighty father, holds her hands
> over it. But it is the citizens themselves who by their
> acts of foolishness and subservience to money are
> willing to destroy a great city, and the mind of the
> people's leaders is unjust; they are certain to suffer
> much pain as a result of their great arrogance. For
> they do not know how to restrain excess or to con-
> duct in an orderly and peaceful manner the festivi-
> ties of the banquet that are at hand . . . they grow
> wealthy, yielding to unjust deeds . . . sparing neither

οὔθ᾽ ἱερῶν κτεάνων οὔτε τι δημοσίων
φειδόμενοι κλέπτουσιν ἀφαρπαγῇ ἄλλοθεν
   ἄλλος,
οὐδὲ φυλάσσονται σεμνὰ Δίκης θέμεθλα,
15 ἣ σιγῶσα σύνοιδε τὰ γιγνόμενα πρό τ᾽ ἐόντα,
   τῷ δὲ χρόνῳ πάντως ἦλθ᾽ ἀποτεισομένη.
τοῦτ᾽ ἤδη πάσῃ πόλει ἔρχεται ἕλκος ἄφυκτον,
   ἐς δὲ κακὴν ταχέως ἤλυθε δουλοσύνην,
ἣ στάσιν ἔμφυλον πόλεμόν θ᾽ εὕδοντ᾽ ἐπεγείρει,
20 ὃς πολλῶν ἐρατὴν ὤλεσεν ἡλικίην·
ἐκ γὰρ δυσμενέων ταχέως πολυήρατον ἄστυ
   τρύχεται ἐν συνόδοις τοῖς ἀδικέουσι φίλαις.
ταῦτα μὲν ἐν δήμῳ στρέφεται κακά· τῶν δὲ
   πενιχρῶν
ἱκνέονται πολλοὶ γαῖαν ἐς ἀλλοδαπὴν
25 πραθέντες δεσμοῖσί τ᾽ ἀεικελίοισι δεθέντες

. . . .

οὕτω δημόσιον κακὸν ἔρχεται οἴκαδ᾽ ἑκάστῳ,
   αὔλειοι δ᾽ ἔτ᾽ ἔχειν οὐκ ἐθέλουσι θύραι,
ὑψηλὸν δ᾽ ὑπὲρ ἕρκος ὑπέρθορεν, εὗρε δὲ πάντως,
   εἰ καί τις φεύγων ἐν μυχῷ ᾖ θαλάμου.
30 ταῦτα διδάξαι θυμὸς Ἀθηναίους με κελεύει,
   ὡς κακὰ πλεῖστα πόλει Δυσνομίη παρέχει,
Εὐνομίη δ᾽ εὔκοσμα καὶ ἄρτια πάντ᾽ ἀποφαίνει,
   καὶ θαμὰ τοῖς ἀδίκοις ἀμφιτίθησι πέδας·
τραχέα λειαίνει, παύει κόρον, ὕβριν ἀμαυροῖ,
35 αὐαίνει δ᾽ ἄτης ἄνθεα φυόμενα,

sacred nor private property, they steal with rapaciousness, one from one source, one from another, and they have no regard for the august foundations of Justice, who bears silent witness to the present and the past and who in time assuredly comes to exact retribution. This[1] is now coming upon the whole city as an inescapable wound and the city has quickly approached wretched slavery,[2] which arouses civil strife and slumbering war, the loss for many of their lovely youth. For at the hands of its enemies the much-loved city is being swiftly worn down amid conspiracies dear to the unjust. These are the evils that are rife among the people, and many of the poor are going to a foreign land, sold and bound in shameful fetters . . . And so the public evil comes home to each man and the courtyard gates no longer have the will to hold it back, but it leaps over the high barrier and assuredly finds him out, even if he takes refuge in an innermost corner of his room. This is what my heart bids me teach the Athenians, that Lawlessness brings the city countless ills, but Lawfulness[3] reveals all that is orderly and fitting, and often places fetters round the unjust. She makes the rough smooth, puts a stop to excess, weakens insolence, dries up the blooming

ELEGIAC POETRY

εὐθύνει δὲ δίκας σκολιάς, ὑπερήφανά τ' ἔργα
    πραΰνει, παύει δ' ἔργα διχοστασίης,
παύει δ' ἀργαλέης ἔριδος χόλον, ἔστι δ' ὑπ' αὐτῆς
    πάντα κατ' ἀνθρώπους ἄρτια καὶ πινυτά.

ἀκούετ', ὦ ἄνδρες Ἀθηναῖοι, περὶ τῶν τοιούτων ἀνθρώ-
πων οἷα Σόλων λέγει καὶ περὶ τῶν θεῶν, οὕς φησι τὴν
πόλιν σῴζειν.

1 ἡμετέρα codd., corr. Camerarius   11 πλουτοῦσιν
codd., corr. Fick   13 ἐφ' ἁρπαγῇ codd. recc.
16 ἀποτισομένη B p.c., -αμένη cett., corr. Hiller
22 ἀδικοῦσι codd., corr. West: ἀδίκοισι Richards   φίλους F
p.c. (retin. West), φίλοις cett., φίλαις Bergk   24 ἱκνοῦνται
codd., corr. Fick   29 ἢ θαλάμῳ codd., corr. Schneidewin
31 Δυσνομία codd., corr. Bergk   32 Εὐνομία codd., corr.
Bergk

4a Arist. *Ath. Pol.* 5

τοιαύτης δὲ τῆς τάξεως οὔσης ἐν τῇ πολιτείᾳ, καὶ τῶν
πολλῶν δουλευόντων τοῖς ὀλίγοις, ἀντέστη τοῖς γνω-
ρίμοις ὁ δῆμος. ἰσχυρᾶς δὲ τῆς στάσεως οὔσης καὶ
πολὺν χρόνον ἀντικαθημένων ἀλλήλοις εἵλοντο κοινῇ
διαλλακτὴν καὶ ἄρχοντα Σόλωνα, καὶ τὴν πολιτείαν
ἐπέτρεψαν αὐτῷ, ποιήσαντι τὴν ἐλεγείαν ἧς ἐστιν
ἀρχή·

γινώσκω, καί μοι φρενὸς ἔνδοθεν ἄλγεα κεῖται,
    πρεσβυτάτην ἐσορῶν γαῖαν [Ἰ]αονίης
κλινομένην

116

flowers of ruin,[4] straightens out crooked judge-
ments, tames deeds of pride, and puts an end to acts
of sedition and to the anger of grievous strife. Under
her all things among men are fitting and rational.[5]

You hear, men of Athens, what Solon has to say about such
men and about the gods who, he says, keep our city safe.

[1] It is unclear what 'this' refers to. Perhaps it is to the pun-
ishment of Justice.　　　[2] Probably a reference to tyranny.
[3] On these two personifications see M. Ostwald, *Nomos and the
Beginnings of Athenian Democracy* (Oxford 1969) 64-69: "They
are 'poetic persons' which symbolize, respectively, the orderly and
disorderly state of affairs in the city" (p. 66).　　　[4] Or "infatua-
tion."　　　[5] Except for lacunae of indeterminate length, the
poem may be complete.

4a Aristotle, *Constitution of Athens*

When such was the organization of the state and many
were enslaved to the few, the people rose up against the
men of note. After bitter strife and protracted opposition
to one another, they agreed to choose Solon as reconciler
and archon [594/3], and they entrusted the state to him.
He had composed the elegy which begins:

I know (and pain lies within my heart), as I look on
the eldest land of Ionia[1] tottering, that . . .[2]

ἐν ᾗ πρὸς ἑκατέρους ὑπὲρ ἑκατέρων μάχεται καὶ διαμ-
φισβητεῖ, καὶ μετὰ ταῦτα κοινῇ παραινεῖ καταπαύειν
τὴν ἐνεστῶσαν φιλονικίαν.

1 γινώσκω pap. (retin. West), γιγν- Blass, alii
2 ['I]αονίας pap., corr. West   3 κλιν- agnovit Wilcken, καιν-
Blass

4c Pergit Arist.

ἦν δὲ ὁ Σόλων τῇ μὲν φύσει καὶ τῇ δόξῃ τῶν πρώτων,
τῇ δ' οὐσίᾳ καὶ τοῖς πράγμασι τῶν μέσων, ὡς ἔκ τε
τῶν ἄλλων ὁμολογεῖται καὶ αὐτὸς ἐν τοῖσδε τοῖς
ποιήμασιν μαρτυρεῖ, παραινῶν τοῖς πλουσίοις μὴ
πλεονεκτεῖν·

> ὑμεῖς δ' ἡσυχάσαντες ἐνὶ φρεσὶ καρτερὸν ἦτορ,
>   οἳ πολλῶν ἀγαθῶν ἐς κόρον [ἠ]λάσατε,
> ἐν μετρίοισι τίθεσθε μέγαν νόον· οὔτε γὰρ ἡμεῖς
>   πεισόμεθ', οὔθ' ὑμῖν ἄρτια τα[ῦ]τ' ἔσεται.

2 [ἠ]λάσατε suppl. Postgate

4b Pergit Arist.

καὶ ὅλως αἰεὶ τὴν αἰτίαν τῆς στάσεως ἀνάπτει τοῖς
πλουσίοις· διὸ καὶ ἐν ἀρχῇ τῆς ἐλεγείας δεδοικέναι
φησὶ τήν τε φ[. .] . . [. .] . . τιαν τήν τε ὑπερηφαν[ί]αν, ὡς
διὰ ταῦτα τῆς ἔχθρας ἐνεστώσης.

In this poem he fights and disputes with each side on behalf of each side, and afterwards he urges them to join in bringing an end to the contention dwelling among them.

1 Athens claimed to be the mother city of all Ionians.
2 My translation assumes that the sentence is incomplete, but if it is complete I would translate as follows: "I realize that I am looking on the eldest land of Ionia tottering, and pain lies within my heart."

4c Aristotle continues

Solon was by birth and reputation one of the leading citizens, but by property and business dealings one of the middle class, as is agreed on from other sources and as he himself attests in these poems, where he urges the rich not to be greedy:

> You who had more than your fill of many good things, calm the stern heart within your breast and moderate your ambition; for we shall not comply nor will these things be fitting for you.

4b Aristotle continues

And in short he always lays the blame for the strife on the rich. That is why he says at the beginning of the elegy that he fears their . . . and their arrogance,[1] suggesting that this was the cause of the hostility.

ELEGIAC POETRY

Plut. *Sol.* 14.2

ἀλλ’ αὐτός φησιν ὁ Σόλων ὀκνῶν τὸ πρῶτον ἅψασθαι
τῆς πολιτείας καὶ δεδοικὼς τῶν μὲν τὴν φιλοχρη-
ματίαν, τῶν δὲ τὴν ὑπερηφανίαν.

5 Arist. *Ath. Pol.* 11.2-12.1

ὁ δὲ ἀμφοτέροις ἠναντιώθη, καὶ ἐξὸν αὐτῷ μεθ’ ὁπο-
τέρων ἐβούλετο συστά[ντ]α τυραννεῖν, εἵλετο πρὸς
ἀμφοτέρους ἀπεχθέσθαι σώσας τὴν πατρίδα καὶ τὰ
βέ[λτι]στα νομοθετήσας. ταῦτα δὲ ὅτι τοῦτον ⟨τὸν⟩
τρόπον ἔσχεν οἵ τε ἄλλοι συμφωνοῦσι πάντες καὶ
αὐτὸς ἐν τῇ ποιήσει μέμνηται περὶ αὐτῶν ἐν τοῖσδε·

δήμῳ μὲν γὰρ ἔδωκα τόσον γέρας ὅσσον
    ἀπαρκεῖν
τιμῆς οὔτ’ ἀφελὼν οὔτ’ ἐπορεξάμενος·
οἳ δ’ εἶχον δύναμιν καὶ χρήμασιν ἦσαν ἀγητοί,
    καὶ τοῖς ἐφρασάμην μηδὲν ἀεικὲς ἔχειν·
5 ἔστην δ’ ἀμφιβαλὼν κρατερὸν σάκος
    ἀμφοτέροισι,
νικᾶν δ’ οὐκ εἴασ’ οὐδετέρους ἀδίκως.

Plut. *Sol.* 18.5

1 κράτος pro γέρας Plut.   ἀπαρκεῖ pap., corr. Ziegler;
ἐπαρκεῖ Plut., ἐπαρκεῖν Brunck (prob. West)   2 ἀπορ- pap.,
ἐπορ- Plut.

120

SOLON

Plutarch, *Life of Solon*

But Solon himself says that at first he undertook public life reluctantly and in fear of one side's love of money and the other side's arrogance.

[1] On the basis of Plutarch many see a pentameter lurking here, τὴν φιλοχρηματίαν (vel sim.) τήν θ᾽ ὑπερηφανίαν, and some suggest that δέδοικα ended the previous hexameter. "I fear their love of money and their arrogance." West agrees that the general thought was present in the poem, but not in this form.

5 Aristotle, *Constitution of Athens*

But Solon opposed both sides, and while he could have joined with whichever side he wished and become tyrant, he chose to incur the enmity of both by saving his homeland and legislating for the best. Everyone else agrees that he acted in this way and he himself in his poetry has made mention of this, as follows:

> I have given the masses as much privilege as is sufficient, neither taking away from their honour nor adding to it. And as for those who had power and were envied for their wealth, I saw to it that they too should suffer no indignity. I stood with a mighty shield cast round both sides and did not allow either to have an unjust victory.

ELEGIAC POETRY

6 Pergit Aristotle

πάλιν δὲ ἀποφαινόμενος περὶ τοῦ πλήθους, ὡς αὐτῷ
δεῖ χρῆσθαι·

> δῆμος δ' ὧδ' ἂν ἄριστα σὺν ἡγεμόνεσσιν ἕποιτο,
>   μήτε λίην ἀνεθεὶς μήτε βιαζόμενος·
> τίκτει γὰρ κόρος ὕβριν, ὅταν πολὺς ὄλβος
>   ἕπηται
> ἀνθρώποις ὁπόσοις μὴ νόος ἄρτιος ᾖ.

Sequitur fr. 34.

Plut. *comp. Sol. et Publ.* 2.6 (vv. 1-2)
Theogn. 153-54 (vv. 3-4)
Clem. *Strom.* 6.8.7 (v. 3)

2 λίαν pap., λίην v.l. in Plut.   πιεζόμενος Plut.   3 τοι pro
γὰρ et κακῷ pro πολὺς Theogn.   4 ἀνθρώπῳ καὶ ὅτῳ Theogn.

7 Plut. *Sol.* 25.6

. . . ὅλως δὲ ταῖς ἀπορίαις ὑπεκστῆναι βουλόμενος καὶ
διαφυγεῖν τὸ δυσάρεστον καὶ τὸ φιλαίτιον τῶν πολι-
τῶν—

> ἔργμασι ⟨γὰρ⟩ ἐν μεγάλοις πᾶσιν ἁδεῖν χαλεπόν,

ὡς αὐτὸς εἴρηκε—πρόσχημα τῆς πλάνης τὴν ναυκλη-
ρίαν ποιησάμενος ἐξέπλευσε, δεκαετῆ παρὰ τῶν Ἀθη-
ναίων ἀποδημίαν αἰτησάμενος.

ἔργμασιν vel ἔργμασι δ' Heinemann

122

SOLON

6 Aristotle continues

And again showing how the masses should be treated:

> And in this way the masses would best follow their
> leaders, if they are neither given too much free-
> dom nor subjected to too much restraint. For excess
> breeds insolence,[1] whenever great prosperity
> comes to men who are not sound of mind.

[1] This became proverbial.

7 Plutarch, *Life of Solon*

. . . and wishing to be wholly free of these difficulties and
to escape from the displeasure and censoriousness of the
citizens—

> in matters of great importance it is hard to please
> everyone,

as he himself said—he gave the ownership of a vessel as an
excuse for travel and set sail, after asking the Athenians for
a ten-year absence abroad.

9 Diod. Sic. 9.20.2

λέγεται δὲ Σόλων καὶ προειπεῖν τοῖς Ἀθηναίοις τὴν
ἐσομένην τυραννίδα δι᾽ ἐλεγείων·

> ἐκ νεφέλης πέλεται χιόνος μένος ἠδὲ χαλάζης,
>   βροντὴ δ᾽ ἐκ λαμπρῆς γίγνεται ἀστεροπῆς·
> ἀνδρῶν δ᾽ ἐκ μεγάλων πόλις ὄλλυται, ἐς δὲ
>   μονάρχου
>   δῆμος ἀϊδρίῃ δουλοσύνην ἔπεσεν.
> 5 λίην δ᾽ ἐξάραντ᾽ ⟨οὐ⟩ ῥᾴδιόν ἐστι κατασχεῖν
>   ὕστερον, ἀλλ᾽ ἤδη χρή ⟨τινα⟩ πάντα νοεῖν.

Sequitur fr. 11.

> Diog. Laert. 1.50 (vv. 1-4)
> Plut. *Sol.* 3.6 (vv. 1-2)
> Diod. Sic. 19.1.4 (vv. 3-4)

> 1 φέρεται Diog.   θαλάττης Diod., θαλάσσης cod. P
> Diogenis   2 λαμπρᾶς Diod., Plut.   3 τυράννου Diod.
> 19   4 ἀϊδρείη Diod. 9   5 λείης δ᾽ ἐξέραντα Diod.,
> corr. Schneidewin   οὐ suppl. Dindorf   6 τινα suppl. Sintenis,
> alii alia

10 Diog. Laert. 1.49

ἄξας γὰρ εἰς τὴν ἐκκλησίαν μετὰ δόρατος καὶ ἀσπί-
δος προεῖπεν αὐτοῖς τινα ἐπίθεσιν τοῦ Πεισιστράτου
. . . καὶ ἡ βουλή, Πεισιστρατίδαι ὄντες, μαίνεσθαι
ἔλεγον αὐτόν· ὅθεν εἶπε ταυτί·

9 Diodorus Siculus, *World History*

Solon is said to have foretold the Athenians of the coming tyranny (i.e., Pisistratus) in elegiac verses:

> From a cloud comes the force of snow and hail, thunder from a flash of lightning, from powerful men a city's destruction, and through ignorance the masses fall enslaved to a tyrant. If they raise a man too high, it's not easy to restrain him afterwards; it is now that one should consider everything.

10 Diogenes Laertius, *Lives of the Philosophers*

Rushing into the assembly armed with spear and shield, he warned them of the designs of Pisistratus . . . And the council, consisting of Pisistratus' supporters, declared that he was mad; as a result of which he uttered these verses:

125

δείξει δὴ μανίην μὲν ἐμὴν βαιὸς χρόνος ἀστοῖς,
δείξει ἀληθείης ἐς μέσον ἐρχομένης.

11 Pergit Diod. Sic. (v. ad fr. 9)

καὶ μετὰ ταῦτα τυραννοῦντος ἔφη·

εἰ δὲ πεπόνθατε λυγρὰ δι᾽ ὑμετέρην κακότητα,
μὴ θεοῖσιν τούτων μοῖραν ἐπαμφέρετε·
αὐτοὶ γὰρ τούτους ηὐξήσατε ῥύματα δόντες,
καὶ διὰ ταῦτα κακὴν ἔσχετε δουλοσύνην.
5   ὑμέων δ᾽ εἷς μὲν ἕκαστος ἀλώπεκος ἴχνεσι βαίνει,
σύμπασιν δ᾽ ὑμῖν χαῦνος ἔνεστι νόος·
ἐς γὰρ γλῶσσαν ὁρᾶτε καὶ εἰς ἔπη αἱμύλου
ἀνδρός,
εἰς ἔργον δ᾽ οὐδὲν γιγνόμενον βλέπετε.

Diog. Laert. 1.51 (vv. 1-8)
Plut. *Sol.* 30.8 (vv. 1-4)
Plut. *Sol.* 30.3 (= Clem. Alex. *Strom.* 1.23.1), vv. 5-7 (7,5,6)

1 δεινὰ Diog.   ὑμετέραν Diod., cod. F Diogenis
2 τι θεοῖς Diog., v.l. in Plut.   μῆνιν Plut.   3 ῥύσια Diog.
6 χαῦνος Plut., κοῦφος Diod., Diog.   7 ἔπη αἱμύλου Plut.,
ἔπος αἰόλον Diod., Diog.

12 Plut. *Sol.* 3.6

ἐξ ἀνέμων δὲ θάλασσα ταράσσεται· ἢν δέ τις
αὐτὴν
μὴ κινῇ, πάντων ἐστὶ δικαιοτάτη.

126

A little time will show the citizens how mad I am,
when the truth comes out in the open.

11 Diodorus Siculus (following fr. 9)

And afterwards, when Pisistratus was tyrant, he said:

> If you have suffered grief because of your wrong ac-
> tion, do not lay the blame for this on the gods. You
> yourselves increased the power of these men by pro-
> viding a bodyguard and that is why you have foul
> slavery. Each one of you follows the fox's tracks, and
> collectively you are empty-headed. You look to the
> tongue and words of a crafty man, but not to what he
> does.

12 Plutarch, *Life of Solon*

> The sea is disturbed by winds, but if none moves it,
> it is the evenest[1] of all things.

[1] The imagery is no doubt being applied to a political situation,
as in fr. 9. See B. Gentili, *QUCC* 20 (1975) 159-62. Plutarch actu-
ally cites the verses as a continuation of fr. 9.1-2 which he ineptly
introduced with the words ἐν δὲ τοῖς φυσικοῖς ἁπλοῦς ἐστι λίαν
καὶ ἀρχαῖος, "but in physical matters he is extremely simple-
minded and primitive."

13 Stob. 3.9.23

Σόλωνος·

Μνημοσύνης καὶ Ζηνὸς Ὀλυμπίου ἀγλαὰ τέκνα,
Μοῦσαι Πιερίδες, κλῦτέ μοι εὐχομένῳ·
ὄλβον μοι πρὸς θεῶν μακάρων δότε καὶ πρὸς
ἁπάντων
ἀνθρώπων αἰεὶ δόξαν ἔχειν ἀγαθήν·
5 εἶναι δὲ γλυκὺν ὧδε φίλοις, ἐχθροῖσι δὲ πικρόν,
τοῖσι μὲν αἰδοῖον, τοῖσι δὲ δεινὸν ἰδεῖν.
χρήματα δ᾽ ἱμείρω μὲν ἔχειν, ἀδίκως δὲ πεπᾶσθαι
οὐκ ἐθέλω· πάντως ὕστερον ἦλθε δίκη.
πλοῦτον δ᾽ ὃν μὲν δῶσι θεοί, παραγίγνεται ἀνδρὶ
10 ἔμπεδος ἐκ νεάτου πυθμένος ἐς κορυφήν·
ὃν δ᾽ ἄνδρες τιμῶσιν ὑφ᾽ ὕβριος, οὐ κατὰ κόσμον
ἔρχεται, ἀλλ᾽ ἀδίκοις ἔργμασι πειθόμενος
οὐκ ἐθέλων ἕπεται, ταχέως δ᾽ ἀναμίσγεται ἄτῃ·
ἀρχὴν δ᾽ ἐξ ὀλίγης γίγνεται ὥστε πυρός,
15 φλαύρη μὲν τὸ πρῶτον, ἀνιηρὴ δὲ τελευτᾷ·
οὐ γὰρ δὴν θνητοῖς ὕβριος ἔργα πέλει,
ἀλλὰ Ζεὺς πάντων ἐφορᾷ τέλος, ἐξαπίνης δὲ
ὥστ᾽ ἄνεμος νεφέλας αἶψα διεσκέδασεν
ἠρινός, ὃς πόντου πολυκύμονος ἀτρυγέτοιο
20 πυθμένα κινήσας, γῆν κάτα πυροφόρον
δῃώσας καλὰ ἔργα θεῶν ἕδος αἰπὺν ἱκάνει
οὐρανόν, αἰθρίην δ᾽ αὖτις ἔθηκεν ἰδεῖν·
λάμπει δ᾽ ἠελίοιο μένος κατὰ πίονα γαῖαν
καλόν, ἀτὰρ νεφέων οὐδ᾽ ἓν ἔτ᾽ ἐστὶν ἰδεῖν—

128

13 Stobaeus, *Anthology*

From Solon:

Resplendent daughters of Memory and Olympian
Zeus, Pierian[1] Muses, hearken to my prayer. Grant
that I have prosperity from the blessed gods and a
good reputation always from all men; grant that in
these circumstances I be sweet to my friends and
bitter to my enemies, viewed with respect by the
former and with dread by the latter.

I long to have money, but I am unwilling to pos-
sess it unjustly, for retribution assuredly comes af-
terwards. Wealth which the gods give remains with
a man, secure from the lowest foundation to the
top,[2] whereas wealth which men honour with vio-
lence comes in disorder, an unwilling attendant per-
suaded by unjust actions, and it is quickly mixed
with ruin. Ruin has a small beginning, like that of
fire, insignificant at first but grievous in the end, for
mortals' deeds of violence do not live long. Zeus
oversees every outcome, and suddenly, just as the
clouds are quickly scattered by a spring wind which
stirs up the bottom of the swelling and un-
draining(?) sea, ravages the lovely fields over the
wheat-bearing land, reaches the gods' high seat in
heaven, and again brings a clear sky to view; the
strong sun shines in beauty over the fertile land and
no longer can even a single cloud be seen—such is

25 τοιαύτη ΖηνϏς πέλεται τίσις· οϟδ’ ἐφ’ ἑκάστω
ὦσπερ θνητός ἀνήρ γίγνεται ὀξύχολος,
αἰεὶ δ’ οὔ έ λέληθε διαμπερές, ὅστις ἀλιτρὸν
θυμὸν ἔχει, πάντως δ’ ἐς τέλος ἐξεφάνη·
ἀλλ’ ὁ μὲν αὐτίκ’ ἔτεισεν, ὁ δ’ ὕστερον· οἱ δὲ
φύγωσιν
30 αὐτοί, μηδὲ θεῶν μοῖρ’ ἐπιοῦσα κίχη,
ἤλυθε πάντως αὖτις· ἀναίτιοι ἔργα τίνουσιν
ἢ παῖδες τούτων ἢ γένος ἐξοπίσω.
θνητοὶ δ’ ὧδε νοέομεν ὁμῶς ἀγαθός τε κακός τε,
†ἐν δηνην† αὐτὸς δόξαν ἕκαστος ἔχει,
35 πρίν τι παθεῖν· τότε δ’ αὖτις ὀδύρεται· ἄχρι δὲ
τούτου
χάσκοντες κούφαις ἐλπίσι τερπόμεθα.
χῶστις μὲν νούσοισιν ὑπ’ ἀργαλέησι πιεσθῇ,
ὡς ὑγιὴς ἔσται, τοῦτο κατεφράσατο·
ἄλλος δειλὸς ἐὼν ἀγαθὸς δοκεῖ ἔμμεναι ἀνήρ,
40 καὶ καλὸς μορφὴν οὐ χαρίεσσαν ἔχων·
εἰ δέ τις ἀχρήμων, πενίης δέ μιν ἔργα βιάται,
κτήσεσθαι πάντως χρήματα πολλὰ δοκεῖ.
σπεύδει δ’ ἄλλοθεν ἄλλος· ὁ μὲν κατὰ πόντον
ἀλᾶται
ἐν νηυσὶν χρήζων οἴκαδε κέρδος ἄγειν
45 ἰχθυόεντ’ ἀνέμοισι φορεόμενος ἀργαλέοισιν,
φειδωλὴν ψυχῆς οὐδεμίαν θέμενος·
ἄλλος γῆν τέμνων πολυδένδρεον εἰς ἐνιαυτὸν
λατρεύει, τοῖσιν καμπύλ’ ἄροτρα μέλει·
ἄλλος Ἀθηναίης τε καὶ Ἡφαίστου πολυτέχνεω

130

the vengeance of Zeus. He is not, like a mortal man, quick to anger at every incident, but anyone who has a sinful heart never ever escapes his notice and in the end he is assuredly revealed. But one man pays the penalty at once, another later, and if they themselves escape the penalty and the pursuing destiny of the gods does not overtake them, it assuredly comes at another time; the innocent pay the penalty, either their children or a later progeny. And thus we mortals, whatever our estate, think that the expectation which each one has is progressing well(?), until he suffers some mishap, and then afterwards he wails. But until then we take eager delight in empty hopes. Whoever is oppressed by grievous sickness thinks that he will be healthy; another man of low estate considers that it's high and that he's handsome, though his form is without beauty. If someone is lacking means and is constrained by the effects of poverty, he thinks that he will assuredly acquire much money. Everyone has a different pursuit. One roams over the fish-filled sea in ships, longing to bring home profit; tossed by cruel winds, he has no regard for life. Another, whose concern is the curved plough, cleaves the thickly wooded land and slaves away for a year. Another who has learned the works of Athena and Hephaestus,[3] the

50   ἔργα δαεὶς χειροῖν ξυλλέγεται βίοτον,
        ἄλλος Ὀλυμπιάδων Μουσέων πάρα δῶρα
             διδαχθείς,
        ἱμερτῆς σοφίης μέτρον ἐπιστάμενος·
        ἄλλον μάντιν ἔθηκεν ἄναξ ἑκάεργος Ἀπόλλων,
        ἔγνω δ᾽ ἀνδρὶ κακὸν τηλόθεν ἐρχόμενον,
55   ᾧ συνομαρτήσωσι θεοί· τὰ δὲ μόρσιμα πάντως
        οὔτε τις οἰωνὸς ῥύσεται οὔθ᾽ ἱερά·
        ἄλλοι Παιῶνος πολυφαρμάκου ἔργον ἔχοντες
        ἰητροί· καὶ τοῖς οὐδὲν ἔπεστι τέλος·
        πολλάκι δ᾽ ἐξ ὀλίγης ὀδύνης μέγα γίγνεται ἄλγος,
60   κοὐκ ἄν τις λύσαιτ᾽ ἤπια φάρμακα δούς·
        τὸν δὲ κακαῖς νούσοισι κυκώμενον ἀργαλέαις τε
        ἁψάμενος χειροῖν αἶψα τίθησ᾽ ὑγιῆ.
        Μοῖρα δέ τοι θνητοῖσι κακὸν φέρει ἠδὲ καὶ
             ἐσθλόν,
        δῶρα δ᾽ ἄφυκτα θεῶν γίγνεται ἀθανάτων.
65   πᾶσι δέ τοι κίνδυνος ἐπ᾽ ἔργμασιν, οὐδέ τις οἶδεν
        ᾗ μέλλει σχήσειν χρήματος ἀρχομένου·
        ἀλλ᾽ ὁ μὲν εὖ ἔρδειν πειρώμενος οὐ προνοήσας
        ἐς μεγάλην ἄτην καὶ χαλεπὴν ἔπεσεν,
        τῷ δὲ κακῶς ἔρδοντι θεὸς περὶ πάντα δίδωσιν
70   συντυχίην ἀγαθήν, ἔκλυσιν ἀφροσύνης.
        πλούτου δ᾽ οὐδὲν τέρμα πεφασμένον ἀνδράσι
             κεῖται·
        οἳ γὰρ νῦν ἡμέων πλεῖστον ἔχουσι βίον,
        διπλασίως σπεύδουσι· τίς ἂν κορέσειεν ἅπαντας;
        κέρδεά τοι θνητοῖς ὤπασαν ἀθάνατοι,

132

god of many crafts, gathers in his livelihood with his hands; another, taught the gifts that come from the Olympian Muses and knowing the rules of the lovely art of poetry, makes his living. Another has been made a seer by lord Apollo who works from afar and, if the gods are with him, he sees a distant calamity coming upon a man; but assuredly neither augury nor sacrifice will ward off what is destined. Others, engaged in the work of Paeon,[4] rich in drugs, are physicians; for them too there is no guarantee. Often agony results from a slight pain and no one can provide relief by giving soothing drugs, whereas another, in the throes of a terrible and grievous disease, he quickly restores to health with the touch of his hands. Fate brings good and ill to mortals and the gifts of the immortal gods are inescapable. In all actions there is risk and no one knows, when something starts, how it is going to turn out. The man who tries to act rightly falls unawares into great and harsh calamity, while to the one who acts badly the god gives success in all things, an escape from his folly. But of wealth no limit lies revealed to men, since those of us who now have the greatest livelihood show twice as much zeal. What could satisfy everyone? In truth the immortals give men profit, but from it (them?)[5] there is revealed ruin, which

75   ἄτη δ' ἐξ αὐτῶν ἀναφαίνεται, ἢν ὁπότε Ζεὺς
      πέμψῃ τεισομένην, ἄλλοτε ἄλλος ἔχει.

Crates fr. 1.1-2 (vv. 1-2)
Clem. *Strom.* 6.11.1 (v. 1)
Plut. *Sol.* 2.4, *Publ.* 24.7 (*comp. Sol. et Publ.* 1.7), vv. 7-8
Theognis 585-90, Stob. 4.47.16 (vv. 65-70)
Theognis 227-32 (vv. 71-76)
Arist. *Pol.* 1.8.1256b31, Plut. *de cupid. div.* 4.524e, Basil. *ad adul.* 9.103 (p. 58 Boulenger, p. 34 Wilson), v. 71

11 μετίωσιν Ahrens, alii alia   13 ἄτη v.l.   14 ἀρχὴ Stob., corr. Arnott, ἀρχῆς δ' ἐξ ὀλίγης West   16 δὴ Stob., δὴν Paris. 1985 et Regin. gr. 146   22 αὖθις Stob., corr. Bach   27 οὔτε Stob., corr. Hermann   29 ἔτισεν Stob., corr. Hiller   31 αὐτίκ' Stob., corr. Brunck   ἀναίτια Stob., corr. nescioquis ante Schow   32 ἡγεμόνων ὀπίσω Stob., corr. Paris. 1985 et Pierson   33 νοεῦμεν Stob., corr. West   34 εὖ ῥεῖν ἦν Büchner et Theiler (prob. West), alii alia   37 χὤστις Stob., corr. Stephanus   42 κτήσασθαι Stob. (retin. West), corr. Sylburg   πάντων Stob., corr. Gesner   45 φορεύμενος Stob., corr. West   46 οὐδεμίην Stob., corr. Schneidewin   48 τοῖσι Stob., corr. Grotius   μένει Stob., corr. Gesner   51 Μουσάων Stob., corr. Turnebus   61 κακώμενον Stob., corr. Gesner   62 χεροῖν Stob., corr. Trincavelli   65 πᾶσίν τοι Theogn.   66 πῇ et ποῖ Theogn.   σχήσειν μέλλει πρήγματος Theogn.   67 εὐδοκιμεῖν Theogn.   69 καλῶς ποιεῦντι Theogn., καλὸν ποιοῦντι Stob. 4.47.16   70 ἀγαθῶν Stob. 4.47.16   71 ἀνδράσι κεῖται Stob., Arist., Basil.; ἀνθρώποισι Theogn., Plut.   73 διπλάσιον Theogn. (retin. West)   74 χρήματά τοι θνητοῖς γίνεται ἀφροσύνη Theogn.   75 αὐτῆς Theogn.   ὁπόταν Stob.   76 πέμψει Stob. et Theogn. (v.l.)   τισομένην Stob., corr. Hiller; τειρομένοις Theogn.

now one, now another has, whenever Zeus sends it
to punish them.

[1] Hesiod (*Theog.* 53) states that the Muses were born in Pieria,
in southern Macedonia northwest of Mt. Olympus.   [2] Vari-
ous metaphors have been postulated (building, tree, grain, stor-
age jar), but nothing specific need be intended.   [3] Patron
deities of craftsmen, especially potters. They shared cult wor-
ship in Athens.   [4] The god of healing, often identified with
Apollo.   [5] The reference of αὐτῶν is unclear, some arguing
for 'profit' (assuming this to mean unjustly gained), others for
'men' (i.e., men themselves are the cause of their own ruin), and
others for 'immortals.'

According to Clem. *Strom.* 6.11.1 we have the beginning of
the poem and it has the appearance of completeness.

ELEGIAC POETRY

14 Stob. 4.34.23

Σόλωνος·

οὐδὲ μάκαρ οὐδεὶς πέλεται βροτός, ἀλλὰ πονηροὶ
πάντες ὅσους θνητοὺς ἠέλιος καθορᾷ.

15 Plut. Sol. 3.2

ὅτι δὲ ἑαυτὸν ἐν τῇ τῶν πενήτων μερίδι μᾶλλον ἢ τῇ
τῶν πλουσίων ἔταττε, δῆλόν ἐστιν ἐκ τούτων·

πολλοὶ γὰρ πλουτέουσι κακοί, ἀγαθοὶ δὲ πένονται·
ἀλλ᾽ ἡμεῖς αὐτοῖς οὐ διαμειψόμεθα
τῆς ἀρετῆς τὸν πλοῦτον, ἐπεὶ τὸ μὲν ἔμπεδον αἰεί,
χρήματα δ᾽ ἀνθρώπων ἄλλοτε ἄλλος ἔχει.

Theogn. 315-18 (vv. 1-4)
Plut. de prof. virt. 6.78c, de tranqu. animi 13.472d, Basil. ad
adul. 5.45 (p. 48 Boulenger, p. 25 Wilson), vv. 2-4
Plut. de inim. util. 11.92e (vv. 2-3, ἀλλ᾽—πλοῦτον)

1 τοι pro γὰρ Theogn.   πλουτεῦσι Plut. v.l., -οῦσι Plut. v.l.,
Theogn., corr. West   2 τούτοις Theogn. (rec. West)   3 αἰεὶ
Theogn., Basil., Plut. Sol. cod. C: ἔστιν Plut. alias

16 Clem. Strom. 5.81.1

σοφώτατα τοίνυν γέγραπται τῷ Σόλωνι ταῦτα περὶ
θεοῦ·

γνωμοσύνης δ᾽ ἀφανὲς χαλεπώτατόν ἐστι νοῆσαι
μέτρον, ὃ δὴ πάντων πείρατα μοῦνον ἔχει.

SOLON

14 Stobaeus, *Anthology*

From Solon:

> No mortal is blessed, but all whom the sun looks
> down upon are in a sorry state.

15 Plutarch, *Life of Solon*

That he classified himself among the poor rather than the
rich is clear from the following:

> Many base men are rich and many good men poor:
> but we will not take their wealth in exchange for vir-
> tue, since this is always secure, while wealth belongs
> now to one man, now to another.

16 Clement of Alexandria, *Miscellanies*

Solon has written these very wise words about God:

> Wisdom's hidden essence, which alone holds the
> key to everything, is the most difficult to discern.[1]

[1] Clement may have misunderstood or misinterpreted Solon's
words, since the context is probably political, with 'wisdom' being
a requirement of good government.

ELEGIAC POETRY

17 Clem. *Strom.* 5.129.5

ἀλλὰ καὶ Ἡσίοδος δι' ὧν γράφει συνᾴδει τοῖς προ-
ειρημένοις· (fr. 303 M.-W.) . . . εἰκότως ἄρα Σόλων
ὁ Ἀθηναῖος ἐν ταῖς ἐλεγείαις καὶ αὐτὸς κατακολου-
θήσας Ἡσιόδῳ

πάντῃ δ' ἀθανάτων ἀφανὴς νόος ἀνθρώποισιν

γράφει. Exscripsit Euseb. *praep. ev.* 13.13.57

πάμπαν Euseb.

18 Ps.-Plat. *Amat.* 133c

τί δ' ἄλλο γε (τὸ φιλοσοφεῖν) ἢ κατὰ τὸ τοῦ Σόλωνος;
Σόλων γάρ που εἶπε·

γηράσκω δ' αἰεὶ πολλὰ διδασκόμενος.

19 Plut. *Sol.* 26.2-4

ἔπειτα πλεύσας εἰς Κύπρον ἠγαπήθη διαφερόντως
ὑπὸ Φιλοκύπρου τινὸς τῶν ἐκεῖ βασιλέων, ὃς εἶχεν οὐ
μεγάλην πόλιν . . . ἔπεισεν οὖν αὐτὸν ὁ Σόλων,
ὑποκειμένου καλοῦ πεδίου, μεταθέντα τὴν πόλιν ἡδί-
ονα καὶ μείζονα κατασκευάσαι, καὶ παρὼν ἐπεμελήθη
τοῦ συνοικισμοῦ . . . καὶ αὐτὸς δὲ μέμνηται τοῦ
συνοικισμοῦ· προσαγορεύσας γὰρ ἐν ταῖς ἐλεγείαις
τὸν Φιλόκυπρον

17 Clement of Alexandria, *Miscellanies*

But Hesiod in his writings agrees with what has been said
earlier . . . It is reasonable then that Solon the Athenian,
following Hesiod, writes in his elegies:

> The mind of the immortals is altogether hidden
> from men.

18 Pseudo-Plato, *Lovers*

What else is philosophizing than the statement of Solon?
For he said:

> As I grow old I am always learning many things.[1]

[1] This became proverbial and is cited in a great many sources.

19 Plutarch, *Life of Solon*

Then he sailed (from Egypt) to Cyprus and received an ex-
ceptionally warm welcome from Philocyprus, one of the
local kings, who had a small city . . . Solon persuaded him
to move the city to the lovely plain that lay below and to
make it more attractive and spacious, and he took personal
charge of the consolidation . . . Solon himself mentions this
in the elegiac verses which he addressed to Philocyprus:

νῦν δὲ (φησί) σὺ μὲν Σολίοισι πολὺν χρόνον
   ἐνθάδ᾽ ἀνάσσων
τήνδε πόλιν ναίοις καὶ γένος ὑμέτερον·
αὐτὰρ ἐμὲ ξὺν νηῒ θοῇ κλεινῆς ἀπὸ νήσου
   ἀσκηθῆ πέμποι Κύπρις ἰοστέφανος·
5   οἰκισμῷ δ᾽ ἐπὶ τῷδε χάριν καὶ κῦδος ὀπάζοι
   ἐσθλὸν καὶ νόστον πατρίδ᾽ ἐς ἡμετέρην.

Vita Arati (p. 7.14 Martin), vv. 1-4

2 δύοις Vita

20 Diog. Laert. 1.60 (v. ad Mimn. fr. 6)

ἀλλ᾽ εἴ μοι κἂν νῦν ἔτι πείσεαι, ἔξελε τοῦτο—
   μηδὲ μέγαιρ᾽, ὅτι σέο λῷον ἐπεφρασάμην—
καὶ μεταποίησον, Λιγυαιστάδη, ὧδε δ᾽ ἄειδε·
   "ὀγδωκονταέτη μοῖρα κίχοι θανάτου."

1 καὶ νῦν Thiersch (prob. West)   τοῦτον v.l.   2 σεῦ
codd., corr. West   τοῖον codd., λῷον Boissonade, λῷον᾽
Ziegler, λώιον ἐφρ- Christianus   3 ναιγιαστάδη vel
α(ι)γιαστάδί codd., corr. Bergk (Λιγυαστ-) et Diels (Λιγυᾳστ-),
Λιγιαστ- West

21 Plut. Publ. 24.5 (comp. Sol. et Publ. 1.5)

ἔτι τοίνυν οἷς πρὸς Μίμνερμον ἀντειπὼν περὶ χρόνου
ζωῆς ἐπιπεφώνηκε,

μηδέ μοι ἄκλαυστος θάνατος μόλοι, ἀλλὰ φίλοισι
   καλλείποιμι θανὼν ἄλγεα καὶ στοναχάς,

Now may you and your progeny dwell in this city
and rule over Soloi[1] for a long time; and may Cypris
of the violet crown send me unscathed from your fa-
mous island on a swift ship. May she bestow favour
and glory on this settlement and a fair return to my
homeland.

[1] Plutarch states that Aepeia was renamed Soloi by Philocy-
prus out of gratitude for Solon's assistance. Herodotus 5.113.2
and the *Life of Aratus* mention more briefly Solon's involvement
with Philocyprus, the *Life* calling him Cypranor.

20 Diogenes Laertius, *Lives of the Philosophers*

But if even now you will still listen to me, remove
this[1]—and do not be offended because my thoughts
are better than yours—and changing it, Ligyai-
stades,[2] sing as follows: "May my fated death come
at eighty."

[1] I.e., what Mimnermus said in fr. 6. West argues that Solon
quoted Mimn. fr. 6.2 immediately before v. 1 of our fragment.
[2] The precise form is disputed. See Mimn. test. 1.

21 Plutarch, *Comparison of Solon and Publicola*

Furthermore, from what Solon said on the duration of life,
in opposition to Mimnermus,

May death not come to me without tears, but when I
die may I leave my friends with sorrow and lamenta-
tion,[1]

εὐδαίμονα τὸν Ποπλικόλαν ἄνδρα ποιεῖ.

Stob. 4.54.3 (vv. 1-2); cf. Cic. *Tusc.* 1.117 et *de senect.* 73

1 ἄκλαυτος van Herwerden (prob. West)
2 καλλείποιμι Stob. (-λίπ- codd., corr. Gesner), cf. Cic.
(*linquamus*); ποιήσαιμι Plut.

22 Plat. *Tim.* 20e

ἦν μὲν οὖν (Σόλων) οἰκεῖος ἡμῖν καὶ σφόδρα φίλος
Δρωπίδου τοῦ προπάππου, καθάπερ λέγει πολλαχοῦ
καὶ αὐτὸς ἐν τῇ ποιήσει.

Plat. *Charm.* 157e

ἥ τε γὰρ πατρῴα ὑμῖν οἰκία, ἡ Κριτίου τοῦ Δρωπίδου,
καὶ ὑπὸ Ἀνακρέοντος (fr. 495 *PMG*) καὶ ὑπὸ Σόλωνος
καὶ ὑπ᾽ ἄλλων πολλῶν ποιητῶν ἐγκεκωμιασμένη
παραδέδοται ἡμῖν, ὡς διαφέρουσα κάλλει τε καὶ
ἀρετῇ καὶ τῇ ἄλλῃ λεγομένῃ εὐδαιμονίᾳ.

22a Procl. in *Tim.* l.c. (i.81.27 Diehl); cf. schol. Plat.
(p. 280 Greene)

ἡ μὲν ἱστορία ἡ κατὰ τὸ Σόλωνος γένος καὶ τὴν
Πλάτωνος πρὸς αὐτὸν συγγένειαν τοιαύτη τίς ἐστιν·
Ἐξηκεστίδου παῖδες ἐγένοντο Σόλων καὶ Δρωπίδης,
καὶ Δρωπίδου μὲν Κριτίας, οὗ μνημονεύει καὶ Σόλων
ἐν τῇ ποιήσει, λέγων·

εἰπεῖν μοι Κριτίῃ ξανθότριχι πατρὸς ἀκούειν·

142

he makes Publicola a happy man.

1 Because of the reference to Mimnermus many assume that these verses came from the same poem as fr. 20.

22 Plato, *Timaeus*

Now Solon was related to us and was a close friend of Dropides, my great-grandfather, as he himself says many times in his poetry.

Plato, *Charmides*

For your ancestral house (i.e., of Charmides and Critias), the house of Critias son of Dropides, has been praised by Anacreon, Solon, and many other poets and has come down to us in tradition as one that is distinguished for beauty, virtue, and whatever is called happiness.

22a Proclus on Plato, *Timaeus*

The history of Solon's family and of Plato's kinship with him is as follows: Solon and Dropides were the sons of Execestides, and the son of Dropides was Critias,[1] whom Solon mentions in his poetry, saying:

Please tell flaxen-haired Critias to listen to his

οὐ γὰρ ἁμαρτινόῳ πείσεται ἡγεμόνι.

Arist. *Rhet.* 1.1375b31; Paraphr. Anon. ad loc. (*Comm. in Arist. Graeca* xxi(2).81.13), v. 1

1 εἰπεῖν μοι Arist. (εἰπεῖν τῷ Paraphr.), εἰπέμεναι Procl., schol. Plat.   Κριτίᾳ πυρρότριχι Arist.

23 Plat. *Lys.* 212d-e

ἢ φιλοῦσι μὲν ταῦτα ἕκαστοι, οὐ μέντοι φίλα ὄντα;—
ἀλλὰ ψεύδεται ὁ ποιητὴς ὃς ἔφη·

ὄλβιος, ᾧ παῖδές τε φίλοι καὶ μώνυχες ἵπποι
καὶ κύνες ἀγρευταὶ καὶ ξένος ἀλλοδαπός.

Hermias in Plat. *Phaedr.* 231e (p. 38.14 Couvreur); Theogn.
1253-54 (vv. 1-2)
Ps.-Luc. *amores* 48 (v. 1)

1 νέοι pro φίλοι ps.-Luc.   2 θηρευταί τε κύνες καὶ ξένοι
ἀλλοδαποί Theogn.

24 Stob. 4.33.7 (Θεόγνιδος); Theognis 719-28; Plut. *Sol.*
2.3 (1-6, πολὺς—ἁρμοδία)

ἶσόν τοι πλουτέουσιν, ὅτῳ πολὺς ἄργυρός ἐστι
καὶ χρυσὸς καὶ γῆς πυροφόρου πεδία
ἵπποι θ᾿ ἡμίονοί τε, καὶ ᾧ μόνα ταῦτα πάρεστι,
γαστρί τε καὶ πλευραῖς καὶ ποσὶν ἁβρὰ παθεῖν,
5   παιδός τ᾿ ἠδὲ γυναικός, ἐπὴν καὶ ταῦτ᾿ ἀφίκηται,
ὥρη, σὺν δ᾿ ἥβη γίνεται ἁρμοδίη.

father; for he will be heeding a guide of unerring judgement.

[1] See also Critias test. 1.

23 Plato, *Lysis*

Or does each group love these things, without these things loving them?—thereby giving the lie to the poet who said:

> Happy is he who has dear boys,[1] horses of uncloven hoof, hunting dogs, and a friend in foreign parts.

[1] Or "dear sons," but a pederastic sense seems more probable. Plato has sophistically misrepresented Solon as applying φίλοι (with active meaning, 'loving') to the following nouns as well. Only Hermias names Solon as author.

24 Stobaeus, *Anthology* (from Theognis); Theognis; Plutarch, *Life of Solon*

> Equally rich is he who has much silver and gold, fields of wheat-bearing land, and horses and mules, and he who has only this, comfort for his stomach, sides, and feet,[1] and whenever this too comes, the season for a boy and for a wife, accompanied by a youthful vigour that fits his needs.[2] This is wealth for

ταῦτ᾽ ἄφενος θνητοῖσι· τὰ γὰρ περιώσια πάντα
χρήματ᾽ ἔχων οὐδεὶς ἔρχεται εἰς Ἀΐδεω,
οὐδ᾽ ἂν ἄποινα διδοὺς θάνατον φύγοι, οὐδὲ
βαρείας

10   νούσους, οὐδὲ κακὸν γῆρας ἐπερχόμενον.

1 πλουτοῦσιν codd., corr. West   ὅσοις Stob.
3 μόνα ταῦτα Plut., τὰ δέοντα Theogn., τάδε πάντα Stob.
4 πλευρῆ Plut.   5 ἐπὴν καὶ ταῦτ᾽ Plut., ὅταν δέ κε τῶν(δ᾽)
Theogn. (Stob.)   6 ἥβη, σὺν δ᾽ ὥρη(ι) Plut.   ἁρμοδία
v.l. Stob. et Theogn., corr. Schneidewin

25 Plut. *amat.* 5.751b

εὖ γε νὴ Δία, ἔφη, τοῦ Σόλωνος ἐμνήσθης, καὶ χρη-
στέον αὐτῷ γνώμονι τοῦ ἐρωτικοῦ ἀνδρός·

ἔσθ᾽ ἥβης ἐρατοῖσιν ἐπ᾽ ἄνθεσι παιδοφιλήσῃ,
μηρῶν ἱμείρων καὶ γλυκεροῦ στόματος.

Ath. 13.602e; Apul. *apol.* 9 (v. 2)

1 -ήσεις Brunck, -ήσῃς Ziegler, -ήσει Boissonade
2 ἱμείρων om. codd. Plut.

26 Plut. *amat.* 5.751e

ὅθεν, οἶμαι, καὶ Σόλων ἐκεῖνα μὲν (fr. 25) ἔγραψε νέος
ὢν ἔτι καὶ "σπέρματος πολλοῦ μεστός," ὡς ὁ Πλάτων
φησί (*Leges* 8.839b)· ταυτὶ δὲ πρεσβύτης γενόμενος·

ἔργα δὲ Κυπρογενοῦς νῦν μοι φίλα καὶ Διονύσου
καὶ Μουσέων, ἃ τίθησ᾽ ἀνδράσιν εὐφροσύνας,

mortals, since no one goes to Hades with all his enormous possessions nor can he pay a price to escape death or grim diseases or the onset of evil old age.

[1] I.e., sufficient food, clothing, and footwear.   [2] Text and translation of v. 6 are uncertain.

25 Plutarch, *Dialogue on Love*

You did well, he said, to mention Solon, and we ought to use him as an index of the erotic man:

until (so long as?) one falls in love with a boy in the lovely flower of youth, desiring thighs and a sweet mouth.

26 Plutarch, *Dialogue on Love*

Hence I think Solon wrote those verses (fr. 25) while he was still young and "full of abundant seed," as Plato puts it, but the following when he was old:

But now the works of the Cyprus-born[1] and of Dionysus and the Muses are dear to me; they bring men good cheer,

147

ELEGIAC POETRY

ὥσπερ ἐκ ζάλης καὶ χειμῶνος {καὶ} τῶν παιδικῶν
ἐρώτων ἔν τινι γαλήνῃ τῇ περὶ γάμον καὶ φιλοσοφίαν
θέμενος τὸν βίον.

Plut. Sol. 31.7, sept. sap. conv. 13.155e; Hermias in Pl. Phaedr.
231e (p. 38.17 Couvreur); P. Hercul. 1384 fr. 1 (vv. 1-2)

27 Philo, de opif. mundi 104 (i.36.8 Cohn-Wendland)

τὰς ἡλικίας ταύτας ἀνέγραψε καὶ Σόλων ὁ τῶν Ἀθη-
ναίων νομοθέτης, ἐλεγεῖα ποιήσας τάδε·

παῖς μὲν ἄνηβος ἐὼν ἔτι νήπιος ἕρκος ὀδόντων
  φύσας ἐκβάλλει πρῶτον ἐν ἕπτ᾽ ἔτεσιν.
τοὺς δ᾽ ἑτέρους ὅτε δὴ τελέσῃ θεὸς ἕπτ᾽ ἐνιαυτούς,
  ἥβης ἐκφαίνει σήματα γεινομένης.
5 τῇ τριτάτῃ δὲ γένειον ἀεξομένων ἔτι γυίων
  λαχνοῦται, χροιῆς ἄνθος ἀμειβομένης.
τῇ δὲ τετάρτῃ πᾶς τις ἐν ἑβδομάδι μέγ᾽ ἄριστος
  ἰσχύν, ᾗ τ᾽ ἄνδρες σήματ᾽ ἔχουσ᾽ ἀρετῆς.
πέμπτῃ δ᾽ ὥριον ἄνδρα γάμου μεμνημένον εἶναι
10 καὶ παίδων ζητεῖν εἰσοπίσω γενεήν.
τῇ δ᾽ ἕκτῃ περὶ πάντα καταρτύεται νόος ἀνδρός,
  οὐδ᾽ ἔρδειν ἔθ᾽ ὁμῶς ἔργ᾽ ἀπάλαμνα θέλει.
ἑπτὰ δὲ νοῦν καὶ γλῶσσαν ἐν ἑβδομάσιν μέγ᾽
    ἄριστος
  ὀκτώ τ᾽· ἀμφοτέρων τέσσαρα καὶ δέκ᾽ ἔτη.
15 τῇ δ᾽ ἐνάτῃ ἔτι μὲν δύναται, μαλακώτερα δ᾽ αὐτοῦ
  πρὸς μεγάλην ἀρετὴν γλῶσσά τε καὶ σοφίη.

148

as though after the storm and stress of loving boys he placed his life in the calm of marriage and philosophy.

[1] Aphrodite.

27 Philo, *On the Creation of the World*

Solon, the Athenian lawgiver, described these ages of life in the following elegy:

A boy, while still an immature child, in seven years grows a fence of teeth and loses them for the first time. When the god completes another seven years, he shows the signs of coming puberty. In the third hebdomad his body is still growing, his chin becomes downy, and the skin changes its hue. In the fourth everyone is far the best in strength, whereby men show their signs of manliness. In the fifth it is time for a man to be mindful of marriage and to look for a line of sons to come after him. In the sixth a man's mind is being trained for everything and he is no longer as willing to commit acts of foolishness. In the seventh and eighth, a total of fourteen years, he is far the best in thought and speech. In the ninth he still has ability, but his speech and wisdom give weaker proof of a high level of excellence. If one

τὴν δεκάτην δ᾽ εἴ τις τελέσας κατὰ μέτρον ἵκοιτο,
οὐκ ἂν ἄωρος ἐὼν μοῖραν ἔχοι θανάτου.

Clem. *Strom.* 6.144.3; Par. 1843 (*Anecd. Par.* i.46 Cramer);
Anatol. π. δεκάδος (p. 37 Heiberg); Apostol. 14.94 (*Paroem. Gr.*
ii.626), vv. 1-18

5 ἐπὶ testes, corr. Bergk   8 ἤν τ᾽ Clem., ἤν τ᾽ Sylburg
πείρατ᾽ Stadtmüller (prob. West)   14 δ᾽ testes, corr. Mangey

28 Plut. *Sol.* 26.1

πρῶτον μὲν οὖν εἰς Αἴγυπτον ἀφίκετο, καὶ διέτριψεν
ὡς καὶ †πρότερον† αὐτός φησι

Νείλου ἐπὶ προχοῇσι, Κανωβίδος ἐγγύθεν ἀκτῆς.

προχοαῖσι v.l.

29 Ps.-Plat. π. δικαίου 374a

ἀλλά τοι, ὦ Σώκρατες, εὖ ἡ παλαιὰ παροιμία ἔχει ὅτι

πολλὰ ψεύδονται ἀοιδοί.

30 Diogen. 2.99 (*Paroem. Gr.* i.213.11) = Apostol. 4.3
(*Paroem. Gr.* ii.310.14)

"ἀρχῶν ἄκουε καὶ δικαίως κἀδίκως"· ἐκ τῶν τοῦ Σόλω-
νος ἐλεγείων, παραινετική.

κἂν δίκη κἂν μὴ δίκη v.l. in Diogen.

were to complete stage after stage and reach the
tenth, he would not have death's allotment prema-
turely.[1]

[1] For a more detailed apparatus of Solon's poem and for Latin
paraphrases see West's edition or that of Gentili-Prato (fr. 23).

28 Plutarch, *Life of Solon*

First he went to Egypt and, as he himself says, spent time

at the mouth of the Nile, near Canopus'[1] shore

[1] The name given to the westernmost branch of the Nile.

29 Pseudo-Plato, *On Justice*

But, Socrates, the ancient proverb is well said, that

Poets tell many lies.[1]

[1] The schol. ad loc. (p. 402 Greene) states that the proverb is
mentioned by Philochorus (*FGrHist* 328 F 1) and by Solon.

30 Diogenianus, *Proverbs*

"Obey rulers, however right or wrong." From the elegies[1]
of Solon, hortatory.

[1] The meter is iambic, not elegiac. For different versions of the
proverb see West's edition.

ELEGIAC POETRY

30a Io. Diac. in Hermog. (Rabe, *RhM* 63 [1908] 150)

τῆς δὲ τραγῳδίας πρῶτον δρᾶμα Ἀρίων ὁ Μηθυ-
μναῖος εἰσήγαγεν, ὥσπερ Σόλων ἐν ταῖς ἐπιγραφο-
μέναις Ἐλεγείαις ἐδίδαξε.

Hexametri

31 Plut. *Sol.* 3.5

ἔνιοι δέ φασιν ὅτι καὶ τοὺς νόμους ἐπεχείρησεν ἐντεί-
νας εἰς ἔπος ἐξενεγκεῖν, καὶ διαμνημονεύουσι τὴν
ἀρχὴν οὕτως ἔχουσαν·

> πρῶτα μὲν εὐχώμεσθα Διὶ Κρονίδῃ βασιλῆϊ
> θεσμοῖς τοῖσδε τύχην ἀγαθὴν καὶ κῦδος
> ὀπάσσαι.

32-35. Tetrametri

32 Plut. *Sol.* 14.8

τούτων οὐδὲν ἐξέκρουσε τὸν Σόλωνα τῆς αὑτοῦ προ-
αιρέσεως, ἀλλὰ πρὸς μὲν τοὺς φίλους εἶπεν ὡς λέγε-
ται καλὸν μὲν εἶναι τὴν τυραννίδα χωρίον, οὐκ ἔχειν
δ᾽ ἀπόβασιν, πρὸς δὲ Φῶκον ἐν τοῖς ποιήμασι
γράφων

> εἰ δὲ γῆς (φησιν) ἐφεισάμην
> πατρίδος, τυραννίδος δὲ καὶ βίης ἀμειλίχου

30a John the Deacon on Hermogenes

Arion of Methymna introduced the first tragic drama, as Solon has informed us in the elegies ascribed to him.

Dactylic Hexameters

31 Plutarch, *Life of Solon*

And some say that he attempted to put his laws into epic verse and publish them, and they record the beginning as follows:

> First let us pray to Zeus the king, son of Cronus, to grant these laws success and fame.[1]

[1] Attribution to Solon is improbable, since there is no other evidence that he composed in hexameters.

32-35. Trochaic Tetrameters

32 Plutarch, *Life of Solon*

None of this (sc. pressure from his friends to become tyrant) shook Solon from his resolve, but he is said to have told his friends that although tyranny was a fine position, there was no way to leave it. And writing in his poems to Phocus[1] he says:

> If I spared my homeland and did not grasp tyranny

οὐ καθηψάμην μιάνας καὶ καταισχύνας κλέος,
οὐδὲν αἰδέομαι· πλέον γὰρ ὧδε νικήσειν δοκέω
5   πάντας ἀνθρώπους.

ὅθεν εὔδηλον ὅτι καὶ πρὸ τῆς νομοθεσίας μεγάλην
δόξαν εἶχεν.

4 αἰδεῦμαι codd., corr. West

33 Pergit Plut. (14.9-15.1)

ἃ δὲ φυγόντος αὐτοῦ τὴν τυραννίδα πολλοὶ κατα-
γελῶντες ἔλεγον, γέγραφεν οὕτως·

"οὐκ ἔφυ Σόλων βαθύφρων οὐδὲ βουλήεις ἀνήρ·
ἐσθλὰ γὰρ θεοῦ διδόντος αὐτὸς οὐκ ἐδέξατο·
περιβαλὼν δ᾽ ἄγρην ἀγασθεὶς οὐκ ἐπέσπασεν
    μέγα
δίκτυον, θυμοῦ θ᾽ ἁμαρτῇ καὶ φρενῶν
    ἀποσφαλείς·
5   ἤθελον γάρ κεν κρατήσας, πλοῦτον ἄφθονον
    λαβὼν
καὶ τυραννεύσας Ἀθηνέων μοῦνον ἡμέρην μίαν,
ἀσκὸς ὕστερον δεδάρθαι κἀπιτετρίφθαι γένος."

ταῦτα τοὺς πολλοὺς καὶ φαύλους περὶ αὐτοῦ πεποίηκε
λέγοντας.

3 ἄγραν codd., corr. Bergk   5 ἤθελεν codd., corr.
Xylander   6 ἀθηνῶν codd., corr. Schneidewin   ἡμέραν
codd., corr. Bergk

154

and brute force, bringing stain and disgrace on my reputation, I am not ashamed. For I think that in this way I shall be more able to outstrip everyone.

It is quite clear from this that he had a high reputation even before his legislation.

[1] Person unknown.

33 Plutarch continues

And regarding the ridicule which many heaped upon him for shunning tyranny, he has written as follows:

"Solon is by nature a man of shallow mind and a fool. When the god offered him good things, he did not accept them. He cast a great net round his quarry, but stood in wonderment and did not draw it tight, bereft of courage and sense alike. If I had gained power, obtained vast wealth, and become tyrant of Athens for only a single day, I'd be willing to be flayed into a wineskin afterwards and to have my line wiped out."

This is what he represented many of the common sort as saying about him.

34 Arist. *Ath. Pol.* 12.3 (quae praecedunt v. ad fr. 6)

καὶ πάλιν δὲ ἑτέρωθί που λέγει περὶ τῶν διανείμασθαι
τὴν γῆν βουλομένων·

οἱ δ' ἐφ' ἁρπαγῇσιν ἦλθον· ἐλπίδ' εἶχον ἀφνεήν,
κἀδόκ[ε]ον ἕκαστος αὐτῶν ὄλβον εὑρήσειν πολύν,
καί με κωτίλλοντα λείως τραχὺν ἐκφανεῖν νόον.
χαῦνα μὲν τότ' ἐφράσαντο, νῦν δέ μοι χολούμενοι
5   λοξὸν ὀφθαλμοῖς ὁρῶσι πάντες ὥστε δήϊον.
οὐ χρεών· ἃ μὲν γὰρ εἶπα, σὺν θεοῖσιν ἤνυσα,
ἄλλα δ' οὐ μάτην ἔερδον, οὐδέ μοι τυραννίδος
ἁνδάνει βίηι τι [. .] ε[ι]ν, οὐδὲ πιεί[ρ]ης χθονὸς
πατρίδος κακοῖσιν ἐσθλοὺς ἰσομοιρίην ἔχειν.

Sequitur fr. 36.

Plut. *Sol.* 16.3 (vv. 4-5)
Aristides *or.* 28.137 (ii.184.29 Keil), vv. 6-7

1 οἱ δ'. . . ἦλθον editores plerique: οἱ δ'. . . ἦλθον Richards,
West, alii   αρπαγαισιν pap., corr. West   ἁρπαγῇ
συνῆλθον Richards   αφνεαν pap., corr. West   2]υν
pap., corr. West   8 ἥνδανεν Richards   βια pap., corr.
West   [ῥέζ]ειν Kenyon   πιει[ ]ας pap., corr. West
9 ισομοιριαν pap., corr. West

36-40. Trimetri

36 Pergit Arist. (v. ad fr. 34) = L; hic accedit P. Berol.

[πάλιν] (suppl. Kenyon) δὲ καὶ περὶ τῆς ἀπ[οκ]οπῆς
τῶν χ[ρε]ῶν καὶ τῶν δουλευόντων μὲν πρότερον, ἐλευ-

156

34 Aristotle, *Constitution of Athens*

And again in another place he speaks of those who wanted
a redistribution of the land:

> And others[1] came for plunder; they had hopes of
> wealth, each one of them thinking that he would
> find much prosperity and that I, for all my gentle
> prattle, would reveal a harsh disposition. They had
> foolish thoughts then, and now they are angry and
> they all look askance at me as if I were their enemy.
> They should not. With the help of the gods I have
> accomplished what I said I would, and other fruit-
> less measures I did not take; it gives me no pleasure
> to act(?) with the violence of tyranny or to share the
> country's rich land equally between the lower and
> upper classes.[2]

[1] Or reading οἵ, "those who came for plunder had . . ."
[2] On the interpretation of this final segment see V. J. Rosivach,
"Redistribution of Land in Solon, Fragment 34 West," *JHS* 112
(1992) 153-57.

36-40. Iambic Trimeters

36 Aristotle continues

And again on the cancellation of debts and on those who

θερωθέντων δὲ διὰ τὴν σεισάχθειαν·

ἐγὼ δὲ τῶν μὲν οὕνεκα ξυνήγαγον
δῆμον, τί τούτων πρὶν τυχεῖν ἐπαυσάμην;
συμμαρτυροίη ταῦτ᾽ ἂν ἐν δίκῃ χρόνου
μήτηρ μεγίστη δαιμόνων Ὀλυμπίων
5   ἄριστα, Γῆ μέλαινα, τῆς ἐγώ ποτε
ὅρους ἀνεῖλον πολλαχῇ πεπηγότας·
πρόσθεν δὲ δουλεύουσα, νῦν ἐλευθέρη.
πολλοὺς δ᾽ Ἀθήνας πατρίδ᾽ ἐς θεόκτιτον
ἀνήγαγον πραθέντας, ἄλλον ἐκδίκως,
10   ἄλλον δικαίως, τοὺς δ᾽ ἀναγκαίης ὑπὸ
χρειοῦς φυγόντας, γλῶσσαν οὐκέτ᾽ Ἀττικὴν
ἱέντας, ὡς ἂν πολλαχῇ πλανωμένους·
τοὺς δ᾽ ἐνθάδ᾽ αὐτοῦ δουλίην ἀεικέα
ἔχοντας, ἤθη δεσποτέων τρομεομένους,
15   ἐλευθέρους ἔθηκα. ταῦτα μὲν κράτει
ὁμοῦ βίην τε καὶ δίκην ξυναρμόσας
ἔρεξα, καὶ διῆλθον ὡς ὑπεσχόμην·
θεσμοὺς δ᾽ ὁμοίως τῷ κακῷ τε κἀγαθῷ
εὐθεῖαν εἰς ἕκαστον ἁρμόσας δίκην
20   ἔγραψα. κέντρον δ᾽ ἄλλος ὡς ἐγὼ λαβών,
κακοφραδής τε καὶ φιλοκτήμων ἀνήρ,
οὐκ ἂν κατέσχε δῆμον· εἰ γὰρ ἤθελον
ἃ τοῖς ἐναντίοισιν ἥνδανεν τότε,
αὖτις δ᾽ ἃ τοῖσιν οὕτεροι φρασαίατο,
25   πολλῶν ἂν ἀνδρῶν ἥδ᾽ ἐχηρώθη πόλις.
τῶν οὕνεκ᾽ ἀλκὴν πάντοθεν ποιεόμενος

were slaves before and were set free by the shaking-off of burdens:[1]

> Before achieving what of the goals for which I brought the people together[2] did I stop? In the verdict of time I will have as my best witness the mighty mother of the Olympian gods, dark Earth, whose boundary markers[3] fixed in many places I once removed; enslaved before, now she is free. And I brought back to Athens, to their homeland founded by the gods, many who had been sold, one legally another not, and those who had fled under necessity's constraint, no longer speaking the Attic tongue, as wanderers far and wide are inclined to do. And those who suffered shameful slavery right here, trembling before the whims of their masters, I set free. These things I did by the exercise of my power, blending together force and justice, and I persevered to the end as I promised. I wrote laws for the lower and upper classes alike, providing a straight legal process for each person. If another had taken up the goad as I did, a man who gave bad counsel and was greedy, he would not have restrained the masses. For if I had been willing to do what then was pleasing to their opponents and in turn whatever the others [i.e., the masses] planned for them, this city would have been bereft of many men. For that reason I set up a defence on every

ELEGIAC POETRY

ὡς ἐν κυσὶν πολλῆσιν ἐστράφην λύκος.

Aristides *or.* 28.138-40 (ii.185.6 Keil), vv. 3-27
Plut. *Sol.* 15.6 (vv. 6-7, 11-14, γλῶσσαν—ἔχοντας)
Plut. *Sol.* 15.1 (v. 16)

3 Χρόνου praeferunt aliqui   7 ἐλευθέρα libri, corr.
Ahrens   12 δὴ pro ἂν West   14 δεσποτῶν libri, corr.
Schneidewin   τρομευμένους libri, corr. West
26 ποιούμενος L, corr. West   27 πολλαι [.] L, πολλαῖσιν
Aristid., corr. Wilcken

37 Pergit Arist.

καὶ πάλιν ὀνειδίζων πρὸς τὰς ὕστερον αὐτῶν μεμψι-
μοιρίας ἀμφοτέρων·

> δήμωι μὲν εἰ χρὴ διαφάδην ὀνειδίσαι,
> ἃ νῦν ἔχουσιν οὔποτ᾽ ὀφθαλμοῖσιν ἂν
> εὕδοντες εἶδον . . .
> ὅσοι δὲ μείζους καὶ βίην ἀμείνονες,
> 5   αἰνοῖεν ἄν με καὶ φίλον ποιοίατο.

εἰ γάρ τις ἄλλος, φησί, ταύτης τῆς τιμῆς ἔτυχεν,

> οὐκ ἂν κατέσχε δῆμον, οὐδ᾽ ἐπαύσατο,
> πρὶν ἀνταράξας πῖαρ ἐξεῖλεν γάλα.
> ἐγὼ δὲ τούτων ὥσπερ ἐν μεταιχμίωι
> ὅρος κατέστην.

Plut. *Sol.* 16.4 (vv. 6-7)

1 διαφραδην pap., corr. Kondos   4 βιαν pap., corr. West
6 οὔτ᾽ . . . οὔτ᾽ Plut.   7 πναρ pap., πῖαρ Plut.   ἐξέλη Plut.

160

side and turned about like a wolf among a pack of dogs.

[1] A literal translation of *seisachtheia*. The term was given to Solon's cancellation of debts and according to Plutarch (*Solon* 15.2) it was a euphemism actually coined by Solon.   [2] Precise meaning disputed.   [3] As a sign of mortgaged land.

37 Aristotle continues

And again rebuking both sides for the complaints they made afterwards:

> If I must rebuke the masses openly, their eyes would never have seen in their dreams what they now have . . . And those who are greater and stronger would praise me and treat me as their friend.

For if someone else, he says, had obtained this office,

> he would not have restrained the masses nor would he have stopped until he had stirred up the milk and got rid of the cream.[1] But I stood in no-man's-land[2] between them like a boundary marker.

[1] Meaning and syntax disputed. My translation assumes that milk = the state and cream = the aristocracy, but perhaps preferable is "until he had stirred up the masses and removed the cream from the milk," although the general meaning remains the same. See T. C. W. Stinton, *JHS* 96 (1976) 159-62.   [2] A military metaphor, here perhaps standing for Athens itself.

38 Ath. 14.645f

γοῦρος ὅτι πλακοῦντος εἶδος ὁ Σόλων ἐν τοῖς ἰάμβοις
φησίν·

> πίνουσι· καὶ τρώγουσιν οἱ μὲν ἴτρια,
> οἱ δ' ἄρτον αὐτῶν, οἱ δὲ συμμεμιγμένους
> γούρους φακοῖσι· κεῖθι δ' οὔτε πεμμάτων
> ἄπεστιν οὐδ' ἕν, ἄσσ' ἐν ἀνθρώποισι γῆ
> 5   φέρει μέλαινα, πάντα δ' ἀφθόνως πάρα.

4 ἔνασσεν cod., corr. West: alii alia

39 Pollux 10.103

καὶ ἴγδιν δὲ αὐτὴν (τὴν θυείαν) κεκλήκασι Σόλων τε ἐν
τοῖς ἰάμβοις λέγων·

> σπεύδουσι δ' οἱ μὲν ἴγδιν, οἱ δὲ σίλφιον,
> οἱ δ' ὄξος.

1 σπεῦ, σπευσίδα etc. codd., corr. Casaubon

40 Phryn. *Ecl.* 374 (pp. 102 et 122 Fischer)

ἔτι καὶ νῦν κόκκωνα οἱ πολλοὶ λέγουσιν ὀρθῶς· καὶ
γὰρ ὁ Σόλων ἐν τοῖς αὐτοῦ ποιήμασιν οὕτω χρῆται·

> †κόκκωνας δὲ† ἄλλος, †ἕτερος† δὲ σήσαμα.

κόκκωνας ἄλλος vel κόκκωνα δ' ἄλλος Lobeck   οὕτερος
Kalinka

SOLON

38 Athenaeus, *Scholars at Dinner*

Solon says in his iambics that *gouros* is a kind of cake:

> They are drinking; and some are eating cakes,[1] others bread, and others *gouroi* mixed with lentils. No pastry which the dark earth brings forth among mankind is lacking there, but everything is present in abundance.

[1] Athenaeus goes on (646d) to define *itrion* as a thin cake made with sesame and honey. The word *gouros* is not attested elsewhere.

39 Pollux, *Vocabulary*

They call mortar *igdis*, as does Solon in his iambics:

> Some are hurrying for a mortar, others for *silphium*, and others for vinegar.[1]

[1] It is unclear what kind of situation is being described here. *Silphium* is a plant whose juice was used as a medicine and as a pungent food flavouring. In the latter sense it goes well enough with vinegar, but neither seems an appropriate combination with mortar. There is some evidence that *igdis* could also be a type of dance and perhaps Pollux misunderstood Solon's meaning. Some assume that frr. 38-41 came from the same poem.

40 Phrynichus, *Attic Words and Phrases*

Even to this day the majority rightly call the pomegranate seed *kokkōn*. In fact Solon uses it thus in his poetry:

> One (hurries for?, brings?) pomegranate seeds, another sesame.

ELEGIAC POETRY

41 Phot. *lex.* (ii.136 Naber)

ῥοῦν· τὸ ἥδυσμα. Σόλων.

43 Choric. *or.* 2.5 (p. 29.10 Foerster-Richtsteig)

γῆ μὲν γὰρ τοῖς ἐνοικοῦσιν ἐπίσταται φέρειν ὅσα
τίκτουσιν Ὧραι, ὑπτία τε πᾶσα καθειμένη καὶ τὸ τοῦ
Σόλωνος

λιπαρὴ κουροτρόφος.

45 Arist. *Eth. Nic.* 10.7.1177b31

οὐ χρὴ δὲ κατὰ τοὺς παραινοῦντας ἀνθρώπινα φρο-
νεῖν ἄνθρωπον ὄντα.

Michael ad loc. (*Comm. in Arist. Graeca* xx.591.14)

τινὲς μὲν Θεόγνιδός φασιν εἶναι τὴν γνώμην ταύτην,
οἱ δὲ Σόλωνος.

41 Photius, *Lexicon*

ῥοῦς ('sumach') as a seasoning occurs in Solon.

43 Choricius, *Declamations*

For the earth knows how to produce for its inhabitants all that the Seasons give birth to, since it stretches down entirely on its back and is, in the words of Solon,

a rich nurse of children[1]

[1] Probably from an elegiac pentameter.

45 Aristotle, *Nicomachean Ethics*

We ought not to follow those who recommend that a man have thoughts suitable to a man.

Michael on the passage

Some say that this maxim belongs to Theognis, others to Solon.

THEOGNIS

TESTIMONIA

1 *Suda* (ii.692.13 Adler)

Θέογνις, Μεγαρεύς, τῶν ἐν Σικελίᾳ Μεγάρων, γεγο-
νὼς ἐν τῇ νθ΄ ὀλυμπιάδι. ἔγραψεν ἐλεγείαν εἰς τοὺς
σωθέντας τῶν Συρακουσίων ἐν τῇ πολιορκίᾳ, γνώμας
δι᾽ ἐλεγείας ὡς (εἰς ed. pr.) ἔπη ͵βω΄, καὶ πρὸς Κύρ-
⟨ν⟩ον τὸν αὑτοῦ ἐρώμενον γνωμολογίαν δι᾽ ἐλεγείων,
καὶ ἑτέρας ὑποθήκας παραινετικάς, τὰ πάντα ἐπικῶς
(ἔπη ͵βω΄ Ditzen). ὅτι μὲν παραινέσεις ἔγραψε Θέο-
γνις, ⟨χρήσιμος·⟩ ἀλλ᾽ ἐν μέσῳ τούτων παρεσπαρ-

166

THEOGNIS

Listed below are the sigla for the manuscripts recorded in the apparatus. For further details see West's edition (pp. xi-xiii) and Young's Teubner edition (pp. vii-ix, xx, xxviii-xxix).

A = Paris. suppl. gr. 388 (early 10th century)
O = Vat. gr. 915 (early 14th century)
X = Lond. Add. 16409 (c. 1300)
D = Paris. gr. 2739 (mid 15th century)
Ur = Vat. Urb. gr. 95 (c. 1430)
I = Marc. gr. 774 (mid 15th century)
o = a lost MS of which O is a copy (c. 1300)
p = a lost MS of which X is a copy (c. 1299)

TESTIMONIA

1 *Suda*

Theognis, a Megarian from the Megara in Sicily,[1] flourished in the 59th Olympiad (544/41).[2] He wrote an elegy on those saved from the Syracusans in the siege,[3] elegiac maxims totaling about 2800 verses,[4] a collection of elegiac maxims addressed to Cyrnus his beloved, and other hortatory precepts,[5] all in the epic dialect. Theognis (is useful) because he wrote exhortations. But in the midst of these

μέναι μιαρίαι καὶ παιδικοὶ ἔρωτες καὶ ἄλλα ὅσα ὁ
ἐνάρετος ἀποστρέφεται βίος.

γνώμας—βω΄ del. West   ⟨χρήσιμος⟩ add. West

2 Pl. *Leges* 1.630a

ἡμεῖς δέ γε ἀγαθῶν ὄντων τούτων ἔτι φαμὲν ἀμείνους
εἶναι καὶ πολὺ τοὺς ἐν τῷ μεγίστῳ πολέμῳ γιγνο-
μένους ἀρίστους διαφανῶς· ποιητὴν δὲ καὶ ἡμεῖς
μάρτυρ᾽ ἔχομεν, Θέογνιν, πολίτην τῶν ἐν Σικελίᾳ
Μεγαρέων, ὅς φησιν (vv. 77-78).

3 Schol. ad loc. (p. 301 Greene)

περὶ Θεόγνιδος καὶ τῆς κατ᾽ αὐτὸν ταύτης ἱστορίας
ἀμφιβολία πολλὴ ἐγένετο τοῖς παλαιοῖς. καὶ οἱ μέν
φασιν αὐτὸν ἐκ Μεγάρων γεγενῆσθαι τῆς Ἀττικῆς·
οὕτως ὁ Δίδυμος, ἐπιφυόμενος τῷ Πλάτωνι ὡς παρ-
ιστοροῦντι· οἱ δὲ ὅτι ἐκ Σικελίας. εἰ δὲ μὴ καὶ εἴη ἐκ
Σικελίας, οὐδὲν λυμαίνεται τὸ προκείμενον, ἀλλὰ καὶ

are scattered foul and pederastic poems and other verses on which the virtuous life turns its back.[6]

[1] See testt. 2-4.   [2] Other sources give the 58th or 57th Olympiad (p. 57 Garzya).   [3] Nothing is known of this poem and some attribute it to the tragic poet Theognis whom the *Suda* goes on to record as one of the 30 tyrants.   [4] Roughly double the size of the present corpus and perhaps "a mistake in the reckoning occasioned by the addition of two totals found in different sources" (Hudson-Williams 101).   [5] It is unclear whether these and the maxims addressed to Cyrnus are being represented as separate works or as parts of the 2800.   [6] These were collected in Book II, although the segregation actually occurred before the date of the *Suda*, since MS A, which alone preserves Book II, is earlier than the compilation of the *Suda* (2nd half of the 10th cent.).

2 Plato, *Laws*

But brave though these men are, we still say that even much braver are those who are conspicuously brave in the greatest of wars. And we also have as witness a poet, Theognis, a citizen of the Megarians in Sicily,[1] who says (vv. 77-78).

[1] See test. 3.

3 Scholiast on the passage

There was much controversy among the ancients concerning Theognis and this information about him. Some say that he was from Attic Megara (this is the view of Didymus who attacks Plato for giving false information), while others say that he was from Sicily. Even if he were not from Sicily, the present passage does not mistreat him, but does

τοὐναντίον· οὐ γὰρ ὑπὲρ Ἀττικοῦ ὡς Ἀθηναῖος λέγει,
ἀλλὰ καίτοι πρὸς Ἀθηναῖον αὐτὸν παραβάλλων τὸν
Τυρταῖον, τὸ ἀληθὲς περὶ τὴν κρίσιν ἐφύλαξεν καὶ τὸν
Θέογνιν καὶ ξένον ὄντα προέκρινεν. τί δὲ ἐκώλυεν
αὐτὸν ἐκ ταύτης μὲν εἶναι τῆς Μεγαρίδος, ἀπελθόντα
δὲ εἰς Σικελίαν, ὡς ἱστορία ἔχει, γενέσθαι νόμῳ
Μεγαρέα ἐκεῖ, ὡς καὶ τὸν Τυρταῖον Λακεδαιμόνιον;

4 Harpocration (pp. 126-27 Keaney)

Θέογνις· οὗτος δ᾽ ἦν Μεγαρεύς, ἀπὸ τῶν πρὸς τῇ
Ἀττικῇ Μεγάρων. αὐτὸς γάρ φησιν ὁ ποιητής (v. 783).
ὃ μὴ ἐπιστήσας Πλάτων ἐν α΄ Νόμων (test. 2) τῶν ἐν
Σικελίᾳ Μεγαρέων πολίτην ἔφασκεν. κατηκολού-
θησαν δὲ τῷ Πλάτωνι οὐκ ὀλίγοι.

5 Isoc. Nicocl. 42-43

ἐπεὶ κἀκεῖνό μοι πρόδηλον ἦν, ὅτι τὰ συμβουλεύοντα
καὶ τῶν ποιημάτων καὶ τῶν συγγραμμάτων χρησι-
μώτατα μὲν ἅπαντες νομίζουσιν, οὐ μὴν ἥδιστά γ᾽
αὐτῶν ἀκούουσιν, ἀλλὰ πεπόνθασιν ὅπερ πρὸς τοὺς

the opposite. For Plato is not speaking as an Athenian
on behalf of an Athenian, but although comparing him
with an Athenian, Tyrtaeus, he kept to the truth in judging
them and preferred Theognis even though a foreigner.
What prevented his being from this Megara and after
going to Sicily, as Plato's account implies, becoming a
Megarian there according to the law, just as Tyrtaeus be-
came a Spartan?[1]

[1] The scholiast interprets Plato to mean that just as Tyrtaeus
was an Athenian by birth but became a Spartan (see Tyrt. test. 2),
so Theognis was from Megara on the Isthmus of Corinth but be-
came a citizen of Megara's colony (Hyblaean Megara) in Sicily.
This interpretation of Plato's words may be correct, but there is no
evidence in the corpus that Theognis was a citizen of Hyblaean
Megara and the modern consensus is that he came from mainland
Megara. See also test. 4.

4 Harpocration, *Lexicon of the Ten Attic Orators*

Theognis was a Megarian from Attic Megara. The poet
says this himself (v. 783).[1] Plato did not pay attention to
this when he said in Book 1 of the *Laws* that Theognis was
a citizen of Megara in Sicily. And many have followed
Plato.

[1] 783 merely states that the speaker visited Sicily. See notes on
773-88.

5 Isocrates, *To Nicocles*

Moreover this too was clear to me, that although all con-
sider words of advice both in poetry and in prose to be
most useful, they certainly do not derive the greatest plea-
sure from listening to them, but their attitude towards

νουθετοῦντας· καὶ γὰρ ἐκείνους ἐπαινοῦσι μέν, πλη-
σιάζειν δὲ βούλονται τοῖς συνεξαμαρτάνουσιν, ἀλλ'
οὐ τοῖς ἀποτρέπουσιν. σημεῖον δ' ἄν τις ποιήσαιτο
τὴν Ἡσιόδου καὶ Θεόγνιδος καὶ Φωκυλίδου ποίησιν·
καὶ γὰρ τούτους φασὶ μὲν ἀρίστους γεγενῆσθαι συμ-
βούλους τῷ βίῳ τῷ τῶν ἀνθρώπων, ταῦτα δὲ λέγοντες
αἱροῦνται συνδιατρίβειν ταῖς ἀλλήλων ἀνοίαις μᾶλ-
λον ἢ ταῖς ἐκείνων ὑποθήκαις. ἔτι δ' εἴ τις ἐκλέξειε τῶν
προεχόντων ποιητῶν τὰς καλουμένας γνώμας, ἐφ' αἷς
ἐκεῖνοι μάλιστ' ἐσπούδασαν, ὁμοίως ἂν καὶ πρὸς
ταύτας διατεθεῖεν· ἥδιον γὰρ ἂν κωμῳδίας τῆς φαυλο-
τάτης ἢ τῶν οὕτω τεχνικῶς πεποιημένων ἀκούσειαν.

6 Stob. 4.29.53

Ξενοφῶντος ἐκ τοῦ περὶ Θεόγνιδος. "Θεόγνιδός ἐστιν
ἔπη τοῦ Μεγαρέως" (22-23). οὗτος δὲ ὁ ποιητὴς περὶ
οὐδενὸς ἄλλου λόγον πεποίηται ἢ περὶ ἀρετῆς καὶ
κακίας ἀνθρώπων, καί ἐστιν ἡ ποίησις σύγγραμμα
περὶ ἀνθρώπων, ὥσπερ εἴ τις ἱππικὸς ὢν συγγράψειεν
περὶ ἱππικῆς. ἡ οὖν ἀρχή μοι δοκεῖ τῆς ποιήσεως
ὀρθῶς ἔχειν· ἄρχεται γὰρ πρῶτον ἀπὸ τοῦ εὖ γενέ-
σθαι. ᾤετο γὰρ οὔτ' ἄνθρωπον οὔτε τῶν ἄλλων οὐδὲν
ἂν ἀγαθὸν εἶναι, εἰ μὴ τὰ γεννήσοντα ἀγαθὰ εἴη.
ἔδοξεν οὖν αὐτῷ παραδείγμασι τοῖς ἄλλοις ζῴοις
χρήσασθαι, ὅσα μὴ εἰκῇ τρέφεται, ἀλλὰ μετὰ τέχνης
ἕκαστα θεραπεύεται, ὅπως γενναιότατα ἔσονται.
δηλοῖ δ' ἐν τοῖς ἔπεσι· (183-90). ταῦτα τὰ ἔπη λέγει

them is the same as their attitude towards those who admonish; for although they praise the latter, they prefer to associate with those who share in their follies and not with those who seek to dissuade them. As proof one could cite the poetry of Hesiod, Theognis, and Phocylides;[1] for people say that these have been the best advisers for human life, but while saying this they prefer to occupy themselves with one another's follies than with the precepts of those poets. And furthermore, if one were to select from the foremost poets those maxims, as they are called, to which they had given their most serious attention, people would treat these in the same way too; for they would more gladly listen to the most paltry comedy than to such proficient compositions.

1 Phocylides and Theognis are frequently combined.

6 Stobaeus, *Anthology*

From Xenophon's[1] work on Theognis. "They are the verses of Theognis of Megara" (22-23). This poet's composition is about nothing else than human excellence and vice, and his poetry is a treatise on people, just as if a horseman were to write about horsemanship. And so the primary element[2] of his poetry seems to me to be correct, since it is about good birth. For he believed that neither a person nor anything else could be good unless the progenitors were good. He therefore decided to use as examples other living creatures which are not raised at random, but which are systematically attended to in each case so that they will be of the best descent. He makes this clear in his verses (183-

τοὺς ἀνθρώπους οὐκ ἐπίστασθαι γεννᾶν ἐξ ἀλλήλων,
κᾆτα γίγνεσθαι τὸ γένος τῶν ἀνθρώπων κάκιον ἀεὶ
μειγνύμενον τὸ χεῖρον τῷ βελτίονι. οἱ δὲ πολλοὶ ἐκ
τούτων τῶν ἀνθρώπων κατηγορεῖν καὶ ἀντὶ χρημάτων
ἀγένειαν καὶ κακίαν ἀντικαταλλάττεσθαι εἰδότας.
ἐμοὶ δὲ δοκεῖ ἄγνοιαν κατηγορεῖν περὶ τὸν αὐτῶν
βίον.

ELEGIAC POEMS

Book I

1-4

ὦ ἄνα, Λητοῦς υἱέ, Διὸς τέκος, οὔποτε σεῖο
λήσομαι ἀρχόμενος οὐδ᾽ ἀποπαυόμενος,
ἀλλ᾽ αἰεὶ πρῶτόν τε καὶ ὕστατον ἔν τε μέσοισιν
ἀείσω· σὺ δέ μοι κλῦθι καὶ ἐσθλὰ δίδου.

5-10

5   Φοῖβε ἄναξ, ὅτε μέν σε θεὰ τέκε πότνια Λητώ,
φοίνικος ῥαδινῆς χερσὶν ἐφαψαμένη,

90). These verses mean that people do not know how to procreate from one another and as a result the human race is becoming worse because the worse is ever mingled with the better. But many think on the basis of these verses that the poet is leveling accusations against human greed and against those who know how to make money compensate for low birth and vice.[3] But it seems to me that he is accusing them of lack of knowledge about their own lives.

[1] There is much debate about whether this is the well-known Athenian writer born c. 430 B.C. or some unknown figure. The only other reference to a work on Theognis is the two books recorded by Diogenes Laertius 6.16 in his list of Antisthenes' writings. [2] Since ἀρχή can also mean 'beginning,' some argue that the edition of Theognis used by Xenophon began with the verses cited below (183-90). [3] This sentence is ungrammatical and presumably has suffered corruption. I have translated what seems to be the general sense.

ELEGIAC POEMS

Book I

1-4

O lord, son of Leto, child of Zeus,[1] I will never forget you at the beginning or at the end, but I will ever sing of you first, last, and in between; and do you give ear to me and grant me success.

[1] Apollo.

5-10

Lord Phoebus, when the august goddess Leto gave birth to you, fairest of the immortals, as she clasped

ἀθανάτων κάλλιστον, ἐπὶ τροχοειδέι λίμνῃ,
  πᾶσα μὲν ἐπλήσθη Δῆλος ἀπειρεσίη
ὀδμῆς ἀμβροσίης, ἐγέλασσε δὲ γαῖα πελώρη,
10   γήθησεν δὲ βαθὺς πόντος ἁλὸς πολιῆς.

6 ῥαδινῆς codd. plerique

11-14

Ἄρτεμι θηροφόνη, θύγατερ Διός, ἣν Ἀγαμέμνων
  εἷσαθ᾽ ὅτ᾽ ἐς Τροίην ἔπλεε νηυσὶ θοῇς,
εὐχομένῳ μοι κλῦθι, κακὰς δ᾽ ἀπὸ κῆρας ἄλαλκε·
  σοὶ μὲν τοῦτο, θεά, σμικρόν, ἐμοὶ δὲ μέγα.

Arist. Eth. Eud. 7.10.1243a18 (v. 14)

12 θοαῖς v.l.   14 θεᾶ (cum rasura) μικρὸν A, θεὸς μικρὸν codd. Arist.

15-18

15   Μοῦσαι καὶ Χάριτες, κοῦραι Διός, αἵ ποτε
      Κάδμου
  ἐς γάμον ἐλθοῦσαι καλὸν ἀείσατ᾽ ἔπος,
"ὅττι καλὸν φίλον ἐστί, τὸ δ᾽ οὐ καλὸν οὐ φίλον
  ἐστί"·
  τοῦτ᾽ ἔπος ἀθανάτων ἦλθε διὰ στομάτων.

19-38

Κύρνε, σοφιζομένῳ μὲν ἐμοὶ σφρηγὶς ἐπικείσθω
20   τοῖσδ᾽ ἔπεσιν· λήσει δ᾽ οὔποτε κλεπτόμενα,

the palm-tree with her slender arms beside the cir-
cular lake,[1] all Delos was filled from end to end with
an ambrosial aroma, the vast earth beamed, and the
deep expanse of the white-capped sea rejoiced.

[1] Actually a pond used as a reservoir.

11-14

Artemis, slayer of wild beasts, daughter of Zeus, for
whom Agamemnon set up a temple[1] when he was
preparing to sail on his swift ships to Troy, give ear to
my prayer and ward off the evil death-spirits. For
you, goddess, this is a small thing, but for me it is
critical.[2]

[1] According to Pausanias 1.43.1 Agamemnon set up this tem-
ple in Megara when he went there to persuade Calchas to accom-
pany him to Troy.   [2] The author, identified by Aristotle as
Theognis, is presumably about to go on a voyage and is praying to
Artemis in her capacity as the protector of seafarers.

15-18

Muses and Graces, daughters of Zeus, who came
once to the wedding of Cadmus[1] and sang the lovely
verse, "What is beautiful is loved, what is not beauti-
ful is not loved." This is the verse that went through
your immortal lips.

[1] The wedding in Thebes of Cadmus and Harmonia, daughter
of Ares and Aphrodite, was attended by the gods.

19-38[1]

For me, a skilled and wise poet, let a seal,[2] Cyrnus,[3]
be placed on these verses. Their theft will never pass

177

οὐδέ τις ἀλλάξει κάκιον τοὐσθλοῦ παρεόντος,
  ὧδε δὲ πᾶς τις ἐρεῖ· "Θεόγνιδός ἐστιν ἔπη
τοῦ Μεγαρέως· πάντας δὲ κατ' ἀνθρώπους
  ὀνομαστός"·
ἀστοῖσιν δ' οὔπω πᾶσιν ἁδεῖν δύναμαι.
25 οὐδὲν θαυμαστόν, Πολυπαΐδη· οὐδὲ γὰρ ὁ Ζεὺς
  οὔθ' ὕων πάντεσσ' ἁνδάνει οὔτ' ἀνέχων.
σοὶ δ' ἐγὼ εὖ φρονέων ὑποθήσομαι, οἷάπερ αὐτός,
  Κύρν', ἀπὸ τῶν ἀγαθῶν παῖς ἔτ' ἐὼν ἔμαθον.
πέπνυσο, μηδ' αἰσχροῖσιν ἐπ' ἔργμασι μηδ'
  ἀδίκοισιν
30 τιμὰς μηδ' ἀρετὰς ἕλκεο μηδ' ἄφενος.
ταῦτα μὲν οὕτως ἴσθι· κακοῖσι δὲ μὴ προσομίλει
  ἀνδράσιν, ἀλλ' αἰεὶ τῶν ἀγαθῶν ἔχεο·
καὶ μετὰ τοῖσιν πῖνε καὶ ἔσθιε, καὶ μετὰ τοῖσιν
  ἵζε, καὶ ἅνδανε τοῖς, ὧν μεγάλη δύναμις.
35 ἐσθλῶν μὲν γὰρ ἄπ' ἐσθλὰ μαθήσεαι· ἢν δὲ
  κακοῖσι
συμμίσγῃς, ἀπολεῖς καὶ τὸν ἐόντα νόον.
ταῦτα μαθὼν ἀγαθοῖσιν ὁμίλει, καί ποτε φήσεις
  εὖ συμβουλεύειν τοῖσι φίλοισιν ἐμέ.

Xenophon ap. Stob. 4.29.53 (v. test. 6), vv. 22-23 (Θεόγνι-
δος—Μεγαρέως)

P. Berol. 12319 (ostracon), vv. 25-26 (οὐδε—ανεχειν)

Plat. *Meno* 95d; Musonius (p. 62 Hense) ap. Stob. 4.15.18 (vv.
33-36)

Nicostratus π. γάμου ap. Stob. 4.23.64 (vv. 33-35 confuse)

Xen. *conv.* 2.4; id. *mem.* 1.2.20 (+ Stob. 3.29.95); Clem. *Strom.*

unnoticed, nor will anyone take something worse in
exchange when that which is good is at hand, but
everyone will say, "They are the verses of Theognis
of Megara, and he is famous among all men;"[4] but I
am not yet able to please all the townsmen. It's not
surprising, Polypaïdes, since not even Zeus pleases
everyone when he sends rain or holds back.[5] It is
with kind thoughts for you that I shall give you ad-
vice such as I myself, Cyrnus, learned from noble
men while still a child. Be sensible and do not, at the
cost of shameful or unjust acts, seize for yourself
prestige, success or wealth. Know that this is so, and
do not seek the company of base men, but always
cling to the noble.[6] Drink and dine with them, sit
with them, and be pleasing to those whose power is
great. For from the noble you will learn noble
things, but if you mingle with the base, you will lose
even the sense you have. Knowing this, associate
with the noble, and one day you will say that I give
good advice to my friends.

[1] There is no agreement whether these verses represent one
poem, two poems (19-30, 31-38) or three (19-26, 27-30, 31-38).
On this, and also on Theognis' date, see H. Friis Johansen, *C&M*
42 (1991) 5-37, 44 (1993) 5-29, and 47 (1996) 9-23.   [2] The
most disputed word in the entire corpus. Among the explanations
are: Theognis' name (v. 22), Cyrnus' name, poetic style, political
and ethical contents, and a literal seal affixed to a written copy of
Theognis' poems.   [3] Theognis' beloved boy. The name, to-
gether with the patronymic (v. 25), appears numerous times in the
corpus.   [4] Many end the quotation with the word Megara.
[5] Cf. vv. 801-4.   [6] The words $\dot{a}\gamma a\theta\delta\varsigma/\dot{\epsilon}\sigma\theta\lambda\delta\varsigma$ and $\kappa a\kappa\delta\varsigma/$
$\delta\epsilon\iota\lambda\delta\varsigma$ occur frequently in the corpus as an indication of social sta-

179

ELEGIAC POETRY

5.52.4; Nicolaus *Progymn.* (p. 27.2 Felten); schol. Arist. *Eth. Nic.*
9.9.7 (*Anecd. Par.* i.229.4 Cramer), vv. 35-36

22 πᾶς ἐρέειρ   23 ὀνομαστοῦ ρ   29 πέπνυο Bergk
33 μετὰ τῶν σύ γε Muson., Nicostr.: παρὰ τοῖσιν Plato
35 διδάξεαι Plato, Xen., Nicol.   36 ἐνόντα Xen. *mem.* cod.
A, Nicol. codd. plerique   37 ὁμίλεε codd., corr. West

39-52

Κύρνε, κύει πόλις ἥδε, δέδοικα δὲ μὴ τέκῃ ἄνδρα
40   εὐθυντῆρα κακῆς ὕβριος ἡμετέρης.
ἀστοὶ μὲν γὰρ ἔθ' οἵδε σαόφρονες, ἡγεμόνες δὲ
    τετράφαται πολλὴν εἰς κακότητα πεσεῖν.
οὐδεμίαν πω, Κύρν', ἀγαθοὶ πόλιν ὤλεσαν
    ἄνδρες·
ἀλλ' ὅταν ὑβρίζειν τοῖσι κακοῖσιν ἅδῃ,
45   δῆμόν τε φθείρωσι δίκας τ' ἀδίκοισι διδῶσιν
οἰκείων κερδέων εἵνεκα καὶ κράτεος,
ἔλπεο μὴ δηρὸν κείνην πόλιν ἀτρεμίεσθαι,
    μηδ' εἰ νῦν κεῖται πολλῇ ἐν ἡσυχίῃ,
εὖτ' ἂν τοῖσι κακοῖσι φίλ' ἀνδράσι ταῦτα
    γένηται,
50   κέρδεα δημοσίῳ σὺν κακῷ ἐρχόμενα.
ἐκ τῶν γὰρ στάσιές τε καὶ ἔμφυλοι φόνοι
    ἀνδρῶν
μούναρχοί τε· πόλει μήποτε τῇδε ἅδοι.

40 ὑμετέρης ο   45 φθείρουσι et διδοῦσι A
47 ἀτρεμέεσθαι codd., corr. Wackernagel: ἀτρεμεῖσθαι Bergk,
ἀτρέμε' ἦσθαι Young, alii alia   52 μούναρχος p   τε pro
δὲ Leutsch   θ'· ἁ Ahrens

THEOGNIS

tus, essentially to distinguish between aristocrats (like Theognis) and the rest, including those who are aristocrats by birth but do not behave as such.

39-52[1]

Cyrnus, this city is pregnant and I am afraid she will give birth to a man who will set right[2] our wicked insolence. These townsmen are still of sound mind, but their leaders[3] have changed and fallen into the depths of depravity. Never yet, Cyrnus, have noble men destroyed a city, but whenever the base take delight in outrageous behaviour and ruin the people and give judgements in favour of the unjust, for the sake of their own profit and power, do not expect that city to remain quiet long, even if it is now utterly calm, whenever this is dear to base men, profit that comes along with public harm.[4] From this arise civil strife, the spilling of kindred blood, and tyrants; may this city never delight in that.

[1] Treated by some as two poems (39-42, 43-52). Vv. 39-42 reappear as 1081-82b, with a difference between only 40 and 1082.
[2] I.e., a tyrant (cf. v. 52). The only tyrant of Megara we know of was Theagenes, whose rule ended c. 600, but Theognis may well be afraid that another tyrant will arise. [3] Presumably the ruling oligarchs, members of the aristocracy, but since they do not behave as 'noble' men should, they can be called 'base' (vv. 44, 49).
[4] The punctuation of vv. 43-50 is disputed, depending in part on whether the subjunctive or indicative is read in v. 45. I have followed West, but with no great confidence.

181

53-68

Κύρνε, πόλις μὲν ἔθ' ἥδε πόλις, λαοὶ δὲ δὴ ἄλλοι
οἳ πρόσθ' οὔτε δίκας ᾔδεσαν οὔτε νόμους,
55   ἀλλ' ἀμφὶ πλευραῖσι δορὰς αἰγῶν κατέτριβον,
ἔξω δ' ὥστ' ἔλαφοι τῆσδ' ἐνέμοντο πόλεος.
καὶ νῦν εἰσ' ἀγαθοί, Πολυπαΐδη· οἱ δὲ πρὶν ἐσθλοὶ
νῦν δειλοί. τίς κεν ταῦτ' ἀνέχοιτ' ἐσορῶν;
ἀλλήλους δ' ἀπατῶσιν ἐπ' ἀλλήλοισι γελῶντες,
60   οὔτε κακῶν γνώμας εἰδότες οὔτ' ἀγαθῶν.
μηδένα τῶνδε φίλον ποιεῦ, Πολυπαΐδη, ἀστῶν
ἐκ θυμοῦ χρείης οὕνεκα μηδεμιῆς·
ἀλλὰ δόκει μὲν πᾶσιν ἀπὸ γλώσσης φίλος εἶναι,
χρῆμα δὲ συμμείξῃς μηδενὶ μηδ' ὁτιοῦν
65   σπουδαῖον· γνώσῃ γὰρ ὀϊζυρῶν φρένας ἀνδρῶν,
ὥς σφιν ἐπ' ἔργοισιν πίστις ἔπ' οὐδεμία,
ἀλλὰ δόλους ἀπάτας τε πολυπλοκίας τ' ἐφίλησαν
οὕτως ὡς ἄνδρες μηκέτι σῳζόμενοι.

55 πλευρῆσι p   56 τήνδ' . . . πόλιν o   62 εἵνεκα o

69-72

μήποτε, Κύρνε, κακῷ πίσυνος βούλευε σὺν ἀνδρί,
70   εὖτ' ἂν σπουδαῖον πρῆγμ' ἐθέλῃς τελέσαι,
ἀλλὰ μετ' ἐσθλὸν ἰὼν βούλευ καὶ πολλὰ
    μογῆσαι
καὶ μακρὴν ποσσίν, Κύρν', ὁδὸν ἐκτελέσαι.

71 βούλευ καὶ A, βούλευε O, βουλεύεο p
71-72 μογήσας et ἐκτελέσας A²p

53-68[1]

Cyrnus, this city is still a city, but the people are different, people who formerly knew neither justice nor laws, but wore tattered goatskins about their sides and lived outside this city like deer. And now they are noble, Polypaïdes, while those who were noble before are now base. Who can endure the sight of this? They deceive one another and mock one another, knowing neither the distinctive marks of the base nor those of the noble.[2] Make none of these townsmen your sincere friend, Polypaïdes, because of any need. Seem in speech to be the friend of everyone, but share with no one any serious matter whatsoever. If you do, you will come to know the minds of men who are wretched, since there is no trust to be placed in their actions, but they love treachery, deceit, and craftiness, just like men beyond salvation.

[1] Some divide into two poems (53-60, 61-68).   [2] Vv. 57-60 recur, with some variation, in 1109-10 and 1113-14. West agrees with Schneidewin that 1111-12 should be inserted after 58.

69-72

Never trust or take counsel with a base man, Cyrnus, whenever you want to accomplish a serious matter, but be willing, Cyrnus, to endure much toil and to cover a long journey in search of a noble man.

73-74

πρῆξιν μηδὲ φίλοισιν ὅλως ἀνακοινέο πᾶσιν·
παῦροί τοι πολλῶν πιστὸν ἔχουσι νόον.

73 ἀνακοίνεο Αο. -έο Par. 2833

75-76

75 παύροισιν πίσυνος μεγάλ' ἀνδράσιν ἔργ'
     ἐπιχείρει,
     μή ποτ' ἀνήκεστον, Κύρνε, λάβῃς ἀνίην.

77-78

πιστὸς ἀνὴρ χρυσοῦ τε καὶ ἀργύρου
     ἀντερύσασθαι
ἄξιος ἐν χαλεπῇ, Κύρνε, διχοστασίῃ.

Plat. Leges 1.630a (v. test. 2), vv. 77-78

79-82

παύρους εὑρήσεις, Πολυπαΐδη, ἄνδρας ἑταίρους
80 πιστοὺς ἐν χαλεποῖς πρήγμασι γινομένους,
οἵτινες ἂν τολμῷεν ὁμόφρονα θυμὸν ἔχοντες
     ἶσον τῶν ἀγαθῶν τῶν τε κακῶν μετέχειν.

Themist. or. 22.265a (vv. 79-80)

83-86

τούτους οὐχ εὕροις διζήμενος οὐδ' ἐπὶ πάντας
     ἀνθρώπους, οὓς ναῦς μὴ μία πάντας ἄγοι,
85 οἷσιν ἐπὶ γλώσσῃ τε καὶ ὀφθαλμοῖσιν ἔπεστιν
     αἰδώς, οὐδ' αἰσχρὸν χρῆμ' ἔπι κέρδος ἄγει.

83 οὔ χ' van der Mey, editores plerique

184

73-74

Don't deliberate at all on an enterprise even with any of your friends; few indeed out of many friends have a mind that is trustworthy.

75-76

Trust few men when you attempt important enterprises, lest one day, Cyrnus, you get pain beyond cure.

77-78

A trustworthy man is worth his weight in gold and silver,[1] Cyrnus, in times of harsh civil strife.

[1] Literally, "is worthy of being weighed against gold and silver."

79-82

You will find few men, Polypaïdes, who are loyal comrades in difficult enterprises, men who can be of one mind with you and can bring themselves to share equally in both the good times and the bad.

83-86

Not even if you searched among all men would you find so many that a single ship could not carry them all, men on whose tongue and eyes there is a sense of shame and whom profit does not lead to a disgraceful act.

87-90

μή μ᾽ ἔπεσιν μὲν στέργε, νόον δ᾽ ἔχε καὶ φρένας
  ἄλλῃ
εἴ με φιλεῖς καί σοι πιστὸς ἔνεστι νόος.
ἤ με φίλει καθαρὸν θέμενος νόον, ἤ μ᾽ ἀποειπὼν
90 ἔχθαιρ᾽ ἀμφαδίην νεῖκος ἀειράμενος.

91-92

ὃς δὲ μιῇ γλώσσῃ δίχ᾽ ἔχει νόον, οὗτος ἑταῖρος
  δεινός, Κύρν᾽· ἐχθρὸς βέλτερος ἢ φίλος ὤν.

92 δειλὸς West (noluit Brunck)

93-100

ἄν τις ἐπαινήσῃ σε τόσον χρόνον ὅσσον ὁρῴης,
  νοσφισθεὶς δ᾽ ἄλλῃ γλῶσσαν ἵησι κακήν,
95 τοιοῦτός τοι ἑταῖρος ἀνὴρ φίλος οὔ τι μάλ᾽
  ἐσθλός.
ὅς κ᾽ εἴπῃ γλώσσῃ λεῖα, φρονῇ δ᾽ ἕτερα.
ἀλλ᾽ εἴη τοιοῦτος ἐμοὶ φίλος, ὃς τὸν ἑταῖρον
  γινώσκων ὀργὴν καὶ βαρὺν ὄντα φέρει
ἀντὶ κασιγνήτου. σὺ δέ μοι, φίλε, ταῦτ᾽ ἐνὶ θυμῷ
100 φράζεο, καί ποτέ μου μνήσεαι ἐξοπίσω.

93 εἴ ρ   ἐπαινήσει ο   ὁρῴη ρ   94 ἄλλη ρ, ἄλλην
AO   96 λῶια AO, λῶστα ρ, corr. Richards

THEOGNIS

87-90

Don't show affection for me in your words but keep
your mind and heart elsewhere, if you love me
and the mind within you is loyal. Either love me
sincerely or renounce me, hate me, and quarrel
openly.[1]

[1] These verses recur, with variation, in 1082c-f. Many combine
87-90 with 91-92, but it seems better, with West, to assume that
1083-84 once followed 90.

91-92

He who says one thing but thinks another is a dan-
gerous comrade, Cyrnus, better an enemy than a
friend.

93-100[1]

If a man praises you as long as you can see him, but
speaks maliciously when apart, such a comrade is in
truth no very good friend, whoever speaks with a
smooth tongue but has different thoughts. May I
have the sort of friend who knows his comrade and,
like a brother, puts up with his disposition even
when he is hard to bear. Please take these things to
heart, my friend, and one day hereafter you will
remember me.

[1] Editors regularly treat these verses as a single poem, but
West may well be right to divide them into three (93-94, 95-96,
97-100), with a lacuna after 94. 97-100 reappear as 1164a-d.

101-112

μηδείς σ᾽ ἀνθρώπων πείσῃ κακὸν ἄνδρα
    φιλῆσαι,
    Κύρνε· τί δ᾽ ἔστ᾽ ὄφελος δειλὸς ἀνὴρ φίλος ὤν;
οὔτ᾽ ἄν σ᾽ ἐκ χαλεποῖο πόνου ῥύσαιτο καὶ ἄτης,
    οὔτε κεν ἐσθλὸν ἔχων τοῦ μεταδοῦν ἐθέλοι.
105 δειλοὺς δ᾽ εὖ ἔρδοντι ματαιοτάτη χάρις ἐστίν·
    ἶσον καὶ σπείρειν πόντον ἁλὸς πολιῆς·
οὔτε γὰρ ἂν πόντον σπείρων βαθὺ λήιον ἀμῷς,
    οὔτε κακοὺς εὖ δρῶν εὖ πάλιν ἀντιλάβοις.
ἄπληστον γὰρ ἔχουσι κακοὶ νόον· ἢν δ᾽ ἓν
    ἁμάρτῃς,
110   τῶν πρόσθεν πάντων ἐκκέχυται φιλότης·
οἱ δ᾽ ἀγαθοὶ τὸ μέγιστον ἐπαυρίσκουσι παθόντες,
    μνῆμα δ᾽ ἔχουσ᾽ ἀγαθῶν καὶ χάριν ἐξοπίσω.

Anon. P. Colon. 64.13 (v. 105)
    Teles (p. 42.7 Hense) ap. Stob. 4.33.31 (sine nom.), v. 109
(- νόον)

104 μεταδούναι θέλοι A¹, μεγάλου δοῦναι θέλει O, μέγα
δοῦν᾽ ἐθέλει p: corr. Buttmann

113-14

μήποτε τὸν κακὸν ἄνδρα φίλον ποιεῖσθαι
    ἑταῖρον,
ἀλλ᾽ αἰεὶ φεύγειν ὥστε κακὸν λιμένα.

115-16

115 πολλοί τοι πόσιος καὶ βρώσιός εἰσιν ἑταῖροι,
    ἐν δὲ σπουδαίῳ πρήγματι παυρότεροι.

101-112[1]

Let no one persuade you, Cyrnus, to make a base man your friend. Of what use is a base man as a friend? He would not rescue you from hard toil or from ruin (delusion?) nor if he has any success would he be willing to give you a share of this. Doing a good turn to the base is an utterly useless act of kindness; it is the same as sowing the expanse of the white-capped sea. You cannot reap a tall crop by sowing the sea and you cannot get anything good in return by doing good to the base. For the base have an insatiable desire; if you make one mistake, the friendship shown by all former acts is wasted. But the noble enjoy to the highest degree the treatment they've received, they remember the good things, and they are grateful thereafter.

[1] Most editors treat 101-4 and 105-12 as separate poems.

113-14

Never make a base man your close comrade, but always avoid him like a bad harbour.

115-16[1]

Many in truth are your comrades when there's food and drink, but not so many when the enterprise is serious.

[1] 116 is repeated in 644, with 643 similar to 115 in thought. 115 re-appears as Ps.-Phocylides 92 (with γάρ for τοι).

117-18

κιβδήλου δ' ἀνδρὸς γνῶναι χαλεπώτερον οὐδέν,
Κύρν', οὐδ' εὐλαβίης ἐστὶ περὶ πλέονος.

119-28

χρυσοῦ κιβδήλοιο καὶ ἀργύρου ἄνσχετος ἄτη,
120   Κύρνε, καὶ ἐξευρεῖν ῥάδιον ἀνδρὶ σοφῷ·
εἰ δὲ φίλου νόος ἀνδρὸς ἐνὶ στήθεσσι λελήθῃ
ψυδρὸς ἐών, δόλιον δ' ἐν φρεσὶν ἦτορ ἔχῃ,
τοῦτο θεὸς κιβδηλότατον ποίησε βροτοῖσιν,
καὶ γνῶναι πάντων τοῦτ' ἀνιηρότατον.
125   οὐδὲ γὰρ εἰδείης ἀνδρὸς νόον οὔτε γυναικός,
πρὶν πειρηθείης ὥσπερ ὑποζυγίου,
οὐδέ κεν εἰκάσσαις †ὥσπερ ποτ' ἐς ὥριον
ἐλθών·†
πολλάκι γὰρ γνώμην ἐξαπατῶσ' ἰδέαι.

Clem. *Strom.* 6.18.6 (vv. 119-24)
Arist. *Eth. Eud.* 7.2.1237b15 (vv. 125-26)

119 ἄσχετος codd., corr. Camerarius   121 λελήθη A,
λελήθει O, λέληθε p et Clem.   122 ψυδρὸς A, ψυχρὸς
Clem., ψυδνὸς p   ἔχῃ ι A, ἔχειρ et Clem.   125 οὐ γὰρ ἂν
p et Arist.   οὐδὲ γυναικός Arist.   126 πειραθείης o et
Arist.   127 ποτ' ἐσώριον O¹p, ποτε σώριον O a.c., ὤνιον
Camerarius, alii alia

129-30

μήτ' ἀρετὴν εὔχου, Πολυπαΐδη, ἔξοχος εἶναι
130   μήτ' ἄφενος· μοῦνον δ' ἀνδρὶ γένοιτο τύχη.

117-18

Nothing, Cyrnus, is more difficult to recognize than a counterfeit man and nothing is of more importance than being on one's guard against him.

119-28

The ruin that results from counterfeit gold and silver is endurable, Cyrnus, and it is easy for an expert to find out (that they are counterfeit). But if a friend's intent is false and lies undetected in his breast and if he has a treacherous heart, this is the most counterfeit thing that the god has made for mortals and to recognize it costs the greatest pain of all. For you cannot know a man's or a woman's intent, until you make trial of it like a beast of burden, nor can you form an estimate of it by coming as it were at the right time(?), since appearances often deceive one's judgement.

129-30

Don't pray for outstanding excellence or wealth, Polypaïdes; the only thing a man can have is luck.

131-32

οὐδὲν ἐν ἀνθρώποισι πατρὸς καὶ μητρὸς ἄμεινον
ἔπλεθ᾽, ὅσοις ὁσίη, Κύρνε, μέμηλε δίκη.

Stob. 4.25.1 (vv. 131-32)

132 οἷς codd., ὅσοις Stob.   ὁσίης . . . δίκης Stob.

133-42

οὐδείς, Κύρν᾽, ἄτης καὶ κέρδεος αἴτιος αὐτός,
ἀλλὰ θεοὶ τούτων δώτορες ἀμφοτέρων·
135   οὐδέ τις ἀνθρώπων ἐργάζεται ἐν φρεσὶν εἰδὼς
ἐς τέλος εἴτ᾽ ἀγαθὸν γίνεται εἴτε κακόν.
πολλάκι γὰρ δοκέων θήσειν κακὸν ἐσθλὸν
       ἔθηκεν,
καί τε δοκῶν θήσειν ἐσθλὸν ἔθηκε κακόν.
οὐδέ τῳ ἀνθρώπων παραγίνεται ὅσσ᾽ ἐθέλησιν·
140   ἴσχει γὰρ χαλεπῆς πείρατ᾽ ἀμηχανίης.
ἄνθρωποι δὲ μάταια νομίζομεν, εἰδότες οὐδέν·
θεοὶ δὲ κατὰ σφέτερον πάντα τελοῦσι νόον.

Orion, anth. 5.12 (p. 48 Schneidewin), vv. 141-42

139 ἐθέλησιν p, θέλησιν AO

143-44

οὐδείς πω ξεῖνον, Πολυπαΐδη, ἐξαπατήσας
οὐδ᾽ ἱκέτην θνητῶν ἀθανάτους ἔλαθεν.

145-48

145   βούλεο δ᾽ εὐσεβέων ὀλίγοις σὺν χρήμασιν οἰκεῖν
ἢ πλουτεῖν ἀδίκως χρήματα πασάμενος.

131-32

There is nothing among mankind better than a father and a mother, Cyrnus, who care about holy justice.

133-42

No one, Cyrnus, is responsible on his own for ruin or profit, but it is the gods who give both. Nor does anyone know in his heart whether his toil will turn out well or badly in the end. For often a man who thought he would fail succeeds and a man who thought he would succeed fails. No one has at hand everything he wants, since the constraints of grievous helplessness hold him back. We mortals have vain thoughts, not knowledge; it is the gods who bring everything to pass according to their own intent.

143-44

No mortal, Polypaïdes, has yet escaped the notice of the immortals, if he deceives a stranger or a suppliant.

145-48

Prefer to live righteously with a few possessions than to become rich by the unjust acquisition of

ἐν δὲ δικαιοσύνῃ συλλήβδην πᾶσ᾽ ἀρετή ᾽στιν,
πᾶς δέ τ᾽ ἀνὴρ ἀγαθός, Κύρνε, δίκαιος ἐών.

Anon. in Arist. *Eth. Nic.* 5.1.15 (*Comm. in Arist. Graeca* xx.210.11), vv. 145-47
Arist. *Eth. Nic.* 5.1.15.1129b29, alii (v. 147)

146 πασσάμενος codd., corr. Brunck   147 ἀρετὴ ἔνι Arist.

149-50

χρήματα μὲν δαίμων καὶ παγκάκῳ ἀνδρὶ
    δίδωσιν,
150   Κύρν᾽· ἀρετῆς δ᾽ ὀλίγοις ἀνδράσι μοῖρ᾽
    ἕπεται.

151-52

ὕβριν, Κύρνε, θεὸς πρῶτον κακῷ ὤπασεν ἀνδρί,
οὗ μέλλει χώρην μηδεμίαν θέμεναι.

151 κακὸν o   152 μηδεμίην A

153-54

τίκτει τοι κόρος ὕβριν, ὅταν κακῷ ὄλβος ἔπηται
ἀνθρώπῳ καὶ ὅτῳ μὴ νόος ἄρτιος ᾖ.

155-58

155   μήποτέ μοι πενίην θυμοφθόρον ἀνδρὶ χαλεφθεὶς
μηδ᾽ ἀχρημοσύνην οὐλομένην πρόφερε·

194

money. For in justice there is the sum total of every excellence,[1] and every man who is just, Cyrnus, is noble.

[1] This proverbial statement is also attributed to Phocylides (fr. 10).

149-50

Fortune gives even an utterly wicked man riches, Cyrnus, but excellence is allotted to few as their companion.

151-52

It is insolence, Cyrnus, that the god gives first to a wicked man whose position he intends to make of no account.

153-54

In truth excess breeds insolence, whenever prosperity comes to a wicked man who is not sound of mind.[1]

[1] For a slightly different version see Solon fr. 6.3-4.

155-58

Never, pray, out of anger at a man throw heart-rending poverty and accursed indigence in his face.

Ζεὺς γάρ τοι τὸ τάλαντον ἐπιρρέπει ἄλλοτε ἄλλως,
ἄλλοτε μὲν πλουτεῖν, ἄλλοτε μηδὲν ἔχειν.

Stob. 4.32.36 (vv. 155-58 + 179-80)
Basil. ad adul. 5 (p. 48 Boulenger, p. 25 Wilson), vv. 157-58

155 τοι codd., μοι Stob.   χολωθεὶς codd., χαλεφθεὶς Stob.
156 οὐλομένην codd., Κύρνε κακὴν Stob.
157 ἄλλῳ codd., ἄλλως Stob., Basil.

159-60

μήποτε, Κύρν', ἀγορᾶσθαι ἔπος μέγα· οἶδε γὰρ
οὐδεὶς
160   ἀνθρώπων ὅ τι νὺξ χἠμέρη ἀνδρὶ τελεῖ.

161-64

πολλοί τοι χρῶνται δειλαῖς φρεσί, δαίμονι δ'
ἐσθλῷ,
οἷς τὸ κακὸν δοκέον γίνεται εἰς ἀγαθόν·
εἰσὶν δ' οἳ βουλῇ τ' ἀγαθῇ καὶ δαίμονι δειλῷ
μοχθίζουσι, τέλος δ' ἔργμασιν οὐχ ἕπεται.

163 δειλῷ A, κακῶ O, φαύλω p

165-66

165   οὐδεὶς ἀνθρώπων οὔτ' ὄλβιος οὔτε πενιχρὸς
οὔτε κακὸς νόσφιν δαίμονος οὔτ' ἀγαθός.

167-68

ἀλλ' ἄλλῳ κακόν ἐστι, τὸ δ' ἀτρεκὲς ὄλβιος
οὐδεὶς
ἀνθρώπων ὁπόσους ἤέλιος καθορᾷ.

THEOGNIS

Be assured that Zeus inclines the scales now on this side, now on that; now to be wealthy, now to have nothing.

159-60

Never talk big, Cyrnus, for no one knows what a day or night will bring to pass for a man.

161-64

Many indeed have worthless brains, but enjoy good fortune, and for them apparent failure turns into success. And there are those who labour wisely, but suffer bad luck, and their efforts accomplish nothing.

165-66

No man is prosperous or poor or of low or high estate[1] without divine aid.

[1] The precise significance of κακός and ἀγαθός is uncertain here. My translation assumes that they are essentially the equivalent, in reverse order, of the two preceding adjectives.

167-68

One man is wretched this way, another that, and no one of all whom the sun looks down upon is truly fortunate.

169-70

ὃν δὲ θεοὶ τιμῶσιν, ὁ καὶ μωμεύμενος αἰνεῖ·
ἀνδρὸς δὲ σπουδὴ γίνεται οὐδεμία.

170

171-72

θεοῖς εὔχου †θεοῖσιν ἔπι κράτος· οὗτοι ἄτερ θεῶν
γίνεται ἀνθρώποις οὔτ' ἀγάθ' οὔτε κακά.

171 θεοῖσιν ἔπι A, οἷς ἐστὶ ο, θεοῖς vel τοῖς ἐστιν ἔπι Bergk,
θεοῖς οἷσιν ἔπι Schmidt

173-78

ἄνδρ' ἀγαθὸν πενίη πάντων δάμνησι μάλιστα,
καὶ γήρως πολιοῦ, Κύρνε, καὶ ἠπιάλου·
ἣν δὴ χρὴ φεύγοντα καὶ ἐς μεγακήτεα πόντον
ῥιπτεῖν καὶ πετρέων, Κύρνε, κατ' ἠλιβάτων.
καὶ γὰρ ἀνὴρ πενίῃ δεδμημένος οὔτε τι εἰπεῖν
οὔτ' ἔρξαι δύναται, γλῶσσα δέ οἱ δέδεται.

175

Chrysipp. ap. Plut. *Sto. repugn.* 14.1039f, *de comm. not.*
22.1069d; Porph. in Hor. *epist.* 1.1.45; Clem. *Strom.* 4.23.3;
Hermog. *Progymn.* 4 (p. 8.21 Rabe); Aphthon. *Progymn.* 4 (p.
8.12 Rabe); Stob. 4.32.38; schol. Thuc. 2.43.5; Elias, *proleg.*
philos. 6 (*Comm. in Arist. Graeca* xviii(1).15.16); alii (vv. 175-76)
Plut. *quomodo aud. poet.* 4.22a; Artem. 1.32; Stob. 4.32.34; alii
(vv. 177-78)

175 ἣν δὴ χρὴ codd., χρὴ πενίην (-αν) testes omnes
μεγακήτεα ο, Plut. 1069d, Hermog., Aphthon., Stob. SM, schol.
Thuc., Elias; βαθυκήτεα A, Plut. 1039f, Porph., Clem., Stob. A
176 πετρέων A, Clem., Stob. MA; πετρῶν alii   177 πᾶς γὰρ
testes

169-70

Even the fault-finder praises one whom the gods honour, whereas a man's zeal counts for nothing.

171-72

Pray to the gods; power rests with the gods. Nothing good or bad happens to men without the gods.

173-78[1]

Poverty, Cyrnus, overwhelms a man of worth more than anything else, including hoary age and fever. To escape from it, Cyrnus, you should throw yourself to the monsters of the sea or down from lofty cliffs. For in effect a man overwhelmed by poverty is powerless to say or accomplish anything, and his tongue is bound fast.

[1] Some editors combine 173-78 with 179-82, but they are better treated as three separate poems.

179-80

χρὴ γὰρ ὁμῶς ἐπὶ γῆν τε καὶ εὐρέα νῶτα
  θαλάσσης
180   δίζησθαι χαλεπῆς, Κύρνε, λύσιν πενίης.

Stob. 4.32.36 (vv. 179-80 + 155-58)

179 χρὴ δ᾽ αἰεὶ κατὰ Stob.   180 δίζεσθαι ο, Stob.

181-82

τεθνάμεναι, φίλε Κύρνε, πενιχρῷ βέλτερον ἀνδρὶ
ἢ ζώειν χαλεπῇ τειρόμενον πενίῃ.

181 τεθνάμεναι A, τεθνᾶναι p

183-92

κριοὺς μὲν καὶ ὄνους διζήμεθα, Κύρνε, καὶ
  ἵππους
εὐγενέας, καί τις βούλεται ἐξ ἀγαθῶν
185   βήσεσθαι· γῆμαι δὲ κακὴν κακοῦ οὐ μελεδαίνει
ἐσθλὸς ἀνήρ, ἤν οἱ χρήματα πολλὰ διδῷ,
οὐδὲ γυνὴ κακοῦ ἀνδρὸς ἀναίνεται εἶναι ἄκοιτις
πλουσίου, ἀλλ᾽ ἀφνεὸν βούλεται ἀντ᾽ ἀγαθοῦ.
χρήματα μὲν τιμῶσι· καὶ ἐκ κακοῦ ἐσθλὸς ἔγημε
190   καὶ κακὸς ἐξ ἀγαθοῦ· πλοῦτος ἔμειξε γένος.
οὕτω μὴ θαύμαζε γένος, Πολυπαΐδη, ἀστῶν
μαυροῦσθαι· σὺν γὰρ μίσγεται ἐσθλὰ κακοῖς.

Xenoph. ap. Stob. 4.29.53 (v. test. 6); Stob. 4.30.11a (vv.
183-90)
Stob. 4.22.99 (vv. 183-86)

179-80

One should search over land and the broad-backed sea alike, Cyrnus, to find a release from grievous poverty.

181-82

It is better, dear Cyrnus, for a poor man to be dead than to live oppressed by grievous poverty.

183-92

We seek out rams and asses and horses that are purebred, Cyrnus, and everyone wishes that they mount (females) of good stock; but a noble man does not mind marrying the base daughter of a base father if the latter gives him a lot of money, and a woman does not refuse to be the wife of a base man who is rich, but she wants a wealthy man instead of one who is noble. It is money people honour; one who is noble marries the daughter of one who is base and one who is base marries the daughter of one who is noble.[1] Wealth has mixed up blood. And so, Polypaïdes, do not be surprised that the townsmen's stock is becoming enfeebled, since what is noble is mixing with what is base.

[1] West suggests that something has been lost after 188, since the transition to 189 is rather harsh.

---

184 ἀγαθοῦ Stob. 29 et 30   185 κτήσεσθαι Stob. 30
(-ασθαι 29)   186 ἤν τις Stob. 29, ἄν τις 30   φέρῃ Stob. 22
189 γὰρ Stob. bis

193-96

αὐτός τοι ταύτην εἰδὼς κακόπατριν ἐοῦσαν
  εἰς οἴκους ἄγεται χρήμασι πειθόμενος,
195 εὔδοξος κακόδοξον, ἐπεὶ κρατερή μιν ἀνάγκη
  ἐντύει, ἥ τ' ἀνδρὸς τλήμονα θῆκε νόον.

193 αὐτός τοι ταύτην excerptoris supplementum censet West
ἀστὸς Heimsoeth τοιαύτην O   196 ἐντύνει codd., corr.
Brunck

197-208

χρῆμα δ' ὃ μὲν Διόθεν καὶ σὺν δίκῃ ἀνδρὶ
    γένηται
  καὶ καθαρῶς, αἰεὶ παρμόνιμον τελέθει·
εἰ δ' ἀδίκως παρὰ καιρὸν ἀνὴρ φιλοκερδέι θυμῷ
200 κτήσεται, εἴθ' ὅρκῳ πὰρ τὸ δίκαιον ἑλών,
αὐτίκα μέν τι φέρειν κέρδος δοκεῖ, ἐς δὲ τελευτὴν
  αὖθις ἔγεντο κακόν, θεῶν δ' ὑπερέσχε νόος.
ἀλλὰ τάδ' ἀνθρώπων ἀπατᾷ νόον· οὐ γὰρ ἐπ'
    αὐτοῦ
  τίνονται μάκαρες πρήγματος ἀμπλακίας,
205 ἀλλ' ὃ μὲν αὐτὸς ἔτεισε κακὸν χρέος, οὐδὲ
    φίλοισιν
  ἄτην ἐξοπίσω παισὶν ἐπεκρέμασεν·
ἄλλον δ' οὐ κατέμαρψε δίκη· θάνατος γὰρ
    ἀναιδὴς
  πρόσθεν ἐπὶ βλεφάροις ἕζετο κῆρα φέρων.

203 ἐπ' Vat. Urb. gr. 160, ἔτ' αὐτοὺς Ao
206 ὑπεκρέμασεν O, unde ὑπερ- Boeckh

202

THEOGNIS

193-96

With full knowledge that she is of base stock he
brings her home as wife, persuaded by wealth, al-
though he has a fine reputation and she a poor one;
powerful necessity, which makes a man's spirit capa-
ble of endurance, urges him on.

197-208

Whatever possession comes to a man from Zeus and
is obtained with justice and without stain, is forever
lasting. But if a man acquires it unjustly, inoppor-
tunely, and with a greedy heart or seizes it wrongly
by a false oath, for the moment he thinks he's win-
ning profit, but in the end it turns out badly and the
will of the gods prevails. The minds of men, how-
ever, are misled, since the blessed gods do not pun-
ish sin at the time of the very act, but one man pays
his evil debt himself and doesn't cause doom to hang
over his dear progeny later, while another is not
overtaken by justice; before that ruthless death
settles on his eyelids, bringing doom.[1]

[1] For the same general thought cf. portions of Solon fr. 13.9-
32.

209-210

οὐδείς τοι φεύγοντι φίλος καὶ πιστὸς ἑταῖρος·
210   τῆς δὲ φυγῆς ἐστιν τοῦτ᾽ ἀνιηρότερον.

211-12

οἶνόν τοι πίνειν πουλὺν κακόν· ἢν δέ τις αὐτὸν
    πίνῃ ἐπισταμένως, οὐ κακὸς ἀλλ᾽ ἀγαθός.

213-18

θυμέ, φίλους κατὰ πάντας ἐπίστρεφε ποικίλον
    ἦθος,
    ὀργὴν συμμίσγων ἥντιν᾽ ἕκαστος ἔχει.
215 πουλύπου ὀργὴν ἴσχε πολυπλόκου, ὃς ποτὶ
    πέτρῃ,
    τῇ προσομιλήσῃ, τοῖος ἰδεῖν ἐφάνη.
νῦν μὲν τῇδ᾽ ἐφέπου, τότε δ᾽ ἀλλοῖος χρόα γίνου.
κρέσσων τοι σοφίη γίνεται ἀτροπίης.

Plut. de amic. multit. 9.96f, aet. phys. 19.916c, sollert. anim. 27.978e; Ath. 7.317a; alii (vv. 215-16)

213 Κύρνε pro θυμέ ο   215 πο(υ)λύποδος νόον ἴσχε πολυχρόου Plut. ter   216 τῇπερ   ὁμ. Plut. 96 (v.l.), 978 -ήσει AOXDUr, Plut. 916 et v.l. 96, 978

219-20

μηδὲν ἄγαν ἄσχαλλε ταρασσομένων πολιητέων,
220   Κύρνε, μέσην δ᾽ ἔρχευ τὴν ὁδὸν ὥσπερ ἐγώ.

THEOGNIS

209-210[1]

In truth an exile has no friend or loyal comrade, and
this is more painful than the exile.

[1] Identical to 332ab, except for the first two words and the last.

211-12[1]

Drinking wine in large quantities is indeed a bane,
but if one drinks it wisely, wine is not a bane but a
blessing.

[1] Repeated with slight variations in 509-510.

213-18[1]

My heart, keep turning a versatile disposition in ac-
cordance with all your friends, mingling with it the
mood which each one has. Adopt the mood of the
cunning octopus[2] which seems to resemble the rock
to which it clings. Now follow along in this direction,
now take on a different complexion. Cleverness is in
truth superior to inflexibility.

[1] 213-14 and 217-18 reappear, with variations, as 1071-74.
Some, including West, treat 213-14 as a separate poem.
[2] There is much information on the octopus in Athenaeus 7.316a-
318f. The adjective translated as "cunning" may also refer literally
to the many convolutions of the octopus, and the noun "complex-
ion" in the next sentence reflects the imagery of the octopus.

219-20

Because (when?) the citizens are in turmoil do not
be too distressed, Cyrnus, but go along the middle
of the road, as I do.

221-26

ὅστις τοι δοκέει τὸν πλησίον ἴδμεναι οὐδέν,
  ἀλλ᾽ αὐτὸς μοῦνος ποικίλα δήνε᾽ ἔχειν,
κεῖνός γ᾽ ἄφρων ἐστί, νόου βεβλαμμένος ἐσθλοῦ·
  ἴσως γὰρ πάντες ποικίλ᾽ ἐπιστάμεθα·
225 ἀλλ᾽ ὁ μὲν οὐκ ἐθέλει κακοκερδείῃσιν ἕπεσθαι,
  τῷ δὲ δολοπλοκίαι μᾶλλον ἄπιστοι ἄδον.

Stob. 3.4.26 (vv. 221-26)

221 ἔμμεναι Stob.   226 μᾶλλον ἔτ᾽ εἰσὶ φίλαι Stob.

227-32

πλούτου δ᾽ οὐδὲν τέρμα πεφασμένον ἀνθρώποισιν·
  οἳ γὰρ νῦν ἡμῶν πλεῖστον ἔχουσι βίον,
διπλάσιον σπεύδουσι. τίς ἂν κορέσειεν ἅπαντας;
230 χρήματά τοι θνητοῖς γίνεται ἀφροσύνη,
ἄτη δ᾽ ἐξ αὐτῆς ἀναφαίνεται, ἣν ὁπότε Ζεὺς
  πέμψῃ τειρομένοις, ἄλλοτε ἄλλος ἔχει.

233-34

ἀκρόπολις καὶ πύργος ἐὼν κενεόφρονι δήμῳ,
  Κύρν᾽, ὀλίγης τιμῆς ἔμμορεν ἐσθλὸς ἀνήρ.

235-36

235 οὐδὲν ἐπιπρέπει ἦμιν ἅτ᾽ ἀνδράσι σῳζομένοισιν,
  ἀλλ᾽ ὡς πάγχυ πόλει, Κύρνε, ἁλωσομένῃ.

235 οὐδὲν ἐπιτρέπει A, corr. Bekker; οὐδέ τι πρέπει o, οὐδὲν
ἔτι πρέπει Ahrens (prob. West)

221-26

Anyone who thinks that his neighbour knows nothing, while he himself is the only one to make crafty plans, is a fool, his good sense impaired. For all of us alike have crafty thoughts, but while one man is unwilling to pursue base gains, another takes pleasure rather in deceitful guile.

227-32[1]

Of wealth no limit is revealed to men, since those of us who now have the greatest livelihood are eager to double it. What could satisfy everyone? In truth possessions result in folly for mortals, and from folly there is revealed ruin, which now one, now another has, whenever Zeus sends it to wretched men.

[1] A version of Solon fr. 13.71-76.

233-34

Although a noble man is a citadel and a tower for the empty-headed people, Cyrnus, his share of honour is slight.

235-36

We cannot regard ourselves as men who are saved, Cyrnus, but as a city that will be utterly captured.[1]

[1] Probably not in the literal sense, but as a city that will be 'taken over' by those who are, in Theognis' view, members of the lower class. It is also possible that the verb has its legal meaning, 'condemned.'

237-54

σοὶ μὲν ἐγὼ πτέρ᾽ ἔδωκα, σὺν οἷς ἐπ᾽ ἀπείρονα
πόντον
πωτήσῃ καὶ γῆν πᾶσαν ἀειρόμενος
ῥηϊδίως· θοίνῃς δὲ καὶ εἰλαπίνῃσι παρέσσῃ
240   ἐν πάσαις, πολλῶν κείμενος ἐν στόμασιν,
καί σε σὺν αὐλίσκοισι λιγυφθόγγοις νέοι ἄνδρες
εὐκόσμως ἐρατοὶ καλά τε καὶ λιγέα
ᾄσονται. καὶ ὅταν δνοφερῆς ὑπὸ κεύθεσι γαίης
βῇς πολυκωκύτους εἰς Ἀΐδαο δόμους,
245   οὐδέποτ᾽ οὐδὲ θανὼν ἀπολεῖς κλέος, ἀλλὰ
μελήσεις
ἄφθιτον ἀνθρώποις αἰὲν ἔχων ὄνομα,
Κύρνε, καθ᾽ Ἑλλάδα γῆν στρωφώμενος ἠδ᾽ ἀνὰ
νήσους
ἰχθυόεντα περῶν πόντον ἐπ᾽ ἀτρύγετον,
οὐχ ἵππων νώτοισιν ἐφήμενος, ἀλλά σε πέμψει
250   ἀγλαὰ Μουσάων δῶρα ἰοστεφάνων·
πᾶσι δ᾽ ὅσοισι μέμηλε καὶ ἐσσομένοισιν ἀοιδὴ
ἔσσῃ ὁμῶς, ὄφρ᾽ ἂν γῆ τε καὶ ἠέλιος·
αὐτὰρ ἐγὼν ὀλίγης παρὰ σεῦ οὐ τυγχάνω αἰδοῦς,
ἀλλ᾽ ὥσπερ μικρὸν παῖδα λόγοις μ᾽ ἀπατᾷς.

238 κατὰ codd., corr. Bergk   251 πᾶσι διὸσ οἶσι A,
πᾶσιν οἶσι O, πᾶσι γὰρ οἶσι p, corr. Lachmann

THEOGNIS

237-54[1]

I have given you wings with which you will fly, soaring easily, over the boundless sea and all the land. You will be present at every dinner and feast, lying on the lips of many, and lovely youths accompanied by the clear sounds of pipes[2] will sing of you in orderly fashion with beautiful, clear voices. And whenever you go to Hades' house of wailing, down in the dark earth's depths, never even in death will you lose your fame, but you will be in men's thoughts, your name ever immortal, Cyrnus, as you roam throughout the land of Greece and among the islands, crossing over the fish-filled, undraining(?) sea, not riding on the backs of horses,[3] but it is the splendid gifts of the violet-wreathed Muses that will escort you. For all who care about their gifts, even for future generations, you will be alike the subject of song, as long as earth and sun exist. And yet I do not meet with a slight[4] respect from you, but you deceive me with your words, as if I were a small child.

[1] These verses seem to form a kind of epilogue to 19-26, although they need not have been composed for that purpose.
[2] The Greek word is a diminutive, apparently describing a pipe suitable for young voices.   [3] The significance of this is disputed.   [4] A few prefer to connect the negative with the adjective, "I meet with no slight respect," i.e., "with much respect," arguing that Cyrnus shows considerable respect, but it is not genuine, as the next verse indicates.

255-56

255   κάλλιστον τὸ δικαιότατον· λῷστον δ' ὑγιαίνειν·
       πρᾶγμα δὲ τερπνότατον, τοῦ τις ἐρᾷ, τὸ τυχεῖν.

P. Oxy. xxiii.2380 (saec. II/III p. Chr.); Arist. *Eth. Nic.*
1.8.14.1099a27; Arist. *Eth. Eud.* 1.1.1214a5; Stob. 4.39.8 (vv. 255-
56)

257-60

ἵππος ἐγὼ καλὴ καὶ ἀεθλίη, ἀλλὰ κάκιστον
   ἄνδρα φέρω, καί μοι τοῦτ' ἀνιηρότατον.
πολλάκι δὴ 'μέλλησα διαρρήξασα χαλινὸν
260   φεύγειν ὠσαμένη τὸν κακὸν ἡνίοχον.

259 δὴ 'μ- X p.c., D; δ' ἠμ- AOUrI   260 ὠσαμένη p,
ἀπωσαμένη AO (φεύγεν Bergk)

261-66

οὔ μοι πίνεται οἶνος, ἐπεὶ παρὰ παιδὶ τερείνῃ
   ἄλλος ἀνὴρ κατέχει πολλὸν ἐμοῦ κακίων.
ψυχρόν μοι παρὰ τῇδε φίλοι πίνουσι τοκῆες,
   ὡς θαμά θ' ὑδρεύει καί με γοῶσα φέρει·
265   ἔνθα μέσην περὶ παῖδα λαβὼν ἀγκῶν' ἐφίλησα
   δειρήν, ἡ δὲ τέρεν φθέγγετ' ἀπὸ στόματος.

262 κάλ' ἔχει West   263 που pro μοι West
264 ὥσθ' ἅμα θ' malunt multi   265 βαλὼν Hermann

---

1 Meaning and text are much disputed, and West may well be
right to separate 261-62 from 263-66. Some critics treat the verses
as a riddle.

THEOGNIS

255-56[1]

Fairest is that which is most just, best is health, and
the most pleasurable thing is to obtain what one
loves.[2]

[1] Aristotle (*Eth. Nic.*) cites these lines as "the Delian inscrip-
tion" (τὸ Δηλιακὸν ἐπίγραμμα) and (*Eth. Eud.*) as inscribed
in the shrine of Leto on Delos. The text printed is that of the
Theognidean MSS, the other sources giving a variety of readings,
especially in the first half of the pentameter. The papyrus contains
vv. 254-78, in a fragmentary state.   [2] Not necessarily in an
erotic sense.

257-60

I am a fine, prize-winning horse, but I carry a man
who is utterly base, and this causes me the greatest
pain. Often I was on the point of breaking the bit,
throwing my bad rider, and running off.[1]

[1] Various explanations of the imagery have been offered. The
likeliest, in my opinion, is that the horse represents a woman of
the upper class married off to a man of the lower class, and resent-
ing the union.

261-66

No wine is being drunk for me (?), since at the ten-
der maiden's side another man, much inferior to me,
has the upper hand. At her place (?) her dear par-
ents drink cool water in my opinion (?), since she
often draws and carries it, crying for me; there I
grasped her round the waist in my arms and kissed
her neck, while from her lips came tender words.[1]

ELEGIAC POETRY

267-70

γνωτή τοι Πενίη γε καὶ ἀλλοτρίη περ ἐοῦσα·
  οὔτε γὰρ εἰς ἀγορὴν ἔρχεται οὔτε δίκας·
πάντη γὰρ τοὔλασσον ἔχει, πάντη δ' ἐπίμυκτος,
270   πάντη δ' ἐχθρὴ ὁμῶς γίνεται, ἔνθα περ ᾖ.

267 τε A, corr. Friedemann   269 ἐπίμυκτος A,
ἐπίμικτος o (-ον O) et pap. (]πιμι[)   270 ε]νθ[α] παρ[ηι
pap.

271-78

ἴσως τοι τὰ μὲν ἄλλα θεοὶ θνητοῖς ἀνθρώποις
  γῆράς τ' οὐλόμενον καὶ νεότητ' ἔδοσαν,
τῶν πάντων δὲ κάκιστον ἐν ἀνθρώποις θανάτου τε
  καὶ πασέων νούσων ἐστὶ πονηρότατον,
275   παῖδας ἐπεὶ θρέψαιο καὶ ἄρμενα πάντα
          παράσχοις,
  χρήματα δ' ἐγκαταθῇς πόλλ' ἀνιηρὰ παθών,
τὸν πατέρ' ἐχθαίρουσι, καταρῶνται δ' ἀπολέσθαι,
  καὶ στυγέουσ' ὥσπερ πτωχὸν ἐσερχόμενον.

274 πονηρότερον Hartung   278 ἐπερχ- o et pap. (]περ[)

279-82

εἰκὸς τὸν κακὸν ἄνδρα κακῶς τὰ δίκαια νομίζειν,
280   μηδεμίαν κατόπισθ' ἀζόμενον νέμεσιν·
δειλῷ γάρ τ' ἀπάλαμνα βροτῷ πάρα πόλλ'
          ἀνελέσθαι
  πὰρ ποδός, ἡγεῖσθαί θ' ὡς καλὰ πάντα τιθεῖ.

280 κατόπιν o

212

267-70

Poverty is indeed well known, even though she belongs to someone else. She does not visit the marketplace or the courts, since everywhere her status is inferior, everywhere she is scorned, and everywhere she is equally hated, regardless of where she is.

271-78

The gods have given mortal men an equal share of other things, accursed old age and youth, but there is something that is the worst and most grievous of all things in human life, including death and every kind of sickness, (namely, that) whenever you have raised sons, provided everything that is fitting, and stored up wealth (for them) after much bitter suffering, they hate their father, pray for his death, and loathe him as if he were a beggar at the door.[1]

[1] The punctuation of this segment is unclear and many treat θανάτου—πονηρότατον as a parenthesis.

279-82

It is natural that the base man have a base view of justice and have no regard for resentment to follow, since it is possible for a base man to have ready access to many criminal acts and to consider that everything he does is fine.

283-86

ἀστῶν μηδενὶ πιστὸς ἐὼν πόδα τῶνδε πρόβαινε,
μήθ᾿ ὅρκῳ πίσυνος μήτε φιλημοσύνῃ,
285 μηδ᾿ εἰ Ζῆν᾿ ἐθέλῃ παρέχειν βασιλῆα μέγιστον
ἔγγυον ἀθανάτων πιστὰ τιθεῖν ἐθέλων

283 τόνδε codd., corr. Hermann   286 πιστὰ—ἐθέλων
excerptoris supplementum censet West

287-92

ἐν γάρ τοι πόλει ὧδε κακοψόγῳ ἀνδάνει οὐδέν·
†ωσδετοσωσαιει† πολλοὶ ἀνολβότεροι.
νῦν δὲ τὰ τῶν ἀγαθῶν κακὰ γίνεται ἐσθλὰ
    κακοῖσιν
290 ἀνδρῶν· γαίονται δ᾿ ἐκτραπέλοισι νόμοις·
αἰδὼς μὲν γὰρ ὄλωλεν, ἀναιδείη δὲ καὶ ὕβρις
νικήσασα δίκην γῆν κατὰ πᾶσαν ἔχει.

288 ita A, ὡς δὲ τὸ σῶσαι οἱ o, δὶς δὲ τόσως αἰεὶ Bergk, alii
alia   290 ανδρωηγεονται A, ἀνδρῶν γίνεται o, corr. West:
ἀνδρῶν· ἡγέονται Bekker (fort. recte)

293-94

οὐδὲ λέων αἰεὶ κρέα δαίνυται, ἀλλά μιν ἔμπης
καὶ κρατερόν περ ἐόνθ᾿ αἱρεῖ ἀμηχανίη.

294 ἐόντ᾿ αἴρει A

295-98

295 κωτίλῳ ἀνθρώπῳ σιγᾶν χαλεπώτατον ἄχθος,
φθεγγόμενος δ᾿ ἀδὴς οἷσι παρῇ πέλεται,

214

283-86

Do not take a step forward with trust in any of these townsmen and do not rely on their oaths and claims of friendship, not even if they want to offer Zeus, the greatest king of the immortals, as guarantor in their desire to establish trust.

287-92[1]

In a city so given to malicious faultfinding nothing pleases (the citizens); ... many are less well off. Now what the noble consider vices are deemed virtues by the base, and they rejoice in perverted ways (laws?). For respect is lost and shameless outrage, having overcome justice, prevails in all the land.

[1] Some join 287-88 (or 287-92) to 283-86. West suggests that something like 367-68 preceded 287-92.

293-94

Not even a lion always feasts on meat, but (sometimes), for all his strength, he is in the grip of helplessness.

295-98

For a chatterbox the hardest burden to bear is silence, but when he talks he is a bore to those present

ἐχθαίρουσι δὲ πάντες· ἀναγκαίη δ' ἐπίμειξις
ἀνδρὸς τοιούτου συμποσίῳ τελέθει.

296 ἀδαὴς codd., corr. Ahrens   μέλεται codd., corr.
Camerarius   297 πάντας A

299-300

οὐδεὶς λῇ φίλος εἶναι ἐπὴν κακὸν ἀνδρὶ γένηται,
οὐδ' ᾧ κ' ἐκ γαστρός, Κύρνε, μιᾶς γεγόνῃ.

299 οὐδεις δη A, corr. Sauppe: οὐδὲ θέλει O, οὐδ' ἐθέλει p
300 ωκ' A, expl. Bekker: ἦν o   γεγόνει o

301-302

πικρὸς καὶ γλυκὺς ἴσθι καὶ ἁρπαλέος καὶ
ἀπηνὴς
λάτρισι καὶ δμωσὶν γείτοσί τ' ἀγχιθύροις.

303-304

οὐ χρὴ κιγκλίζειν ἀγαθὸν βίον, ἀλλ' ἀτρεμίζειν,
τὸν δὲ κακὸν κινεῖν ἔστ' ἂν ἐς ὀρθὰ βάλῃς.

304 λάβῃς codd., corr. Stephanus

305-308

οἱ κακοὶ οὐ πάντως κακοὶ ἐκ γαστρὸς γεγόνασιν,
ἀλλ' ἄνδρεσσι κακοῖς συνθέμενοι φιλίην
ἔργα τε δείλ' ἔμαθον καὶ ἔπη δύσφημα καὶ
ὕβριν,
ἐλπόμενοι κείνους πάντα λέγειν ἔτυμα.

305 τοι A   πάντες A

and everyone dislikes him; not from choice does one
join such a man at a symposium.

299-300

No one wants to be a friend whenever hard times
befall a man, Cyrnus, even though he be born of the
same womb.

301-302

Be bitter and sweet, kind and harsh, to hired ser-
vants and slaves[1] and the neighbours next door.

[1] Or perhaps a contrast is intended between female and male
slaves.

303-304

You should leave the good life undisturbed and not
jerk it about, but you should stir up the bad life until
you set it straight.

305-308

The base are not always born base from the womb,
but by establishing friendship with base men they
learn bad actions, foul speech, and outrageous be-
haviour, in the belief that everything those friends
say is true.

217

309-12

ἐν μὲν συσσίτοισιν ἀνὴρ πεπνυμένος εἶναι,
310   πάντα δέ μιν λήθειν ὡς ἀπεόντα δοκοῖ,
εἰς δὲ φέροι τὰ γελοῖα· θύρηφι δὲ καρτερὸς εἴη,
γινώσκων ὀργὴν ἥντιν' ἕκαστος ἔχει.

309 εἶναι A, ἴσθι o   310 δοκει A, δόκει O, δόκει p, corr.
Geel

313-14

ἐν μὲν μαινομένοις μάλα μαίνομαι, ἐν δὲ δικαίοις
πάντων ἀνθρώπων εἰμὶ δικαιότατος.

315-18

315   πολλοί τοι πλουτοῦσι κακοί, ἀγαθοὶ δὲ πένονται·
ἀλλ' ἡμεῖς τούτοις οὐ διαμειψόμεθα
τῆς ἀρετῆς τὸν πλοῦτον, ἐπεὶ τὸ μὲν ἔμπεδον αἰεί,
χρήματα δ' ἀνθρώπων ἄλλοτε ἄλλος ἔχει.

Stob. 3.1.8 (Θεόγνιδος), vv. 315-18

319-22

Κύρν', ἀγαθὸς μὲν ἀνὴρ γνώμην ἔχει ἔμπεδον αἰεί,
320   τολμᾷ δ' ἔν τε κακοῖς κείμενος ἔν τ' ἀγαθοῖς·
εἰ δὲ θεὸς κακῷ ἀνδρὶ βίον καὶ πλοῦτον ὀπάσσῃ,
ἀφραίνων κακίην οὐ δύναται κατέχειν.

Stob. 3.37.3 (vv. 319-22)

320 ἔν τ' ἀγαθοῖς . . . ἔν τε κακοῖς p, Stob.   321 ὀπάσσει o,
ὀπάσει Stob. A

THEOGNIS

309-12

Among one's fellow diners let a man have his wits
about him, let everything seem to escape his notice
as if he were not there, and let him contribute jokes,
but when he's outside let him be firm,[1] recognizing
the temperament which each one has.

[1] The precise significance of καρτερός is uncertain. I take the
general meaning to be that when a man is in the company of others
he should pretend to share their views, but when he leaves he
should show the strength of his convictions. Editors disagree on
punctuation and on some readings. I have followed West.

313-14

Among those who rave I rave with the best,[1] but
among the level-headed I am the most level-headed
of all.

[1] An adaptation of a proverb attested elsewhere. See R.
Renehan, *CR* n.s. 13 (1963) 131-32.

315-18[1]

Many base men are rich and many noble men poor;
but we'll not take their wealth in exchange for vir-
tue, since this is always secure, while wealth belongs
now to one man, now to another.

[1] A version of Solon fr. 15. See ad loc. for the slight variations.

319-22

Cyrnus, a noble man has a judgement that is ever se-
cure and he endures whether his situation is bad or
good, but if the god gives a base man livelihood and
wealth, because of his foolishness he cannot restrain
his baseness.

323-28

μήποτ᾽ ἐπὶ σμικρᾷ προφάσει φίλον ἄνδρ᾽
    ἀπολέσσαι
πειθόμενος χαλεπῇ, Κύρνε, διαβολίῃ.
325   εἴ τις ἁμαρτωλῇσι φίλων ἐπὶ παντὶ χολοῖτο,
    οὔποτ᾽ ἂν ἀλλήλοις ἄρθμιοι οὐδὲ φίλοι
εἶεν· ἁμαρτωλαὶ γὰρ ἐν ἀνθρώποισιν ἕπονται
    θνητοῖς, Κύρνε· θεοὶ δ᾽ οὐκ ἐθέλουσι φέρειν.

323 ἀπολέσσης o   324 διαβολίη Bergk
325 ἁμαρτωλοῖσι o   χολῷτο codd., corr. Kalinka

329-30

καὶ βραδὺς εὔβουλος εἶλεν ταχὺν ἄνδρα διώκων,
330   Κύρνε, σὺν εὐθείῃ θεῶν δίκῃ ἀθανάτων.

331-32

ἥσυχος ὥσπερ ἐγὼ μέσσην ὁδὸν ἔρχεο ποσσίν,
    μηδετέροισι διδούς, Κύρνε, τὰ τῶν ἑτέρων.

Stob. 3.15.6 (vv. 331-32)
332 δίδου Stob.

332ab

οὐκ ἔστιν φεύγοντι φίλος καὶ πιστὸς ἑταῖρος·
    τῆς δὲ φυγῆς ἐστιν τοῦτ᾽ ἀνιηρότατον.

Clem. Strom. 6.8.1 (v. 332a)
332ab om. o

THEOGNIS

323-28

Cyrnus, never lose a friend on trivial grounds by malicious slander. If one were to be angry at the faults of friends on every occasion, there would never be mutual harmony or friendship; for in the world of humans faults accompany mortals,[1] Cyrnus, but the gods refuse to tolerate them.

[1] I.e., it is natural for mortals to make mistakes. Some connect θνητοῖς with ἀνθρώποισι and treat the verb as absolute, "among mortal men faults are inherent." The end result is the same.

329-30

With good planning, Cyrnus, even a slow man overtakes the swift,[1] aided by the direct justice of the immortal gods.

[1] Modeled on *Od.* 8.329-30.

331-32

Walk quietly along the middle of the road as I do, Cyrnus, giving to neither side what belongs to the other.

332ab[1]

An exile has no friend or loyal comrade, and this is the most painful part of exile.

[1] See 209-10 for a slightly different version.

ELEGIAC POETRY

333-34

μήποτε φεύγοντ᾽ ἄνδρα ἐπ᾽ ἐλπίδι, Κύρνε,
  φιλήσῃς·
οὐδὲ γὰρ οἴκαδε βὰς γίνεται αὐτὸς ἔτι.

334 αὐτὸς dub. Bergk

335-36

335 μηδὲν ἄγαν σπεύδειν· πάντων μέσ᾽ ἄριστα· καὶ
    οὕτως,
  Κύρν᾽, ἕξεις ἀρετήν, ἥν τε λαβεῖν χαλεπόν.

337-40

Ζεύς μοι τῶν τε φίλων δοίη τίσιν, οἵ με
  φιλεῦσιν,
  τῶν τ᾽ ἐχθρῶν μεῖζον, Κύρνε, δυνησόμενον.
χοὔτως ἂν δοκέοιμι μετ᾽ ἀνθρώπων θεὸς εἶναι,
340 εἴ μ᾽ ἀποτεισάμενον μοῖρα κίχῃ θανάτου.

340 ἀποτισ- codd., corr. Hiller

341-50

ἀλλά, Ζεῦ, τέλεσόν μοι, Ὀλύμπιε, καίριον εὐχήν·
  δὸς δέ μοι ἀντὶ κακῶν καί τι παθεῖν ἀγαθόν·
τεθναίην δ᾽, εἰ μή τι κακῶν ἄμπαυμα μεριμνέων
  εὑροίμην. δοίην δ᾽ ἀντ᾽ ἀνιῶν ἀνίας·
345 αἶσα γὰρ οὕτως ἐστί, τίσις δ᾽ οὐ φαίνεται ἡμῖν
  ἀνδρῶν οἳ τἀμὰ χρήματ᾽ ἔχουσι βίῃ
συλήσαντες· ἐγὼ δὲ κύων ἐπέρησα χαράδρην
  χειμάρρῳ ποταμῷ, πάντ᾽ ἀποσεισάμενος.

222

333-34

Never be the friend of an exile with a view to the future, Cyrnus; for not even when he comes home is he any longer the man he was.

335-36

Don't show too much zeal;[1] the middle course is the best of all.[2] This way, Cyrnus, you will have merit and that's hard to come by.

[1] Cf. 401.   [2] Cf. Phoc. fr. 12.

337-40

May Zeus grant that I requite the friends who love me and that I requite my enemies by having greater power in the future. This way I'd seem to be a god among men, if my allotted death overtakes me with requital paid.

341-50

Come, Olympian Zeus, fulfil my timely prayer; grant that I experience something good to be set against my ills, or may I die if I do not find some relief from the anxieties that plague me. May I give pain in return for pain; for that is my due. But there is no retribution in sight for me against the men who have my possessions which they robbed from me by force. I am like the dog that crossed the mountain stream in winter's flood and shook everything off.[1]

τῶν εἴη μέλαν αἷμα πιεῖν· ἐπί τ᾽ ἐσθλὸς ὄροιτο
350   δαίμων ὃς κατ᾽ ἐμὸν νοῦν τελέσειε τάδε.

347 δ᾽ ἐκνέων Cerri   348 ἀποτεισόμενος Murray

351-54

ἆ δειλὴ Πενίη, τί μένεις προλιποῦσα παρ᾽ ἄλλον
    ἄνδρ᾽ ἰέναι; μὴ δή μ᾽ οὐκ ἐθέλοντα φίλει,
ἀλλ᾽ ἴθι καὶ δόμον ἄλλον ἐποίχεο, μηδὲ μεθ᾽
        ἡμέων
    αἰεὶ δυστήνου τοῦδε βίου μέτεχε.

352 μὴ δή μ᾽ Bekker, μ᾽ ἢν δὴν A, τί δή μ᾽ O, τί δὲ δή μ᾽ p
φιλεῖς o

355-60
355   τόλμα, Κύρνε, κακοῖσιν, ἐπεὶ κἀσθλοῖσιν
        ἔχαιρες,
    εὖτέ σε καὶ τούτων μοῖρ᾽ ἐπέβαλλεν ἔχειν·
ὡς δέ περ ἐξ ἀγαθῶν ἔλαβες κακόν, ὣς δὲ καὶ
        αὖθις
    ἐκδῦναι πειρῶ θεοῖσιν ἐπευχόμενος.
μηδὲ λίην ἐπίφαινε· κακὸν δέ τε, Κύρν᾽,
        ἐπιφαίνειν·
360   παύρους κηδεμόνας σῆς κακότητος ἔχεις.

356 οὔτε A

224

May I drink their dark blood! And may an avenging
spirit rise up[2] so as to bring this to pass in accor-
dance with my intent.

[1] The meaning is obscure. West (*Studies* 153) assumes that
"the poet had a brief unpleasant experience which made him rid
himself of his property all at once," just as a dog shakes itself after
crossing a stream, but neither this nor any of the emendations pro-
posed is convincing. Perhaps there is an allusion to some fable.
[2] Or "may my guardian spirit watch over me."

351-54

O wretched Poverty,[1] why do you delay to leave me
and go to another man? Don't be attached to me
against my will, but go, visit another house, and
don't always share this miserable life with me.

[1] Cf. 649.

355-60

Put up with bad times, Cyrnus, since you rejoiced in
good times when fortune fell your way to have a
share of them. And just as you got bad luck after
good, so strive to emerge again by praying to the
gods. Don't let it show too much; it's bad to let it
show, Cyrnus. You have few sympathizers in your
plight.

361-62

ἀνδρός τοι κραδίη μινύθει μέγα πῆμα παθόντος,
Κύρν᾽· ἀποτεινυμένου δ᾽ αὔξεται ἐξοπίσω.

362 -τινν- ADI, -τιννν- OXD[1], corr. Hiller

363-64

εὖ κώτιλλε τὸν ἐχθρόν· ὅταν δ᾽ ὑποχείριος ἔλθῃ,
τεῖσαί μιν πρόφασιν μηδεμίαν θέμενος.

364 τῖσαί codd., corr. Hiller   νιν codd., corr. Sylburg

365-66

365   ἴσχε νόῳ, γλώσσῃ δὲ τὸ μείλιχον αἰὲν ἐπέστω·
δειλῶν τοι τελέθει καρδίη ὀξυτέρη.

365 νόον ο   γλώσσης A   ἐπέσθω ο

367-70

οὐ δύναμαι γνῶναι νόον ἀστῶν ὅντιν᾽ ἔχουσιν·
οὔτε γὰρ εὖ ἔρδων ἁνδάνω οὔτε κακῶς·
μωμεῦνται δέ με πολλοί, ὁμῶς κακοὶ ἠδὲ καὶ
ἐσθλοί·
370   μιμεῖσθαι δ᾽ οὐδεὶς τῶν ἀσόφων δύναται.

371-72

μή μ᾽ ἀέκοντα βίῃ κεντῶν ὑπ᾽ ἄμαξαν ἔλαυνε
εἰς φιλότητα λίην, Κύρνε, προσελκόμενος.

226

THEOGNIS

361-62

When a man has suffered a great disaster, Cyrnus, his heart[1] diminishes, but afterwards, when he gets revenge, it increases.

[1] Here almost in the sense of 'confidence' or 'self-assurance.'

363-64

Flatter your enemy well, but whenever you get the upper hand, pay him back, and don't give any pretext.

365-66

Hold back on your thoughts, but let there always be sweetness on your tongue; a heart that is too quick to show emotions is assuredly a mark of the base.[1]

[1] Cf. 1030.

367-70[1]

I can't understand the attitude the townsmen have, since neither by good actions nor by bad do I please them. Many, base and noble alike, find fault with me, but none of the fools can match me.

[1] 367-68 are virtually identical to 1184ab. Cf. also 24.

371-72

Don't ply the goad and drive me under the yoke by force against my will, Cyrnus, drawing me too far into friendship.[1]

[1] Perhaps to be understood in an erotic sense.

373-400

Ζεῦ φίλε, θαυμάζω σε· σὺ γὰρ πάντεσσιν
    ἀνάσσεις
  τιμὴν αὐτὸς ἔχων καὶ μεγάλην δύναμιν,
375 ἀνθρώπων δ' εὖ οἶσθα νόον καὶ θυμὸν ἑκάστου,
  σὸν δὲ κράτος πάντων ἔσθ' ὕπατον, βασιλεῦ·
πῶς δή σευ, Κρονίδη, τολμᾷ νόος ἄνδρας
    ἀλιτροὺς
  ἐν ταὐτῇ μοίρῃ τόν τε δίκαιον ἔχειν,
ἤν τ' ἐπὶ σωφροσύνην τρεφθῇ νόος ἤν τε πρὸς
    ὕβριν
380 ἀνθρώπων, ἀδίκοις ἔργμασι πειθομένων;
  οὐδέ τι κεκριμένον πρὸς δαίμονός ἐστι
    βροτοῖσιν,
  οὐδ' ὁδὸς ἥντιν' ἰὼν ἀθανάτοισιν ἅδοι;
. . . .
  ἔμπης δ' ὄλβον ἔχουσιν ἀπήμονα· τοὶ δ' ἀπὸ
    δειλῶν
  ἔργων ἴσχοντες θυμὸν ὅμως πενίην,
385 μητέρ' ἀμηχανίης, ἔλαβον τὰ δίκαια φιλεῦντες,
  ἥ τ' ἀνδρῶν παράγει θυμὸν ἐς ἀμπλακίην
βλάπτουσ' ἐν στήθεσσι φρένας, κρατερῆς ὑπ'
    ἀνάγκης·
  τολμᾷ δ' οὐκ ἐθέλων αἴσχεα πολλὰ φέρειν
χρημοσύνῃ εἴκων, ἣ δὴ κακὰ πολλὰ διδάσκει,
390 ψεύδεά τ' ἐξαπάτας τ' οὐλομένας τ' ἔριδας,
  ἄνδρα καὶ οὐκ ἐθέλοντα, κακὸν δέ οἱ οὐδὲν ἔοικεν·
  ἡ γὰρ καὶ χαλεπὴν τίκτει ἀμηχανίην.

373-400[1]

Dear Zeus, I'm surprised at you. You are lord over
all, you alone have great power and prestige, you
know well the mind and heart of every man, and
your rule, king, is the highest of all. How then, son of
Cronus, does your mind bear to hold sinners and the
just man in the same esteem, whether the mind of
men is disposed to prudent discretion or to wan-
ton outrage, when they yield to unjust acts? Have
no rules been set by divinity for mortals, is there
no path along which one can go and please the im-
mortals? [Some people rob and steal quite shame-
lessly,][2] but for all that they have a prosperity free
from harm, while others who refrain from wicked
deeds nevertheless get poverty, the mother of help-
lessness, despite their love of justice, poverty which
leads men's hearts astray to sinful action, impairing
their wits under the force of necessity. Against his
will a man brings himself to endure much that is
shameful. yielding to need which teaches many bad
ways, including lies, deceit, and deadly strife, even
though he is unwilling. There is no ill comparable to
need, for it gives birth to painful helplessness. In

ἐν πενίῃ δ᾽ ὅ τε δειλὸς ἀνὴρ ὅ τε πολλὸν ἀμείνων
    φαίνεται, εὖτ᾽ ἂν δὴ χρημοσύνη κατέχῃ·
395 τοῦ μὲν γὰρ τὰ δίκαια φρονεῖ νόος, οὗ τέ περ αἰεὶ
    ἰθεῖα γνώμη στήθεσιν ἐμπεφύῃ·
τοῦ δ᾽ αὖτ᾽ οὔτε κακοῖς ἕπεται νόος οὔτ᾽ ἀγαθοῖσιν.
    τὸν δ᾽ ἀγαθὸν τολμᾶν χρὴ τά τε καὶ τὰ φέρειν,
αἰδεῖσθαι δὲ φίλους φεύγειν τ᾽ ὀλεσήνορας ὅρκους
. . . .
400   ἐντράπελ᾽, ἀθανάτων μῆνιν ἀλευάμενον.

379 τερφθῇ codd., corr. Camerarius   post v. 382 lacunam
susp. Hudson-Williams   386 προάγει o   395 ουτε A
(expl. Bekker), οὔτε o   397 τῷ δ᾽ Bergk   ἔχεται dub.
West   post v. 399 lacunam susp. Bergk   400 ἐντράπελ᾽
A, ἔντρεπε δ᾽ o   αλευάμενον A, -άμενος o,   -όμενος I
(cf. 750)

401-406

μηδὲν ἄγαν σπεύδειν· καιρὸς δ᾽ ἐπὶ πᾶσιν
    ἄριστος
ἔργμασιν ἀνθρώπων. πολλάκι δ᾽ εἰς ἀρετὴν
σπεύδει ἀνὴρ κέρδος διζήμενος, ὅντινα δαίμων
    πρόφρων εἰς μεγάλην ἀμπλακίην παράγει,
405 καί οἱ ἔθηκε δοκεῖν, ἃ μὲν ᾖ κακά, ταῦτ᾽ ἀγάθ᾽
    εἶναι,
εὐμαρέως, ἃ δ᾽ ἂν ᾖ χρήσιμα, ταῦτα κακά.

THEOGNIS

poverty, whenever need takes hold, both the base
man and he who is much better are brought to light.
For the latter's mind has its thoughts on justice and
straight judgement is ever implanted in his breast,
while the former's mind does not go along with ei-
ther bad times or good.[3] The noble man must bring
himself to endure both, to respect his friends, and to
shun false oaths that bring ruin to men. . . . care-
fully, avoiding the wrath of the immortals.

[1] Editors regularly divide into two or more segments (usually
373-92, 393-400 or 373-80, 381-82, 383-92, 393-400), but I agree
with West (*Studies* 153-54) that it is best to assume one poem with
two lacunae.   [2] West's suggestion for the contents of the la-
cuna.   [3] It is difficult to obtain adequate sense from ἕπεται,
'follow' or 'accompany,' and there may well be textual corruption,
but perhaps the meaning is that the base man cannot accommo-
date himself to either bad or good fortune.

401-406

Don't show too much zeal.[1] Proper measure is best
in all men's actions.[2] Often a man is zealous of merit,
seeking gain, a man whom divinity on purpose leads
astray into great wickedness, and easily makes what
is bad seem to him to be good, and what is worth-
while seem to be bad.

[1] Cf. 335.   [2] Cf. Critias fr. 7.2.

231

407-408

φίλτατος ὢν ἥμαρτες· ἐγὼ δέ τοι αἴτιος οὐδέν,
ἀλλ᾽ αὐτὸς γνώμης οὐκ ἀγαθῆς ἔτυχες.

407 σοι A

409-10

οὐδένα θησαυρὸν παισὶν καταθήσῃ ἀμείνω
410   αἰδοῦς, ἥ τ᾽ ἀγαθοῖς ἀνδράσι, Κύρν᾽, ἔπεται.

409 παισὶ καταθήσει ΑΟ

411-12

οὐδενὸς ἀνθρώπων κακίων δοκεῖ εἶναι ἑταῖρος
ᾧ γνώμη θ᾽ ἕπεται, Κύρνε, καὶ ᾧ δύναμις.

411 οὐδενὸς et δοκει Α, μηδενὸς et δόκει ο

413-14

πίνων δ᾽ οὐχ οὕτως θωρήξομαι, οὐδέ με οἶνος
ἐξάγει, ὥστ᾽ εἰπεῖν δεινὸν ἔπος περὶ σοῦ.

413 μέ γ᾽ Ο, μετ᾽ Α, με ρ

415-18

415   οὐδέν᾽ ὁμοῖον ἐμοὶ δύναμαι διζήμενος εὑρεῖν
πιστὸν ἑταῖρον, ὅτῳ μή τις ἔνεστι δόλος·
ἐς βάσανον δ᾽ ἐλθὼν παρατρίβομαι ὥστε
      μολύβδῳ
χρυσός, ὑπερτερίης δ᾽ ἄμμιν ἔνεστι λόγος.

417 μολίβδῳ codd., corr. van Herwerden   418 νόος ο

232

407-408

You who are (were?) dearest[1] have slipped up. I'm not responsible, but it's you yourself who fell short of good judgement.

[1] Without a context the force of the participle ὤν cannot be determined. See van Groningen's commentary for the various possibilities.

409-10[1]

You will not leave your sons a better treasure than a sense of shame; it accompanies the noble, Cyrnus.

[1] Cf. the version in 1161-62.

411-12

A comrade who is endowed with judgement and power, Cyrnus, is held to be inferior to none.

413-14

I'll not so arm myself with wine, nor does wine lead me on, that I speak ill of you.

415-18[1]

I can find none like myself in my search for a loyal comrade, one in whom there is no deceit. When I come to the touchstone I am rubbed like gold beside lead,[2] and the balance[3] of superiority is in me.

[1] Cf. 1164e-h.   [2] The imagery is that of the touchstone used to distinguish pure gold from gold adulterated with lead. Cf. 450.   [3] I have hesitantly followed Hudson-Williams who explains λόγος as an accounting term, but various other explanations have been given.

419-20

πολλά με καὶ συνιέντα παρέρχεται· ἀλλ᾽ ὑπ᾽
    ἀνάγκης
420 σιγῶ, γινώσκων ἡμετέρην δύναμιν.

421-24

πολλοῖς ἀνθρώπων γλώσσῃ θύραι οὐκ ἐπίκεινται
    ἁρμόδιαι, καί σφιν πόλλ᾽ ἀμέλητα μέλει·
πολλάκι γὰρ τὸ κακὸν κατακείμενον ἔνδον
    ἄμεινον,
    ἐσθλὸν δ᾽ ἐξελθὸν λώιον ἢ τὸ κακόν.

Stob. 3.36.1 (vv. 421-24)

421-22 θύρα οὐκ ἐπίκειται ἁρμοδίη Stob.
422 ἀλάλητα Stob. (λαλητὰ Bücheler)   πέλει Stob. (prob.
West)   423 ἔνδοθεν ἦλθεν Stob.   424 ἐξελθὼν ΑΟ,
-εῖν Stob.

425-28

425 πάντων μὲν μὴ φῦναι ἐπιχθονίοισιν ἄριστον,
    μηδ᾽ ἐσιδεῖν αὐγὰς ὀξέος ἠελίου,
    φύντα δ᾽ ὅπως ὤκιστα πύλας Ἀίδαο περῆσαι
    καὶ κεῖσθαι πολλὴν γῆν ἐπαμησάμενον.

Sext. Emp. Pyrrh. hypot. 3.231; Stob. 4.52.30 (vv. 425-28)
Clem. Strom. 3.15.1; Suda i.374.27 Adler; Paroem. Gr. ii.148.4
(vv. 425-27)

    Stob. 4.52.22 (ἐκ τοῦ Ἀλκιδάμαντος Μουσείου); Cert. Hom.
et Hes. 78-79; alii (vv. 425 et 427)

    425 ἀρχὴν μὲν testes praeter Clem.   426 ἰδέειν Sext.,

419-20

I understand much that passes by, but I am forced
into silence, knowing my own power.

421-24

Many men do not have on their tongue a door that
closes with a well-adjusted fit, and they care about
much that does not concern them. Often it is better
for the bad to be stored away within and better for
the good to come out than the bad.

425-28

It is best of all for mortals not to be born and not to
look upon the rays of the piercing sun, but once born
it is best to pass the gates of Hades as quickly as pos-
sible and to lie under a large heap of earth.[1]

[1] This pessimistic outlook appears in many authors and be-
came proverbial. Only some of the sources name Theognis as the
author. Since a number cite only the hexameters and since the
pentameters add nothing new, it can be safely assumed that the
poet has formed an elegy out of two pre-existing hexameters.

ἐπιδεῖν *Paroem.*, ἐσορᾶν *Clem.*   ὀξέας *Stob.*   427 ὅμως
Cert., *Paroem.*   428 γῆν ἀπαμησάμενον *Stob.*, γαῖαν
ἐφεσσάμενον *Sext.*

429-38

φῦσαι καὶ θρέψαι ῥᾷον βροτὸν ἢ φρένας ἐσθλὰς
430 ἐνθέμεν· οὐδείς πω τοῦτό γ' ἐπεφράσατο,
ᾧ τις σώφρον' ἔθηκε τὸν ἄφρονα κἀκ κακοῦ
ἐσθλόν.
εἰ δ' Ἀσκληπιάδαις τοῦτό γ' ἔδωκε θεός,
ἰᾶσθαι κακότητα καὶ ἀτηρὰς φρένας ἀνδρῶν,
πολλοὺς ἂν μισθοὺς καὶ μεγάλους ἔφερον.
435 εἰ δ' ἦν ποιητόν τε καὶ ἔνθετον ἀνδρὶ νόημα,
οὔποτ' ἂν ἐξ ἀγαθοῦ πατρὸς ἔγεντο κακός,
πειθόμενος μύθοισι σαόφροσιν· ἀλλὰ διδάσκων
οὔποτε ποιήσει τὸν κακὸν ἄνδρ' ἀγαθόν.

Anon. P. Oxy. ined. (vv. 432-33)
Dio Chrys. 1.8; Plut. *quaest. Plat.* 3.1000c (v. 432)
Plat. *Meno* 95e confuse; P. Berol. 12310 (ostr.), vv. 434-38

431 ὅτις A, ὅστις *o*, corr. Bergk   432 οὐδ' O, testes
438 ποιήσεις *o*, Plato, -ης ostr.

439-40

νήπιος, ὃς τὸν ἐμὸν μὲν ἔχει νόον ἐν φυλακῇσιν,
440 τῶν δ' αὐτοῦ †κίδιον† οὐδὲν ἐπιστρέφεται.

440 τὸν *o*   κῐδιον A, κίδιον O, ἴδιον *p*, ἰδίων Jacobs

441-46

οὐδεὶς γὰρ πάντ' ἐστὶ πανόλβιος· ἀλλ' ὁ μὲν
ἐσθλὸς
τολμᾷ ἔχων τὸ κακὸν κοὐκ ἐπίδηλος ὅμως,

THEOGNIS

429-38

It is easier to beget and rear a man than to put good sense in him. No one has yet devised a means whereby one has made the fool wise and a noble man out of one who is base. If the god had granted this power to the Asclepiads,[1] to cure men's baseness and muddled wits, they would be earning many a handsome fee. And if good sense could be made and placed in a man, there would never be a base son of a noble father, since he would heed words of wisdom. But you will never make the base man noble through teaching.

[1] Literally, 'descendants of Asclepius,' the god of healing, but here simply 'physicians.'

439-40

Foolish is he who stands guard over my intentions, but pays no heed to his own (?).[1]

[1] For a defence of Jacobs' emendation see R. Renehan, *HSCP* 87 (1983) 23-24.

441-46[1]

For no one is wholly prosperous in every respect. The noble man puts up with bad luck and for all that

δειλὸς δ' οὔτ' ἀγαθοῖσιν ἐπίσταται οὔτε κακοῖσιν
θυμὸν ἔχων μίμνειν. ἀθανάτων δὲ δόσεις
445 παντοῖαι θνητοῖσιν ἐπέρχοντ'· ἀλλ' ἐπιτολμᾶν
χρὴ δῶρ' ἀθανάτων οἷα διδοῦσιν ἔχειν.

441 γὰρ A, τοι p, om. O   442 ἔχειν o   ὁμῶς A
443 οὔτε κακοῖσιν . . . οὔτ' ἀγαθοῖσιν o   444 δὲ O, τε A et p

447-52

εἴ μ' ἐθέλεις πλύνειν, κεφαλῆς ἀμίαντον ἀπ'
    ἄκρης
    αἰεὶ λευκὸν ὕδωρ ῥεύσεται ἡμετέρης,
εὑρήσεις δέ με πᾶσιν ἐπ' ἔργμασιν ὥσπερ
    ἄπεφθον
450   χρυσόν, ἐρυθρὸν ἰδεῖν τριβόμενον βασάνῳ,
τοῦ χροιῆς καθύπερθε μέλας οὐχ ἅπτεται ἰὸς
    οὐδ' εὐρώς, αἰεὶ δ' ἄνθος ἔχει καθαρόν.

453-56

ὤνθρωπ', εἰ γνώμης ἔλαχες μέρος ὥσπερ ἀνοίης
    καὶ σώφρων οὕτως ὥσπερ ἄφρων ἐγένου,
455 πολλοῖς ἂν ζηλωτὸς ἐφαίνεο τῶνδε πολιτῶν
    οὕτως ὥσπερ νῦν οὐδενὸς ἄξιος εἶ.

457-60

οὔτοι σύμφορόν ἐστι γυνὴ νέα ἀνδρὶ γέροντι·
    οὐ γὰρ πηδαλίῳ πείθεται ὡς ἄκατος,

238

makes no show of it, but the base man does not know how to control his emotions and stand firm in good or in bad times. The gifts of the gods come to mortals in all forms, but we must endure to possess their gifts, whatever it is they give.

[1] Cf. 1162a-f.

447-52

If you want to rinse me, the water will always flow unpolluted and clear from the top of my head, and you will find that in every activity I am like refined gold, yellow to the view when rubbed by the touchstone.[1] Above its surface no dark verdigris or mould takes hold, and it keeps its sheen ever pure.

[1] Cf. 417 and D. E. Eichholz, *Theophrastus, De Lapidibus* (Oxford 1965) 118: "The gold to be tested was rubbed on a touchstone already marked by a streak made by gold known to be pure. The new streak could thus be compared with the original one, and the relative impurity of the specimen under test detected by the different appearance of the streak left by it on the stone."

453-56

If you, sir, had been allotted as much judgement as stupidity and if you had been as sensible as you are foolish, you would seem to many of these citizens to be as deserving of admiration as you are now worth nothing.

457-60

A young wife is not suitable for a husband who is old. For she is like a boat that does not obey the rudder,

οὐδ' ἄγκυραι ἔχουσιν· ἀπορρήξασα δὲ δεσμὰ
460   πολλάκις ἐκ νυκτῶν ἄλλον ἔχει λιμένα.

Ath. 13.560a; Stob. 4.22.110 (vv. 457-60)
Clem. *Strom.* 6.14.5 (vv. 457-58)

457 σύμφορόν ἐστι Ath., Stob.: σύμφρον ἔνεστι fere codd.
Theogn.: χρήσιμόν ἐστι Clem.   νέα γυνὴ Clem.
459 ἄγκυραν Ath.

461-62

μήποτ' ἐπ' ἀπρήκτοισι νόον ἔχε μηδὲ μενοίνα
χρήμασι· τῶν ἄνυσις γίνεται οὐδεμία.

463-64

εὐμαρέως τοι χρῆμα θεοὶ δόσαν οὔτε τι δειλὸν
οὔτ' ἀγαθόν· χαλεπῷ δ' ἔργματι κῦδος ἔπι.

464 ἔπι A p.c., ἔπει a.c., ἔχει o

465-66

465   ἀμφ' ἀρετῇ τρίβου, καί τοι τὰ δίκαια φίλ' ἔστω,
μηδέ σε νικάτω κέρδος ὅ τ' αἰσχρὸν ἔῃ.

467-96

μηδένα τῶνδ' ἀέκοντα μένειν κατέρυκε παρ' ἡμῖν,
μηδὲ θύραζε κέλευ' οὐκ ἐθέλοντ' ἰέναι·
μηδ' εὕδοντ' ἐπέγειρε, Σιμωνίδη, ὅντιν' ἂν ἡμῶν
470   θωρηχθέντ' οἴνῳ μαλθακὸς ὕπνος ἕλῃ,

nor do the anchors hold. She breaks her moorings
and often finds another harbour at night.[1]

[1] For a close imitation of this passage cf. Theophilus fr. 6 K.-A.

461-62

Never set your mind and heart on things that can't
be done; there is nothing to be gained.[1]

[1] Literally, "there is no accomplishment of them."

463-64

The gods do not give anything readily, either bad or
good; but in hard work there is glory.[1]

[1] The meaning of the couplet is obscure and various emenda-
tions, none convincing, have been proposed in 463.

465-66

Wear yourself out in the pursuit of excellence, let
justice be dear to you, and don't let any gain that is
shameful win you over.

467-96

Don't hold back anyone of these so that he remain
with us against his will, don't tell anyone to depart
who does not want to, don't waken from his sleep,
Simonides, anyone of us who, fortified with wine,
has been overcome by gentle sleep, and don't tell

ELEGIAC POETRY

μηδὲ τὸν ἀγρυπνέοντα κέλευ᾽ ἀέκοντα καθεύδειν·
πᾶν γὰρ ἀναγκαῖον χρῆμ᾽ ἀνιηρὸν ἔφυ.
τῷ πίνειν δ᾽ ἐθέλοντι παρασταδὸν οἰνοχοείτω·
οὐ πάσας νύκτας γίνεται ἀβρὰ παθεῖν.
475 αὐτὰρ ἐγώ, μέτρον γὰρ ἔχω μελιηδέος οἴνου,
ὕπνου λυσικάκου μνήσομαι οἴκαδ᾽ ἰών.
ἥκω δ᾽ ὡς οἶνος χαριέστατος ἀνδρὶ πεπόσθαι·
οὔτε τι γὰρ νήφων οὔτε λίην μεθύων·
ὃς δ᾽ ἂν ὑπερβάλλῃ πόσιος μέτρον, οὐκέτι κεῖνος
480 τῆς αὑτοῦ γλώσσης καρτερὸς οὐδὲ νόου,
μυθεῖται δ᾽ ἀπάλαμνα, τὰ νήφοσι γίνεται αἰσχρά,
αἰδεῖται δ᾽ ἔρδων οὐδὲν ὅταν μεθύῃ,
τὸ πρὶν ἐὼν σώφρων, τότε νήπιος. ἀλλὰ σὺ ταῦτα
γινώσκων μὴ πῖν᾽ οἶνον ὑπερβολάδην,
485 ἀλλ᾽ ἢ πρὶν μεθύειν ὑπανίστασο—μή σε βιάσθω
γαστὴρ ὥστε κακὸν λάτριν ἐφημέριον—
ἢ παρεὼν μὴ πῖνε. σὺ δ᾽ "ἔγχεε·" τοῦτο μάταιον
κωτίλλεις αἰεί· τούνεκά τοι μεθύεις·
ἡ μὲν γὰρ φέρεται φιλοτήσιος, ἡ δὲ πρόκειται,
490 τὴν δὲ θεοῖς σπένδεις, τὴν δ᾽ ἐπὶ χειρὸς ἔχεις,
ἀρνεῖσθαι δ᾽ οὐκ οἶδας. ἀνίκητος δέ τοι οὗτος,
ὃς πολλὰς πίνων μή τι μάταιον ἐρεῖ.
ὑμεῖς δ᾽ εὖ μυθεῖσθε παρὰ κρητῆρι μένοντες,
ἀλλήλων ἔριδας δὴν ἀπερυκόμενοι,
495 εἰς τὸ μέσον φωνεῦντες, ὁμῶς ἑνὶ καὶ συνάπασιν·
χοὔτως συμπόσιον γίνεται οὐκ ἄχαρι.

Pherecrates fr. 162.11-12 K.-A. (vv. 467 + 469 -Σιμωνίδη)

242

one who's wide awake to sleep against his will. All force is disagreeable.[1] And let (a slave) stand by and pour wine for him who wants to drink; it's not possible to have a good time every night. But I'll go home—I've had my limit of honey-sweet wine— and I'll take thought for sleep that brings release from ills. I've reached the stage where the consumption of wine is most pleasant for a man, since I am neither sober nor too drunk. Whoever exceeds his limit of drink is no longer in command of his tongue or his mind; he says wild things which are disgraceful in the eyes of the sober, and he's not ashamed of anything he does when he's drunk. Formerly he was sensible, but then he's a fool. Aware of this, don't drink wine to excess, but either rise before you're drunk—don't let your belly overpower you as if you were a wretched hired help for the day—or stay without drinking. But you say "fill it up!" This is always your idle chatter; that's why you get drunk. One cup is a toast to friendship, another is set before you, another you offer as a libation to the gods, another you have as a penalty,[2] and you don't know how to say no. That man is truly the champion who after drinking many cups will say nothing foolish. If you stay by the mixing bowl, make good conversation, long avoiding quarrels with one another and speaking openly[3] to one and all alike. In this way a symposium turns out to be not half bad.

[1] This verse, with $\pi\rho\hat{a}\gamma\mu'$ in place of $\chi\rho\hat{\eta}\mu'$, is cited by Arist. *Metaph.* 4.5.1015a28 and assigned to Euenus (fr. 8). Because of this and the presence of Simonides, who appears in 667-82 and

Ath. 10.428c (vv. 477-86)
Stob. 3.18.13 (vv. 479-86)

467 μηδένα μήτ᾽ Pherecr.   469 μήθ᾽ Pherecr.
476 λησικάκου I p.c.   477 ἥκω Ath., ἥξω codd.
478 οὔτε τι νήφων εἴμ᾽ οὔτε λίαν μεθύων Ath., οὔτε τι γὰρ νήφω
οὔτε λίην μεθύω codd.: ut supra Friedemann   479 οὐκέτ᾽
ἐκεῖνος Ath., Stob.   492 πολλὸν A   494 ἐριδος A
495 συνάπατι A (συνάπαντι Kalinka)

497-98

ἄφρονος ἀνδρὸς ὁμῶς καὶ σώφρονος οἶνος, ὅταν δὴ
    πίνῃ ὑπὲρ μέτρον, κοῦφον ἔθηκε νόον.

Stob. 3.18.14-16 (vv. 497-508)

499-502

ἐν πυρὶ μὲν χρυσόν τε καὶ ἄργυρον ἴδριες ἄνδρες
500   γινώσκουσ᾽, ἀνδρὸς δ᾽ οἶνος ἔδειξε νόον,
καὶ μάλα περ πινυτοῦ, τὸν ὑπὲρ μέτρον ἤρατο
    πίνων,
ὥστε καταισχῦναι καὶ πρὶν ἐόντα σοφόν.

500 (ἀνδρὸς—νόον) Ath. 2.37e
501-502 κακότητα δὲ πᾶσαν ἐλέγχει, ὥστε καταισχύνειν
καὶ τὸν ἐόντα σοφόν Stob.

503-508

οἰνοβαρέω κεφαλήν, Ὀνομάκριτε, καί με βιᾶται
    οἶνος, ἀτὰρ γνώμης οὐκέτ᾽ ἐγὼ ταμίης
505   ἡμετέρης, τὸ δὲ δῶμα περιτρέχει. ἀλλ᾽ ἄγ᾽
    ἀναστὰς
πειρηθῶ, μή πως καὶ πόδας οἶνος ἔχει

244

1341-50, some editors, perhaps rightly, attribute all three poems to Euenus. The identity of Simonides is unknown.   [2] For a breach of conduct, but the meaning of the Greek is unclear.
[3] Or "in common."

497-98

The mind of the foolish and sensible man alike is made light-headed, whenever he drinks beyond his limit.

499-502

Experts recognize gold and silver by fire, but wine reveals the mind of a man, even though he is very prudent, if he takes and drinks it beyond his limit, so that it puts to shame even one who[1] was formerly wise.

[1] Or "a mind which."

503-508

My head is heavy with wine, Onomacritus,[1] it over-powers me, I am no longer the manager of my judgement, and the room is going round and round. But, come, let me stand and find out whether the wine has hold of my feet as well as the mind

καὶ νόον ἐν στήθεσσι· δέδοικα δὲ μή τι μάταιον
ἔρξω θωρηχθεὶς καὶ μέγ᾽ ὄνειδος ἔχω.

506 πειρήσω Stob.　　ἔχῃ p, Stob. SA

509-10

οἶνος πινόμενος πουλὺς κακόν· ἢν δέ τις αὐτὸν
510　　πίνῃ ἐπισταμένως, οὐ κακὸν ἀλλ᾽ ἀγαθόν.

511-22

ἦλθες δή, Κλεάριστε, βαθὺν διὰ πόντον ἀνύσσας
512　　ἐνθάδ᾽ ἐπ᾽ οὐδὲν ἔχοντ᾽, ὦ τάλαν, οὐδὲν ἔχων·
515　　τῶν δ᾽ ὄντων τἄριστα παρέξομεν· ἢν δέ τις ἔλθῃ
　　σεῦ φίλος ὤν, κατάκεισ᾽ ὡς φιλότητος ἔχεις.
οὔτε τι τῶν ὄντων ἀποθήσομαι, οὔτε τι μείζω
　　σῆς ἕνεκα ξενίης ἄλλοθεν οἰσόμεθα.
513　　νηός τοι πλευρῇσιν ὑπὸ ζυγὰ θήσομεν ἡμεῖς,
514　　Κλεάρισθ᾽, οἷ᾽ ἔχομεν χοῖα διδοῦσι θεοί.
ἢν δέ τις εἰρωτᾷ τὸν ἐμὸν βίον, ὧδέ οἱ εἰπεῖν·
520　　"ὡς εὖ μὲν χαλεπῶς, ὡς χαλεπῶς δὲ μάλ᾽ εὖ,
ὥσθ᾽ ἕνα μὲν ξεῖνον πατρώιον οὐκ ἀπολείπειν,
　　ξείνια δὲ πλεόνεσσ᾽ οὐ δυνατὸς παρέχειν."

517 μεῖζον o　　　513-14 transposuit West　　　519 τί σ᾽
van Herwerden

246

within me. I'm afraid that in my fortified state I may do something foolish and bring great disgrace upon me.

1 Identity unknown.

509-10

Wine drunk in large quantities is a bane, but if one drinks it wisely, it is not a bane but a blessing.[1]

1 A slightly different version occurs at 211-12. See West's edition for five additional sources and for variant readings, none of which alters the sense.

511-22

You've crossed the deep sea, Clearistus,[1] and come here penniless, poor fellow, to one who's penniless. But I'll provide the best of what there is, and if any friend of yours comes along, recline as suits your degree of friendship.[2] I'll not hold back anything of what I have nor bring in more from elsewhere to entertain you. I'll stow under the benches at the side of your ship, Clearistus, such as I have and the gods provide. And if anyone asks how I live, reply to him as follows: "Poorly by good standards, but quite well by poor standards,[3] and so he doesn't fail one friend of the family, but is unable to offer entertainment to more."

1 Identity unknown. 2 For the significance of seating arrangements see Plato *Symp*. 222e. 3 More literally, "compared to one who lives well, he lives poorly, but compared to one who lives poorly, he lives quite well," ζῇ being understood from βίον with each adverb.

523-26

οὐ σὲ μάτην, ὦ Πλοῦτε, βροτοὶ τιμῶσι μάλιστα·
  ἦ γὰρ ῥηϊδίως τὴν κακότητα φέρεις.
525 καὶ γάρ τοι πλοῦτον μὲν ἔχειν ἀγαθοῖσιν ἔοικεν,
  ἡ πενίη δὲ κακῷ σύμφορος ἀνδρὶ φέρειν.

Stob. 4.31.1 (vv. 523-24)
Stob. 4.31.3a (vv. 525-26)

523 θεοὶ Stob.   524 σὺ γὰρ Stob.   525 ἔδωκεν Stob.
526 σοφῷ σύμφορον Stob.

527-28

ὦ μοι ἐγὼν ἥβης καὶ γήραος οὐλομένοιο,
  τοῦ μὲν ἐπερχομένου, τῆς δ' ἀπονισομένης.

Stob. 4.50.44; Anth. Pal. 9.118 (Βησαντίνου), vv. 527-28

528 ἀπονισ(σ)αμένης Stob. A, Anth. Pal., ἀπανισταμένης p

529-30

οὐδέ τινα προύδωκα φίλον καὶ πιστὸν ἑταῖρον,
530   οὐδ' ἐν ἐμῇ ψυχῇ δούλιον οὐδὲν ἔνι.

529 οὐδένα A, οὔτε τινα et 530 οὔτ' p

531-34

αἰεί μοι φίλον ἦτορ ἰαίνεται, ὁππότ' ἀκούσω
  αὐλῶν φθεγγομένων ἱμερόεσσαν ὄπα·
χαίρω δ' εὖ πίνων καὶ ὑπ' αὐλητῆρος ἀείδων,
  χαίρω δ' εὔφθογγον χερσὶ λύρην ὀχέων.

533 fin. ἀκούων codd. ex 531, corr. Pierson

523-26

Not to no purpose, Wealth, do mortals honour you
most of all, for you easily put up with baseness.[1]
In fact, it is fitting for the noble to have wealth,
whereas poverty is appropriate for the base man to
endure.

[1] The poet seems to be saying sarcastically that Wealth is honoured because he does not mind conferring his benefits on the base. The second couplet then provides a correction. The majority of editors treat the couplets as separate.

527-28

Alas for youth and alas for cursed old age, the latter
because it comes on, the former because it leaves.

529-30

I have not betrayed any friend or loyal comrade, and
there's nothing of the slave[1] in my soul.

[1] The poet means that a slave would feel no obligation to be loyal.

531-34

My heart is always warmed whenever I hear the
pipes sounding a lovely voice. I delight in drinking
well and singing to the piper's accompaniment, and
I delight in holding in my hands the tuneful lyre.[1]

[1] Some editors treat the couplets as separate.

535-38

535   οὔποτε δουλείη κεφαλὴ ἰθεῖα πέφυκεν,
       ἀλλ' αἰεὶ σκολιή, καὐχένα λοξὸν ἔχει.
       οὔτε γὰρ ἐκ σκίλλης ῥόδα φύεται οὐδ' ὑάκινθος,
       οὔτε ποτ' ἐκ δούλης τέκνον ἐλευθέριον.

Philo, *omnis probus liber* 155 (vi.43.11 C.-W.); Stob. 4.19.36
(vv. 535-36)

535 εὐθεῖα ο, testes   537-38 οὔθ' . . . οὐδέ codd., οὐδ' . . . οὔτε
Bekker

539-40

       οὗτος ἀνήρ, φίλε Κύρνε, πέδας χαλκεύεται αὑτῷ,
540   εἰ μὴ ἐμὴν γνώμην ἐξαπατῶσι θεοί.

539 οὗτις ο

541-42

       δειμαίνω μὴ τήνδε πόλιν, Πολυπαΐδη, ὕβρις
       ἤ περ Κενταύρους ὠμοφάγους ὀλέσῃ.

542 ὀλέσῃ p, ὄλεσε(ν) ΑΟ

543-46

       χρή με παρὰ στάθμην καὶ γνώμονα τήνδε
             δικάσσαι,
       Κύρνε, δίκην, ἶσόν τ' ἀμφοτέροισι δόμεν,
545   μάντεσί τ' οἰωνοῖς τε καὶ αἰθομένοις ἱεροῖσιν,
       ὄφρα μὴ ἀμπλακίης αἰσχρὸν ὄνειδος ἔχω.

THEOGNIS

535-38

Never is a slave's head by nature straight, but it is always crooked, and he holds his neck aslant. For from a squill grow neither roses nor hyacinth and the child of a slave mother is never free in spirit.

539-40

This man, dear Cyrnus, is forging fetters for himself, unless the gods deceive my judgement.[1]

[1] West suggests that the couplet was preceded by 1101-1102.

541-42

I'm afraid, Polypaïdes, that lawlessness will destroy this city,[1] just as it did the Centaurs, eaters of raw flesh.[2]

[1] Cf. 1103-1104. [2] Not a normal attribute of the Centaurs, but it is said of the Centaur Pholus in Apollodorus 2.5.4.

543-46

I must render this judgement by rule and square, Cyrnus, and give an equal share to both sides, with the aid of seers, auguries, and burning sacrifices, so that I not incur the shameful reproach of having erred.[1]

[1] Some editors treat the couplets as separate (the second being incomplete) and some assume a lacuna after 544.

547-48

μηδένα πω κακότητι βιάζεο· τῷ δὲ δικαίῳ
τῆς εὐεργεσίης οὐδὲν ἀρειότερον.

549-54

ἄγγελος ἄφθογγος πόλεμον πολύδακρυν ἐγείρει,
550   Κύρν᾽, ἀπὸ τηλαυγέος φαινόμενος σκοπιῆς.
ἀλλ᾽ ἵπποις ἔμβαλλε ταχυπτέρνοισι χαλινούς·
    δῄων γάρ σφ᾽ ἀνδρῶν ἀντιάσειν δοκέω.
οὐ πολλὸν τὸ μεσηγύ· διαπρήξουσι κέλευθον,
    εἰ μὴ ἐμὴν γνώμην ἐξαπατῶσι θεοί.

553 διαπρήσσουσι Par. 2883, prob. West ("participium video")

555-60

555   χρὴ τολμᾶν χαλεποῖσιν ἐν ἄλγεσι κείμενον ἄνδρα,
    πρός τε θεῶν αἰτεῖν ἔκλυσιν ἀθανάτων.
φράζεο δ᾽—ὁ κλῆρός τοι ἐπὶ ξυροῦ ἵσταται ἀκμῆς·
    ἄλλοτε πόλλ᾽ ἕξεις, ἄλλοτε παυρότερα—
ὥστε σε μήτε λίην ἀφνεὸν κτεάτεσσι γενέσθαι,
560   μήτε σέ γ᾽ ἐς πολλὴν χρημοσύνην ἐλάσαι.

557 κίνδυνός codd., κλῆρός tentavit West (δ᾽ ὁ om. o)
559 λῷστά σε Geel (plene interpungens post 558)

---

[1] Text and translation highly uncertain. See West, *Studies* 156. Except for West, editors treat 555-56, which are almost identical to 1178ab, as a separate couplet, and some assume three separate couplets.

THEOGNIS

547-48

Don't at all apply force on anyone by base means;
nothing is better for the just man than a kindly act.[1]

[1] West punctuates differently, taking τῷ δὲ δικαίῳ with what
precedes, but "don't apply force by base means, but by justice"
gives an unlikely combination.

549-54

The voiceless messenger,[1] shining from the far-
gleaming lookout, is rousing tearful war, Cyrnus.
Come, place bits on the swift-heeled horses, for I
think they'll meet the enemy. The distance between
is not great; they'll get there,[2] unless the gods de-
ceive my judgement.

[1] A beacon fire.   [2] West (*Studies* 156) considers this "in-
ane" and prefers the dative διαπρήσσουσι, "I think they will
meet the foe—the distance is not far—already on the way," but
the presence of both genitive and dative with ἀντιάσειν in the
same sentence is intolerably harsh, even though both construc-
tions are found. West, following Hudson-Williams, treats 554 as
inserted from 540 to replace a lost verse, and this is highly prob-
able.

555-60

The man laid low in painful hardships must endure
and ask the immortal gods for release. Take heed—
your estate is balanced on a razor's edge; at one time
you will have much, at another less—so as not to be-
come exceedingly rich in possessions nor to enter
into great poverty.[1]

253

561-62

εἴη μοι τὰ μὲν αὐτὸν ἔχειν, τὰ δὲ πόλλ' ἐπιδοῦναι
χρήματα τῶν ἐχθρῶν τοῖσι φίλοισιν ἔχειν.

563-66

κεκλῆσθαι δ' ἐς δαῖτα, παρέζεσθαι δὲ παρ' ἐσθλὸν
ἄνδρα χρεὼν σοφίην πᾶσαν ἐπιστάμενον.
565   τοῦ συνιεῖν, ὁπόταν τι λέγῃ σοφόν, ὄφρα
        διδαχθῇς,
        καὶ τοῦτ' εἰς οἶκον κέρδος ἔχων ἀπίῃς.

567-70

ἥβῃ τερπόμενος παίζω· δηρὸν γὰρ ἔνερθεν
γῆς ὀλέσας ψυχὴν κείσομαι ὥστε λίθος
ἄφθογγος, λείψω δ' ἐρατὸν φάος ἠελίοιο·
570   ἔμπης δ' ἐσθλὸς ἐὼν ὄψομαι οὐδὲν ἔτι.

571-72

δόξα μὲν ἀνθρώποισι κακὸν μέγα, πεῖρα δ'
        ἄριστον·
πολλοὶ ἀπείρητοι δόξαν ἔχουσ' ἀγαθῶν.

573-74

εὖ ἔρδων εὖ πάσχε· τί κ' ἄγγελον ἄλλον ἰάλλοις;
τῆς εὐεργεσίης ῥῃδίη ἀγγελίη.

573 πράττε ο

254

THEOGNIS

561-62

May I have some of my enemies' property for myself
and hand over most of theirs to my friends to keep.

563-66

You should get invited to dinner and sit beside a
man of worth who knows every kind of skill. When-
ever he says something clever, take note of it so that
you may learn and go home with this as profit.

567-70

I have fun, delighting in my youth; for I will lie a long
time beneath the earth, mute as a stone, when my
life is over and I leave the sun's lovely light. For all
my merit I'll have sight no more.

571-72

(Mere) reputation is a great evil for men; trial is
best. Many who have not been tested have a reputa-
tion for merit.[1]

[1] Repeated at 1104ab. West takes δόξα to mean "hope or ex-
pectation" and ἀγαθῶν "good things to come," translating: "Vain
fantasy's no good, experience is the thing. Many imagine joys
they've never known."

573-74

Experience good by doing good. Why would you
send another messenger? News of a good deed trav-
els easily.

575-76

575 οἵ με φίλοι προδιδοῦσιν, ἐπεὶ τόν γ' ἐχθρὸν
ἀλεῦμαι
ὥστε κυβερνήτης χοιράδας εἰναλίας.

577-78

"ῥήιον ἐξ ἀγαθοῦ θεῖναι κακὸν ἢ 'κ κακοῦ
ἐσθλόν."
—μή με δίδασκ'· οὔτοι τηλίκος εἰμὶ μαθεῖν.

577 ῥηΐδιον A, ῥήδιον o, corr. Schneider

579-82

ἐχθαίρω κακὸν ἄνδρα, καλυψαμένη δὲ πάρειμι,
580 σμικρῆς ὄρνιθος κοῦφον ἔχουσα νόον·
ἐχθαίρω δὲ γυναῖκα περίδρομον, ἄνδρα τε
μάργον,
ὃς τὴν ἀλλοτρίην βούλετ' ἄρουραν ἀροῦν.

580 μικρῆς o   ἔχοντα West

583-84

ἀλλὰ τὰ μὲν προβέβηκεν, ἀμήχανόν ἐστι
γενέσθαι
ἀργά· τὰ δ' ἐξοπίσω, τῶν φυλακὴ μελέτω.

584 ἔργα codd., corr. Eldick

THEOGNIS

575-76

It's my friends who betray me, for I avoid my enemy
just as the helmsman avoids reefs in the sea.[1]

[1] Well paraphrased by Hudson-Williams: "'It is my friends
who betray me; for I can easily keep off my declared enemies, just
as a pilot can keep his ship clear of the reefs that stand out above
the surface of the sea.' A false friend is like a hidden reef."

577-78

"It is easier to make bad from good than good from
bad." —Don't try to teach me; I'm too old to learn.[1]

[1] The pentameter seems to be a sarcastic reply to a well-known
saying.

579-82

I hate a scoundrel and I veil myself as I pass by, with
as little thought for him as a small bird would have.[1]
And I hate a woman who runs around, and a lecher
who wants to plough a field belonging to another.[2]

[1] Translation uncertain. With West's emendation the verse de-
scribes the man, "a creature with a small bird's empty brains," as
he translates it.   [2] Some editors treat the couplets as sepa-
rate and some combine them with 583-84. Attempts have been
made to identify the speaker with figures from mythology or with
a personification such as Tyche, Dike etc.

583-84

But what is past cannot be undone; let precaution
against what is to come be your concern.

585-90

585 πᾶσίν τοι κίνδυνος ἐπ' ἔργμασιν, οὐδέ τις οἶδεν
     πῇ σχήσειν μέλλει πρήγματος ἀρχομένου·
     ἀλλ' ὁ μὲν εὐδοκιμεῖν πειρώμενος οὐ προνοήσας
     εἰς μεγάλην ἄτην καὶ χαλεπὴν ἔπεσεν·
     τῷ δὲ κακῶς ποιεῦντι θεὸς περὶ πάντα τίθησιν
590 συντυχίην ἀγαθήν, ἔκλυσιν ἀφροσύνης.

Stob. 4.47.16; 3.9.23 (Solonis), vv. 585-90

585 πᾶσι δέ τοι Sol.   586 ποῖο, Stob.: ᾗ μέλλει σχήσειν
χρήματος Sol.   587 εὖ ἔρδειν Sol.
589 καλῶς ποιεῦντι codd., καλὸν ποιοῦντι Stob., κακῶς ἔρδοντι
Sol. καλὰ πάντα Stob.   δίδωσιν Sol.   590 ἀγαθῶν Stob.
ἔκδυσιν δ' Stob. SA

591-94

     τολμᾶν χρὴ τὰ διδοῦσι θεοὶ θνητοῖσι βροτοῖσιν,
     ῥηϊδίως δὲ φέρειν ἀμφοτέρων τὸ λάχος,
     μήτε κακοῖσιν ἀσῶντα λίην φρένα, μήτ' ἀγαθοῖσιν
     τερφθῇς ἐξαπίνης πρὶν τέλος ἄκρον ἰδεῖν.

593 κακοῖσι νοσοῦντα λυποῦ φρένα ο   594 τερφθέντ'
Bekker

595-98

595 ἄνθρωπ', ἀλλήλοισιν ἀπόπροθεν ὦμεν ἑταῖροι·
     πλὴν πλούτου παντὸς χρήματός ἐστι κόρος.
     δὴν δὴ καὶ φίλοι ὦμεν· ἀτάρ τ' ἄλλοισιν ὁμίλει
     ἀνδράσιν, οἳ τὸν σὸν μᾶλλον ἴσασι νόον.

597 cf. 1243   ὁμιλεῖν ο

585-90

In truth, there is risk in every action and no one
knows, when something starts, how it is going to
turn out. The man who tries for a good reputation
falls unawares into great and harsh calamity, while
to the one who acts badly the god gives success in all
things, an escape from his folly.[1]

[1] A version of Solon fr. 13.65-70.

591-94

One must endure what the gods give mortal men
and calmly bear both lots,[1] neither too sick at heart
in bad times nor suddenly rejoicing[2] in good times,
until the final outcome is seen.

[1] I.e., good and bad fortune.   [2] Literally, "and don't sud-
denly rejoice." For the syntax see West, *Studies* 156-57.

595-98

Let's be comrades at a distance, fellow. There is sati-
ety in everything except for wealth. In fact, let's be
friends for a long time, but associate with other men
who have a better understanding of how you think.[1]

[1] Hudson-Williams' explanation seems to be correct: "I am
willing to be your friend as long as you like, but never let me see
your face again."

599-602

οὔ μ' ἔλαθες φοιτῶν κατ' ἀμαξιτόν, ἦν ἄρα καὶ
      πρὶν
600 ἠλάστρεις, κλέπτων ἡμετέρην φιλίην.
ἔρρε θεοῖσίν ⟨τ'⟩ ἐχθρὲ καὶ ἀνθρώποισιν ἄπιστε,
ψυχρὸν ὃς ἐν κόλπῳ ποικίλον εἶχες ὄφιν.

601 τ' add. p   602 ὃν . . . εἶχον Sintenis

603-604

τοιάδε καὶ Μάγνητας ἀπώλεσεν ἔργα καὶ ὕβρις,
οἷα τὰ νῦν ἱερὴν τήνδε πόλιν κατέχει.

605-606

605 πολλῷ τοι πλέονας λιμοῦ κόρος ὤλεσεν ἤδη
ἄνδρας, ὅσοι μοίρης πλεῖον' ἔχειν ἔθελον.

Stob. 3.18.9 (vv. 605-606)
Teles (p. 45 Hense) ap. Stob. 4.32.21 (v. 605)

605 πλείους Teles   606 πλεῦν' ἐθέλουσιν ἔχειν Stob.

607-10

ἀρχῇ ἔπι ψεύδους μικρὰ χάρις· εἰς δὲ τελευτὴν
αἰσχρὸν δὴ κέρδος καὶ κακόν, ἀμφότερον,
γίνεται, οὐδέ τι καλόν, ὅτῳ ψεῦδος προσομαρτῇ
610 ἀνδρὶ καὶ ἐξέλθῃ πρῶτον ἀπὸ στόματος.

Stob. 3.12.16 (vv. 607-10)

608 ἀμφότερα Stob. MA   609 προσαμαρτῇ A, προσ-
ομαρτεῖ O, Stob. MA, -ῇ Stob. S

599-602

I was well aware that you were travelling along the common road you used to drive before, cheating on my friendship. To hell with you, hated by the gods and distrusted by men, you who kept a cold and cunning serpent in your bosom.

603-604

Such acts of lawlessness destroyed Magnesia[1] as now prevail in this holy city.

[1] Cf. Archilochus fr. 20.

605-606

Excess to be sure has already destroyed many more men than famine, men who wanted to have more than their allotment.

607-10

At the beginning of a lie there's a small pleasure; but in the end the gain is both shameful and foul, and there's no honour for a man when once a lie accompanies him and issues from his mouth.

611-14

οὐ χαλεπὸν ψέξαι τὸν πλησίον, οὐδὲ μὲν αὐτὸν
αἰνῆσαι· δειλοῖς ἀνδράσι ταῦτα μέλει.
σιγᾶν δ᾽ οὐκ ἐθέλουσι κακοὶ κακὰ λεσχάζοντες,
οἱ δ᾽ ἀγαθοὶ πάντων μέτρον ἴσασιν ἔχειν.

615-16

615   οὐδένα παμπήδην ἀγαθὸν καὶ μέτριον ἄνδρα
τῶν νῦν ἀνθρώπων ἠέλιος καθορᾷ.

617-18

οὔ τι μάλ᾽ ἀνθρώποις καταθύμια πάντα τελεῖται·
πολλὸν γὰρ θνητῶν κρέσσονες ἀθάνατοι.

Stob. 4.34.55 (vv. 617-18)

618 πολλῶν O, Stob. (unde πολλῷ Gesnerus)

619-22

πόλλ᾽ ἐν ἀμηχανίῃσι κυλίνδομαι ἀχνύμενος κῆρ·
620   ἄκρην γὰρ πενίην οὐχ ὑπερεδράμομεν.
πᾶς τις πλούσιον ἄνδρα τίει, ἀτίει δὲ πενιχρόν·
πᾶσιν δ᾽ ἀνθρώποις αὐτὸς ἔνεστι νόος.

Stob. 4.33.15 (vv. 619-22)

622 αὐτὸς codd., corr. Blaydes

623-24

παντοῖαι κακότητες ἐν ἀνθρώποισιν ἔασιν,
παντοῖαι δ᾽ ἀρεταὶ καὶ βιότου παλάμαι.

THEOGNIS

611-14

It's not hard to find fault with your neighbour nor indeed to praise oneself; these things are the concern of base men. The base, with their base gossip, refuse to be silent, but the noble know how to observe due measure in all things.

615-16

Of those whom the sun now looks down upon, there's not a man who is wholly good and moderate.

617-18

By no means is everything accomplished according to men's desires; for the immortals are far superior to mortals.

619-22

Often I toss about in helplessness, distressed at heart; for I have not run over the crest of poverty.[1] Everyone honours a rich man, but despises a pauper; all men have the same attitude.

[1] Cf. 1114ab.

623-24

There are all kinds of badness in men, and all kinds of excellence and means of livelihood.

625-26

625   ἀργαλέον φρονέοντα παρ' ἄφροσι πόλλ' ἀγορεύειν
        καὶ σιγᾶν αἰεί· τοῦτο γὰρ οὐ δυνατόν.

Stob. 3.34.13 (vv. 625-26)
Suda i.339.28 Adler; *Paroem. Gr.* i.211.11, 357.3, ii.101.7
(v. 625)

627-28

αἰσχρόν τοι μεθύοντα παρ' ἀνδράσι νήφοσιν
     εἶναι,
αἰσχρὸν δ' εἰ νήφων πὰρ μεθύουσι μένει.

Stob. 3.18.10 (vv. 627-28)

627 ἐχθρὸν Stob. (item 628)   νήφουσ' ο   νήφοσι
μεῖναι Leutsch (fort. recte)

629-30

ἥβη καὶ νεότης ἐπικουφίζει νόον ἀνδρός,
630   πολλῶν δ' ἐξαίρει θυμὸν ἐς ἀμπλακίην.

Stob. 4.11.12 (vv. 629-30)

631-32

ᾧτινι μὴ θυμοῦ κρέσσων νόος, αἰὲν ἐν ἄταις,
     Κύρνε, καὶ ἐν μεγάλαις κεῖται ἀμηχανίαις.

632 καὶ μεγάλαις κεῖται ἐν ἀμπλακίαις codd., corr. Bergk cl.
646

625-26

It's painful for a man of sense to speak at length in
the presence of fools and painful to be always silent;
for this is impossible.[1]

[1] West, following Hudson-Williams, treats the last four words
as a later addition to fill a gap. This seems highly probable, in spite
of van Groningen's defence.

627-28

It's disgraceful for a drunk to be in sober company
and disgraceful if a sober man keeps company with
drunks.

629-30

Youthful impetuosity makes a man's mind frivolous
and arouses the heart of many to wrongdoing.

631-32

He whose mind does not control his heart always
finds himself in trouble, Cyrnus, and in great per-
plexity.

633-34

βουλεύου δὶς καὶ τρίς, ὅ τοί κ᾽ ἐπὶ τὸν νόον ἔλθῃ·
ἀτηρὸς γάρ τοι λάβρος ἀνὴρ τελέθει.

635-36

635   ἀνδράσι τοῖς ἀγαθοῖς ἔπεται γνώμη τε καὶ αἰδώς·
οἳ νῦν ἐν πολλοῖς ἀτρεκέως ὀλίγοι.

Stob. 3.37.16 (vv. 635-36)

637-38

ἐλπὶς καὶ κίνδυνος ἐν ἀνθρώποισιν ὁμοῖοι·
οὗτοι γὰρ χαλεποὶ δαίμονες ἀμφότεροι.

Stob. 4.46.11 (vv. 637-38)

637 ὁμοῖα Stob.

639-40

πολλάκι πὰρ δόξαν τε καὶ ἐλπίδα γίνεται εὖ ῥεῖν
640   ἔργ᾽ ἀνδρῶν, βουλαῖς δ᾽ οὐκ ἐπέγεντο τέλος.

Stob. 4.47.15 (vv. 639-40)

639 ευρεῖν A, εὑρεῖν cett.: expl. Ahrens   640 ἔπεσεν τὸ
Stob., unde ἐπέθεντο coniecit West

641-44

οὔτοι κ᾽ εἰδείης οὔτ᾽ εὔνουν οὔτε τὸν ἐχθρόν,
εἰ μὴ σπουδαίου πρήγματος ἀντιτύχοις.
πολλοὶ πὰρ κρητῆρι φίλοι γίνονται ἑταῖροι,
ἐν δὲ σπουδαίῳ πρήγματι παυρότεροι.

THEOGNIS

633-34

Reflect two or three times on whatever comes into your head; for a reckless man assuredly ends up in ruin.

635-36

Good judgement and discretion accompany the noble; there are now precious few of them among many.

637-38

Expectation and risk are similar among mankind; for they are both harsh forces.

639-40

It often happens that the activities of men flow along well contrary to expectation and hope, while their plans meet with no success.

641-44

You can't know either your friend or your enemy, unless you find yourself engaged in a serious enterprise. Many are your friends and comrades at the mixing bowl, but not so many when the enterprise is serious.[1]

[1] Cf. 115-16.

---

641 εὔνοον Wordsworth   642 πράγματος A
ἀντιτύχης O   644 πράγματι A

ELEGIAC POETRY

645-46

645 παύρους κηδεμόνας πιστοὺς εὕροις κεν ἑταίρους
κείμενος ἐν μεγάλῃ θυμὸν ἀμηχανίῃ.

647-48

ἦ δὴ νῦν αἰδὼς μὲν ἐν ἀνθρώποισιν ὄλωλεν,
αὐτὰρ ἀναιδείη γαῖαν ἐπιστρέφεται.

Stob. 3.32.8 (vv. 647-48)

647 ἤδη codd., corr. Bergk

649-52

ἆ δειλὴ Πενίη, τί ἐμοῖς ἐπικειμένη ὤμοις
650 σῶμα καταισχύνεις καὶ νόον ἡμέτερον;
αἰσχρὰ δέ μ' οὐκ ἐθέλοντα βίῃ καὶ πολλὰ
διδάσκεις
ἐσθλὰ μετ' ἀνθρώπων καὶ κάλ' ἐπιστάμενον.

Stob. 4.32.34 (vv. 649-52 + 177-78)

649 ἐμοῖσι καθημένη o   651 καὶ codd., κακὰ Stob.
652 παρ' o

653-54

εὐδαίμων εἴην καὶ θεοῖς φίλος ἀθανάτοισιν,
Κύρν'· ἀρετῆς δ' ἄλλης οὐδεμιῆς ἔραμαι.

Stob. 4.39.12 (vv. 653-54)

653 κε A

268

645-46

You can find few comrades who care about you and are loyal, when your heart lies in great perplexity.

647-48

Now inhibition is lost among men and shameless-ness roams over the land.

649-52

Ah wretched Poverty, why do you lie upon my shoulders and deform my body and mind? Forcibly and against my will you teach me much that is shameful, although I know what is noble and honourable among men.

653-54

May I have divine favour and be dear to the immortal gods, Cyrnus. I crave no other merit.

655-56

655   σύν τοι, Κύρνε, παθόντι κακῶς ἀνιώμεθα πάντες·
    ἀλλά τοι ἀλλότριον κῆδος ἐφημέριον.

657-66

μηδὲν ἄγαν χαλεποῖσιν ἀσῶ φρένα μηδ᾽
    ἀγαθοῖσιν
χαῖρ᾽, ἐπεὶ ἔστ᾽ ἀνδρὸς πάντα φέρειν ἀγαθοῦ.
οὐδ᾽ ὀμόσαι χρὴ τοῦθ᾽, ὅτι "μήποτε πρῆγμα τόδ᾽
    ἔσται·"
660   θεοὶ γάρ τοι νεμεσῶσ᾽, οἷσιν ἔπεστι τέλος.
κἄπρηξαν μέντοι τι· καὶ ἐκ κακοῦ ἐσθλὸν ἔγεντο
    καὶ κακὸν ἐξ ἀγαθοῦ· καί τε πενιχρὸς ἀνὴρ
αἶψα μάλ᾽ ἐπλούτησε, καὶ ὃς μάλα πολλὰ πέπαται
    ἐξαπίνης †ἀπὸ πάντ᾽ οὖν† ὤλεσε νυκτὶ μιῇ·
665   καὶ σώφρων ἥμαρτε, καὶ ἄφρονι πολλάκι δόξα
    ἕσπετο, καὶ τιμῆς καὶ κακὸς ὢν ἔλαχεν.

Stob. 4.42.5 (vv. 665-66)

659 τοῦτο τί codd. (τί om. O): expl. Camerarius
661 καὶ πρῆξαι codd., κἄπρηξαν West, alii alia
663 πέπασται codd., corr. Brunck   664 αποτοῦν A, πάντ᾽
οὖν p, πάντα O, ἀπὸ πάντ᾽ Bergk

667-82

εἰ μὲν χρήματ᾽ ἔχοιμι, Σιμωνίδη, οἷά περ ἤδη,
    οὐκ ἂν ἀνιώμην τοῖς ἀγαθοῖσι συνών.
νῦν δέ με γινώσκοντα παρέρχεται, εἰμὶ δ᾽ ἄφωνος
670   χρημοσύνῃ, πολλῶν γνοὺς ἂν ἄμεινον ἔτι,

THEOGNIS

655-56

We all share your pain, Cyrnus, in your misfortune,
but grief for another is short-lived.

657-66

Don't be too vexed at heart in hard times or rejoice
too much in good times, since it is the mark of a no-
ble man to endure everything.[1] And you shouldn't
swear, "this will never be," for the gods are resentful
and the outcome depends on them. They act, what's
more:[2] good comes from bad and bad from good; a
poor man suddenly gets very rich, and he who has
acquired a great deal suddenly loses it all in one
night; a sensible man errs, fame often accompanies
the fool, and even a base man wins honour.

[1] Cf. 593-94. Many editors treat 657-58 as separate.
[2] West's translation of his emendation, but the correct text is per-
haps still to be found.

667-82

If I had wealth, Simonides,[1] such as I once had, I
wouldn't feel distressed in the company of the
noble. But now I am aware that it passes me by and
want deprives me of a voice, although I would have
recognized[2] still better than many that we are now
being carried along,[3] with white sails lowered, be-

271

οὕνεκα νῦν φερόμεσθα καθ᾽ ἱστία λευκὰ
βαλόντες
Μηλίου ἐκ πόντου νύκτα διὰ δνοφερήν,
ἀντλεῖν δ᾽ οὐκ ἐθέλουσιν, ὑπερβάλλει δὲ
θάλασσα
ἀμφοτέρων τοίχων. ᾗ μάλα τις χαλεπῶς
675 σῴζεται, οἷ᾽ ἔρδουσι· κυβερνήτην μὲν ἔπαυσαν
ἐσθλόν, ὅτις φυλακὴν εἶχεν ἐπισταμένως·
χρήματα δ᾽ ἁρπάζουσι βίῃ, κόσμος δ᾽ ἀπόλωλεν,
δασμὸς δ᾽ οὐκέτ᾽ ἴσος γίνεται ἐς τὸ μέσον·
φορτηγοὶ δ᾽ ἄρχουσι, κακοὶ δ᾽ ἀγαθῶν
καθύπερθεν.
680 δειμαίνω, μή πως ναῦν κατὰ κῦμα πίῃ.
ταῦτά μοι ᾐνίχθω κεκρυμμένα τοῖς ἀγαθοῖσιν·
γινώσκοι δ᾽ ἄν τις καὶ κακόν, ἂν σοφὸς ᾖ.

667 ᾔδειν p   670 γνοῦσαν A, γνοὺς O, γνοὺς ἄρ᾽ Do-
ver, γνοὺς ἐν van Groningen   675 οἳ δ᾽ codd. (εὕδουσι p),
corr. Bekker   682 κακός Brunck (probb. West, alii)

683-86
πολλοὶ πλοῦτον ἔχουσιν ἀίδριες· οἱ δὲ τὰ καλὰ
ζητοῦσιν χαλεπῇ τειρόμενοι πενίῃ.
685 ἔρδειν δ᾽ ἀμφοτέροισιν ἀμηχανίη παράκειται·
εἴργει γὰρ τοὺς μὲν χρήματα, τοὺς δὲ νόος.

Stob. 4.31.44 (vv. 683-86)

686 εἴργει τοὺς μὲν δὴ Stob.

272

THEOGNIS

yond the Melian sea[4] through the dark night, and
they refuse to bail, even though the sea is washing
over both sides. In very truth, safety is difficult for
anyone, such things are they doing; they have de-
posed the noble helmsman[5] who skilfully kept
watch, they seize possessions by force, and disci-
pline is lost; no longer is there an equal distribution
in the common interest; the porters rule, and the
base are above the noble. I'm afraid that perhaps a
wave will swallow the ship. Let these be my riddling
words with hidden meaning for the noble. But any-
one, if he is wise, can recognize the actual calamity.[6]

[1] See n. 1 on 467-96.   [2] Text uncertain. Van Groningen's
emendation is attractive, "although I knew one thing still better
than many."   [3] From 671 to 680 we have the imagery of the
ship of state. A social and political revolution is underway and the
nobility are apparently making little effort to avoid a total over-
throw.   [4] Melos is at the southwest edge of the Cyclades, be-
yond which is open sea.   [5] Presumably the nobles who held
power rather than an individual.   [6] With Brunck's emenda-
tion, accepted by most, the meaning will be, "But even a base man,
if he is clever, can recognize (the meaning of my riddling words)."

683-86

Many who are fools have wealth, while others who
are oppressed by harsh poverty strive for what is
honourable. But both are helpless to act, for the lat-
ter are constrained by possessions, the former by in-
telligence.[1]

[1] I.e., lack of possessions and lack of intelligence.

687-88

οὐκ ἔστι θνητοῖσι πρὸς ἀθανάτους μαχέσασθαι,
οὐδὲ δίκην εἰπεῖν οὐδενὶ τοῦτο θέμις.

689-90

οὐ χρὴ πημαίνειν, ὅτε μὴ πημαντέον εἴη,
690 οὐδ' ἔρδειν ὅ τι μὴ λώιον ᾖ τελέσαι.

689 ὅτι ed. Aldina   εἴη Schneider   690 ὅτε ο

691-92

Χαίρων, εὖ τελέσειας ὁδὸν μεγάλου διὰ πόντου,
καί σε Ποσειδάων χάρμα φίλοις ἀγάγοι.

691 nomen proprium agnovit Sitzler   ἐκτελέσειας Hecker
692 ἀνάγοι Hecker

693-94

πολλούς τοι κόρος ἄνδρας ἀπώλεσεν
    ἀφραίνοντας·
γνῶναι γὰρ χαλεπὸν μέτρον, ὅτ' ἐσθλὰ παρῇ.

Stob. 3.4.43 (vv. 693-94)

693 πολλός Stob.   ἀφρονέοντας p   694 μέτρον
codd., παῦρον Stob.

695-96

695 οὐ δύναμαί σοι, θυμέ, παρασχεῖν ἄρμενα πάντα·
τέτλαθι· τῶν δὲ καλῶν οὔ τι σὺ μοῦνος ἐρᾷς.

Stob. 3.19.11 (vv. 695-96)

696 οὐχὶ Stob.

THEOGNIS

687-88

It is not possible for mortals to fight against the gods
or to pronounce judgement (on them); no one has
this right.

689-90

One ought not to cause harm, except when harm is
called for, nor do what is better left undone.

691-92

Chaeron,[1] may you safely complete your voyage
over the vast sea and may Poseidon bring you as a joy
to your friends.

[1] Most editors read the participle 'rejoicing,' but West (*Studies*
158) rightly remarks that the proper name avoids the redundancy
with εὖ and gives more point to the play on words with χάρμα.

693-94

Excess has ruined many foolish men; it's difficult to
recognize a limit, whenever prosperity is at hand.

695-96

My heart, I cannot provide you with everything that
is fitting. Be patient: you're not the only one to have
a passion for fine things.

697-98

εὖ μὲν ἔχοντος ἐμοῦ πολλοὶ φίλοι· ἢν δέ τι δεινὸν
συγκύρσῃ, παῦροι πιστὸν ἔχουσι νόον.

697 δειλὸν Bergk (prob. West)   698 ἐγκύρσῃ ο

699-718

πλήθει δ᾽ ἀνθρώπων ἀρετὴ μία γίνεται ἥδε,
700   πλουτεῖν· τῶν δ᾽ ἄλλων οὐδὲν ἄρ᾽ ἦν ὄφελος,
οὐδ᾽ εἰ σωφροσύνην μὲν ἔχοις Ῥαδαμάνθυος
         αὐτοῦ,
πλείονα δ᾽ εἰδείης Σισύφου Αἰολίδεω,
ὅς τε καὶ ἐξ Ἀΐδεω πολυιδρίῃσιν ἀνῆλθεν
πείσας Περσεφόνην αἱμυλίοισι λόγοις,
705   ἥ τε βροτοῖς παρέχει λήθην βλάπτουσα νόοιο—
ἄλλος δ᾽ οὔ πώ τις τοῦτό γ᾽ ἐπεφράσατο,
ὅντινα δὴ θανάτοιο μέλαν νέφος ἀμφικαλύψῃ,
ἔλθῃ δ᾽ ἐς σκιερὸν χῶρον ἀποφθιμένων,
κυανέας τε πύλας παραμείψεται, αἵ τε θανόντων
710   ψυχὰς εἴργουσιν καίπερ ἀναινομένας·
ἀλλ᾽ ἄρα κἀκεῖθεν πάλιν ἤλυθε Σίσυφος ἥρως
ἐς φάος ἠελίου σφῇσι πολυφροσύναις—
οὐδ᾽ εἰ ψεύδεα μὲν ποιοῖς ἐτύμοισιν ὁμοῖα,
γλῶσσαν ἔχων ἀγαθὴν Νέστορος ἀντιθέου,
715   ὠκύτερος δ᾽ εἴησθα πόδας ταχέων Ἁρπυιῶν
καὶ παίδων Βορέω, τῶν ἄφαρ εἰσὶ πόδες.

276

697-98

When I am faring well, many are my friends, but if
something dire befalls me, few have a trustworthy
mind.[1]

[1] West, unlike other editors, combines the couplet with what
follows.

699-718

For the majority of people this alone is best: wealth.
Nothing else after all is of use, not even if you have
the good judgement of Rhadamanthys[1] himself or
know more than Sisyphus,[2] son of Aeolus, who by
his wits came up even from Hades, after persuad-
ing with wily words Persephone who impairs the
mind of mortals and brings them forgetfulness. No
one else has ever yet contrived this, once death's
dark cloud has enveloped him and he has come to
the shadowy place of the dead and passed the black
gates which hold back the souls of the dead, for all
their protestations. But even from there the hero
Sisyphus returned to the light of the sun by his
cleverness. (Nothing else is of use), not even if you
compose lies that are like the truth, with the elo-
quent tongue of godlike Nestor,[3] and were faster of
foot than the swift Harpies[4] and the fleet-footed

ἀλλὰ χρὴ πάντας γνώμην ταύτην καταθέσθαι,
ὡς πλοῦτος πλείστην πᾶσιν ἔχει δύναμιν.

Stob. 4.31.3 (vv. 699-702)
Stob. 4.31.8 (vv. 717-18)

699 πᾶσιν δ᾽ ἀνθρώποις Stob.   701 ἔχεις O, ἔχοι Stob.
MA p.c.   702 εἰδείη Stob.   αἰολίδου σισύφου o
703 ἀΐδαο o   705 νόημα p   708 ἀποφθιμένος A,
ἀποφθίμενος? Young (fort. recte)   713 ψευδέα A
ποιεῖς o   716 βορέου o   717 ταύτην γνώμην πάντας
Stob. (-ως Stob. A)

719-28

ἰσόν τοι πλουτοῦσιν, ὅτῳ πολὺς ἄργυρός ἐστιν
720   καὶ χρυσὸς καὶ γῆς πυροφόρου πεδία
ἵπποι θ᾽ ἡμίονοί τε, καὶ ᾧ τὰ δέοντα πάρεστι
    γαστρί τε καὶ πλευραῖς καὶ ποσὶν ἁβρὰ
        παθεῖν,
παιδός τ᾽ ἠδὲ γυναικός, ὅταν καὶ τῶν ἀφίκηται,
    ὥρη, σὺν δ᾽ ἥβη γίνεται ἁρμοδία.
725   ταῦτ᾽ ἄφενος θνητοῖσι· τὰ γὰρ περιώσια πάντα
    χρήματ᾽ ἔχων οὐδεὶς ἔρχεται εἰς Ἀΐδεω,
οὐδ᾽ ἂν ἄποινα διδοὺς θάνατον φύγοι, οὐδὲ
        βαρείας
    νούσους, οὐδὲ κακὸν γῆρας ἐπερχόμενον.

Stob. 4.33.7 (vv. 719-28)
Plut. Sol. 2.3 (vv. 719-24, πολὺς—ἁρμοδία)

sons of Boreas.[5] No, everyone should store up[6] this thought, that for all people wealth has the greatest power.

[1] Son of Zeus and Europa and one of the judges in the underworld.   [2] He instructed his wife to neglect his burial rites after his death, so that he could use punishment of her as an excuse to be allowed to return to the upperworld.   [3] The aged warrior from Pylos whose eloquence is praised in the *Iliad* (cf. esp. 1.247 f.).   [4] Female wind spirits who snatch ($\dot{\alpha}\rho\pi\dot{\alpha}\zeta\omega$) people away (cf. *Od.* 20.66-78).   [5] Zetes and Calaïs, who are also wind spirits and are represented as winged (Pind. *Pyth.* 4.182 f.).

[6] The precise meaning of the infinitive is disputed. Van Groningen argues for 'abandon,' but the last couplet seems to repeat rather than oppose the opening statement.

719-28

Equally rich is he who has much silver and gold, fields of wheat-bearing land, and horses and mules, and he who has at hand what is necessary to provide comfort for his stomach, sides, and feet, and the season for a boy and for a wife, whenever the season for this comes, accompanied by a youthful vigour that fits his needs. This is wealth for mortals, since no one goes to Hades with all his enormous possessions nor can he pay a price to escape death or grim diseases or the onset of evil old age.[1]

[1] A version of Solon fr. 24. See ad loc. for apparatus and notes.

729-30

φροντίδες ἀνθρώπων ἔλαχον, πτερὰ ποικίλ'
ἔχουσαι,
730   μυρόμεναι ψυχῆς εἵνεκα καὶ βιότου.

731-52

Ζεῦ πάτερ, εἴθε γένοιτο θεοῖς φίλα τοῖς μὲν
ἀλιτροῖς
    ὕβριν ἀδεῖν, καί σφιν τοῦτο γένοιτο φίλον
θυμῷ, σχέτλια ἔργα· †διατάφρεσι† δ' ὅστις
    †ἀθήνης†
    ἐργάζοιτο, θεῶν μηδὲν ὀπιζόμενος,
735   αὐτὸν ἔπειτα πάλιν τεῖσαι κακά, μηδ' ἔτ' ὀπίσσω
    πατρὸς ἀτασθαλίαι παισὶ γένοιντο κακόν·
παῖδες δ' οἵ τ' ἀδίκου πατρὸς τὰ δίκαια νοεῦντες
    ποιῶσιν, Κρονίδη, σὸν χόλον ἀζόμενοι,
ἐξ ἀρχῆς τὰ δίκαια μετ' ἀστοῖσιν φιλέοντες,
740   μήτιν' ὑπερβασίην ἀντιτίνειν πατέρων.
ταῦτ' εἴη μακάρεσσι θεοῖς φίλα· νῦν δ' ὁ μὲν
    ἔρδων
    ἐκφεύγει, τὸ κακὸν δ' ἄλλος ἔπειτα φέρει.
καὶ τοῦτ', ἀθανάτων βασιλεῦ, πῶς ἐστι δίκαιον,
    ἔργων ὅστις ἀνὴρ ἐκτὸς ἐὼν ἀδίκων,
745   μήτιν' ὑπερβασίην κατέχων μήθ' ὅρκον ἀλιτρόν,
    ἀλλὰ δίκαιος ἐών, μὴ τὰ δίκαια πάθῃ;
τίς δή κεν βροτὸς ἄλλος ὁρῶν πρὸς τοῦτον ἔπειτα
    ἄζοιτ' ἀθανάτους, καὶ τίνα θυμὸν ἔχων,

729-30

Mankind's allotment is anxieties; they have wings of
varied hue and they lament for life and livelihood.[1]

[1] The meaning seems to be that semi-personified cares or anxi-
eties bewail the condition of life and substance to which mankind
is subjected. The 'wings of varied hue' may symbolize the swift-
ness with which they appear and the varied forms they take.

731-52

Father Zeus, would that it pleased the gods that
wanton outrage delighted sinners and that wicked
deeds pleased the hearts of the gods,[1] but that who-
ever acted . . ., without regard for the gods, should
then pay woeful requital in person, and the father's
sins should no longer be a bane for his sons after-
wards;[2] and would that sons of an unjust father who
act with just intent, dreading your anger, son of
Cronus, and loving justice from the start in their
dealings with fellow townsmen, should not pay for
the transgressions of their fathers. May this be
pleasing to the blessed gods. But now the perpetra-
tor escapes and another then suffers misery. Also,
king of the immortals, how is it right that a man who
keeps from unjust deeds and does not commit trans-
gressions and perjury, but is just, suffers unjustly?
What other mortal, looking upon him, would then
be in awe of the immortals? What frame of mind

ὁππότ᾽ ἀνὴρ ἄδικος καὶ ἀτάσθαλος, οὔτε τευ
 ἀνδρὸς
750 οὔτε τευ ἀθανάτων μῆνιν ἀλευόμενος,
ὑβρίζῃ πλούτῳ κεκορημένος, οἱ δὲ δίκαιοι
τρύχονται χαλεπῇ τειρόμενοι πενίῃ;

733 μετὰ φρεσὶ ο   θ᾽ Ο   ἀθειρὴς Bergk, alii alia
734 μηδέν᾽ Hermann   735 μηδέ τ᾽ fere codd., corr.
Hermann   736 ἀτασθαλίᾳ Ο, -ίη ρ   γένοιτο ο
737 παῖδας Laur. 31.20 (prob. West)   δ᾽ ρ, τ᾽ Α, θ᾽ Ο
738 παιῶσιν Α, ποιοῦσι ο, corr. Bekker   746 παθεῖν
Turnebus   747 καὶ ο   751 ὑβρίζει ο
752 τρύχωνται Bekker

753-56

ταῦτα μαθών, φίλ᾽ ἑταῖρε, δικαίως χρήματα
 ποιοῦ,
σώφρονα θυμὸν ἔχων ἐκτὸς ἀτασθαλίης,
755 αἰεὶ τῶνδ᾽ ἐπέων μεμνημένος· εἰς δὲ τελευτὴν
αἰνήσεις μύθῳ σώφρονι πειθόμενος.

757-64

Ζεὺς μὲν τῆσδε πόληος ὑπειρέχοι αἰθέρι ναίων
αἰεὶ δεξιτερὴν χεῖρ᾽ ἐπ᾽ ἀπημοσύνῃ
ἄλλοι τ᾽ ἀθάνατοι μάκαρες θεοί· αὐτὰρ Ἀπόλλων
760 ὀρθώσαι γλῶσσαν καὶ νόον ἡμέτερον·
φόρμιγξ δ᾽ αὖ φθέγγοιθ᾽ ἱερὸν μέλος ἠδὲ καὶ
 αὐλός·
ἡμεῖς δὲ σπονδὰς θεοῖσιν ἀρεσσάμενοι

would he have whenever an unjust and wicked man who does not avoid the wrath of any man or god commits wanton outrage and rolls in wealth, while the just are worn out and consumed by harsh poverty?

1 Presumably sarcastic.   2 Cf. Solon fr. 13.29-32.

753-56

Learning this lesson, dear friend, make wealth by just means, keeping your heart sensible and free of wickedness, ever mindful of these words, and in the end you will rejoice at having heeded my sensible advice.[1]

1 I follow those who connect verb and participle (literally, "you will applaud being persuaded"), but some understand "these words" or "me" as the object of the verb. The verses have the appearance of concluding either a longer poem or a collection of poems.

757-64

May Zeus who dwells in the sky ever hold his right hand over this city to keep off harm, and may the other blessed immortal gods (do likewise); and may Apollo make straight our tongue and mind. Let the lyre sound forth holy song and the pipe also, and

πίνωμεν χαρίεντα μετ᾽ ἀλλήλοισι λέγοντες,
μηδὲν τὸν Μήδων δειδιότες πόλεμον.

760 ἀρθῶσαι O, -ώσαι XD   761 φορμιγγ᾽δ᾽ A,
φόρμιγγ᾽ ο, corr. Brunck   φθέγγοισθ᾽ Ap
762 ἀρεσσόμενοι A p.c., O: ἀρυσσάμενοι Emperius, alii alia

765-68

765   ὧδ᾽ εἶναι καὶ ἄμεινον, εὔφρονα θυμὸν ἔχοντας
νόσφι μεριμνάων εὐφροσύνως διάγειν
τερπομένους· τηλοῦ δὲ κακὰς ἀπὸ κῆρας ἀμῦναι
γῆράς τ᾽ οὐλόμενον καὶ θανάτοιο τέλος.

765 ειν A, εἴη κεν Ahrens, editores plerique

769-72

χρὴ Μουσῶν θεράποντα καὶ ἄγγελον, εἴ τι
περισσὸν
770   εἰδείη, σοφίης μὴ φθονερὸν τελέθειν,
ἀλλὰ τὰ μὲν μῶσθαι, τὰ δὲ δεικνύναι, ἄλλα δὲ
ποιεῖν·
τί σφιν χρήσηται μοῦνος ἐπιστάμενος;

771 δεικνύειν AO, δεικνύεν Schmidt   δεικνύναι· ἄλλα δὲ
ποιῶν dub. West

773-88

Φοῖβε ἄναξ, αὐτὸς μὲν ἐπύργωσας πόλιν ἄκρην,
Ἀλκαθόῳ Πέλοπος παιδὶ χαριζόμενος·
775   αὐτὸς δὲ στρατὸν ὑβριστὴν Μήδων ἀπέρυκε
τῆσδε πόλευς, ἵνα σοι λαοὶ ἐν εὐφροσύνῃ

after offering libations satisfying to the gods let us drink, making pleasant conversation with one another and fearing not the Median war.[1]

[1] Since "this city" cannot be identified, the war could be as early as that against the Ionian cities in the 540s or as late as Xerxes' invasion of 480.

765-68

May it be thus or better,[1] to pass the time with cheerful hearts in festive pleasure free of cares; and may malevolent spirits, accursed old age, and death's finality be kept far away.

[1] Text and translation uncertain.

769-72

The servant and messenger of the Muses, if he should have any exceptional knowledge, must not be stinting of it, but meditate on (seek out?) some things, display some things, and compose other things.[1] What use would it be for him if he alone knows it?

[1] The three infinitives in 771 refer to poetic activity, but their precise significance is obscure. For numerous interpretations see van Groningen 297-99 and L. Woodbury, *Collected Writings* (Atlanta 1991) 483-90.

773-88

Lord Phoebus, since it was you who built the towering citadel, as a favour to Pelops' son Alcathous,[1] so now keep the Median army's aggression away from this city,[2] so that at the coming of spring the

ELEGIAC POETRY

ἦρος ἐπερχομένου κλειτὰς πέμπων' ἑκατόμβας,
τερπόμενοι κιθάρῃ καὶ ἐρατῇ θαλίῃ
παιάνων τε χοροῖς ἰαχῇσί τε σὸν περὶ βωμόν.
780   ἦ γὰρ ἔγωγε δέδοικ' ἀφραδίην ἐσορῶν
καὶ στάσιν Ἑλλήνων λαοφθόρον· ἀλλὰ σύ,
Φοῖβε,
ἵλαος ἡμετέρην τήνδε φύλασσε πόλιν.
ἦλθον μὲν γὰρ ἔγωγε καὶ εἰς Σικελήν ποτε
γαῖαν,
ἦλθον δ' Εὐβοίης ἀμπελόεν πεδίον,
785   Σπάρτην τ' Εὐρώτα δονακοτρόφου ἀγλαὸν ἄστυ,
καί μ' ἐφίλευν προφρόνως πάντες
ἐπερχόμενον·
ἀλλ' οὔτις μοι τέρψις ἐπὶ φρένας ἦλθεν ἐκείνων·
οὕτως οὐδὲν ἄρ' ἦν φίλτερον ἄλλο πάτρης.

Harpocration (= test. 4), v. 783

779 ἰαχαῖσίο, -οισί A, corr. Bekker   τὸν O   785 δ' AO

789-94
μήποτέ μοι μελέδημα νεώτερον ἄλλο φανείη
790   ἀντ' ἀρετῆς σοφίης τ', ἀλλὰ τόδ' αἰὲν ἔχων
τερποίμην φόρμιγγι καὶ ὀρχηθμῷ καὶ ἀοιδῇ,
καὶ μετὰ τῶν ἀγαθῶν ἐσθλὸν ἔχοιμι νόον,
μήτε τινὰ ξείνων δηλεύμενος ἔργμασι λυγροῖς
μήτε τιν' ἐνδήμων, ἀλλὰ δίκαιος ἐών.

790 τ' om. o

286

people may send you glorious hecatombs amid festivity, delighting in the lyre and in lovely feasting and in the dances of paeans[3] and in cries round your altar. For indeed I am afraid when I look upon the mindless, people-destroying strife of the Greeks. Come, Phoebus, graciously protect this city of ours.[4] For I went once to the land of Sicily and I went to the vine-rich plain of Euboea and to Sparta, the splendid city of the reed-nourishing Eurotas, and they all treated me with kindly friendship on my arrival. But no delight came to my heart from them, so true it is after all that nothing else is dearer than one's homeland.

[1] For the myth see Hudson-Williams ad loc. Apollo was the patron deity of Megara.   [2] Since "this city" is Megara, the reference must be to Xerxes' invasion of 480, and the poet cannot be Theognis. Carrière, followed by West, suggests that the author may be Philiadas, an obscure Megarian poet who composed a poem on the dead at Thermopylae.   [3] Here, as often, songs of thanksgiving.   [4] What follows is usually treated as a separate segment and as proof that Theognis could not have been a native of Sicilian Megara (see testt. 2-4). I hesitantly follow West in combining the verses.

789-94

May no other new pursuit arise for me in place of excellence and learning, but ever holding on to this may I enjoy lyre, dance, and song, and may I have noble thoughts in company with the noble, harming with hurtful deeds neither foreigner nor citizen, but living righteously.[1]

[1] Many editors combine the last couplet with 795-96.

795-96

795 τὴν σαυτοῦ φρένα τέρπε· δυσηλεγέων δὲ πολιτῶν
ἄλλος τοί σε κακῶς, ἄλλος ἄμεινον ἐρεῖ.

797-98

τοὺς ἀγαθοὺς ἄλλος μάλα μέμφεται, ἄλλος
ἐπαινεῖ,
τῶν δὲ κακῶν μνήμη γίνεται οὐδεμία.

799-800

ἀνθρώπων δ’ ἄψεκτος ἐπὶ χθονὶ γίνεται οὐδείς·
800 ἀλλ’ ὡς λώιον, εἰ μὴ πλεόνεσσι μέλοι.

800 ειλώϊον A, λώϊον ὁ ο (οὖ XD, οὐ I), (ἄλλως) λώιον εἰ
Hermann

801-804

οὐδεὶς ἀνθρώπων οὔτ’ ἔσσεται οὔτε πέφυκεν
ὅστις πᾶσιν ἁδὼν δύσεται εἰς Ἀΐδεω·
οὐδὲ γὰρ ὃς θνητοῖσι καὶ ἀθανάτοισιν ἀνάσσει,
Ζεὺς Κρονίδης, θνητοῖς πᾶσιν ἀδεῖν δύναται.

805-10

805 τόρνου καὶ στάθμης καὶ γνώμονος ἄνδρα θεωρὸν
εὐθύτερον χρὴ <ἔ>μεν, Κύρνε, φυλασσόμενον,
ᾧτινί κεν Πυθῶνι θεοῦ χρήσασ’ ἱέρεια
ὀμφὴν σημήνῃ πίονος ἐξ ἀδύτου·

THEOGNIS

795-96

Enjoy yourself. Some of the harsh citizens will speak ill of you, some better.[1]

[1] The couplet also occurs as Mimnermus fr. 7. See ad loc. for variant readings.

797-98

Some vehemently blame the noble and others praise them, but of the base there is no recollection at all.

799-800

There is no one on earth who escapes blame; but it is better thus, if the majority pay no heed.

801-804

There never has been nor will there be a man who will please everyone before he goes down to Hades. For not even he who is lord of mortals and immortals, Zeus the son of Cronus, can please all men.[1]

[1] Cf. 24-26.

805-10

A man sent to consult the oracle must take care, Cyrnus, to be straighter than a carpenter's compass, rule, and square, that man to whom the priestess of the god[1] at Delphi in her response reveals the god's voice from the wealthy shrine. For you can no

289

οὔτε τι γὰρ προσθεὶς οὐδέν κ᾽ ἔτι φάρμακον
    εὕροις,
810   οὐδ᾽ ἀφελὼν πρὸς θεῶν ἀμπλακίην προφύγοις.

805 θεωρῶν codd., corr. Vinetus   806 χρὴ μὲν codd.,
corr. Ahrens   807 vel κ᾽ ἐν (Hudson-Williams)   809 κέ
τι o

811-14

χρῆμ᾽ ἔπαθον θανάτου μὲν ἀεικέος οὔτι κάκιον,
    τῶν δ᾽ ἄλλων πάντων, Κύρν᾽, ἀνιηρότατον·
οἵ με φίλοι προύδωκαν· ἐγὼ δ᾽ ἐχθροῖσι πελασθεὶς
    εἰδήσω καὶ τῶν ὄντιν᾽ ἔχουσι νόον.

814 τὸν AO

815-18

815   βοῦς μοι ἐπὶ γλώσσῃ κρατερῷ ποδὶ λὰξ
    ἐπιβαίνων
ἴσχει κωτίλλειν καίπερ ἐπιστάμενον,
Κύρν᾽· ἔμπης δ᾽ ὅ τι μοῖρα παθεῖν οὐκ ἔσθ᾽
    ὑπαλύξαι.
ὅττι δὲ μοῖρα παθεῖν, οὔτι δέδοικα παθεῖν.

815 γλώσσης o

819-20

ἐς πολυάρητον κακὸν ἤκομεν, ἔνθα μάλιστα,
820   Κύρνε, συναμφοτέρους μοῖρα λάβοι θανάτου.

819 πολὺ ἄρρητον o

longer find any remedy[2] if you add anything nor can you avoid sinning in the eyes of the gods if you take anything away.

[1] Apollo.   [2] According to West (*Studies* 159), "the remedy supplied by the oracle for the situation which prompted its consultation."

811-14

I have suffered something that is not actually worse than ugly death, Cyrnus, but that is more bitter than anything else: my friends have betrayed me. I'll approach my enemies and see how they're disposed.

815-18

An ox steps on my tongue with his powerful foot,[1] Cyrnus, and prevents me from flattering, although I know how to. After all, it's impossible to escape from what one is destined to suffer; and I'm not at all afraid to suffer what it is my fate to suffer.[2]

[1] A proverbial statement used of those who cannot speak freely.   [2] Except for West, editors treat the two couplets as separate. West deletes the last verse, attributing it to some Stoic editor, and this is a decided improvement.

819-20

Cyrnus, we have reached the terrible situation against which our prayers were often directed,[1] a situation in which it would be best if our allotted death were to seize us both together.

[1] Or possibly, "a terrible situation that is utterly accursed."

821-22

οἵ κ᾽ ἀπογηράσκοντας ἀτιμάζωσι τοκῆας,
τούτων τοι χώρη, Κύρν᾽, ὀλίγη τελέθει.

821 δ᾽ ρ   ἀτιμάζουσι codd., corr. Bergk

823-24

μήτε τιν᾽ αὖξε τύραννον ἐπ᾽ ἐλπίσι, κέρδεσιν
    εἴκων.
μήτε κτεῖνε θεῶν ὅρκια συνθέμενος.

823 ἐλπίδι Bekker cl. 333 (prob. West)   824 κτεῖναι ο

825-30

825   πῶς ὑμῖν τέτληκεν ὑπ᾽ αὐλητῆρος ἀείδειν
           θυμός; γῆς δ᾽ οὖρος φαίνεται ἐξ ἀγορῆς,
       ἥ τε τρέφει καρποῖσιν †ἐν εἰλαπίναις φορέοντας
           ξανθῆσίν τε κόμαις πορφυρέους στεφάνους.†
       ἀλλ᾽ ἄγε δή, Σκύθα, κεῖρε κόμην, ἀπόπαυε δὲ
           κῶμον,
830   πένθει δ᾽ εὐώδη χῶρον ἀπολλύμενον.

828 ξανθαῖς ἀμφὶ Schneidewin

831-32

πίστει χρήματ᾽ ὄλεσσα, ἀπιστίῃ δ᾽ ἐσάωσα·
γνώμη δ᾽ ἀργαλέη γίνεται ἀμφοτέρων.

821-22

There's little esteem, Cyrnus, for those who dishon-
our parents when they're growing old.

823-24

Don't be led on by hopes of gain to increase a ty-
rant's power, and don't swear an oath by the gods to
kill him.

825-30

How do you endure in your hearts to sing to
the piper's accompaniment? From the marketplace
there is visible the mortgage-marker of the land that
feeds with its fruits those who wear crimson gar-
lands on their blond hair at feasts.[1] Come, Scythes,
crop your hair, bring the revelry to an end, and
grieve for the fragrant land that is being lost.[2]

---

[1] The text is corrupt, but the general sense is clear.
[2] There is much obscurity in these verses. B. Bravo, *Annales
Littéraires de l'Univ. de Besançon* 429 (1990) 41-51, argues that
Scythes (a man's name, not an ethnic designation) is holding an
elaborate symposium in his house even though his land is mort-
gaged and that the poet is urging him to crop his hair in grief for
the land he will soon lose. My translation reflects this interpreta-
tion, but this hinges on the problematic explanation of οὖρος,
traditionally understood as the (diminished) boundary of the
town's land.

831-32

Through trust I lost my possessions, through dis-
trust I rescued them; awareness of both brings
bitterness.

833-36

πάντα τάδ᾽ ἐν κοράκεσσι καὶ ἐν φθόρῳ· οὐδέ τις
ἡμῖν
αἴτιος ἀθανάτων, Κύρνε, θεῶν μακάρων,
835 ἀλλ᾽ ἀνδρῶν τε βίη καὶ κέρδεα δειλὰ καὶ ὕβρις
πολλῶν ἐξ ἀγαθῶν ἐς κακότητ᾽ ἔβαλεν.

837-40

δισσαί τοι πόσιος κῆρες δειλοῖσι βροτοῖσιν,
δίψα τε λυσιμελὴς καὶ μέθυσις χαλεπή·
τούτων δ᾽ ἂν τὸ μέσον στρωφήσομαι, οὐδέ με
πείσεις
840 οὔτε τι μὴ πίνειν οὔτε λίην μεθύειν.

841-42

οἶνος ἐμοὶ τὰ μὲν ἄλλα χαρίζεται, ἐν δ᾽
ἀχάριστος,
εὖτ᾽ ἂν θωρήξας μ᾽ ἄνδρα πρὸς ἐχθρὸν ἄγῃ.

841 ἀχάριστον A

843-44

ἀλλ᾽ ὁπόταν καθύπερθεν ἐὼν ὑπένερθε γένηται,
τουτάκις οἴκαδ᾽ ἴμεν παυσάμενοι πόσιος.

843 ἐὸν Epkema   844 παυσάμενον Camerarius

THEOGNIS

833-36

Everything here has gone to the dogs[1] and to ruin,
Cyrnus, and we can't hold any of the blessed immortal gods responsible. It's the violence of men, their
base gains and insolence that have cast us from prosperity into misery.

[1] Literally, "to the crows."

837-40

Two demons of drink beset wretched mortals, enfeebling thirst and harsh drunkenness. I'll steer a
middle course between them and you won't persuade me either not to drink or to drink too much.

841-42

For the most part wine gives me pleasure, but in one
respect it does not, whenever it intoxicates me and
leads me to my enemy.

843-44

But whenever one who was above becomes the one
below,[1] then stop drinking and go home.

[1] Variously explained, as a disruption of the proper arrangement of the guests, as a collapse to the floor from an upright position, as a sign that one's head is spinning (cf. 505), etc. Some
combine the couplet with 841-42.

845-46

845   εὖ μὲν κείμενον ἄνδρα κακῶς θέμεν εὐμαρές ἐστιν,
   εὖ δὲ θέμεν τὸ κακῶς κείμενον ἀργαλέον.

845 ἀνδρὶ Hermann

847-50

  λὰξ ἐπίβα δήμῳ κενεόφρονι, τύπτε δὲ κέντρῳ
   ὀξέι καὶ ζεύγλην δύσλοφον ἀμφιτίθει·
  οὐ γὰρ ἔθ᾽ εὑρήσεις δῆμον φιλοδέσποτον ὧδε
850   ἀνθρώπων ὁπόσους ἥλιος καθορᾷ.

851-52

  Ζεὺς ἄνδρ᾽ ἐξολέσειεν Ὀλύμπιος, ὃς τὸν ἑταῖρον
   μαλθακὰ κωτίλλων ἐξαπατᾶν ἐθέλει.

853-54

  ἤδεα μὲν καὶ πρόσθεν, ἀτὰρ πολὺ λώιον ἤδη,
   οὕνεκα τοῖς δειλοῖς οὐδεμί᾽ ἐστὶ χάρις.

853 ἤδέα codd. (spir. et acc. erasis in A): expl. Camerarius
λώιον ἤδη 1038a, λώϊα δὴ νῦν A, λώϊα ἢ νῦν O, λῴονα ἢ νῦν XD
854 τούνεκα A (τ del. A f) p

855-56

855   πολλάκις ἡ πόλις ἥδε δι᾽ ἡγεμόνων κακότητα
   ὥσπερ κεκλιμένη ναῦς παρὰ γῆν ἔδραμεν.

855 πολλάκι δὴ Schneider

845-46

It's easy to displace a man who is well placed, but hard to place well what is badly placed.

847-50

Trample the empty-headed people, jab them with a sharp goad, and place a painful yoke round their necks. For among the people whom the sun looks down upon you'll find none so much in love with tyranny.

851-52

May Olympian Zeus utterly destroy the man who is willing to deceive his comrade with gentle blandishments.

853-54

I knew it before, but I know it much better now, that the base have no gratitude.[1]

[1] Identical to 1038ab, if the text printed is correct.

855-56

Because of the depravity of its leaders[1] this city has often run along the shore[2] like a listing (veering?)[3] ship.

[1] Cf. 41-42 with n. 3.   [2] Presumably in the sense of 'too close to the shore.'   [3] Either 'listing' because its cargo is unevenly distributed or 'veering' off its proper course.

857-60

τῶν δὲ φίλων εἰ μέν τις ὁρᾷ μέ τι δειλὸν ἔχοντα,
αὐχέν᾽ ἀποστρέψας οὐδ᾽ ἐσορᾶν ἐθέλει·
ἦν δέ τί μοί ποθεν ἐσθλόν, ἃ παυράκι γίνεται
ἀνδρί,
860   πολλοὺς ἀσπασμοὺς καὶ φιλότητας ἔχω.

857 δεινὸν o   859 πολλάκι o

861-64

οἵ με φίλοι προδιδοῦσι καὶ οὐκ ἐθέλουσί τι δοῦναι
ἀνδρῶν φαινομένων· ἀλλ᾽ ἐγὼ αὐτομάτη
ἑσπερίη τ᾽ ἔξειμι καὶ ὀρθρίη αὖτις ἔσειμι,
ἦμος ἀλεκτρυόνων φθόγγος ἐγειρομένων.

863 αὖθις A, αὖτις p, αὐτῆς O

865-68

865   πολλοῖς ἀχρήστοισι θεὸς διδοῖ ἀνδράσιν ὄλβον
ἐσθλόν, ὃς οὔτ᾽ αὐτῷ βέλτερος, οὐδὲν ἐών,
οὔτε φίλοις· ἀρετῆς δὲ μέγα κλέος οὔποτ᾽ ὀλεῖται·
αἰχμητὴς γὰρ ἀνὴρ γῆν τε καὶ ἄστυ σαοῖ.

Stob. 4.42.6 (vv. 865-68)

869-72

ἔν μοι ἔπειτα πέσοι μέγας οὐρανὸς εὐρὺς ὕπερθεν
870   χάλκεος, ἀνθρώπων δεῖμα χαμαιγενέων,
εἰ μὴ ἐγὼ τοῖσιν μὲν ἐπαρκέσω οἵ με φιλεῦσιν,
τοῖς δ᾽ ἐχθροῖς ἀνίη καὶ μέγα πῆμ᾽ ἔσομαι.

870 παλαιγενέων o

THEOGNIS

857-60

If any of my friends sees that I am in some distress,
he turns his neck aside and refuses to look at me; but
if something good befalls me from some source, a
rare occurrence for a man, I receive many embraces
and signs of affection.

861-64

My friends betray me and refuse to give me any-
thing when men appear. Well, of my own accord I'll
go out at evening and return at dawn, when the
roosters awaken and crow.[1]

[1] The speaker is feminine, but beyond that there is no agree-
ment. The many, often bizarre, attempts to explain the verses are
surveyed by J. Labarbe in *Serta Leodiensia Secunda* (Liège 1992)
237-45, but his own identification of the speaker as an owl is no
less bizarre. According to West (*Studies* 160), "the speaker is in
the position of a beggar" and is the wife or daughter of the master
of the house.

865-68

To many worthless men the god gives splendid pros-
perity, which is of no advantage to the man himself
or to his friends, since it is nothing, whereas the
great fame of valour will never die. For a spearman
keeps his land and city safe.

869-72

May the great wide bronze sky fall upon me from
above, the fear of earth-born men, if I do not aid
those who are my friends and cause my enemies
pain and great misery.

873-76

οἶνε, τὰ μέν σ᾽ αἰνῶ, τὰ δὲ μέμφομαι· οὐδέ σε
  πάμπαν
οὔτε ποτ᾽ ἐχθαίρειν οὔτε φιλεῖν δύναμαι.
875 ἐσθλὸν καὶ κακόν ἐσσι. τίς ἂν σέ γε μωμήσαιτο,
  τίς δ᾽ ἂν ἐπαινήσαι μέτρον ἔχων σοφίης;

875 γε ρ, τε AO   876 ἐπαινήσῃ Ap, -σει O, corr. Brunck

877-78

ἥβα μοι, φίλε θυμέ· τάχ᾽ αὖ τινες ἄλλοι ἔσονται
  ἄνδρες, ἐγὼ δὲ θανὼν γαῖα μέλαιν᾽ ἔσομαι.

877 ηβανοι A, ἡβά οἱ O, ἡβάοις p, corr. Ahrens   ἂν ο
ἔσοιντο p

879-84

πῖν᾽ οἶνον, τὸν ἐμοὶ κορυφῆς ὕπο Τηϋγέτοιο
880   ἄμπελοι ἤνεγκαν τὰς ἐφύτευσ᾽ ὁ γέρων
οὔρεος ἐν βήσσῃσι θεοῖσι φίλος Θεότιμος,
  ἐκ Πλατανιστοῦντος ψυχρὸν ὕδωρ ἐπάγων.
τοῦ πίνων ἀπὸ μὲν χαλεπὰς σκεδάσεις
  μελεδώνας,
θωρηχθεὶς δ᾽ ἔσεαι πολλὸν ἐλαφρότερος.

879 κορυφῆς ἀπὸ codd., corr. Sylburg   883 μελεδώνας
Camerarius, -ῶνας codd.

885-86

885 εἰρήνη καὶ πλοῦτος ἔχοι πόλιν, ὄφρα μετ᾽ ἄλλων
  κωμάζοιμι· κακοῦ δ᾽ οὐκ ἔραμαι πολέμου.

873-76

I praise you, wine, in some respects and find fault with you in others; I can never totally hate or love you. You are a blessing and a bane. What man who's truly wise would blame or praise you?

877-78

Enjoy your youth, my dear heart; soon it will be the turn of other men, and I'll be dead and become dark earth.[1]

[1] Identical to 1070ab, except for the first word.

879-84

Drink the wine which was produced for me beneath the peaks of Taygetus[1] from vines planted on the mountain glens by old Theotimus, loved by the gods, who drew cool water from Platanistous. Drinking this, you will scatter troublesome cares and when fortified you'll be much more relaxed.

[1] Above Sparta. Neither Theotimus nor Platanistous has been identified.

885-86

May peace and prosperity attend this city, so that I may hold revelry with others. I have no love of cruel war.

887-88

μηδὲ λίην κήρυκος ἀν᾿ οὖς ἔχε μακρὰ βοῶντος·
οὐ γὰρ πατρῴας γῆς πέρι μαρνάμεθα.

889-90

ἀλλ᾿ αἰσχρὸν παρεόντα καὶ ὠκυπόδων ἐπιβάντα
890   ἵππων μὴ πόλεμον δακρυόεντ᾿ ἐσιδεῖν.

891-94

ὤ μοι ἀναλκίης· ἀπὸ μὲν Κήρινθος ὄλωλεν,
Ληλάντου δ᾿ ἀγαθὸν κείρεται οἰνόπεδον·
οἱ δ᾿ ἀγαθοὶ φεύγουσι, πόλιν δὲ κακοὶ διέπουσιν.
ὡς δὴ Κυψελιδῶν Ζεὺς ὀλέσειε γένος.

891 οἴμοι codd., corr. nescioquis   894 κυψελίζων A,
κυψελλίζον (om. δὴ) o, corr. Hermann

895-96

895   γνώμης δ᾿ οὐδὲν ἄμεινον ἀνὴρ ἔχει αὐτὸς ἐν
αὑτῷ,
οὐδ᾿ ἀγνωμοσύνης, Κύρν᾿, ὀδυνηρότερον.

895 αὑτῷ Orelli   896 ἀνιηρότερον o

897-900

Κύρν᾿, εἰ πάντ᾿ ἄνδρεσσι καταθνητοῖς
χαλέπαινεν
γινώσκων θεὸς νοῦν οἷον ἕκαστος ἔχει

302

887-88

Don't strain your ear for the herald's loud shout; it's
not for our homeland that we are fighting.

889-90

But it is shameful, when one is present and mounted
on swift-footed horses, not to behold tearful war.

891-94

Shame on weakness! Cerinthus is destroyed and
Lelantum's fine vineyards are being ravaged; the
nobles are in exile and base men govern the city.
May Zeus destroy the race of Cypselids.[1]

[1] Cypselus was tyrant of Corinth c. 655-625, but it is un-
clear which ones of his descendants are meant here and so
the fighting cannot be dated. Cerinthus is in northeast Euboea
and the Lelantine plain further south. In general see V. Parker,
*Untersuchungen zum Lelantischen Krieg und verwandten
Problemen der frühgriechischen Geschichte* (Stuttgart 1997), esp.
pp. 82-88.

895-96

Cyrnus, a man has nothing better in him than sense
and nothing more painful than the lack of it.

897-900

Cyrnus, if god were angry at mortal men for every
fault, knowing the inward thoughts each one has

αὐτὸς ἐνὶ στήθεσσι καὶ ἔργματα τῶν τε δικαίων
900 τῶν τ᾽ ἀδίκων, μέγα κεν πῆμα βροτοῖσιν ἐπῆν.

897 κύρν᾽ εἰ A, κύρνε μὴ ο (οὐ I)   (θεὸς θνητοῖς)
χαλέπαινεν Hermann, χαλεπαίνειν codd.   898 γινώσκων
ο, -σκειν A   θεὸς West, ὡς codd.   899-900 τῷ δὲ (τε
recc.) δικαίῳ τῷ τ᾽ (δ᾽ O, I a.c.) ἀδίκῳ codd., corr. Hermann

901-902
ἔστιν ὁ μὲν χείρων, ὁ δ᾽ ἀμείνων ἔργον ἕκαστον·
οὐδεὶς δ᾽ ἀνθρώπων αὐτὸς ἅπαντα σοφός.

901 ἑκάστου codd., corr. Bekker   ἀμείνων· ἔργον
ἑκάστου West ("each has his role")   902 αἰστὸς A, unde
ἔσθ᾽ ὃς Meineke

903-30
ὅστις ἀνάλωσιν τηρεῖ κατὰ χρήματα †θηρῶν†,
κυδίστην ἀρετὴν τοῖς συνιεῖσιν ἔχει.
905 εἰ μὲν γὰρ κατιδεῖν βιότου τέλος ἦν, ὁπόσον τι
ἤμελλ᾽ ἐκτελέσας εἰς Ἀΐδαο περᾶν,
εἰκὸς ἂν ἦν, ὃς μὲν πλείω χρόνον αἶσαν ἔμιμνεν,
φείδεσθαι μᾶλλον τοῦτον, ἵν᾽ εἶχε βίον·
νῦν δ᾽ οὐκ ἔστιν, ὃ δὴ καὶ ἐμοὶ μέγα πένθος
          ὄρωρεν
910 καὶ δάκνομαι ψυχήν, καὶ δίχα θυμὸν ἔχω.
ἐν τριόδῳ δ᾽ ἕστηκα· δύ᾽ εἰσὶ τὸ πρόσθεν ὁδοί μοι·
φροντίζω τούτων ἥντιν᾽ ἴω προτέρην·
ἢ μηδὲν δαπανῶν τρύχω βίον ἐν κακότητι,
ἢ ζώω τερπνῶς ἔργα τελῶν ὀλίγα.

304

and the deeds of just and unjust alike, it would be a great bane for mortals.[1]

[1] Text and translation highly uncertain.

901-902

In every activity one man is worse, another better.
No one on his own is skilled in everything.

903-30

He who watches over his spending according to his means is held in the highest esteem by men of understanding. For if it were possible to see the end of life, how much one was destined to complete before passing into Hades, it would be reasonable for the man who expected a longer period of life to be more sparing, so that he might have livelihood. But as things are, it's impossible. Because of this I am greatly saddened, torn at heart, and of two minds. I'm standing at the crossroads, with two ways ahead of me, and deliberating which of them to choose, whether to spend nothing and wear away my life in misery or to live a life of pleasure, accomplishing

915 εἶδον μὲν γὰρ ἔγωγ᾽ ὃς ἐφείδετο, κοὔποτε γαστρὶ
σῖτον ἐλευθέριον πλούσιος ὢν ἐδίδου·
ἀλλὰ πρὶν ἐκτελέσαι κατέβη δόμον Ἄϊδος εἴσω,
χρήματα δ᾽ ἀνθρώπων οὑπιτυχὼν ἔλαβεν·
ὥστ᾽ ἐς ἄκαιρα πονεῖν καὶ μὴ δόμεν ᾧ κ᾽ ἐθέλῃ τις.

920 εἶδον δ᾽ ἄλλον ὃς ᾗ γαστρὶ χαριζόμενος
χρήματα μὲν διέτριψεν, ἐφ᾽ ἡδυφάγῳ φρένα
τέρψας·
πτωχεύει δὲ φίλους πάντας, ὅπου τιν᾽ ἴδῃ.
οὕτω, Δημόκλεις, κατὰ χρήματ᾽ ἄριστον ἁπάντων
τὴν δαπάνην θέσθαι καὶ μελέτην ἐχέμεν·

925 οὔτε γὰρ ἂν προκαμὼν ἄλλῳ κάματον μεταδοίης,
οὔτ᾽ ἂν πτωχεύων δουλοσύνην τελέοις.
οὐδ᾽ εἰ γῆρας ἵκοιο τὰ χρήματα πάντ᾽ ἀποδραίη·
ἐν δὲ τοιῷδε γένει χρήματ᾽ ἄριστον ἔχειν.
ἢν μὲν γὰρ πλουτῇς, πολλοὶ φίλοι, ἢν δὲ πένηαι,

930 παῦροι, κοὐκέθ᾽ ὁμῶς αὐτὸς ἀνὴρ ἀγαθός.

P. Berol. 21220: v. R. Kotansky, ZPE 96 (1993) 1-5 (vv. 917-33)

903 θήσων Fraccaroli et Cataudella, alii alia
905 ὁπόσος τίς O, ὁπόσον τις p   921 ἐφ᾽ ἡδυφάγωι
Kotansky, ἔφη δ᾽ ὑπάγω codd.,]υφαγωι φ[pap.
925 κάματον Αο et pap., καμάτου Marc. 317 (prob. West)
927 ἵκοιτο p   929 εἰ μὲν γὰρ πλουτεῖς o

931-32
φείδεσθαι μὲν ἄμεινον, ἐπεὶ οὐδὲ θανόντ᾽
ἀποκλαίει
οὐδείς, ἢν μὴ ὁρᾷ χρήματα λειπόμενα.

little. For I have seen one who was sparing and though wealthy never gave his belly the food of a freeman, but he went down to the house of Hades before spending his money(?) and some chance person got his property; as a result he toiled to no purpose and did not give (his money) to whomever he wished. And I have seen another who gratifying his belly squandered his money, having delighted his heart with the eating of sweet food; he begs from all his friends, wherever he sees any. So, Democles, it is best of all to spend according to one's means and to be careful. For you won't give another the fruit of your labours after a life of toil nor will you be a beggar and endure slavery. Not even if you reach old age will all your means run out. In such a generation as this it's best to have money. For if you are wealthy, many are your friends, but few if you are poor, and you are no longer the same worthy man you once were.[1]

[1] On linguistic grounds this is one of the most recent poems in the collection, probably to be assigned to the 5th century. The addressee, Democles, cannot be identified.

931-32

It is better to save, since not even after your death does anyone mourn, unless he sees property left behind.

933-38

παύροις ἀνθρώπων ἀρετὴ καὶ κάλλος ὀπηδεῖ·
  ὄλβιος, ὃς τούτων ἀμφοτέρων ἔλαχεν.
935 πάντες μιν τιμῶσιν· ὁμῶς νέοι οἵ τε κατ' αὐτὸν
  χώρης εἴκουσιν τοί τε παλαιότεροι.
γηράσκων ‹δ'› ἀστοῖσι μεταπρέπει, οὐδέ τις
    αὐτὸν
  βλάπτειν οὔτ' αἰδοῦς οὔτε δίκης ἐθέλει.

Floril. Monac. 118 (vv. 933-34)
cf. Tyrt. fr. 12.37-42 (vv. 935-38)

933 κῦδος Floril.   935 νέοι A, Tyrt.: ἴσοι ο   936 χώροις et οἴ
ο (εἴκουσιν χώροις p, η sscr. XI, χώρης D), εἴκουσ' ἐκ χώρης
Tyrt.   937 δ' add. Camerarius e Tyrt. (ubi v.l.)

939-42

οὐ δύναμαι φωνῇ λίγ' ἀειδέμεν ὥσπερ ἀηδών·
940   καὶ γὰρ τὴν προτέρην νύκτ' ἐπὶ κῶμον ἔβην.
οὐδὲ τὸν αὐλητὴν προφασίζομαι· ἀλλά μ' ἑταῖρος
  ἐκλείπει σοφίης οὐκ ἐπιδευόμενος.

939 ᾀδέμεν codd. (λιγύρ' ο), corr. Schneidewin   941-42
με γῆρυς . . . -όμενον Emperius

943-44

ἐγγύθεν αὐλητῆρος ἀείσομαι ὧδε καταστὰς
  δεξιός, ἀθανάτοις θεοῖσιν ἐπευχόμενος.

944 θεοῖσ AO

933-38

Success and good looks go hand in hand with few men. Fortunate the one who is allotted both of these. All honour him: the young, those of his own age, and his elders alike yield their place. In his old age he stands out among the townsmen and no one seeks to deprive him of respect or his just rights.

939-42

I cannot sing with the high, clear voice of a nightingale, for last night too I went on a revel. And I won't give the piper as an excuse. But my companion, who's not lacking in artistic ability, leaves me in the lurch.[1]

[1] Presumably this means that because of the absence of his musical friend he has to sing, even though carousing has made him hoarse. Emperius' emendation, however, is attractive: "But my voice fails me, though I'm not lacking in artistic ability."

943-44

I'll stand here close to the piper on his right and sing, with prayers to the immortal gods.

945-46

945 εἶμι παρὰ στάθμην ὀρθὴν ὁδόν, οὐδετέρωσε
κλινόμενος· χρὴ γάρ μ᾽ ἄρτια πάντα νοεῖν.

947-48

πατρίδα κοσμήσω, λιπαρὴν πόλιν, οὔτ᾽ ἐπὶ δήμῳ
τρέψας οὔτ᾽ ἀδίκοις ἀνδράσι πειθόμενος.

Stob. 3.39.15 (vv. 947-48)

948 πρέψας Stob.

949-54

νεβρὸν ὑπὲξ ἐλάφοιο λέων ὣς ἀλκὶ πεποιθὼς
950 ποσσὶ καταμάρψας αἵματος οὐκ ἔπιον·
τειχέων δ᾽ ὑψηλῶν ἐπιβὰς πόλιν οὐκ ἀλάπαξα·
ζευξάμενος δ᾽ ἵππους ἅρματος οὐκ ἐπέβην·
πρήξας δ᾽ οὐκ ἔπρηξα, καὶ οὐκ ἐτέλεσσα
τελέσσας,
δρήσας δ᾽ οὐκ ἔδρησ᾽, ἤνυσα δ᾽ οὐκ ἀνύσας.

955-56

955 δειλοὺς εὖ ἔρδοντι δύω κακά· τῶν τε γὰρ αὐτοῦ
χηρώσει πολλῶν, καὶ χάρις οὐδεμία.

Stob. 2.46.12 (vv. 955-56)

955 δ᾽ εὖ p   956 χήρωσις κτεάνων Stob.

945-46

I'll go along a path as straight as a rule, veering to neither side. For all my thoughts must be fitting.

947-48

I will adorn my homeland, a shining city, neither turning it over to the populace nor giving in to unjust men.[1]

[1] Some editors combine with the previous couplet and some assign them to Solon. Both language and thought are similar to passages in Solon.

949-54

Like a lion trusting in its might, I snatched a fawn from the doe with my claws, and did not drink its blood; I scaled the city's high walls, and did not sack it; I yoked a team, and did not mount the chariot; I have done, and not done; completed, and not completed; performed, and not performed; accomplished, and not accomplished.[1]

[1] 949-50 also appear as 1278cd, where the compiler must have judged the imagery to be erotic, and some assume that the whole segment describes one who had the object of his affection within his control, but did nothing about it. The four verbs in 953-54 are essentially synonyms.

955-56

If you do the base a good turn two blows await you; you will lose much of what you have and you'll get no gratitude.

957-58

εἴ τι παθὼν ἀπ' ἐμεῦ ἀγαθὸν μέγα μὴ χάριν
    οἶδας,
χρῄζων ἡμετέρους αὖθις ἵκοιο δόμους.

957 ὑπ' van Herwerden

959-62

ἔστε μὲν αὐτὸς ἔπινον ἀπὸ κρήνης μελανύδρου,
960   ἡδύ τί μοι ἐδόκει καὶ καλὸν ἦμεν ὕδωρ·
νῦν δ' ἤδη τεθόλωται, ὕδωρ δ' ἀναμίσγεται ὕδει·
    ἄλλης δὴ κρήνης πίομαι ἢ ποταμοῦ.

960 ἦμεν A, εἶμεν o, ἔμεν I, ἔμμεν Hermann   961 ἰλυῖ vel
ὕλῃ Ahrens, ὕλει noluit Bergk, οὔδει idem quondam

963-70

μήποτ' ἐπαινήσῃς, πρὶν ἂν εἰδῇς ἄνδρα
    σαφηνέως,
ὀργὴν καὶ ῥυθμὸν καὶ τρόπον ὅστις ἂν ᾖ.
965   πολλοί τοι κίβδηλον ἐπίκλοπον ἦθος ἔχοντες
κρύπτουσ', ἐνθέμενοι θυμὸν ἐφημέριον·
τούτων δ' ἐκφαίνει πάντως χρόνος ἦθος ἑκάστου.
    καὶ γὰρ ἐγὼν γνώμης πολλὸν ἄρ' ἐκτὸς ἔβην·
ἔφθην αἰνήσας πρὶν σοῦ κατὰ πάντα δαῆναι
970   ἤθεα· νῦν δ' ἤδη νηῦς ἅθ' ἑκὰς διέχω.

Stob. 3.1.65 (vv. 963-68)
Floril. Monac. 107 = Orion *anth.* 8.11a (p. 92 Schneidewin),
    v. 963

957-58

If you have received some great benefit from me
and are not grateful, may it be in need that you come
again to my house.

959-62

As long as I was drinking by myself from the spring's
dark water, it seemed sweet and good to me. But
now it's become dirty and water is mixed with water.
I'll drink from another spring rather than a river.[1]

[1] The imagery seems to be erotic, with 'spring' standing for a
faithful lover and 'river' for one who is promiscuous.

963-70

Never praise a man until you know clearly what he is
in temperament, disposition, and way of life. Many
indeed have a false, thievish character and keep it
hidden, taking on an attitude appropriate to the day.
But time assuredly reveals the character of each of
them. In fact I myself went far astray in my judge-
ment. I praised you too soon, before I knew all your
ways; but now I keep a wide berth like a ship.

---

963 σαφηνέως Floril., σαφηνῶς codd., ἄνδρας ἀφανέως
Stob., σώφρονα Orion   964 θυμὸν pro ῥυθμὸν Stob.   ὄντιν᾽
ἔχει Stob.   967 πάντως Vat. gr. 63, πάντων Ao
969 ἔφθην δ᾽ ο   970 ναῦς ο

971-72

τίς δ᾽ ἀρετὴ πίνοντ᾽ ἐπιοίνιον ἆθλον ἑλέσθαι;
πολλάκι τοι νικᾷ καὶ κακὸς ἄνδρ᾽ ἀγαθόν.

973-78

οὐδεὶς ἀνθρώπων, ὃν πρῶτ᾽ ἐπὶ γαῖα καλύψῃ
εἴς τ᾽ ἔρεβος καταβῇ, δώματα Περσεφόνης,
975 τέρπεται οὔτε λύρης οὔτ᾽ αὐλητῆρος ἀκούων
οὔτε Διωνύσου δῶρ᾽ ἐπαειρόμενος.
ταῦτ᾽ ἐσορῶν κραδίη εὖ πείσομαι, ὄφρα τ᾽
ἐλαφρὰ
γούνατα, καὶ κεφαλὴν ἀτρεμέως προφέρω.

973 ὃν ἐπεί ποτε p   καλύψῃ Harl. 6301, -ει Ao
974 δῶμά τε XD, δώματά τε I   976 ἐπ- Diehl, ἐσ- codd.
-όμενος D1, -άμενος Ao   977 κραδίη o, -ην A   ὄφρ᾽ ἔτ᾽
Schneidewin (cf. 984)   978 ἀτρομέων p

979-82

μή μοι ἀνὴρ εἴη γλώσσῃ φίλος, ἀλλὰ καὶ ἔργῳ·
980 χερσίν τε σπεύδοι χρήμασί τ᾽, ἀμφότερα·
μηδὲ παρὰ κρητῆρι λόγοισιν ἐμὴν φρένα θέλγοι,
ἀλλ᾽ ἔρδων φαίνοιτ᾽, εἴ τι δύναιτ᾽, ἀγαθός.

Floril. Monac. 147 (v. 979)

980 σπεύδοι XD, -ει OI, -ου A   ῥήμασί Matthiae
981 κρητῆρι I, κλητῆρι A, κρατῆρσι O, κρητῆρσι XD   τέρποι
o, θέλγοις A, corr. Bekker   982 ἀγαθόν codd., corr. Edmonds

THEOGNIS

971-72

What's the merit in gaining a wine-drinking prize?
Often in fact a base man wins over one who is noble.

973-78

No man, once the earth has covered him and he
has gone down into the darkness, the home of
Persephone, has the pleasure of listening to lyre or
piper or of raising to his lips the gift of Dionysus. In
view of this, I'll give my heart a good time, while my
knees are nimble and my head does not shake.

979-82

Let me have a man who is my friend in deed, not in
words. Let him exert himself (for me) both with
hands and possessions.[1] Let him not beguile me
with words beside the mixing bowl, but let him show
himself to be a man of worth by his actions, if he can.

[1] I.e., let him give me physical and monetary support.

983-88

ἡμεῖς δ' ἐν θαλίῃσι φίλον καταθώμεθα θυμόν,
  ὄφρ' ἔτι τερπωλῆς ἔργ' ἐρατεινὰ φέρῃ.
985 αἶψα γὰρ ὥστε νόημα παρέρχεται ἀγλαὸς ἥβη·
  οὐδ' ἵππων ὁρμὴ γίνεται ὠκυτέρη,
αἵ τε ἄνακτα φέρουσι δορυσσόον ἐς πόνον ἀνδρῶν
  λάβρως, πυροφόρῳ τερπόμεναι πεδίῳ.

983 θαλίεσσι A, θαλίαισι O   984 παρῇ Lavagnini

989-90

πῖν' ὁπόταν πίνωσιν· ὅταν δέ τι θυμὸν ἀσηθῇς,
990   μηδεὶς ἀνθρώπων γνῷ σε βαρυνόμενον.

989 δ' ἔτι A, τοι o, corr. Brunck

991-92

ἄλλοτέ τοι πάσχων ἀνιήσεαι, ἄλλοτε δ' ἔρδων
  χαιρήσεις· δύναται δ' ἄλλοτε ἄλλος ἀνήρ.

991 θ' O, τ' p   992 χαιρῆισι A, -ήσειν o, corr. Epkema
χαιρήσει West   δύνααι ἄλλοτέ τ' o, δύναται· ἄλλοτε δ' A,
corr. Bergk

993-1002

εἰ θείης, Ἀκάδημε, ἐφίμερον ὕμνον ἀείδειν,
  ἆθλον δ' ἐν μέσσῳ παῖς καλὸν ἄνθος ἔχων
995 σοί τ' εἴη καὶ ἐμοὶ σοφίης πέρι δηρισάντοιν,
  γνοίης χ' ὅσσον ὄνων κρέσσονες ἡμίονοι.
τῆμος δ' ἠέλιος μὲν ἐν αἰθέρι μώνυχας ἵππους
  ἄρτι παραγγέλλοι μέσσατον ἦμαρ ἔχων,

983-88

Let us give up our hearts to festivity, while they can still sustain pleasure's lovely activities. For the splendour of youth passes by as quickly as a thought. Not so swift are charging horses which, delighting in the wheat-bearing plain, carry their spear-wielding master furiously to the battle toil of men.

989-90

Drink when they are drinking, but when you are sick at heart, let no one know that you are distressed.

991-92

Sometimes you'll be distressed at what is done to you, sometimes you'll rejoice at what you do. A man's power is never constant.

993-1002[1]

If you were to set a prize, Academus,[2] for the singing of a lovely song, and if a boy with the fair bloom of youth were the prize for you and me as we compete in artistry, you would know how superior mules are to asses.[3] Then the sun in the sky would be urging on his whole-hooved steeds right at midday, we would

δείπνου δὲ λήγοιμεν, ὅπου τινὰ θυμὸς ἀνώγοι,
1000   παντοίων ἀγαθῶν γαστρὶ χαριζόμενοι,
χέρνιβα δ᾽ αἶψα θύραζε φέροι, στεφανώματα δ᾽
      εἴσω,
εὐειδὴς ῥαδιναῖς χερσὶ Λάκαινα κόρη.

Ath. 7.310ab (vv. 993-96 et 997-1002)

993 εἶτ᾽ εἴησακαλὴν μὲν Ath.   ἐφήμερον A, -ριον O
994 καλὸς Ath.   995 δηρησάντοιν o, δηρισάντων AO,
δηριόωσι Ath.   996 τ᾽ A, θ᾽ O   997 ἦμος p
998 πάραντ᾽ ἐλάοι West (ἐλάοι iam Harrison)   999 τε p, δὴ
Ath.   ὅσου Ath.   ἀνώγει o   1001 φέρει et δήσοι o
1002 ῥαδινῆς Ath.

1003-1006

ἥδ᾽ ἀρετή, τόδ᾽ ἄεθλον ἐν ἀνθρώποισιν ἄριστον
      κάλλιστόν τε φέρειν γίνεται ἀνδρὶ σοφῷ,
1005   ξυνὸν δ᾽ ἐσθλὸν τοῦτο πόληί τε παντί τε δήμῳ,
ὅστις ἀνὴρ διαβὰς ἐν προμάχοισι μένῃ.

Tyrt. fr. 12.13-16 (vv. 1003-1006)

1004 ἀνδρὶ νέῳ Tyrt.   1006 μένῃ Stob. in Tyrt., μένει A,
-ν ἔνι o

1007-12

ξυνὸν δ᾽ ἀνθρώποις ὑποθήσομαι, ὄφρα τις ἥβης
      ἀγλαὸν ἄνθος ἔχων καὶ φρεσὶν ἐσθλὰ νοῇ,
τῶν αὐτοῦ κτεάνων εὖ πασχέμεν· οὐ γὰρ ἀνηβᾶν
1010   δὶς πέλεται πρὸς θεῶν, οὐδὲ λύσις θανάτου

be finishing our meal, after gratifying our bellies with all sorts of good dishes as everyone's heart bids him, and a comely Spartan girl with slender hands would quickly carry out the washbasin and bring in garlands.

1 Only West and Young combine these verses, whereas others, perhaps rightly, divide after 996.   2 Person unknown.
3 The point of this is obscure.

1003-1006

This is excellence, this the best human prize and the fairest for a man to win. This is a common benefit for the state and all the people, whenever a man with firm stance holds his ground among the front ranks.[1]

1 Identical to Tyrtaeus fr. 12.13-16 except for one word.

1007-12

I shall give advice for all the world: so long as one has youth's splendid bloom and noble thoughts, let him enjoy his possessions. For it is impossible to obtain a second youth from the gods and there is no

θνητοῖς ἀνθρώποισι, κακὸν δ᾽ ἐπὶ γῆρας ἐλέγχει
οὐλόμενον, κεφαλῆς δ᾽ ἅπτεται ἀκροτάτης.

1007 ἥβᾳ Bergk   1008 ἔχῃ Marc. 317 in ras.

1013-16

ἆ μάκαρ εὐδαίμων τε καὶ ὄλβιος, ὅστις ἄπειρος
ἄθλων εἰς Ἀΐδου δῶμα μέλαν κατέβη,
πρίν τ᾽ ἐχθροὺς πτῆξαι καὶ ὑπερβῆναί περ ἀνάγκῃ
ἐξετάσαι τε φίλους ὅντιν᾽ ἔχουσι νόον.

1013 a A, ὡς o   1014 καταβῆ O   1015 γ᾽ Bekker
1016 δε A

1017-22

αὐτίκα μοι κατὰ μὲν χροιὴν ῥέει ἄσπετος ἱδρώς,
πτοιῶμαι δ᾽ ἐσορῶν ἄνθος ὁμηλικίης
τερπνὸν ὁμῶς καὶ καλόν· ἐπὶ πλέον ὤφελεν εἶναι·
ἀλλ᾽ ὀλιγοχρόνιον γίνεται ὥσπερ ὄναρ
ἥβη τιμήεσσα· τὸ δ᾽ οὐλόμενον καὶ ἄμορφον
αὐτίχ᾽ ὑπὲρ κεφαλῆς γῆρας ὑπερκρέμαται.

1018 πτοιοῦμαι o   1019 ἐπεὶ Ao, ἐπὶ ed. Aldina
1020 ὀλιγοχρόνιος O   1021 ἀργαλέον pro οὐλόμενον
Mimn.   1022 γῆρας . . . αὐτίχ᾽ Mimn.

1023-24

οὔποτε τοῖς ἐχθροῖσιν ὑπὸ ζυγὸν αὐχένα θήσω
δύσλοφον, οὐδ᾽ εἴ μοι Τμῶλος ἔπεστι κάρῃ.

release from death for mortal men, but vile and ac-
cursed old age brings dishonour[1] and takes hold of
the top of one's head.[2]

[1] Or perhaps "puts one to the test."　　[2] Presumably a ref-
erence to grey hair.

1013-16

Ah, blessed, fortunate and happy is he who goes
down to Hades' dark house without experiencing
hardship and before he cowers in the face of ene-
mies, transgresses under duress, and tests what is in
the minds of his friends.

1017-22

Suddenly a copious sweat flows down over my skin
and I am a-flutter when I behold my generation's de-
lightful and fair bloom. Would that it lasted longer!
But precious youth is like a fleeting dream; in no
time accursed and hideous old age hangs over one's
head.[1]

[1] 1020-22 are a version of Mimnermus fr. 5.1-3. See n. 1 ad loc.

1023-24

I'll never place my neck beneath the galling yoke of
my enemies, not even if Tmolus[1] is upon my head.

[1] A mountain in Lydia. This may, but need not, indicate that
the author came from that general area.

1025-26

1025 δειλοί τοι κακότητι ματαιότεροι νόον εἰσίν,
       τῶν δ᾿ ἀγαθῶν αἰεὶ πρήξιες ἰθύτεραι.

1025 δειλοῖς et νόοι ο (γόοι D)

1027-28

ῥηϊδίη τοι πρῆξις ἐν ἀνθρώποις κακότητος,
       τοῦ δ᾿ ἀγαθοῦ χαλεπή, Κύρνε, πέλει παλάμη.

1029-36

       τόλμα, θυμέ, κακοῖσιν ὅμως ἄτλητα πεπονθώς·
1030 δειλῶν τοι κραδίη γίνεται ὀξυτέρη.
       μηδὲ σύ γ᾿ ἀπρήκτοισιν ἐπ᾿ ἔργμασιν ἄλγος ἀέξων
       αὔχει μηδ᾿ αἴσχεα· μηδὲ φίλους ἀνία,
       μηδ᾿ ἐχθροὺς εὔφραινε. θεῶν δ᾿ εἱμαρμένα δῶρα
       οὐκ ἂν ῥηϊδίως θνητὸς ἀνὴρ προφύγοι,
1035 οὔτ᾿ ἂν πορφυρέης καταδὺς ἐς πυθμένα λίμνης,
       οὔθ᾿ ὅταν αὐτὸν ἔχῃ Τάρταρος ἠερόεις.

Stob. 4.56.9 (vv. 1029-34)

1031 γ᾿ ρ et Stob., τ᾿ AD   1032 αὔχει Stob., ἔχθει codd.,
ὄχθει Emperius, alii alia   αἴσχεα Stob., ἄχθει ο (-ουρ), εχθει Α

1037-38

ἄνδρα τοί ἐστ᾿ ἀγαθὸν χαλεπώτατον ἐξαπατῆσαι,
       ὡς ἐν ἐμοὶ γνώμη, Κύρνε, πάλαι κέκριται.

322

THEOGNIS

1025-26

The base are more empty-headed in bad times,[1] whereas the actions of the noble are by comparison always straightforward.

[1] Or "because of their baseness."

1027-28

It's easy, Cyrnus, for men to act badly, but the ability to achieve what is good is difficult.

1029-36

Bear up under misfortunes, my soul, even though you suffer things unbearable. A heart that is too quick to show its emotions is assuredly a mark of the base.[1] And don't add to your grief and shame by boasting of deeds that can't be done.[2] Don't be a source of pain to your friends and joy to your enemies. No mortal man can easily avoid the destined gifts of the gods, either by diving to the bottom of the turbulent sea or when misty Tartarus seizes him.

[1] Cf. 366.   [2] Text and translation uncertain.

1037-38

It is assuredly extremely difficult to deceive a noble man, a judgement I formed long ago, Cyrnus.

1038ab

ἤδεα μὲν καὶ πρόσθεν, ἀτὰρ πολὺ λώιον ἤδη,
οὕνεκα τοῖς δειλοῖς οὐδεμί' ἐστὶ χάρις.

1038a ἠδέα codd., expl. Camerarius

1039-40

ἄφρονες ἄνθρωποι καὶ νήπιοι, οἵτινες οἶνον
1040   μὴ πίνουσ' ἄστρου καὶ κυνὸς ἀρχομένου.

1040 πίνωσ' Par. 2833   ἐρχομένου O

1041-42

δεῦρο σὺν αὐλητῆρι· παρὰ κλαίοντι γελῶντες
πίνωμεν, κείνου κήδεσι τερπόμενοι.

1043-44

εὕδωμεν· φυλακὴ δὲ πόλευς φυλάκεσσι μελήσει
ἀστυφέλης ἐρατῆς πατρίδος ἡμετέρης.

1043 πόλεως A

1045-46

1045   ναὶ μὰ Δί', εἴ τις τῶνδε καὶ ἐγκεκαλυμμένος εὕδει,
ἡμέτερον κῶμον δέξεται ἁρπαλέως.

1047-48

νῦν μὲν πίνοντες τερπώμεθα, καλὰ λέγοντες·
ἄσσα δ' ἔπειτ' ἔσται, ταῦτα θεοῖσι μέλει.

324

THEOGNIS

1038ab (= 853-54)

I knew it before, but I know it much better now, that
the base have no gratitude.

1039-40

Witless and foolish are men[1] who do not drink wine
when the season of the Dog Star[2] commences.

[1] Cf. 1069.   [2] Sirius, Orion's dog, at whose rising in late
July heat and thirst are most intense. Cf. Hes. *Opera* 582-88 and
Alcaeus' adaptation (fr. 347).

1041-42

Come here with a piper. Let's laugh and drink at the
weeper's side, rejoicing in his woes.

1043-44

Let's sleep. The guarding of the city, our fertile[1] and
lovely homeland, will be in the care of its guards.

[1] The first word of 1044 is rare and of uncertain meaning. Its
literal meaning seems to be 'not rugged' and so perhaps 'fertile.'

1045-46

By Zeus, even if one of these is wrapped up and
asleep, he'll gladly welcome us merrymakers.

1047-48

Now let's delight in drink and fine talk. What will
happen afterwards is up to the gods.

1049-54

σοὶ δ' ἐγὼ οἷά τε παιδὶ πατὴρ ὑποθήσομαι αὐτὸς
1050   ἐσθλά· σὺ δ' ἐν θυμῷ καὶ φρεσὶ ταῦτα βάλευ.
μήποτ' ἐπειγόμενος πράξῃς κακόν, ἀλλὰ βαθείῃ
      σῇ φρενὶ βούλευσαι σῷ ἀγαθῷ τε νόῳ.
τῶν γὰρ μαινομένων πέτεται θυμός τε νόος τε,
      βουλὴ δ' εἰς ἀγαθὸν καὶ νόον ἐσθλὸν ἄγει.

1049 δετω A, δὲ o (δέ γε I), corr. Bergk   πατὴρ om. o
(φίλῳ p)   1050 βάλε o   1051 πρήξῃς p
1052 σωτ' A   1053 μαρναμένων μάχεται o

1055-58

1055   ἀλλὰ λόγον μὲν τοῦτον ἐάσομεν, αὐτὰρ ἐμοὶ σὺ
      αὔλει, καὶ Μουσῶν μνησόμεθ' ἀμφότεροι·
αὗται γὰρ τάδ' ἔδωκαν ἔχειν κεχαρισμένα δῶρα
      σοὶ καὶ ἐμοί, ‹μέλο›μεν δ' ἀμφιπερικτίοσιν.

1055 ἐάσομαι o   1058 μενδ' A, μὲν o (νῦν O, μὴν D,
μην I), suppl. Hiller (μελέμεν iam Ahrens): alii alia

1059-62

Τιμαγόρα, πολλῶν ὀργὴν ἀπάτερθεν ὁρῶντι
1060   γινώσκειν χαλεπόν, καίπερ ἐόντι σοφῷ.
οἱ μὲν γὰρ κακότητα κατακρύψαντες ἔχουσιν
      πλούτῳ, τοὶ δ' ἀρετὴν οὐλομένῃ πενίῃ.

Stob. 4.33.9 (vv. 1061-62)

1059 τιμᾶ γὰρ ἀπόλλων fere codd., corr. Camerarius

THEOGNIS

1049-54

I shall personally give you good advice, as a father to a son. Put this in your heart and mind. Never make a mistake through haste, but plan in the depths of your heart and with your good sense. The heart and mind of madmen are flighty, but planning leads to benefit and to good sense.[1]

[1] Or "leads even a good mind to what is beneficial."

1055-58

But let us be done with this talk; play the pipe for me and let us both pay heed to the Muses. For it is they who have given you and me these charming gifts and we are well known to those who live round about.

1059-62

Timagoras,[1] it's difficult, even for one who is skilled, to know the disposition of many by looking from a distance. For some keep their baseness concealed by wealth and others their merit by accursed poverty.

[1] Identity unknown.

1063-68

ἐν δ' ἥβῃ πάρα μὲν ξὺν ὁμήλικι πάννυχον εὕδειν,
ἱμερτῶν ἔργων ἐξ ἔρον ἱέμενον·
1065   ἔστι δὲ κωμάζοντα μετ' αὐλητῆρος ἀείδειν·
τούτων οὐδὲν †τι† ἀλλ' ἐπιτερπνότερον
ἀνδράσιν ἠδὲ γυναιξί. τί μοι πλοῦτός τε καὶ αἰδώς;
τερπωλὴ νικᾷ πάντα σὺν εὐφροσύνῃ.

1063 πάννυχον A, κάλλιστον O, κάλλιον p   1066 τι O,
τοι p, om. A: ἄρ' ἦν Bergk, alii alia

1069-70

ἄφρονες ἄνθρωποι καὶ νήπιοι, οἵ τε θανόντας
1070   κλαίουσ', οὐδ' ἥβης ἄνθος ἀπολλύμενον.

1070ab

τέρπεό μοι, φίλε θυμέ· τάχ' αὖ τινες ἄλλοι
ἔσονται
ἄνδρες, ἐγὼ δὲ θανὼν γαῖα μέλαιν' ἔσομαι.

1070a ἄν o   ἔσοιντο p

1071-74

Κύρνε, φίλους πρὸς πάντας ἐπίστρεφε ποικίλον
ἦθος,
συμμίσγων ὀργὴν οἷος ἕκαστος ἔφυ.
νῦν μὲν τῷδ' ἐφέπου, τότε δ' ἀλλοῖος πέλευ ὀργήν.
κρεῖσσόν τοι σοφίη καὶ μεγάλης ἀρετῆς.

1074 κρείσσων o

1063-68

In youth you are free to sleep all night with an age-mate and satisfy your craving for lovemaking; you may carouse and sing with a piper. No other pleasure compares with these for men and women. What are wealth and respect to me? Pleasure combined with good cheer surpasses everything.

1069-70

Witless and foolish are men[1] who weep for the dead, but not for the fading bloom of youth.

[1] Cf. 1039.

1070ab

Enjoy yourself, my dear heart; soon it will be the turn of other men, and I'll be dead and become dark earth.[1]

[1] Identical to 877-78 except for the first word.

1071-74

Cyrnus, toward all your friends keep turning a versatile disposition, mingling with it a mood according to the nature of each. Now follow along in this direction, now take on a different mood. Cleverness is in truth superior even to great merit.[1]

[1] These are variations on 213-14 and 217-18. West treats the couplets as separate.

1075-78

1075 πρήγματος ἀπρήκτου χαλεπώτατόν ἐστι τελευτὴν
γνῶναι, ὅπως μέλλει τοῦτο θεὸς τελέσαι·
ὄρφνη γὰρ τέταται, πρὸ δὲ τοῦ μέλλοντος ἔσεσθαι
οὐ ξυνετὰ θνητοῖς πείρατ᾽ ἀμηχανίης.

1079-80

οὐδένα τῶν ἐχθρῶν μωμήσομαι ἐσθλὸν ἐόντα,
1080 οὐδὲ μὲν αἰνήσω δειλὸν ἐόντα φίλον.

1081-82b

Κύρνε, κύει πόλις ἥδε, δέδοικα δὲ μὴ τέκῃ ἄνδρα
ὑβριστήν, χαλεπῆς ἡγεμόνα στάσιος·
ἀστοὶ μὲν γὰρ ἔθ᾽ οἷδε σαόφρονες, ἡγεμόνες δὲ
τετράφαται πολλὴν εἰς κακότητα πεσεῖν

1081 τέκοι Ao, η sscr. I   1082a ἔθ᾽ οιδε A, ἔασι o

1082cf-84

c μή μ᾽ ἔπεσιν μὲν στέργε, νόον δ᾽ ἔχε καὶ φρένας
ἄλλας,
d εἴ με φιλεῖς καί σοι πιστὸς ἔνεστι νόος,
e ἀλλὰ φίλει καθαρὸν θέμενος νόον, ἤ μ᾽ ἀποειπὼν
f ἔχθαιρ᾽ ἐμφανέως νεῖκος ἀειράμενος.
οὕτω χρὴ τόν γ᾽ ἐσθλὸν ἐπιστρέψαντα νόημα
ἔμπεδον αἰὲν ἔχειν ἐς τέλος ἀνδρὶ φίλῳ.

1082c ἄλλη o (ut 87)   1082e ἤ με φίλει o (ut 89)
1082f ἀμφαδίην o (ut 90)

THEOGNIS

1075-78

It is very difficult to know how the god is going to bring about the outcome of an action uncompleted. For darkness extends over it, and in advance of what is going to occur mortals cannot comprehend the limits of their helplessness.

1079-80

I'll not find fault with any of my enemies whose behaviour is noble, nor will I praise a friend whose behaviour is base.

1081-82b

Cyrnus, this city is pregnant and I am afraid she will give birth to a man who commits wanton outrage, a leader of grievous strife. These townsmen are still of sound mind, but their leaders have changed and fallen into the depths of depravity.[1]

[1] Identical to 39-42 except for 1082.

1082cf-84

Don't show affection for me in your words, but keep a different mind and heart, if you love me and the mind within you is loyal. But love me sincerely or renounce me, hate me, and quarrel openly. In this way one who is noble should direct his thoughts and hold them ever steadfast to the end for a man who is his friend.[1]

[1] 1082cf are identical to 87-90, with three minor variations.

ELEGIAC POETRY

1085-86

1085   Δημῶναξ, σὺ δὲ πολλὰ φέρειν βαρύς· οὐ γὰρ
    ἐπίστῃ
    τοῦτ᾽ ἔρδειν ὅτι σοι μὴ καταθύμιον ᾖ.

1085 Δημῶναξ σὺ δὲ Bergk (σοὶ Welcker, εἶ Boissonade),
δημωναξιοιδε A, δῆμον δ᾽ ἀξιοῖ o   βαρυ A

1087-90

Κάστορ καὶ Πολύδευκες, οἳ ἐν Λακεδαίμονι δίῃ
    ναίετ᾽ ἐπ᾽ Εὐρώτᾳ καλλιρόῳ ποταμῷ,
εἴ ποτε βουλεύσαιμι φίλῳ κακόν, αὐτὸς ἔχοιμι·
1090   εἰ δέ τι κεῖνος ἐμοί, δὶς τόσον αὐτὸς ἔχοι.

1088 Εὐρώτα praeferunt multi, cl. 785

1091-94

ἀργαλέως μοι θυμὸς ἔχει περὶ σῆς φιλότητος·
    οὔτε γὰρ ἐχθαίρειν οὔτε φιλεῖν δύναμαι,
γινώσκων χαλεπὸν μὲν ὅταν φίλος ἀνδρὶ γένηται
    ἐχθαίρειν, χαλεπὸν δ᾽ οὐκ ἐθέλοντα φιλεῖν.

1095-96

1095   σκέπτεο δὴ νῦν ἄλλον· ἐμοί γε μὲν οὔ τις ἀνάγκη
    τοῦτ᾽ ἔρδειν· τῶν μοι πρόσθε χάριν τίθεσο.

THEOGNIS

1085-86

Demonax,[1] you're often hard to stand, since you don't know how to do what is displeasing to you.

[1] Identity unknown.

1087-90

Castor and Polydeuces, you who dwell in glorious Lacedaemon by the fair-flowing river Eurotas, if I ever plot harm to a friend, may I have it myself; and if he plots harm to me, may he have twice as much himself.

1091-94

My heart is in turmoil with regard to your friendship, since I can neither hate nor love you,[1] realizing that it is difficult to hate, when a man has a friend, and difficult to love when he is unwilling (to love you).

[1] Cf. 874.

1095-96

Look now for someone else; I, however, am under no obligation to do this.[1] Be grateful for what I've done before.[2]

[1] It is unclear what the speaker is not obliged to do.
[2] Identical to 1160ab, except for the beginning and the variation τοῦτ'-ταῦτ'.

1097-1100

ἤδη καὶ πτερύγεσσιν ἐπαίρομαι ὥστε πετεινὸν
ἐκ λίμνης μεγάλης, ἄνδρα κακὸν προφυγών,
βρόχον ἀπορρήξας· σὺ δ᾽ ἐμῆς φιλότητος
  ἁμαρτὼν
1100 ὕστερον ἡμετέρην γνώσῃ ἐπιφροσύνην.

1098 προφυγόν o   1099 βρόκχον Schaefer (prob.
West)

1101-1102

ὅστις σοι βούλευσεν ἐμεῦ πέρι, καί σ᾽ ἐκέλευσεν
οἴχεσθαι προλιπόνθ᾽ ἡμετέρην φιλίην . . .

1103-1104

ὕβρις καὶ Μάγνητας ἀπώλεσε καὶ Κολοφῶνα
καὶ Σμύρνην· πάντως, Κύρνε, καὶ ὔμμ᾽ ἀπολεῖ.

1104 ὔμμας ὀλεῖ o, ἄμμ᾽ Welcker (cf. 40)

1104ab

δόξα μὲν ἀνθρώποισι κακὸν μέγα, πεῖρα δ᾽
  ἄριστον·
πολλοὶ ἀπείρητοι δόξαν ἔχουσ᾽ ἀγαθῶν.

1104b ἀγαθοί A

1097-1100

Now I rise up on my wings like a bird from a large[1]
lake which escapes from an evil man by breaking its
noose.[2] You have lost my friendship and later you'll
recognize my shrewdness.

[1] The epithet seems pointless and various emendations, none
convincing, have been proposed.   [2] The scene envisaged by
the poet is unclear. For one explanation see West, *Studies* 162.

1101-1102

Whoever gave you advice about me and told you to
abandon my friendship and go . . .[1]

[1] 1101-1102 = 1278ab where the relative clause is similarly left
without an apodosis. West inserts 539-40 after 1102, but there are
many other possibilities.

1103-1104

Lawlessness destroyed Magnesia, Colophon, and
Smyrna;[1] it will assuredly destroy you people too,
Cyrnus.

[1] For the destruction of these cities see West, *Studies* 66-67,
although his dating of the couplet to the period 650-600 does not
seem justified. For Magnesia see also 603.

1104ab

(Mere) reputation is a great evil for men; trial is
best. Many who have not been tested have a reputa-
tion for merit.[1]

[1] Identical to 571-72. See n. 1 ad loc.

1105-1106

εἰς βάσανον δ᾽ ἐλθὼν παρατριβόμενός τε
μολύβδῳ
χρυσὸς ἄπεφθος ἐὼν καλὸς ἅπασιν ἔσῃ.

1105 μολίβδῳ Ao, corr. Par. 2883   1106 δῆλος pro
καλὸς Ahrens

1107-1108

ὤ μοι ἐγὼ δειλός· καὶ δὴ κατάχαρμα μὲν ἐχθροῖς,
τοῖς δὲ φίλοισι πόνος δειλὰ παθὼν γενόμην.

1107 οἴμοι A   1108 φίλοις ὁ πόνος A   δεινὰ I

1109-14

Κύρν᾽, οἱ πρόσθ᾽ ἀγαθοὶ νῦν αὖ κακοί, οἱ δὲ
κακοὶ πρὶν
νῦν ἀγαθοί. τίς κεν ταῦτ᾽ ἀνέχοιτ᾽ ἐσορῶν,
τοὺς ἀγαθοὺς μὲν ἀτιμοτέρους, κακίους δὲ
λαχόντας
τιμῆς; μνηστεύει δ᾽ ἐκ κακοῦ ἐσθλὸς ἀνήρ·
ἀλλήλους δ᾽ ἀπατῶντες ἐπ᾽ ἀλλήλοισι γελῶσιν,
οὔτ᾽ ἀγαθῶν μνήμην εἰδότες οὔτε κακῶν.

1114 γνώμην Hecker ex 60

1114ab

πολλὰ δ᾽ ἀμηχανίῃσι κυλίνδομαι ἀχνύμενος κῆρ·
ἀρχὴν γὰρ πενίης οὐχ ὑπερεδράμομεν.

THEOGNIS

1105-1106

If (when?) you come to the touchstone and being rubbed beside lead are refined gold,[1] you will be noble in the eyes of all.

[1] Cf. 417-18 with n. 2 ad loc. Many editors combine this couplet with the preceding one.

1107-1108[1]

O wretch that I am! Because of my wretched suffering I have become a joy to my enemies and a burden to my friends.

[1] Virtually identical to 1318ab.

1109-14

Cyrnus, those who were formerly noble are now base, and those who were base before are now noble. Who can endure the sight of this, the noble dishonoured and the base honoured? A man who is noble seeks marriage with the daughter of one who is base. They deceive one another and mock one another, with no recollection of what is noble or base.[1]

[1] 1109-10 is a variation on 57-58 and 1113-14 on 59-60. For 1112 cf. 189-90.

1114ab

Often I toss about in helplessness, distressed at heart, for I have not run beyond the beginning of poverty.[1]

[1] Cf. 619-20 where ἄκρην is in place of ἀρχήν. The latter may be simply an error (it can hardly mean 'rule' here, as some maintain).

ELEGIAC POETRY

1115-16

1115 χρήματ' ἔχων πενίην μ' ὠνείδισας· ἀλλὰ τὰ μέν μοι
ἔστι, τὰ δ' ἐργάσομαι θεοῖσιν ἐπευξάμενος.

1115 μοι ὀνείδισας Emperius   τὰ μέν μοι p, τὰ μέντοι O,
τεμεμοι A

1117-18

Πλοῦτε, θεῶν κάλλιστε καὶ ἱμεροέστατε πάντων,
σὺν σοὶ καὶ κακὸς ὢν γίνεται ἐσθλὸς ἀνήρ.

1118 γίγνομαι p

1119-22

ἥβης μέτρον ἔχοιμι, φιλοῖ δέ με Φοῖβος Ἀπόλλων
1120 Λητοΐδης καὶ Ζεὺς ἀθανάτων βασιλεύς,
ὄφρα δίκῃ ζώοιμι κακῶν ἔκτοσθεν ἀπάντων,
ἥβῃ καὶ πλούτῳ θυμὸν ἰαινόμενος.

1121 δικηι A, βίον o (δεινδε σώοιμι I)

1123-28

μή με κακῶν μίμνησκε· πέπονθά τοι οἷά τ'
Ὀδυσσεύς,
ὅς τ' Ἀΐδεω μέγα δῶμ' ἤλυθεν ἐξαναδύς.
1125 ὃς δὴ καὶ μνηστῆρας ἀνείλετο νηλέι θυμῷ
Πηνελόπης εὔφρων κουριδίης ἀλόχου,
ἥ μιν δήθ' ὑπέμεινε φίλῳ παρὰ παιδὶ μένουσα,
ὄφρα τε γῆς ἐπέβη †δειμαλέους γε μυχούς†.

1123 μέμνησθε o   1124 ἀΐδου o   1125 ανείλατο A
χαλκῶ o   1126 ἔμφρων o   1127 ἥ μὲν o   πρὸς o

338

THEOGNIS

1115-16

Because you're rich you throw up to me my poverty.
But I have some things and other things I'll earn,
through my prayers to the gods.

1117-18

Wealth, fairest and most desirable of all the gods,
thanks to you even a man who is base becomes
noble.

1119-22

May I have my full measure of youth and may Leto's
son, Phoebus Apollo, and Zeus, king of the immor-
tals, love me, so that I may live righteously, free of
all misfortunes, with youth and wealth to warm my
heart.

1123-28

Don't remind me of my misfortunes. My trials have
been like those of Odysseus who returned, com-
ing up from Hades' great house. With pitiless heart
he joyfully slew the suitors of his wedded wife
Penelope who had long awaited him, remaining at
the side of her dear son, until he set foot on his land
(?) . . .¹

¹ It is unclear whether γῆς depends on the verb or on what
follows and whether ὄφρα means 'until' or 'while.' If it means the
latter, an imperfect would be more natural. Many assume that the
poem is incomplete.

1128 δειλαλεουστε A, δειμαλέους γε o, δείν' ἁλίους τε Sitzler,
alii alia

1129-32

ἐμπίομαι· πενίης θυμοφθόρου οὐ μελεδαίνω,
1130   οὐδ᾽ ἀνδρῶν ἐχθρῶν οἵ με λέγουσι κακῶς.
ἀλλ᾽ ἥβην ἐρατὴν ὀλοφύρομαι, ἥ μ᾽ ἐπιλείπει,
κλαίω δ᾽ ἀργαλέον γῆρας ἐπερχόμενον.

Stob. 4.50.43 (vv. 1129-32)

1129 ἐλπίομαι O, εἰ πίομαι p, οὔτε γε μὴν Stob. (om. ου)
μελεδαίνων A

1133-34

Κύρνε, παροῦσι φίλοισι κακοῦ καταπαύσομεν
    ἀρχήν,
ζητῶμεν δ᾽ ἕλκει φάρμακα φυομένῳ.

1135-50

1135   Ἐλπὶς ἐν ἀνθρώποισι μόνη θεὸς ἐσθλὴ ἔνεστιν,
ἄλλοι δ᾽ Οὔλυμπον ἐκπρολιπόντες ἔβαν.
ᾤχετο μὲν Πίστις, μεγάλη θεός, ᾤχετο δ᾽ ἀνδρῶν
Σωφροσύνη, Χάριτές τ᾽, ὦ φίλε, γῆν ἔλιπον·
ὅρκοι δ᾽ οὐκέτι πιστοὶ ἐν ἀνθρώποισι δίκαιοι,
1140   οὐδὲ θεοὺς οὐδεὶς ἅζεται ἀθανάτους,
εὐσεβέων δ᾽ ἀνδρῶν γένος ἔφθιτο, οὐδὲ θέμιστας
οὐκέτι γινώσκουσ᾽ οὐδὲ μὲν εὐσεβίας.
ἀλλ᾽ ὄφρα τις ζώει καὶ ὁρᾷ φάος ἠελίοιο,
εὐσεβέων περὶ θεοὺς Ἐλπίδα προσμενέτω·
1145   εὐχέσθω δὲ θεοῖσι, καὶ ἀγλαὰ μηρία καίων
Ἐλπίδι τε πρώτῃ καὶ πυμάτῃ θυέτω.

340

THEOGNIS

1129-32

I'll drink my fill, without a thought for soul-destroying poverty or enemies who speak ill of me. But I bewail the lovely youth that is leaving me and weep at the approach of grim old age.

1133-34

Cyrnus, with the friends we have let us check the evil at its beginning, and let us seek a remedy for the ulcer that is growing.

1135-50

Hope is the only good god remaining among mankind; the others have left and gone to Olympus. Trust, a mighty god, has gone, Restraint has gone from men, and the Graces, my friend, have abandoned earth. Men's judicial oaths are no longer to be trusted, nor does anyone revere the immortal gods; the race of pious men has perished and men no longer recognize established rules of conduct or acts of piety. But as long as a man lives and sees the light of the sun, let him show piety to the gods and count on Hope. Let him pray to the gods and burn splendid thigh bones, sacrificing to Hope first and last. And

φραζέσθω δ' ἀδίκων ἀνδρῶν σκολιὸν λόγον αἰεί,
οἳ θεῶν ἀθανάτων οὐδὲν ὀπιζόμενοι
αἰὲν ἐπ' ἀλλοτρίοις κτεάνοις ἐπέχουσι νόημα,
1150   αἰσχρὰ κακοῖς ἔργοις σύμβολα θηκάμενοι.

Stob. 4.46.12 (v. 1135)

1135 ἀνθρώποις μούνη Stob. (sed μόνη cod. A)
1136 Οὔλυμπόν⟨δ'⟩ Camerarius   1143 ζώοι OI, ζώη D
φῶς A   1146 τιθέτω O   1148 μηδὲν o

1151-52

μήποτε τὸν παρεόντα μεθεὶς φίλον ἄλλον ἐρεύνα
δειλῶν ἀνθρώπων ῥήμασι πειθόμενος.

Anth. Pal. 10.40; Anecd. Par. iv.374.13 Cramer (vv. 1151-52)
1151 παρεὶς Anth. Pal.

1153-54

εἴη μοι πλουτοῦντι κακῶν ἀπάτερθε μεριμνέων
ζώειν ἀβλαβέως μηδὲν ἔχοντι κακόν.

Stob. 4.39.14 (vv. 1153-56)
1153 πλουτεῦντι Stob.   μεριμνῶν o, Stob.

1155-56

1155   οὐκ ἔραμαι πλουτεῖν οὐδ' εὔχομαι, ἀλλά μοι εἴη
ζῆν ἀπὸ τῶν ὀλίγων μηδὲν ἔχοντι κακόν.

Anth. Pal. 10.113; Basil. ad adulescentes 9 (p. 58 Boulenger, p. 34 Wilson); gnomol. Georgidis, Anecd. Gr. i.67 Boissonade; imit.

let him ever be on guard against the crooked speech
of unjust men who, with no regard for the immortal
gods, always direct their thoughts to other people's
property, making shameful compacts to further
their evil deeds.

1151-52[1]

Never forsake the friend you have and seek another,
persuaded by what base men say to you.

[1] Identical to 1238ab.

1153-54

May I live without harm,[1] wealthy and free of evil
cares, suffering no ill.

[1] Either 'without harm to myself' or 'without harm to others.'
Probably the former here.

1155-56

I do not crave or pray for wealth, but may I live from
modest means, suffering no ill.

Orac. Sib. 2.109-10; confuse schol. Luc. *apol.* 12 (p. 238.9 Rabe),
v. 1155

    1155 οὐκ ἐθέλω *Anth. Pal.*   οὔτ' *Basil.*, οὐκ *Anth. Pal.*
1156 ἐκ *Anth. Pal.*

1157-60

<πλοῦτος καὶ σοφίη θνητοῖς ἀμαχώτατοι αἰεί·
οὔτε γὰρ ἂν πλούτου θυμὸν ὑπερκορέσαις·>
ὡς δ' αὔτως σοφίην ὁ σοφώτατος οὐκ ἀποφεύγει,
1160   ἀλλ' ἔραται, θυμὸν δ' οὐ δύναται τελέσαι.

Stob. 4.31.26 (1157-58 desunt in codd. Theogn.), vv. 1157-60

1157 ἀμαχώτατον Stob., corr. West   1160 κορέσαι
Stob.

1160ab

†ὧ νέοι οἱ νῦν ἄνδρες·† ἐμοί γε μὲν οὔ τις ἀνάγκη
ταῦτ' ἔρδειν· τῶν μοι πρόσθε χάριν τίθεσο.

1160a ὠνέο σοι νῦν ἄλλον West ex 1095

1161-62

οὐδένα θησαυρὸν παισὶν καταθήσει ἀμείνω
αἰδοῦς, ἣν ἀγαθοῖς ἀνδράσι, Κύρνε, διδῷς.

Stob. 3.31.16 (vv. 1161-62)

1161 παισὶν καταθήσειν A, καταθήσειν παισὶν o, κατα-
θήσεαι ἔνδον Stob. deinde ἄμεινον· αἰτοῦσιν δ' ἀγαθοῖς
ἀνδράσι Κύρνε δίδου codd., ἀμείνω αἰδοῦς, ἣν ... διδῷς Stob.

THEOGNIS

1157-60

Wealth and cleverness[1] are ever most difficult for mortals to conquer; for you cannot glut your desire for wealth. Similarly the cleverest man does not shun (more) cleverness, but craves it and cannot satisfy his desire.

[1] Or "wisdom."

1160ab

. . .;[1] I, however, am under no obligation to do this. Be grateful for what I've done before.

[1] West's text at the beginning ("Make a bid now for someone else") makes the couplet almost identical to 1095-96 and is based on the assumption that the opening "had become partly illegible through damp or some other cause" (*Studies* 163). The pronoun σοι, however, is redundant with the middle and none of the attempts to correct the text is convincing.

1161-62

You will not leave your sons a better treasure than a sense of shame, if you give it to the noble, Cyrnus.[1]

[1] The first half of the couplet repeats 409, but it is uncertain how closely the second half repeats 410. West follows Stobaeus, but the latter's text does not give very appropriate sense and may also be corrupt.

1162af

a   οὐδεὶς γὰρ πάντ᾽ ἐστὶ πανόλβιος· ἀλλ᾽ ὁ μὲν
     ἐσθλὸς
b   τολμᾷ ἔχων τὸ κακὸν κοὐκ ἐπίδηλον ὅμως
c   δειλὸς δ᾽ οὔτ᾽ ἀγαθοῖσιν ἐπίσταται οὔτε κακοῖσιν
d   θυμὸν ὁμῶς μίσγειν. ἀθανάτων τε δόσεις
e   παντοῖαι θνητοῖσιν ἐπέρχοντ᾽· ἀλλ᾽ ἐπιτολμᾶν
f   χρὴ δῶρ᾽ ἀθανάτων οἷα διδοῦσιν ἔχειν.

1162b ὁμῶς A   1162e ἐπέρχεται O   ἐπιτόλμαν A

1163-64

ὀφθαλμοὶ καὶ γλῶσσα καὶ οὔατα καὶ νόος ἀνδρῶν
ἐν μέσσῳ στηθέων ἐν συνετοῖς φύεται.

Stob. 3.3.19 (vv. 1163-64)

1163 ἀνδρὸς Stob.   1164 εὐξύνετος Stob.

1164ad

a   τοιοῦτός τοι ἀνὴρ ἔστω φίλος, ὃς τὸν ἑταῖρον
b   γινώσκων ὀργὴν καὶ βαρὺν ὄντα φέρει
c   ἀντὶ κασιγνήτου. σὺ δέ μοι, φίλε, ταῦτ᾽ ἐνὶ θυμῷ
d   φράζεο, καί ποτέ μου μνήσεαι ἐξοπίσω.

1164eh

e   οὔτιν᾽ ὁμοῖον ἐμοὶ δύναμαι διζήμενος εὑρεῖν
f   πιστὸν ἑταῖρον, ὅτῳ μή τις ἔνεστι δόλος·

346

THEOGNIS

1162af

For no one is wholly prosperous in every respect.
The noble man puts up with bad luck even when it
doesn't show(?), but the base man does not know
how to adapt(?) his emotions to good fortune and
bad alike. The gifts of the immortals come to mor-
tals in all forms, but we must endure to possess their
gifts, whatever it is they give.[1]

1 Essentially identical to 441-46 except for 1162b and d.

1163-64

Among the intelligent eyes, tongue, ears, and mind
are implanted in the middle of their breast.[1]

1 Translation uncertain. For attempts to explain the meaning
and syntax see van Groningen ad loc.

1164ad

Let a friend be the sort of man who knows his com-
rade and, like a brother, puts up with his disposition
even when he is hard to bear. Please take these
things to heart, my friend, and one day hereafter you
will remember me.[1]

1 Identical to 97-100 except for a slight change at the be-
ginning.

1164eh

I can find none like myself in my search for a loyal
comrade in whom there is no deceit. When I come

g   ἐς βάσανόν τ᾽ ἐλθὼν παρατριβόμενός τε
       μολύβδῳ
h   χρυσός, ὑπερτερίης ἄμμιν ἔνεστι λόγος.

1164eh om. *p*   1164g δ᾽ O   μολίβδῳ codd., corr. van
Herwerden   1164h λόγος A, νόος O

1165-66

1165   τοῖς ἀγαθοῖς σύμμισγε, κακοῖσι δὲ μήποθ᾽
       ὁμάρτει,
      εὖτ᾽ ἂν ὁδοῦ στέλλῃ τέρματ᾽ ἐπ᾽ ἐμπορίην.

1166 ἔστ᾽ West   τελέῃς *p*, -οις O, στελεῇ A, corr. Bergk
τέρματ᾽ ἐπ᾽ ἐμπορίην A τέρματά τ᾽ ἐμπορίης *o*, ἀπ᾽ ἐμπορίης
West (et τελέῃς)

1167-68

   τῶν ἀγαθῶν ἐσθλὴ μὲν ἀπόκρισις, ἐσθλὰ δὲ ἔργα·
      τῶν δὲ κακῶν ἄνεμοι δειλὰ φέρουσιν ἔπη.

1169-70

   ἐκ καχεταιρίης κακὰ γίνεται· εὖ δὲ καὶ αὐτὸς
1170   γνώσῃ, ἐπεὶ μεγάλους ἤλιτες ἀθανάτους.

1169 καχεταιρείης OXD   1170 μεγάλως Camerarius

1171-76

   γνώμην, Κύρνε, θεοὶ θνητοῖσι διδοῦσιν ἀρίστην
      ἀνθρώποις· γνώμη πείρατα παντὸς ἔχει.
   ἆ μάκαρ, ὅστις δή μιν ἔχει φρεσίν· ἦ πολὺ
      κρείσσων

to the touchstone and am gold rubbed beside lead,
the balance of superiority is in me.[1]

[1] A version of 415-18, but the alteration in 1164g results in
hanging nominatives.

1165-66

Mingle with the noble and never accompany the
base, whenever you set out for your journey's goal
with a view to trade.

1167-68

Noble is the response of the noble and noble their
actions, but the base words of the base are carried
on the wind.

1169-70

From bad company bad things result. You'll know
that well yourself, since you have sinned against
mighty gods.

1171-76

Judgement, Cyrnus, is the best gift of the gods to
mortal men: judgement holds the key to every-
thing.[1] Blessed is he whose mind possesses it. In-

ὕβριος οὐλομένης λευγαλέου τε κόρου
1175 [ἐστί· κακὸν δὲ βροτοῖσι κόρος, τῶν οὔ τι κάκιον·]
πᾶσα γὰρ ἐκ τούτων, Κύρνε, πέλει κακότης.

1171 ἄριστον Bekker   1172 ἄνθρωπος AO, ἀνθρώπου
p, corr. Bergk   1173 ἃ Naeke (cf. 1013), ὦ codd. (ὦ O)
ἦ A, ἐπεὶ o   1176 τούτου Camerarius

1177-78
εἴ κ᾽ εἴης ἔργων αἰσχρῶν ἀπαθὴς καὶ ἀεργός,
Κύρνε, μεγίστην κεν πεῖραν ἔχοις ἀρετῆς.

1178ab
τολμᾶν χρὴ χαλεποῖσιν ἐν ἄλγεσιν ἦτορ ἔχοντα,
πρὸς δὲ θεῶν αἰτεῖν ἔκλυσιν ἀθανάτων.

1178a ἐπ᾽ O   ἦπαρ O   1178b τε θεῶν δ᾽ O

1179-80
Κύρνε, θεοὺς αἰδοῦ καὶ δείδιθι· τοῦτο γὰρ ἄνδρα
1180 εἴργει μήτ᾽ ἔρδειν μήτε λέγειν ἀσεβῆ.

Orion anth. 3.5 (p. 45 Schneidewin), vv. 1179-80
1180 μήτε παθεῖν Orion

1181-82
δημοφάγον δὲ τύραννον, ὅπως ἐθέλεις, κατακλῖναι·
οὐ νέμεσις πρὸς θεῶν γίνεται οὐδεμία.

1181 ἐθέλης O, sscr. I

deed it is much superior to accursed lawlessness or
baneful excess. [Excess is harmful to mortals;
there's nothing worse.][2] For from these things,
Cyrnus, comes every misery.

[1] Cf. Solon fr. 16.   [2] I agree with West (*Studies* 163-64)
that "the line is a patchwork designed to replace a longer passage
that led to 1176."

1177-78

If you should neither suffer nor commit shameful
acts, Cyrnus, you would possess the greatest proof
of merit.

1178ab

He whose heart is in dire distress must endure and
ask the immortal gods for release.[1]

[1] A variation on 555-56.

1179-80

Cyrnus, respect and fear the gods. For this restrains
a man from impious deed or word.

1181-82

Lay low, by any means you wish, a tyrant who de-
vours the people. The gods show no resentment.

ELEGIAC POETRY

1183-84b

οὐδένα, Κύρν', αὐγαὶ φαεσιμβρότου ἠελίοιο
ἄνδρ' ἐφορῶσ' ᾧ μὴ μῶμος ἐπικρέμαται·

1184a   ἀστῶν δ' οὐ δύναμαι γνῶναι νόον ὅντιν' ἔχουσιν·
οὔτε γὰρ εὖ ἔρδων ἀνδάνω οὔτε κακῶς.

1183-84 om. XD, 1184ab om. p

1185-86

1185   νοῦς ἀγαθόν, καὶ γλῶσσα· τὰ δ' ἐν παύροισι
πέφυκεν
ἀνδράσιν οἳ τούτων ἀμφοτέρων ταμίαι.

1185 ἀγαθὸς o   τ' codd., corr. Stephanus

1187-90

οὔτις ἄποινα διδοὺς θάνατον φύγοι οὐδὲ βαρεῖαν
δυστυχίην, εἰ μὴ μοῖρ' ἐπὶ τέρμα βάλοι,
οὐδ' ἂν δυσφροσύνας, ὅτε δὴ θεὸς ἄλγεα πέμπῃ,

1190   θνητὸς ἀνὴρ δώροις βουλόμενος προφυγεῖν.

1188 δυστυχίαν o   1189 πέμπει o, -οι Bergk
1190 οὐλομένας Matthiae   προφύγῃ A, -οι Camerarius

1191-94

οὐκ ἔραμαι κλισμῷ βασιληΐῳ ἐγκατακεῖσθαι
τεθνεώς, ἀλλά τί μοι ζῶντι γένοιτ' ἀγαθόν.
ἀσπάθαλοι δὲ τάπησιν ὁμοῖον στρῶμα θανόντι·
τῷ ξυνόν, σκληρὸν γίνεται ἢ μαλακόν.

1194 τὸ ξύλον ἢ codd., corr. West: alii alia

352

THEOGNIS

1183-84b

Cyrnus, the rays of the sun that brings light to mortals look upon no man over whom blame does not hang; but I cannot understand the attitude the townsmen have, since neither by good actions nor by bad do I please them.[1]

[1] The second couplet is a variation on 367-68. Some editors treat the couplets as separate.

1185-86

The mind is a good thing and so is the tongue; but they are found in few men who have control over both.

1187-90

No one can pay a ransom and avoid death or heavy misfortune,[1] if fate does not set a limit, nor, although he wish to, can a mortal avoid mental distress through bribery, when the god sends pain.

[1] Cf. Solon fr. 24.9-10.

1191-94

I do not crave to lie on a couch fit for a king when I'm dead; rather, may something good be mine while I'm alive. Thorns are as good a bed for the dead as rugs. It's all the same to him whether the bed is hard or soft.

1195-96

1195 μή τι θεοὺς ἐπίορκον ἐπόμνυθι· οὐ γὰρ ἀνεκτὸν
ἀθανάτους κρύψαι χρεῖος ὀφειλόμενον.

1195 μήτε ο   επιορκος A   ἀνυστὸν Emperius

1197-1202

ὄρνιθος φωνήν, Πολυπαΐδη, ὀξὺ βοώσης
ἤκουσ᾽, ἥ τε βροτοῖς ἄγγελος ἦλθ᾽ ἀρότου
ὡραίου· καί μοι κραδίην ἐπάταξε μέλαιναν,
1200 ὅττι μοι εὐανθεῖς ἄλλοι ἔχουσιν ἀγρούς,
οὐδέ μοι ἡμίονοι κυφὸν ἕλκουσιν ἄροτρον
†τῆς ἄλλης μνηστῆς† εἵνεκα ναυτιλίης.

1198 ἀρότρου ο   1201 κύφων᾽ . . . ἀρότρου p

1203-1206

οὐκ εἶμ᾽, οὐδ᾽ ὑπ᾽ ἐμοῦ κεκλήσεται. οὐδ᾽ ἐπὶ
τύμβῳ
οἰμωχθεὶς ὑπὸ γῆν εἶσι τύραννος ἀνήρ,
1205 οὐδ᾽ ἂν ἐκεῖνος ἐμοῦ τεθνηότος οὔτ᾽ ἀνιῷτο
οὔτε κατὰ βλεφάρων θερμὰ βάλοι δάκρυα.

1204 ἐπὶ ο   1205 τεθνειότος AOI

1207-1208

οὔτε σε κωμάζειν ἀπερύκομεν οὔτε καλοῦμεν·
ἁρπαλέος παρεών, καὶ φίλος εὖτ᾽ ἂν ἀπῇς.

1207 ἀπερύκομαι οὔτε καλοῦμαι ο   1208 ἀργαλέος
codd., corr. Bergk   γὰρ ἐών codd., corr. Camerarius

THEOGNIS

1195-96

Do not swear falsely by the gods; for to hide from
the immortals a debt that is owed is not be tolerated.

1197-1202

I heard the bird's[1] shrill cry, Polypaïdes, which
comes to men as a messenger of the season for
ploughing; and it struck my melancholy heart, since
others possess my flowering fields and mules do not
pull the curved plough for me . . . because of sea-
faring.[2]

[1] I.e., the crane. Cf. Hes. *Opera* 448-50.   [2] The last verse
is judged corrupt by most and none of the many emendations is
persuasive. It seems likely that Theognis has lost his land because
of a disastrous sea voyage.

1203-1206

I shan't go and he won't be invited by me.[1] A tyrant
won't be mourned (by me) even at his tomb when he
goes beneath the earth, any more than he would
grieve or let warm tears fall from his eyes when I am
dead.

[1] This seems to mean, ' I shall not go to his funeral nor will he
be invited to mine.'

1207-1208

We neither exclude you from our revel nor do we
invite you. You are welcome[1] when present and a
friend when absent.

[1] If ἀργαλέος is retained, the meaning would be "you are trou-
blesome" or "a nuisance," but this conflicts with 1207 which sug-
gests that it is all the same whether the person joins in the revel
or not.

1209-10

Αἴθων μὲν γένος εἰμί, πόλιν δ᾽ εὐτείχεα Θήβην

1210   οἰκῶ, πατρῴας γῆς ἀπερυκόμενος.

1211-16

μή μ᾽ ἀφελῶς παίζουσα φίλους δένναζε τοκῆας,

Ἀργυρί· σοὶ μὲν γὰρ δούλιον ἦμαρ ἔπι,

ἡμῖν δ᾽ ἄλλα μέν ἐστι, γύναι, κακὰ πόλλ᾽, ἐπεὶ
ἐκ γῆς

φεύγομεν, ἀργαλέη δ᾽ οὐκ ἔπι δουλοσύνη,

1215   οὔθ᾽ ἡμᾶς περνᾶσι· πόλις γε μέν ἐστι καὶ ἡμῖν
καλή, Ληθαίῳ κεκλιμένη πεδίῳ.

1212 Ἀργυρί Bergk, αργυρι A, ἄργυρι o   σὺ AO
1216 λιθαίω A²OI   ποταμῷ Brunck

1217-18

μήποτε πὰρ κλαίοντα καθεζόμενοι γελάσωμεν
τοῖς αὐτῶν ἀγαθοῖς, Κύρν᾽, ἐπιτερπόμενοι.

1217 "μήποτε ab excerptore illatum videtur" West
κλαίοντι O, κλαίουσι p

THEOGNIS

1209-10

I am Aethon[1] by birth, but I dwell in the well-walled
city of Thebes, excluded from my homeland.

[1] Presumably a fictitious name, but its significance is un-
known. Since this is the name Odysseus takes on in *Od*. 19.183,
an allusion to that passage is often assumed, but there too the
significance is unclear. As an adjective it means 'fiery' in a variety
of senses.

1211-16

Don't make silly jokes and mock my parents,
Argyris.[1] For you there is slavery, but for me, though
I have many other woes, woman, because I am in ex-
ile from my land, there is no dreadful slavery nor am
I for sale. Moreover, I have a city, a fair one that lies
on the Lethaean plain.[2]

[1] Identity unknown. The name would be appropriate for an
hetaera.   [2] Lethaeus was a tributary of the Maeander river,
but some see a reference to the river of the underworld, compar-
ing "the plain of Lethe" (τὸ Λήθης πεδίον) in Arist. *Frogs* 186 and
Plato Rep. 10.621a. Identification depends on how the poem as a
whole is interpreted, and on this there is no agreement. See L.
Kurke, *ClAnt* 16 (1997) 143-45.

1217-18

Let us never[1] laugh if we sit beside one who mourns,
Cyrnus, rejoicing in our own good fortune.[2]

[1] West excises the first word because elsewhere in the corpus
the negative is used with an imperative, not the subjunctive.
[2] For the opposite sentiment cf. 1041-42.

1219-20

ἐχθρὸν μὲν χαλεπὸν καὶ δυσμενῆ ἐξαπατῆσαι,

1220   Κύρνε· φίλον δὲ φίλῳ ῥᾴδιον ἐξαπατᾶν.

1219 δυσμενεῖ Bergk

1221-22

Stob. 3.8.9

πολλὰ φέρειν εἴωθε λόγος θνητοῖσι βροτοῖσιν
    πταίσματα τῆς γνώμης, Κύρνε, ταρασσομένης.

1223-24

Stob. 3.20.1

οὐδέν, Κύρν', ὀργῆς ἀδικώτερον, ἣ τὸν ἔχοντα
    πημαίνει θυμῷ δειλὰ χαριζομένη.

1225-26

Stob. 4.22.5

1225   οὐδέν, Κύρν', ἀγαθῆς γλυκερώτερόν ἐστι
        γυναικός·
        μάρτυς ἐγώ, σὺ δ' ἐμοὶ γίνου ἀληθοσύνης.

1226 δέ μου S, δέ μοι MA, expl. Brunck

THEOGNIS

1219-20

It is difficult for an enemy to deceive even an enemy,
Cyrnus, but easy for a friend to deceive a friend.

1221-30

The first three couplets are preserved only in Stobaeus, the
fourth in Athenaeus. Both sources assign them to Theognis. 1227-
28 are omitted, since Mimnermus fr. 8 was wrongly inserted here.

1221-22

Speech[1] is apt to cause many a slip for mortal men,
Cyrnus, when their judgement is in turmoil.

[1] Or "calculation." Because Stobaeus cites the couplet under
the heading "On cowardice," some emend λόγος to a word for
'fear' (δέος, φόβος), but the error may rest with Stobaeus or the
context may have contained a reference to cowardice.

1223-24

There is nothing more unjust than anger, Cyrnus. It
harms the one who possesses it, gratifying his base
instincts.

1225-26

Nothing is sweeter than a good wife, Cyrnus. I tes-
tify to it; you testify to my truthfulness.[1]

[1] It is unclear whether this means that Cyrnus is to marry a
similar wife or to testify to the character of the poet's wife. Proba-
bly the former.

1229-30

Ath. 10.457a

ἤδη γάρ με κέκληκε θαλάσσιος οἴκαδε νεκρός,
1230   τεθνηκὼς ζωῷ φθεγγόμενος στόματι.

Book II

1231-34

σχέτλι᾽ Ἔρως, Μανίαι τ᾽ ἐτιθηνήσαντο λαβοῦσαι·
    ἐκ σέθεν ὤλετο μὲν Ἰλίου ἀκρόπολις,
ὤλετο δ᾽ Αἰγείδης Θησεὺς μέγας, ὤλετο δ᾽ Αἴας
    ἐσθλὸς Ὀϊλιάδης σῆσιν ἀτασθαλίαις.

1234 ἧσιν West

1235-38

1235   ὦ παῖ, ἄκουσον ἐμεῦ δαμάσας φρένας· οὔτοι
    ἀπειθῆ
    μῦθον ἐρῶ τῇ σῇ καρδίῃ οὐδ᾽ ἄχαριν.

THEOGNIS

1229-30

For a corpse from the sea has summoned me home
now; though dead, it speaks with a living voice.[1]

[1] Athenaeus explains the riddle as referring to a conch. After
the mollusc was removed, the shell could be used as a trumpet.
The poet may be indicating a return from exile.

Book II

1231-1389

The remaining verses are preserved only in ms A, which as-
signs them to Book 2 (ἐλεγείων β). Many are erotic, with empha-
sis on the pederastic.

1231-34

Cruel Eros, the spirits of Madness took you up and
nursed you. Because of you Troy's acropolis was de-
stroyed, and great Theseus, Aegeus' son, and noble
Ajax, Oïleus' son, through your acts of recklessness.[1]

[1] Troy was destroyed because of Helen's elopement with Paris;
Theseus probably because he accompanied Pirithous in an at-
tempt to carry off Persephone (in some accounts he was impris-
oned in Hades, in others he was set free by Heracles); and Ajax
because of his rape of Cassandra (cf. Alcaeus fr. 298).

1235-38

Listen, boy, you who have mastered my soul.[1] I'll
not say anything unpersuasive or displeasing to your

ἀλλὰ τλῆθι νόῳ συνιεῖν ἔπος· οὔτοι ἀνάγκη
τοῦτ᾽ ἔρδειν ὅτι σοι μὴ καταθύμιον ᾖ.

1235 ἀπεχθῆ vel ἀπευθῆ Meineke, ἀπηνῆ dub. West
1236 κραδίηι A, corr. Bekker   1237 συνιδειν A, corr.
Lachmann

1238ab
μήποτε τὸν παρεόντα μεθεὶς φίλον ἄλλον ἐρεύνα
δειλῶν ἀνθρώπων ῥήμασι πειθόμενος.

1239-40
πολλάκι τοι παρ᾽ ἐμοὶ κατὰ σοῦ λέξουσι μάταια,
1240   καὶ παρὰ σοὶ κατ᾽ ἐμοῦ· τῶν δὲ σὺ μὴ ξυνίει.

1240 ξύνιε A, corr. Buttmann

1241-42
χαιρήσεις τῇ πρόσθε παροιχομένῃ φιλότητι,
τῆς δὲ παρερχομένης οὐκέτ᾽ ἔσῃ ταμίης.

heart. Come, have the patience of mind to under-
stand my words. You are under no compulsion to do
what is distasteful to you.

1 Or "listen to me, boy, and gain control of your thoughts," i.e.,
"change your way of thinking"; but $\delta\alpha\mu\acute{a}\zeta\omega$ is so common in erotic
contexts that Vetta's explanation seems preferable to the usual
rendering.

1238ab

Never forsake the friend you have and seek another,
persuaded by what base men say to you.[1]

1 Identical to 1151-52.

1239-40

Often they'll say foolish things against you in my
presence and against me in your presence. Pay no
heed to them.[1]

1 West separates the couplet from 1238ab, but most connect
them and this is unobjectionable.

1241-42

You will derive pleasure from the former love that is
past, but you will no longer be in control of the love
that is coming on.[1]

1 Perhaps the addressee has passed the age at which he was the
one pursued and so could exercise control; now he is at an age
when he will do the pursuing and control will change hands.

1243-44

δὴν δὴ καὶ φίλοι ὦμεν· ἔπειτ' ἄλλοισιν ὁμίλει,
ἦθος ἔχων δόλιον, πίστιος ἀντίτυπον.

1244 πιστεως A, corr. West (πίστεος Bekker et A in ras., prob. Vetta)

1245-46

1245   οὔποθ' ὕδωρ καὶ πῦρ συμμείξεται· οὐδέ ποθ' ἡμεῖς
πιστοὶ ἐπ' ἀλλήλοις καὶ φίλοι ἐσσόμεθα.

1246 ἔτ' Bekker, τ' dub. West

1247-48

φρόντισον ἔχθος ἐμὸν καὶ ὑπέρβασιν, ἴσθι δὲ
        θυμῷ
ὥς σ' ἐφ' ἁμαρτωλῇ τείσομαι ὡς δύναμαι.

1247 εχθρος A, corr. Bekker (ρ in ras. A)

1249-52

παῖ, σὺ μὲν αὔτως ἵππος, ἐπεὶ κριθῶν ἐκορέσθης,
1250   αὖθις ἐπὶ σταθμοὺς ἤλυθες ἡμετέρους
ἡνίοχόν τε ποθῶν ἀγαθὸν λειμῶνά τε καλὸν
κρήνην τε ψυχρὴν ἄλσεά τε σκιερά.

1253-54

ὄλβιος, ᾧ παῖδές τε φίλοι καὶ μώνυχες ἵπποι
θηρευταί τε κύνες καὶ ξένοι ἀλλοδαποί.

1254 καὶ κύνες ἀγρευταὶ καὶ ξένος ἀλλοδαπός Plat. Lys.
212e sine poetae nomine, Hermias in Phaedr. 231e (p. 38
Couvreur) Soloni tribuens

1243-44

Let's be friends for a long time; thereafter[1] associate with others, you whose deceitful ways are the very opposite of loyalty.

[1] 1243 = 597, except that ἔπειτ' ('thereafter') has replaced ἀτάρ τ' ('but'). The sense is unsatisfactory and West may well be right to treat ἔπειτ' as corrupt.

1245-46

Water and fire will never mix, and we will never be true friends to each other.

1247-48

Reflect on my hatred and your transgression,[1] and know in your heart that I will make you pay for your offence to the best of my ability.

[1] Some such translation is common, but it is very harsh to understand "your" after the preceding "my." Perhaps, as Renehan suggests to me, the correct translation here is "my superiority," since the cognate verb can mean "to surpass."

1249-52

Boy, you're just like a horse; when you got your fill of barley, you came back to my stable, longing for your skilled charioteer, lovely meadow, cool spring water, and shady groves.[1]

[1] The horse is a common image in erotic poetry.

1253-54

Happy is he who has dear boys, horses of uncloven hoof, hunting dogs, and friends in foreign parts.[1]

[1] Almost identical to Solon fr. 23 (see n. ad loc.).

1255-56

1255   ὅστις μὴ παῖδάς τε φιλεῖ καὶ μώνυχας ἵππους
        καὶ κύνας, οὔποτέ οἱ θυμὸς ἐν εὐφροσύνῃ.

1257-58

ὦ παῖ, κινδύνοισι πολυπλάγκτοισιν ὁμοῖος
   ὀργὴν ἄλλοτε τοῖς ἄλλοτε τοῖσι φίλην.

1257 ἰκτίνοισι Welcker, alii alia   ὁμοιοῖ Wilamowitz
1258 φιλεῖν A (recep. West), corr. Hermann et Ahrens, τοῖς
φίλος εἶ Schneidewin, alii alia

1259-62

ὦ παῖ, τὴν μορφὴν μὲν ἔφυς καλός, ἀλλ᾽
     ἐπίκειται
1260   καρτερὸς ἀγνώμων σῇ κεφαλῇ στέφανος·
        ἰκτίνου γὰρ ἔχεις ἀγχιστρόφου ἐν φρεσὶν ἦθος,
        ἄλλων ἀνθρώπων ῥήμασι πειθόμενος.

1263-66

ὦ παῖ, ὃς εὖ ἔρδοντι κακὴν ἀπέδωκας ἀμοιβήν,
     οὐδέ τις ἀντ᾽ ἀγαθῶν ἐστι χάρις παρὰ σοί·
1265   οὐδέν πώ μ᾽ ὤνησας· ἐγὼ δέ σε πολλάκις ἤδη
        εὖ ἔρδων αἰδοῦς οὐδεμιῆς ἔτυχον.

1267-70

παῖς τε καὶ ἵππος ὁμοῖον ἔχει νόον· οὔτε γὰρ ἵππος
     ἡνίοχον κλαίει κείμενον ἐν κονίῃ,
        ἀλλὰ τὸν ὕστερον ἄνδρα φέρει κριθαῖσι κορεσθείς·
1270   ὣς δ᾽ αὔτως καὶ παῖς τὸν παρεόντα φιλεῖ.

366

THEOGNIS

1255-56

Whoever does not love boys, horses of uncloven hoof, and dogs, never has good cheer in his heart.

1257-58

Boy, you are like roving perils[1] in your disposition, loving now these, now those.

[1] Welcker's emendation 'kites,' a migratory bird, is attractive, especially in view of 1261, but the corruption is hard to explain.

1259-62

Boy, your form is handsome, but on your head there lies a stubborn and senseless crown. For you have in your heart the disposition of a close-wheeling kite, led on by what other men say.

1263-66

Boy, you have repaid your benefactor badly and there is no gratitude from you for kindnesses rendered. Never yet have you bestowed any benefit on me, and I who have often done you a good turn have met with no respect.

1267-70

A boy and a horse have a similar outlook. A horse does not weep for its charioteer lying in the dust, but carries the man who comes next, when it's had its fill of barley. In the same way also a boy loves the man who's at hand.

1271-74

ὦ παῖ, μαργοσύνης ἀπὸ μὲν νόον ὤλεσας ἐσθλόν,
αἰσχύνη δὲ φίλοις ἡμετέροις ἐγένου·
ἄμμε δ' ἀνέψυξας μικρὸν χρόνον, ἐκ δὲ θυελλῶν
ἠκά γ' ἐνωρμίσθην νυκτὸς ἐπειγομένης.

1271 μαργοσύνης . . . μευ A, corr. Bekker   1273 θελλῶν
A, corr. Bekker   1274 ἐπειγόμενος A, corr. Passow

1275-78

1275   ὡραῖος καὶ Ἔρως ἐπιτέλλεται, ἡνίκα περ γῆ
ἄνθεσιν εἰαρινοῖς θάλλει ἀεξομένη·
τῆμος Ἔρως προλιπὼν Κύπρον περικαλλέα νῆσον
εἶσιν ἐπ' ἀνθρώπους σπέρμα φέρων κατὰ γῆς.

1278 γῆν Weigel

1278ab

ὅστις σοι βούλευσεν ἐμεῦ πέρι, καί σ' ἐκέλευσεν
οἴχεσθαι προλιπόνθ' ἡμετέρην φιλίην . . .

1278cd

νεβρὸν ὑπὲξ <ἐλ>άφοιο λέων ὣς ἀλκὶ πεποιθὼς
ποσσὶ καταμάρψας αἵματος οὐκ ἔπιον.

1278d καταιμάρψας A¹

1279-82

οὐκ ἐθέλω σε κακῶς ἔρδειν, οὐδ' εἴ μοι ἄμεινον
1280   πρὸς θεῶν ἀθανάτων ἔσσεται, ὦ καλὲ παῖ·

THEOGNIS

1271-74

Boy, because of your lustful behaviour you have lost
your good sense, and you have become a source of
shame to my friends. For a short time you gave me
cooling relief and after stormy weather[1] I quietly
put into harbour as night hastened on.[2]

[1] Presumably a metaphor for passion. [2] Or, retaining
the reading of the MS, "hastening during the night."

1275-78

Love too rises in season, when the burgeoning earth
blooms with spring flowers. Then Love leaves the
beautiful island of Cyprus and goes among men,
bringing seed down upon the land.

1278ab

Whoever gave you advice about me and told you to
abandon my friendship and go . . .[1]

[1] The couplet is identical to 1101-1102 and is similarly incomplete, although it is possible, as Vetta argues, that the excerptor
intended καί to mean "also" rather than "and."

1278cd

Like a lion trusting in his might, I snatched a fawn
from the doe with my claws, and did not drink its
blood.[1]

[1] Identical to 949-50. See n. 1 ad loc.

1279-82

I have no wish to treat you badly, dear boy, not even
if it will be better for me in the eyes of the immortal

οὐ γὰρ ἁμαρτωλαῖσιν ἐπὶ σμικραῖσι κάθημαι.
τῶν δὲ καλῶν παίδων †ουτοσετουτ᾽αδικων†.

1282 οὔτις ἔπ᾽ οὐκ ἀδίκων Vetta, οὐ τίσις οὐδ᾽ ἀδίκων
Boissonade, alii alia

1283-94

ὦ παῖ, μή μ᾽ ἀδίκει· ἔτι σοι κα‹τα›θύμιος εἶναι
βούλομαι, εὐφροσύνῃ τοῦτο συνεὶς ἀγαθῇ.
1285   οὐ γάρ τοί με δόλῳ παρελεύσεαι οὐδ᾽ ἀπατήσεις·
νικήσας γὰρ ἔχεις τὸ πλέον ἐξοπίσω,
ἀλλά σ᾽ ἐγὼ τρώσω φεύγοντά με, ὥς ποτέ φασιν
Ἰασίου κούρην παρθένον Ἰασίην
ὡραίην περ ἐοῦσαν ἀναινομένην γάμον ἀνδρῶν
1290   φεύγειν· ζωσαμένη δ᾽ ἔργ᾽ ἀτέλεστα τέλει
πατρὸς νοσφισθεῖσα δόμων ξανθὴ Ἀταλάντη·
ᾤχετο δ᾽ ὑψηλὰς εἰς κορυφὰς ὀρέων
φεύγουσ᾽ ἱμερόεντα γάμον, χρυσῆς Ἀφροδίτης
δῶρα· τέλος δ᾽ ἔγνω καὶ μάλ᾽ ἀναινομένη.

1283 καθύμιος A, corr. Bekker   1285 οὐ—δόλῳ suppl.
m² (saec. X)   ἀπατήσῃς A, corr. Bekker   1290 ζωσαμένην
A, corr. Bekker

gods. For I do not sit in judgement on trifling of-
fences.[1] Of handsome boys . . .[2]

[1] Or "For I sit in judgement on no trifling offences."
[2] The poet may be saying that all handsome boys do wrong or that
handsome boys can do wrong with impunity. In an erotic context
'doing wrong' involves failure to reciprocate the affection shown.

1283-94

Boy, don't wrong me. I still want to please you,[1] and
I make this observation with all good cheer. Rest as-
sured, you will not get the better of me nor will you
trick me. For though (if?) you have won and have
the advantage hereafter,[2] yet I shall wound[3] you
as you flee from me, as they say once the daughter
of Iasius, the maiden Iasie, who was ripe for mar-
riage, refused men and fled. Girding herself, blonde
Atalanta left her father's home and tried to accom-
plish what was not to be accomplished. She went off
to the lofty mountain peaks, fleeing from lovely mar-
riage, the gift of golden Aphrodite. But in the end
she came to know it, in spite of her refusal.[4]

[1] Many editors treat this as parenthetic: "Boy, don't wrong
me—I still want to please you—but understand this with all good
cheer." This is unnecessarily harsh.   [2] Translation uncertain.
[3] An erotic metaphor.   [4] West (Studies 165-67) and Vetta ar-
gue that what follows the middle of 1288 has been inserted from a
different poem on Atalanta, but I agree with those who reject this.
Just as Atalanta refused marriage but eventually succumbed to
Milanion, so the boy has refused the poet's love but in the end will
be won over. No reference to Atalanta's race with Hippomenes
need be seen. For recent discussions of the poem see Lustrum 33
(1991) 213-14.

1295-98

1295 ὦ παῖ, μή με κακοῖσιν ἐν ἄλγεσι θυμὸν ὀρίνῃς,
μηδέ με σῇ φιλότης δώματα Περσεφόνης
οἴχηται προφέρουσα· θεῶν δ' ἐποπίζεο μῆνιν
βάξιν τ' ἀνθρώπων, ἤπια νωσάμενος.

1295 ὀρίναις A, corr. Bekker

1299-1304

ὦ παῖ, μέχρι τίνος με προφεύξεαι; ὥς σε διώκων
1300 δίζημ'· ἀλλά τί μοι τέρμα γένοιτο κιχεῖν
†σησοιγη†· σὺ δὲ μάργον ἔχων καὶ ἀγήνορα
θυμὸν
φεύγεις ἰκτίνου σχέτλιον ἦθος ἔχων.
ἀλλ' ἐπίμεινον, ἐμοὶ δὲ δίδου χάριν· οὐκέτι δηρὸν
ἕξεις Κυπρογενοῦς δῶρον ἰοστεφάνου.

1301 σῆς ὀργῆς Hermann, σῆς ὁρμῆς Gianotti
1302 φεύγοις A, corr. Bekker

1305-10

1305 θυμῷ γνοὺς ὅτι παιδείας πολυηράτου ἄνθος
ὠκύτερον σταδίου, τοῦτο συνεὶς χάλασον
δεσμοῦ, μή ποτε καὶ σὺ βιήσεαι, ὄβριμε παίδων,
Κυπρογενοῦς δ' ἔργων ἀντιάσῃς χαλεπῶν,
ὥσπερ ἐγὼ νῦν ὧδ' ἐπὶ σοί. σὺ δὲ ταῦτα φύλαξαι,
1310 μηδέ σε νικήσῃ †παιδαΐδη† κακότης.

1307 δεσμόν Peek   1308 ἀντιάσεις A, corr. Blaydes
1309 οἶδ' A, corr. Bekker   1310 παῖδ' ἀδαῆ Bergk, alii alia

THEOGNIS

1295-98

Boy, don't stir up my soul in the midst of my cruel torments[1] and don't let my love for you carry me off to the house of Persephone.[2] Respect the wrath of the gods and the talk of men, and conceive kindly thoughts.

[1] Or perhaps "don't stir up my soul with cruel torments."
[2] A reference to suicide.

1299-1304

Boy, how long will you flee from me? How I pursue and seek you out! May there come some end (to my eager desire for you?). But you, with lustful and arrogant heart and with the cruel ways of the kite, keep fleeing. Come, wait up and grant me your favour. Not for long will you possess the gift of the violet-crowned Cyprus-born.[1]

[1] I.e., youth is short-lived and when the young have passed beyond adolescence Aphrodite no longer causes them to inspire passion in others.

1305-10

Realizing in your heart that the bloom of lovely boyhood passes more swiftly than a footrace, reflect on this and release me from my bonds, lest one day you too, mighty boy, be overpowered and encounter the harsh workings of the Cyprus-born, just as I now do with you. Guard against this and do not let bad behaviour get the better of you . . .

1311-18

οὔ μ' ἔλαθες κλέψας, ὦ παῖ—καὶ γάρ σε
†διωμαι†—
τούτοις, οἷσπερ νῦν ἄρθμιος ἠδὲ φίλος
ἔπλευ, ἐμὴν δὲ μεθῆκας ἀτίμητον φιλότητα.
οὐ μὲν δὴ τούτοις γ' ἦσθα φίλος πρότερον,
ἀλλ' ἐγὼ ἐκ πάντων σ' ἐδόκουν θήσεσθαι ἑταῖρον
πιστόν. καὶ δὴ νῦν ἄλλον ἔχοισθα φίλον·
ἀλλ' ὁ μὲν εὖ ἔρδων κεῖμαι· σὲ δὲ μή τις ἁπάντων
ἀνθρώπων ἐσορῶν παιδοφιλεῖν ἐθέλοι.

1315 (left margin, line 5)

1311 οὐκ A, corr. Edmonds   διωμαι A (prob. Vetta),
διώμμαι Hermann, διώκω Ahrens (prob. West)
1312 φίλοις A, corr. Bekker   1314 συ μεν δη τουτοις τ' A,
corr. Hermann   1315 σήσεθαι A, corr. Seidler
1316 ἔχεισθα Bekker (prob. Vetta)   1317 κειμι A, corr.
Bekker   1318 παιδα φιλειν A, corr. Bekker

1318ab

ὤ μοι ἐγὼ δειλός· καὶ δὴ κατάχαρμα μὲν
ἐχθροῖς,
τοῖσι φίλοις δὲ πόνος δεινὰ παθὼν γενόμην.

1319-22

ὦ παῖ, ἐπεί τοι δῶκε θεὰ χάριν ἱμερόεσσαν
Κύπρις, σὸν δ' εἶδος πᾶσι νέοισι μέλει,
τῶνδ' ἐπάκουσον ἐπῶν καὶ ἐμὴν χάριν ἔνθεο θυμῷ,
γνοὺς ἔρος ὡς χαλεπὸν γίνεται ἀνδρὶ φέρειν.

1320 (left margin, line 2)

1320 παισινεοισι A, corr. Bekker   1322 ἔρον ὡς
χαλεπὸς Bergk

THEOGNIS

1311-18

I was aware, boy, that you cheated on me—in fact I
... you—in favour of those with whom you are now a
close friend, throwing aside my friendship as of no
value. You were not their friend before, whereas I
thought that out of all I would make you a loyal com-
rade. Go ahead, take another friend now; but I, your
benefactor, am laid low. Let no one among all men,
viewing you, desire to love a boy.

1318ab[1]

O wretch that I am! Because of my wretched suffer-
ing I have become a joy to my enemies and a burden
to my friends.

[1] Virtually identical to 1107-1108.

1319-22

Boy, since the Cyprian goddess gave you a beauty
that arouses desire and all the young men are ob-
sessed with your looks, listen to these words of mine
and take them to heart as a favour to me, knowing
that love is hard for a man to bear.[1]

[1] As Vetta argues, the connection between the causal and main
clause seems to be that good looks and good sense should be
complementary and that consequently the boy should have the
wisdom to reciprocate the speaker's love.

1323-26

Κυπρογένη, παῦσόν με πόνων, σκέδασον δὲ
μερίμνας
θυμοβόρους, στρέψον δ᾽ αὖθις ἐς εὐφροσύνας·
1325 μερμήρας δ᾽ ἀπόπαυε κακάς, δὸς δ᾽ εὔφρονι θυμῷ
μέτρ᾽ ἥβης τελέσαντ᾽ ἔργματα σωφροσύνης.

1324 τρέψον van der Mey   1325 ευφρόσυνθυμω A,
corr. Bekker

1327-34

ὦ παῖ, ἕως ἂν ἔχῃς λείαν γένυν, οὔποτέ σ᾽ αἰνῶν
παύσομαι, οὐδ᾽ εἴ μοι μόρσιμόν ἐστι θανεῖν.
σοί τε διδόντ᾽ ἔτι καλόν, ἐμοί τ᾽ οὐκ αἰσχρὸν
ἐρῶντι
1330 αἰτεῖν. ἀλλὰ γονέων λίσσομαι ἡμετέρων,
αἴδεό μ᾽, ὦ παῖ ⟨ ⟩, διδοὺς χάριν, εἴ ποτε καὶ σὺ
ἕξεις Κυπρογενοῦς δῶρον ἰοστεφάνου
χρηΐζων καὶ ἐπ᾽ ἄλλον ἐλεύσεαι· ἀλλά σε δαίμων
δοίη τῶν αὐτῶν ἀντιτυχεῖν ἐπέων.

1327 λιαν A, corr. Bekker   σαίνων A, corr. Orelli
1329 διδοῦν Bergk (prob. Vetta)   1331 ⟨καλέ⟩ Welcker, alii
alia

1335-36

1335 ὄλβιος, ὅστις ἐρῶν γυμνάζεται οἴκαδε ἐλθών,
εὕδων σὺν καλῷ παιδὶ πανημέριος.

1335-36 οἴκαδε ⟨δ᾽⟩ ἐλθὼν εὕδει Bekker   1336 ευδειν
A, εὕδων West

376

THEOGNIS

1323-26

Cyprus-born, put an end to my pain, scatter the cares that gnaw at my heart, and restore me to happiness. Keep away cruel worries and with kindly heart grant me the workings of a sound mind, now that I have completed[1] my span of youth.

[1] Less probably, "when I have completed."

1327-34

Boy, as long as you have a chin that is smooth, I'll never stop praising you, not even if it is destined that I die.[1] It's a fine thing still for you the giver and it's not shameful for me the lover to ask. I beseech you, on behalf of our (my?) parents, show me respect, boy, and grant me your favour. If one day you too shall crave the gift of the Cyprus-born crowned with violets and pursue another, then may the god grant that you meet with the same response.[2]

[1] Many editors treat 1327-28 as a separate couplet.
[2] I.e., when you become a lover, may the response you meet with be favourable or unfavourable, depending on how you respond to me.

1335-36

Happy the man who goes home and engages in amorous exercise, sleeping with a handsome boy all day long.

1337-40

οὐκέτ' ἐρῶ παιδός, χαλεπὰς δ' ἀπελάκτισ' ἀνίας,
  μόχθους τ' ἀργαλέους ἄσμενος ἐξέφυγον,
ἐκλέλυμαι δὲ πόθου πρὸς ἐυστεφάνου Κυθερείης·
1340 σοὶ δ', ὦ παῖ, χάρις ἔστ' οὐδεμία πρὸς ἐμοῦ.

1341-50

αἰαῖ, παιδὸς ἐρῶ ἀπαλόχροος, ὅς με φίλοισιν
  πᾶσι μάλ' ἐκφαίνει κοὐκ ἐθέλοντος ἐμοῦ.
τλήσομαι οὐ κρύψας· ἀεκούσι⟨α⟩ πολλὰ βίαια·
  οὐ γὰρ ὑπ' αἰκελίῳ παιδὶ δαμεὶς ἐφάνην.
1345 παιδοφιλεῖν δέ τι τερπνόν, ἐπεί ποτε καὶ
      Γανυμήδους
    ἤρατο καὶ Κρονίδης ἀθανάτων βασιλεύς,
  ἁρπάξας δ' ἐς Ὄλυμπον ἀνήγαγε καί μιν ἔθηκεν
    δαίμονα, παιδείης ἄνθος ἔχοντ' ἐρατόν.
  οὕτω μὴ θαύμαζε, Σιμωνίδη, οὕνεκα κἀγὼ
1350 ἐξεφάνην καλοῦ παιδὸς ἔρωτι δαμείς.

1343 post κρύψας distinxit West   ἀεκουσι A, suppl.
Welcker   1344 ἐπ' A, corr. Hartel   1345 δ' ετι A,
distinxit Bekker   1350 εξεδάμην A, corr. Baiter

1351-52

ὦ παῖ, μὴ κώμαζε, γέροντι δὲ πείθεο ἀνδρί·
  οὔτοι κωμάζειν σύμφορον ἀνδρὶ νέῳ.

1353-56

πικρὸς καὶ γλυκύς ἐστι καὶ ἁρπαλέος καὶ ἀπηνὴς
  ὄφρα τέλειος ἔῃ, Κύρνε, νέοισιν ἔρως.

THEOGNIS

1337-40

I am no longer in love with a boy, I have kicked aside
harsh pain, I have gladly escaped from grievous
hardships, and the fair-crowned Cytherean[1] has re-
leased me from longing. And as for your charms,
boy, they don't exist in my eyes.

[1] See n. 1 on 1386-89.

1341-50

Alas, I am in love with a soft-skinned boy who shows
me off to all my friends in spite of my unwillingness.
I'll put up with the exposure—there are many things
that one is forced to do against one's will—for it's by
no unworthy boy that I was shown to be captivated.[1]
And there is some pleasure in loving a boy, since
once in fact even the son of Cronus, king of the im-
mortals, fell in love with Ganymede,[2] seized him,
carried him off to Olympus, and made him divine,
keeping the lovely bloom of boyhood. So, don't be
astonished, Simonides,[3] that I too have been re-
vealed as captivated by love for a handsome boy.

[1] Many editors treat what follows as a separate poem.
[2] For Zeus' abduction of the Trojan Ganymede see especially *Homeric Hymn to Aphrodite* 200-217.   [3] See n. 1 on 467-96.

1351-52

Don't go carousing, boy, but take an old man's ad-
vice. It's not fitting for a young man to carouse.

1353-56

For the young, Cyrnus, love is bitter and sweet, kind
and harsh,[1] until it is fulfilled. For if one fulfills it, it

1355 ἢν μὲν γὰρ τελέσῃ, γλυκὺ γίνεται· ἢν δὲ διώκων
      μὴ τελέσῃ, πάντων τοῦτ᾽ ἀνιηρότατον.

1354 τέλεος A, corr. Bekker

1357-60

αἰεὶ παιδοφίλησιν ἐπὶ ζυγὸν αὐχένι κεῖται
  δύσλοφον, ἀργαλέον μνῆμα φιλοξενίης.
χρὴ γάρ τοι περὶ παῖδα πονούμενον εἰς φιλότητα
1360 ὥσπερ κληματίνῳ χεῖρα πυρὶ προσάγειν.

1358 δυσμορον A, corr. Ahrens ex 848, 1024

1361-62

ναῦς πέτρῃ προσέκυρσας ἐμῆς φιλότητος
      ἁμαρτών,
  ὦ παῖ, καὶ σαπροῦ πείσματος ἀντελάβου.

1363-64

οὐδαμά σ᾽ οὐδ᾽ ἀπεὼν δηλήσομαι, οὐδέ με πείσει
  οὐδεὶς ἀνθρώπων ὥστε με μή σε φιλεῖν.

1365-66

1365 ὦ παίδων κάλλιστε καὶ ἱμεροέστατε πάντων,
  στῆθ᾽ αὐτοῦ καί μου παῦρ᾽ ἐπάκουσον ἔπη.

1367-68

παιδός τοι χάρις ἐστί· γυναικὶ δὲ πιστὸς ἑταῖρος
  οὐδείς, ἀλλ᾽ αἰεὶ τὸν παρεόντα φιλεῖ.

is sweet, but if one pursues it without fulfilment, it is the most painful of all things.

[1] Cf. 301.

1357-60

Those who love a boy always have a heavy yoke lying on their necks, a harsh reminder of amorous hospitality. For one who toils to win the love of a boy must, as it were, place his hand in a fire of vine twigs.[1]

[1] Such a fire blazes quickly and with great heat. Some treat the couplet as separate.

1361-62

You've lost my love, boy, you're like a ship that has struck a rock, and you've grasped a rotten rope.

1363-64

I'll never cause you harm, even when I am absent, and no one will persuade me not to love you.

1365-66

Most handsome and desirable of all boys, stay where you are and listen to a few words from me.

1367-68

A boy shows gratitude, but a woman is a loyal companion of no one; she always loves the man who's at hand.[1]

[1] Contrast 1267-70 where it is a boy's inconstancy that is stressed.

1369-72

παιδὸς ἔρως καλὸς μὲν ἔχειν, καλὸς δ᾿
    ἀποθέσθαι·
1370   πολλὸν δ᾿ εὑρέσθαι ῥήτερον ἢ τελέσαι.
μυρία δ᾿ ἐξ αὐτοῦ κρέμαται κακά, μυρία δ᾿
    ἐσθλά·
ἀλλ᾿ ἔν τοι ταύτῃ καί τις ἔνεστι χάρις.

1372 τούτῳ Adrados, alii alia

1373-74

οὐδαμά πω κατέμεινας ἐμὴν χάριν, ἀλλ᾿ ὑπὸ
    πᾶσαν
αἰεὶ σπουδαίην ἔρχεαι ἀγγελίην.

1374 σπουδαίως van Herwerden

1375-76

1375   ὄλβιος, ὅστις παιδὸς ἐρῶν οὐκ οἶδε θάλασσαν,
οὐδέ οἱ ἐν πόντῳ νὺξ ἐπιοῦσα μέλει.

1377-80

καλὸς ἐὼν κακότητι φίλων δειλοῖσιν ὁμιλεῖς
ἀνδράσι, καὶ διὰ τοῦτ᾿ αἰσχρὸν ὄνειδος ἔχεις,
ὦ παῖ· ἐγὼ δ᾿ ἀέκων τῆς σῆς φιλότητος ἁμαρτὼν
1380   ὠνήμην, ἔρδων οἷά τ᾿ ἐλεύθερος ὤν.

1377 φιμον A, corr. Bekker: κακότητα φιλῶν Nauck (prob.
Vetta)

THEOGNIS

1369-72

Love of a boy is fine to have and fine to set aside; it is much easier to find than to fulfil. Countless are the woes that hang suspended from it, countless the blessings. But in this way[1] there is in fact some pleasure present.

[1] If ταύτῃ is sound, it must equal οὕτω, with ἐν anticipating ἔνεστι (so Hudson-Williams, Garzya, Vetta), but West, perhaps rightly, judges it to be a corruption for some word expressing the idea of 'pain.'

1373-74

You have never yet stayed for my sake, but you always leave in response to every earnest message.

1375-76

Happy is he who loves a boy and does not know the sea, and is not concerned about the approach of night on the deep.

1377-80

You are handsome, but under the bad influence of friends you associate with base men and because of this, boy, you incur shameful reproach. As for me, although I was reluctant to lose your love, I have benefited from it, acting as a free man should.

1381-85

ἄνθρωποί σ᾽ ἐδόκουν χρυσῆς παρὰ δῶρον ἔχοντα
ἐλθεῖν Κυπρογενοῦς – ‿‿ –‿‿ –
. . . .
– ‿‿ ⟨Κυπρογενοῦς⟩ δῶρον ἰοστεφάνου
γίνεται ἀνθρώποισιν ἔχειν χαλεπώτατον ἄχθος,

1385   ἂν μὴ Κυπρογενὴς δῷ λύσιν ἐκ χαλεπῶν.

1381 ἀνθρώποις A, corr. Bekker   πάρα Vetta
1382-83 lacunam stat. et Κυπρογενοῦς iteravit Bekker

1386-89

Κυπρογενὲς Κυθέρεια δολοπλόκε, σοί τι
    περισσὸν
Ζεὺς τόδε τιμήσας δῶρον ἔδωκεν ἔχειν.
δαμνᾷς δ᾽ ἀνθρώπων πυκινὰς φρένας, οὐδέ τίς
    ἐστιν
οὕτως ἴφθιμος καὶ σοφὸς ὥστε φυγεῖν.

1386 κυπρόγενες κύθειρα A, corr. Bekker   σοι τι A, σοὶ τί
A² (prob. West), σοί τι edd. nonnulli,   1388 δάμνασαι
Bergk, δ᾽ del. Hartung

THEOGNIS

1381-85

Men thought that you had come with a gift from
the golden Cyprus-born . . . (But) the gift of the
violet-crowned (Cyprus-born) becomes a most
painful burden for men to bear, if she does not grant
release from the pain.

1386-89

Cyprus-born Cytherean,[1] weaver of wiles, to honour
you Zeus gave you this special gift. For you over-
whelm the sound minds of men and there is no one
strong or clever enough to escape you.

[1] For an explanation of Aphrodite's connection with both
Cyprus and Cythera, an island off the south coast of the
Peloponnese, see Hes. *Theog.* 190-200.

PHILIADAS

1 Steph. Byz. (p. 310.9 Meineke)

Θέσπεια, πόλις Βοιωτίας . . . καὶ ἐπίγραμμα τῶν
ἀναιρεθέντων ὑπὸ τῶν Περσῶν· ἦν δὲ Φιλιάδου Μεγα-
ρέως·

> ἄνδρες θ᾽ οἳ ποτ᾽ ἔναιον ὑπὸ κροτάφοις
>   Ἑλικῶνος,
> λήματι τῶν αὐχεῖ Θεσπιὰς εὐρύχορος.

Hinc Eust. in Hom. *Il.* 2.498 (i.406.10 V.d.Valk)

1 τοί Brunck   κροτάφῳ Steph.   2 ἄρχει . . .
εὐρύχωρος Steph.

PHILIADAS

1 Stephanus of Byzantium, *Lexicon of Place-names*

Thespeia, a city in Boeotia . . . And there is an epigram on those killed by the Persians.[1] It was by Philiadas of Megara:[2]

> Spacious Thespiae[3] takes pride in the spirit of those men who once dwelled beneath the brows of Helicon.

[1] At Thermopylae in 480. [2] See Page, *Further Greek Epigrams* pp. 78-79: "the fact that the author is named probably means that the epigram is demonstrative, not inscriptional, preserved in an anthology." Philiadas is otherwise unknown, but see n. 2 on Theognis 773-88. [3] A city in south-central Boeotia.

PHOCYLIDES

TESTIMONIA

1 *Suda* (iv.754.19 Adler)

Φωκυλίδης· Μιλήσιος, φιλόσοφος, σύγχρονος Θεό-
γνιδος· ἦν δὲ ἑκάτερος μετὰ χμζ΄ ἔτη τῶν Τρωϊκῶν,
ὀλυμπιάδι γεγονότες νθ΄. ἔγραψεν ἔπη καὶ ἐλεγείας,
παραινέσεις ἤτοι γνώμας· ἅς τινες Κεφάλαια ἐπι-
γράφουσιν· εἰσὶ δὲ ἐκ τῶν Σιβυλλιακῶν κεκλεμμένα.

2 Plut. *de aud.* 13.45a

μέμψαιτο δ᾽ ἄν τις Ἀρχιλόχου μὲν τὴν ὑπόθεσιν,
Παρμενίδου δὲ τὴν στιχοποιΐαν, Φωκυλίδου δὲ τὴν
εὐτέλειαν, Εὐριπίδου δὲ τὴν λαλίαν, Σοφοκλέους δὲ
τὴν ἀνωμαλίαν . . .· ἕκαστός γε μὴν ἐπαινεῖται κατὰ
τὸ ἴδιον τῆς δυνάμεως, ᾧ κινεῖν καὶ ἄγειν πέφυκεν.

PHOCYLIDES

TESTIMONIA

1 *Suda*

Phocylides, a philosopher from Miletus and contemporary of Theognis. Both flourished 647 years after the Trojan War, in the 59th Olympiad (544/41).[1] Phocylides wrote hexameters and elegies[2] containing admonitions or maxims. Some give them the title *Main Topics*; they are lifted from the Sibylline books.[3]

[1] Cf. Theognis test. 1. Other sources give an Olympiad earlier or later. [2] West, *JHS* 98 (1978) 164-67, denies that Phocylides wrote elegies and argues that the hexameter fragments came from one gnomic poem (see n. 2 on fr. 1). [3] A reference to the *Pseudo-Phocylidea*, a collection of 230 gnomic hexameters written probably early in the 1st cent. A.D. For a text, translation, and commentary on these see P. W. Van der Horst, *The Sentences of Pseudo-Phocylides* (Leiden 1978).

2 Plutarch, *On Listening*

One might find fault with Archilochus for his subject matter, Parmenides for his versification, Phocylides for his impoverished language, Euripides for his garrulity, and Sophocles for his unevenness . . . Nevertheless, each is praised for the individual capacity nature has given him to move and lead us on.

3 Cic. *ad Att*. 4.9.1

nos hic cum Pompeio fuimus. multa mecum de re publica,
sane sibi displicens, ut loquebatur (sic est enim in hoc
homine dicendum), Syriam spernens, Hispaniam iactans,
hic quoque ut loquebatur; et, opinor, usquequaque, de hoc
cum dicemus, sit hoc quasi καὶ τόδε Φωκυλίδου.

FRAGMENTS

1. Elegus

1 Strabo 10.5.12

ἔστι δὲ καὶ Ἀμοργὸς τῶν Σποράδων, ὅθεν ἦν Σιμωνί-
δης ὁ τῶν ἰάμβων ποιητής, καὶ Λέβινθος καὶ †Λερία†·

καὶ τόδε Φωκυλίδεω· Λέριοι κακοί, οὐχ ὁ μέν, ὃς
    δ᾽ οὔ·
πάντες πλὴν Προκλέους—καὶ Προκλέης Λέριος.

διεβέβληντο γὰρ ὡς κακοήθεις οἱ ἐνθένδε ἄνθρωποι.

1 -λίδου codd., corr. Fick   2 Πατροκλέους et
Πατροκλέης vv.ll.

---

¹ Strabo's text is corrupt, but however emended it clearly con-
tained the name Leros. Leros is south of Samos, with Amorgos
and Lebinthos to the southwest of Leros.   ² West maintains

3 Cicero, *Letters to Atticus*

I was with Pompey here. He talked with me at length about politics and was quite critical of himself, as he said (for in his case this is a necessary proviso), expressing scorn for Syria and disdain for Spain, here too "as he said," and in my opinion this is to be added everywhere when we speak of him, like the tag "this too is by Phocylides."[1]

[1] Cf. frr. 1-5 and probably 6.

For additional testimonia see Mimn. test. 8, Theognis test. 5, and the introduction to fr. 4.

FRAGMENTS

1. Elegy

1 Strabo, *Geography*

And there is also Amorgos, one of the Sporades, whence came the iambic poet Semonides, and Lebinthos and Leros:[1]

> This too is by Phocylides.[2] The Lerians are base, not just one and another not, but all except Procles[3]— and Procles is a Lerian.

For those who came from there were charged with having a bad character.

that Strabo had a memory lapse and should have said Δημοδόκου (see West's Demodocus fr. 2), but this is based largely on his view that Phocylides did not write elegies. Attribution of the couplet to Phocylides is caustically defended by G. Giangrande, *Studies in Classical Philology* (Amsterdam 1992) 33-37.   [3] Identity unknown.

ELEGIAC POETRY

2-16. Hexametri

2 Stob. 4.22.192

Φωκυλίδου·

> καὶ τόδε Φωκυλίδεω· τετόρων ἀπὸ τῶνδ' ἐγένοντο
> φῦλα γυναικείων· ἢ μὲν κυνός, ἢ δὲ μελίσσης,
> ἢ δὲ συὸς βλοσυρῆς, ἢ δ' ἵππου χαιτηέσσης.
> εὔφορος ἥδε, ταχεῖα, περίδρομος, εἶδος ἀρίστη·
> 5 ἢ δὲ συὸς βλοσυρῆς οὔτ' ἄρ κακὴ οὐδὲ μὲν ἐσθλή·
> ἢ δὲ κυνὸς χαλεπή τε καὶ ἄγριος· ἢ δὲ μελίσσης
> οἰκονόμος τ' ἀγαθὴ καὶ ἐπίσταται ἐργάζεσθαι·
> ἧς εὔχεο, φίλ' ἑταῖρε, λαχεῖν γάμου ἱμερόεντος.

1 τῶν Stob., τῶνδ' Paris. 1985, τῶν⟨δε⟩ γένοντο Trincavelli
8 εὔχευ Stob., corr. Fick

3 Stob. 4.29.28

Φωκυλίδου·

> καὶ τόδε Φωκυλίδεω· τί πλέον, γένος εὐγενὲς εἶναι,
> οἷς οὔτ' ἐν μύθοις ἕπεται χάρις οὔτ' ἐνὶ βουλῇ;

1 -λίδου codd., corr. Brunck   τὸ codd., corr. Brunck

4 Dio Chrys. *or.* 36.10-13

> εἶπον οὖν προσπαίζων πρὸς αὐτόν "πότερόν σοι δο-
> κεῖ, ὦ Καλλίστρατε, ἀμείνων ποιητὴς Ὅμηρος ἢ

PHOCYLIDES

2-16. Dactylic Hexameters

2 Stobaeus, *Anthology*

From Phocylides:

> This too is by Phocylides. The tribes of women origi-
> nated from these four: one from a bitch, one from a
> bee, one from a bristly[1] sow, one from a long-maned
> mare. The last bears herself well, is swift, a gad-
> about, and of the finest form. The one from a bristly
> sow is neither bad nor good. The one from a bitch is
> difficult and wild. The one from a bee is a good
> housekeeper and knows how to work. Pray, dear
> friend, to obtain delightful marriage with her as
> your lot.[2]

[1] Translation uncertain. The word normally describes a fear-
some appearance, but this ill suits what follows.   [2] The
poem is perhaps influenced by Sem. fr. 7, but both could be draw-
ing on a common tradition.

3 Stobaeus, *Anthology*

From Phocylides:

> This too is by Phocylides. Of what advantage is
> noble birth to those who have nothing attractive in
> what they say or plan?

4 Dio Chrysostom, *Discourses*

Therefore I said to him in jest, "Which do you think,
Callistratus, is the better poet, Homer or Phocylides?"

Φωκυλίδης·" καὶ ὃς γελάσας ἔφη "ἀλλ' οὐδὲ ἐπί-
σταμαι ἔγωγε τοῦ ἑτέρου ποιητοῦ τὸ ὄνομα, οἶμαι
δὲ μηδὲ τούτων μηδένα." . . . τὸν δὲ Φωκυλίδην ὑμεῖς
μὲν οὐκ ἐπίστασθε, ὡς λέγεις· πάνυ δὲ τῶν ἐνδόξων
γέγονε ποιητῶν. . . . "οὕτως," ἔφην, "καὶ τῆς Φωκυ-
λίδου ποιήσεως ἔξεστί σοι λαβεῖν δεῖγμα ἐν βραχεῖ.
καὶ γάρ ἐστιν οὐ τῶν μακράν τινα καὶ συνεχῆ ποίησιν
εἰρόντων . . . ἀλλὰ κατὰ δύο καὶ τρία ἔπη αὐτῷ καὶ
ἀρχὴν ἡ ποίησις καὶ πέρας λαμβάνει. ὥστε καὶ προσ-
τίθησι τὸ ὄνομα αὐτοῦ καθ' ἕκαστον διανόημα, ἅτε
σπουδαῖον καὶ πολλοῦ ἄξιον ἡγούμενος, οὐχ ὥσπερ
Ὅμηρος οὐδαμοῦ τῆς ποιήσεως ὠνόμασεν αὐτόν. ἢ οὐ
δοκεῖ σοι εἰκότως προσθεῖναι Φωκυλίδης τῇ τοιαύτῃ
γνώμῃ καὶ ἀποφάσει;

καὶ τόδε Φωκυλίδεω· πόλις ἐν σκοπέλῳ κατὰ
    κόσμον
οἰκέουσα σμικρὴ κρέσσων Νίνου ἀφραινούσης.

1 -λίδου codd., corr. Brunck   2 οἰκεῦσα codd., corr.
Fick

5 Phrynich. *ecl.* 335 (p. 96 Fischer)

γογγυσμὸς καὶ γογγύζειν· ταῦτα ἀδόκιμα μὲν οὐκ
ἔστιν, Ἰακὰ δέ. Φωκυλίδην γὰρ οἶδα κεχρημένον
αὐτῷ τὸν Μιλήσιον, ἄνδρα παλαιὸν σφόδρα·

And he replied with a laugh, "For my part I don't even know the second poet's name, nor do I think any of these men knows it." . . . You people do not know Phocylides, as you state, and yet he is one of the highly renowned poets. . . ."So too," I said, "you may take a brief sample from the poetry of Phocylides. For he is not one of those who string together long and continuous poetry . . . but his poetry has a beginning and end in two or three verses. And so he attaches his name to each sentiment, believing as he does that it is a serious matter and of great importance, unlike Homer who nowhere named himself in his poetry. Or don't you think that Phocylides had good reason to attach his name to such a maxim and pronouncement as this?"

This too is by Phocylides. A small and orderly city on a height is superior to foolish Nineveh.[1]

[1] Nineveh, capital of Assyria, was destroyed by the Medes in 612, but the couplet need not have been composed shortly after the event.

5 Phrynichus, *Selection of Attic Nouns and Verbs*

γογγυσμός ('muttering') and γογγύζειν ('to mutter'): these are not disreputable words, but are Ionic. For I know that Phocylides of Miletus, a very ancient man, used it:

καὶ τόδε Φωκυλίδεω· χρή τοι τὸν ἑταῖρον ἑταίρῳ
φροντίζειν, ἅσσ᾽ ἂν περιγογγύζωσι πολῖται.

1 ἑταίρων Kalinka, ἑταίρου dub. Diehl

6 Schol. Ar. *Nubes* 240 (p. 92 Dübner)

Φωκυλίδης ἐν μὲν τοῖς αὐτοῦ ποιήμασι κατὰ τὴν
συνήθειαν τοὺς χρεωφειλέτας χρήστας καλεῖ λέγων
οὕτως·

   <καὶ τόδε Φωκυλίδεω·> χρήστης κακοῦ ἔμμεναι
        ἀνδρὸς
   φεύγειν, μή σέ γ᾽ ἀνιήσῃ παρὰ καιρὸν ἀπαιτέων.

Suda (i.267.26, iv.825.15 Adler), vv. 1-2

1 suppl. Bergk   χρήστας κακοὺς *Suda* bis
2 ἀνιήσῃ Bergk, ἀνιήσειε διδοὺς codd.

7 Stob. 4.15.6

Φωκυλίδου·

   χρηίζων πλούτου μελέτην ἔχε πίονος ἀγροῦ·
   ἀγρὸν γάρ τε λέγουσιν Ἀμαλθείης κέρας εἶναι.

8 Orion *anth.* 1.22 (p. 43 Schneidewin)

ἐκ τῶν Φωκυλίδου·

   νυκτὸς βουλεύειν, νυκτὸς δέ τοι ὀξυτέρη φρὴν

This too is by Phocylides. Comrade should be concerned for comrade with regard to whatever the citizens mutter.

6 Scholiast on Aristophanes, *Clouds*

Phocylides in his poems uses χρῆσται with the customary meaning of 'debtors,'[1] speaking as follows:

⟨This too is by Phocylides.⟩ Avoid being the debtor of a base man, lest he cause you grief by demanding repayment inappropriately.

[1] Aristophanes had used the word to mean 'creditors.'

7 Stobaeus, *Anthology*

From Phocylides:

If you desire wealth, give your attention to a rich farm; for a farm, they say, is a horn of Amaltheia.[1]

[1] For Amaltheia see Frazer's note on Apollodorus 2.7.5 in the Loeb edition.

8 Orion, *Anthology*

From the works of Phocylides:

Take counsel at night, since at night the mind of

ἀνδράσιν· ἡσυχίη δ' ἀρετὴ‹ν› διζημένῳ ἐσθλή.

2 ἀρετὴ cod., corr. Schneidewin

9 Alex. Aphrod. in Arist. *Top.* 3.118a6 (*Comm. in Arist. Gr.* ii.258.7)

τὸ γοῦν φιλοσοφεῖν τε καὶ θεωρεῖν βέλτιον μέν ἐστι τοῦ χρηματίζεσθαι, οὐ μὴν καὶ αἱρετώτερον τοῖς ἐν ἐνδείᾳ οὖσι καὶ μὴ δυναμένοις ἄλλως εἶναι· κατὰ γὰρ τὸν Φωκυλίδην·

δίζησθαι βιοτήν, ἀρετὴν δ' ὅταν ᾖ βίος ἤδη.

Ps.-Diogen. 4.39 (*Paroem. Gr.* i.237.20), Apost. 6.8a (*Paroem. Gr.* ii.366.10)

δεῖ ζητεῖν vel ζητεῖσθαι Aphrod., δίζεσθαι paroem.: corr. Schneidewin

10 Arist. *Eth. Nic.* 5.1.15.1129b27

καὶ διὰ τοῦτο πολλάκις κρατίστη τῶν ἀρετῶν εἶναι δοκεῖ ἡ δικαιοσύνη . . . καὶ παροιμιαζόμενοί φαμεν·

ἐν δὲ δικαιοσύνῃ συλλήβδην πᾶσ' ἀρετή 'στιν.

men is sharper; quiet is good for one who seeks excellence.[1]

[1] The thought became proverbial. See the many sources cited by Gentili-Prato.

9 Alexander of Aphrodisias on Aristotle, *Topica*

To be a philosopher and to theorize is better than to make money, but it is not preferable for those who are in need and are unable to escape from it. For, in the words of Phocylides:

Seek a livelihood, and whenever you have it, seek excellence.[1]

[1] Plato *Rep.* 3.407a seems to have this passage in mind when he attributes to Phocylides the necessity to practise excellence (ἀρετὴν ἀσκεῖν) whenever anyone has made his livelihood (ὅταν τῳ ἤδη βίος ᾖ).

10 Aristotle, *Nicomachean Ethics*

And because of this justice is often deemed to be the best virtue . . . and we have the proverbial saying:

In justice there is the sum total of every excellence.[1]

[1] Aristotle does not name the author, but the verse appears as Theognis 147 (q.v.). Michael of Ephesus (*Comm. in Arist. Gr.* xxii(3).8.10; cf. xx.210.11) cites Theophrastus as the authority for assigning the verse to both Theognis and Phocylides.

11 Stob. 2.15.8

Φωκυλίδου·

πολλοί τοι δοκέουσι σαόφρονες ἔμμεναι ἄνδρες
σὺν κόσμῳ στείχοντες, ἐλαφρόνοοί περ ἐόντες.

1 σώφρονες cod., corr. Gaisford   2 ἐλαφρόνοί cod.,
corr. Gaisford

12 Arist. *Pol.* 4.1295b25

βούλεται δέ γε ἡ πόλις ἐξ ἴσων εἶναι καὶ ὁμοίων ὅτι
μάλιστα, τοῦτο δ᾽ ὑπάρχει μάλιστα τοῖς μέσοις . . .
διὰ τοῦτο καλῶς ηὔξατο Φωκυλίδης·

πολλὰ μέσοισιν ἄριστα· μέσος θέλω ἐν πόλει
εἶναι.

13 Plut. *de aud.* 18.47e

οὐ γὰρ μόνον, ὥς φησι Φωκυλίδης,

πόλλ᾽ ἀέκοντα παθεῖν διζήμενον ἔμμεναι ἐσθλόν,

ἀλλὰ καὶ γελασθῆναι δεῖ πολλὰ καὶ ἀδοξῆσαι . . .

Clem. *Strom.* 5.140.6; *Anecd. Paris.* (i.166.14 Cramer)

παθεῖν πολλὰ ἀέκοντα Anecd., corr. Bergk   πόλλ᾽
ἀπατηθῆναι Plut., πολλὰ πλανηθῆναι Clem.

PHOCYLIDES

11 Stobaeus, *Anthology*

From Phocylides:

> Many men who walk about in an orderly manner[1]
> seem to be of sound mind, although their wits are
> actually shallow.

[1] Or "with ornate dress."

12 Aristotle, *Politics*

But surely the city wishes to consist as much as possible of
people who are equal and alike, and this is found most of
all in the middle classes . . . For this reason it was a fine
prayer Phocylides made:

> There are many advantages for those who adopt a
> middle course; that's the course I want in the city.[1]

[1] Presumably in the context of class turmoil. Cf. Theognis 219-
20, 331, 335.

13 Plutarch, *On Listening*

For not only must one, as Phocylides says,

> suffer much unwillingly in a search for merit,

but also be much laughed at and meet with disrepute . . .

14 Ath. 10.427f-428b

διὸ καὶ καλῶς οἱ παροιμιαζόμενοι λέγουσι τὸν οἶνον
οὐκ ἔχειν πηδάλια . . . ὁ δὲ Φωκυλίδης ἔφη·

χρὴ δ᾽ ἐν συμποσίῳ κυλίκων περινισομενάων
ἡδέα κωτίλλοντα καθήμενον οἰνοποτάζειν.

15 Ps.-Plut. *de lib. educ.* 5.3f

κινδυνεύει δὲ καὶ Φωκυλίδης ὁ ποιητὴς καλῶς
παραινεῖν λέγων·

‹– ‾‾ – ‾‾ – ‾‾ –› χρὴ παῖδ᾽ ἔτ᾽ ἐόντα
καλὰ διδάσκειν ἔργα ‹∪ – ‾‾ – ∪∪ – –›.

16 Clem. *Strom.* 5.127.4

ἔτι πρὸς τοῖσδε Φωκυλίδης μὲν τοὺς ἀγγέλους
δαίμονας καλῶν, τοὺς μὲν εἶναι ἀγαθοὺς αὐτῶν, τοὺς
δὲ φαύλους διὰ τούτων παρίστησιν, ἐπεὶ καὶ ἡμεῖς
ἀποστάτας τινὰς παρειλήφαμεν·

ἀλλ᾽ ἄρα δαίμονές εἰσιν ἐπ᾽ ἀνδράσιν ἄλλοτε
ἄλλοι
οἱ μὲν ἐπερχομένου κακοῦ ἀνέρας ἐκλύσασθαι.

2 κακὸν ἀνέρος codd., corr. Schneidewin

PHOCYLIDES

14 Athenaeus, *Scholars at Dinner*

Consequently those who speak in proverbs well say that wine has no rudder . . . and Phocylides said:

> When the cups go round at the symposium one should sit and chat pleasantly while drinking.

15 Pseudo-Plutarch, *On the Education of Children*

And the poet Phocylides seems to give good advice when he says:

> While still a child one should learn noble deeds.

16 Clement of Alexandria, *Miscellanies*

Moreover Phocylides who calls the angels *daimones* (spirits) represents some of them as good and some as bad, since we have ascertained that certain ones are rebels:

> But, as it seems, there are different spirits at different times that attend upon men, some to grant men escape from coming ill . . .[1]

[1] The passage presumably went on to say something like, "and others to inflict ill."

I have omitted the epigram ascribed to Phocylides in *Anth. Pal.* 10.117, since it is obviously much later. See Page, *Further Greek Epigrams* p. 159.

DEMODOCUS

TESTIMONIUM

1 Anon. in Arist. *Eth. Nic.* (*Comm. in Arist. Graeca* xx.439.15)

ὁ Δημόδοκος Μιλήσιος Λέριος ἦν τὸ γένος.

FRAGMENTS

1 Arist. *Eth. Nic.* 7.8.1151a5

ὅτι μὲν οὖν κακία ἡ ἀκρασία οὔκ ἐστι, φανερόν. ἀλλά πη ἴσως· τὸ μὲν γὰρ παρὰ προαίρεσιν, τὸ δὲ κατὰ τὴν προαίρεσίν ἐστιν· οὐ μὴν ἀλλ' ὅμοιόν γε κατὰ τὰς πράξεις, ὥσπερ τὸ Δημοδόκου εἰς Μιλησίους·

<καὶ τόδε Δημοδόκου·> Μιλήσιοι ἀξύνετοι μὲν
οὔκ εἰσιν, δρῶσιν δ' οἷά περ ἀξύνετοι.

καὶ οἱ ἀκρατεῖς ἄδικοι μὲν οὔκ εἰσιν, ἀδικοῦσι δέ.

1 suppl. Bergk

404

DEMODOCUS

TESTIMONIUM

1 Anonymous on Aristotle, *Nicomachean Ethics*

Demodocus of Miletus was a Lerian by birth.[1]

[1] The source then comments on fr. 1. Nothing more is known about Demodocus, but he has been tentatively assigned to the 6th century.

FRAGMENTS

1 Aristotle, *Nicomachean Ethics*

That unrestraint is not a vice is clear (although in a way perhaps it is), since unrestraint is over and above deliberate choice, whereas vice is in accordance with it. Nevertheless, it is the same in its actions, as in what Demodocus said about the Milesians:

<This too is by Demodocus.> The Milesians are not fools, but they act as fools do.

Similarly the unrestrained are not unjust, but they act unjustly.

2 *Anth. Pal.* 11.235 (Δημοδόκου)

καὶ τόδε Δημοδόκου· Χῖοι κακοί, οὐχ ὁ μέν, ὃς δ᾽
οὔ·
πάντες πλὴν Προκλέους—καὶ Προκλέης δὲ
Χίος.

Tetrameter

6 Diog. Laert. 1.84

λέγεται δὲ (ὁ Βίας) καὶ δίκας δεινότατος γεγονέναι
εἰπεῖν, ἐπ᾽ ἀγαθῷ μέντοι τῇ τῶν λόγων ἰσχύι προσ-
εχρῆτο· ὅθεν καὶ Δημόδοκος (δημόδικος codd., corr.
Bochart) ὁ Λέριος (ὁ ἀλιείριος vel ὁ ἀλείριος codd., corr.
Menagius) τοῦτο αἰνίττεται λέγων·

ἢν τύχῃς τίνων, δικάζεο τὴν Πριηνίην δίκην.

τίνων, τηνων, τήνων (η in ras.), πίνων, κρίνων codd., Τηίων
dub. West   δικάζευ codd., corr. West

DEMODOCUS

2 *Palatine Anthology*

From Demodocus:

> This too is by Demodocus. The Chians are base, not
> just one and another not, but all except Procles—
> and Procles is a Chian.[1]

[1] Unless West is right that Phoc. fr. 1 (see n. 2 ad loc.) is actu-
ally the work of Demodocus, we should treat this as a spurious
couplet modeled on Phocylides. The last word in v. 2 is arbitrarily
accented Χίος instead of Χῖος so as to make it scan.

West prints as frr. 3-5 three epigrams from the *Palatine An-
thology* which follow immediately after fr. 2 and which have the
heading τοῦ αὐτοῦ ("by the same"). They are treated by West and
others as spurious and so are omitted here. A translation can be
found in the Loeb *Greek Anthology* iv.183.

Trochaic Tetrameter

6 Diogenes Laertius, *Lives of the Philosophers*

Bias is also said to have been very skilful at pleading cases,
but he used the power of his oratory to a good end. Hence
Demodocus of Leros alludes to this when he says:

> If you happen to be paying requital,[1] plead your case
> in the Prienian manner.[2]

[1] Text and translation uncertain. [2] I.e., as Bias would.
Bias, one of the Seven Sages, came from Priene (cf. Hipponax fr.
123).

XENOPHANES

TESTIMONIA

1 Diog. Laert. 9.18-20

Ξενοφάνης Δεξίου ἤ, ὡς Ἀπολλόδωρος (*FGrHist* 244 F 68a), Ὀρθομένους Κολοφώνιος ἐπαινεῖται πρὸς τοῦ Τίμωνος· φησὶ γοῦν (fr. 60.1 Di Marco)· "Ξεινοφάνη θ' ὑπάτυφον, Ὁμηραπάτην ἐπικόπτην." οὗτος ἐκπεσὼν τῆς πατρίδος ἐν Ζάγκλῃ τῆς Σικελίας ***, διέτριβε δὲ καὶ ἐν Κατάνῃ. . . . γέγραφε δὲ ἐν ἔπεσι καὶ ἐλεγείας καὶ ἰάμβους καθ' Ἡσιόδου καὶ Ὁμήρου, ἐπικόπτων αὐτῶν τὰ περὶ θεῶν εἰρημένα. ἀλλὰ καὶ αὐτὸς ἐρρα-ψῴδει τὰ ἑαυτοῦ. ἀντιδοξάσαι τε λέγεται Θαλῇ καὶ Πυθαγόρᾳ, καθάψασθαι δὲ καὶ Ἐπιμενίδου. μακρο-βιώτατός τε γέγονεν, ὥς που καὶ αὐτός φησι (fr. 8). . . . ἐποίησε δὲ καὶ Κολοφῶνος κτίσιν καὶ τὸν εἰς Ἐλέαν τῆς Ἰταλίας ἀποικισμὸν ἔπη δισχίλια. καὶ ἤκμαζε κατὰ τὴν ἑξηκοστὴν ὀλυμπιάδα. . . . γέγονε δὲ καὶ

XENOPHANES

TESTIMONIA

Only the elegiac fragments and two of the many testimonia are included here. All the fragments and testimonia are printed by Gentili-Prato and all are translated by J. H. Lesher, *Xenophanes of Colophon* (Toronto 1992). Most of the testimonia refer to his philosophical views.

1 Diogenes Laertius, *Lives of the Philosophers*

Xenophanes, the son of Dexius or, according to Apollodorus, of Orthomenes, from Colophon, is praised by Timon.[1] At any rate he says: "Xenophanes, moderately free of vanity, censorious of Homer's deceit."[2] Banished from his homeland,[3] (he spent time?) in Zancle in Sicily ***[4] and he also spent time in Catana. . . . He wrote in hexameters as well as elegiac and iambic poems against Hesiod and Homer, censuring what they said about the gods.[5] But he also recited his own works. He is said to have opposed the views of Thales and Pythagoras,[6] and he also attacked Epimenides. He lived a very long life, as he himself states somewhere (fr. 8). . . . He composed poems on both the foundation of Colophon and the colonization of Elea in Italy, two thousand verses.[7] And he flourished in the 60th Olympiad (540-537).[8] . . . There was also another

ἄλλος Ξενοφάνης Λέσβιος ποιητὴς ἰάμβων.

2 Procl. in Hes. *Op.* 286 (p. 96 Pertusi) = Plut. fr. 19
   Bernard.

Ξενοφάνην διὰ δή τινα πρὸς τοὺς κατ᾽ αὐτὸν φιλοσό-
φους καὶ ποιητὰς μικροψυχίαν Σίλλους ἀτόπους συν-
θεῖναι κατὰ πάντων φιλοσόφων καὶ ποιητῶν.

Xenophanes, an iambic poet from Lesbos.[9]

[1] A sceptic philosopher and poet, 3rd c. B.C.   [2] Sextus Empiricus, *Outlines of Pyrrhonism* 1.224, quotes the same verse, but in the nominative.   [3] See n. 3 on fr. 8.   [4] Diels was probably right to propose a reference in the lacuna to the poet's sojourn in Elea (on the west coast of Italy).   [5] An example is fr. 11 D.-K.: "Homer and Hesiod have attributed to the gods all that are matters of reproach and blame among men: theft, adultery, and mutual deceit." There are no iambic poems extant, but fr. 14 D.-K. consists of an iambic trimeter followed by an hexameter. This reminds us of 'Homer,' *Margites*, and F. Bossi, *Studi sul Margite* (Ferrara 1986) 39-43, suggests that this poem was composed by Xenophanes.   [6] See frr. 7, 7a.   [7] It is unknown whether these were in hexameters or in elegiac verse. [8] Several other sources record the same or almost the same date, but Clement, *Miscellanies* 1.64.2, states that according to Apollodorus (*FGrHist* 244 F 68c) Xenophanes was born in the 40th Olympiad (620-617). This date has been generally rejected: for a detailed study of the question see L. Woodbury, *Collected Writings* (Atlanta 1991) 96-117.   [9] Nothing is known of this poet.

2 Proclus on Hesiod, *Works and Days*

Because of some mean-spiritedness towards contemporary philosophers and poets, Xenophanes composed strange *Silloi*[1] against all philosophers and poets.

[1] This was the title of a work in hexameters by Timon of Phlius (see test. 1) who frequently praised Xenophanes and actually dedicated his *Silloi* to him. We do not know the etymology of the word, but it clearly means something like "lampoons" and it may be a synonym of *Parodies* (Παρῳδίαι) which Athenaeus (2.54c) uses to introduce Xen. fr. 22 D.-K. Xenophanes' *Silloi* comprised at least five books and were in hexameters, perhaps with occasional iambic trimeters interspersed.

411

ELEGIAC POETRY

FRAGMENTS

Elegi

1 Ath. 11.462c

ὁρῶν οὖν ὑμῶν καὶ αὐτὸς τὸ συμπόσιον κατὰ τὸν
Κολοφώνιον Ξενοφάνη πλῆρες ὂν πάσης θυμηδίας·

> νῦν γὰρ δὴ ζάπεδον καθαρὸν καὶ χεῖρες ἀπάντων
> καὶ κύλικες· πλεκτοὺς δ᾽ ἀμφιτιθεῖ στεφάνους,
> ἄλλος δ᾽ εὐῶδες μύρον ἐν φιάλῃ παρατείνει·
> κρητὴρ δ᾽ ἔστηκεν μεστὸς εὐφροσύνης·
>
> 5 ἄλλος δ᾽ οἶνος ἑτοῖμος, ὃς οὔποτέ φησι προδώσειν,
> μείλιχος ἐν κεράμοις, ἄνθεος ὀσδόμενος·
> ἐν δὲ μέσοις ἁγνὴν ὀδμὴν λιβανωτὸς ἵησιν,
> ψυχρὸν δ᾽ ἐστὶν ὕδωρ καὶ γλυκὺ καὶ καθαρόν·
> πάρκεινται δ᾽ ἄρτοι ξανθοὶ γεραρή τε τράπεζα
>
> 10 τυροῦ καὶ μέλιτος πίονος ἀχθομένη·
> βωμὸς δ᾽ ἄνθεσιν ἂν τὸ μέσον πάντῃ πεπύκασται,
> μολπὴ δ᾽ ἀμφὶς ἔχει δώματα καὶ θαλίη.
> χρὴ δὲ πρῶτον μὲν θεὸν ὑμνεῖν εὔφρονας ἄνδρας
> εὐφήμοις μύθοις καὶ καθαροῖσι λόγοις,
>
> 15 σπείσαντάς τε καὶ εὐξαμένους τὰ δίκαια δύνασθαι
> πρήσσειν—ταῦτα γὰρ ὦν ἐστι προχειρότερον,
> οὐχ ὕβρεις—· πίνειν δ᾽ ὁπόσον κεν ἔχων ἀφίκοιο
> οἴκαδ᾽ ἄνευ προπόλου μὴ πάνυ γηραλέος·
> ἀνδρῶν δ᾽ αἰνεῖν τοῦτον ὃς ἐσθλὰ πιὼν ἀναφαίνει,
>
> 20 ὡς ᾖ μνημοσύνη καὶ τόνος ἀμφ᾽ ἀρετῆς·

412

FRAGMENTS

Elegies

1 Athenaeus, *Scholars at Dinner*

Since then I myself see that your symposium, in accordance with Xenophanes of Colophon, is full of every delight:

For now the floor is clean and clean the hands of everyone and the cups;[1] (one servant) places woven garlands round (the heads of the guests), and another offers sweet-smelling perfume in a saucer; the mixing-bowl stands filled with good cheer; on hand is additional wine, which promises never to run out, mellow in its jars and fragrant with its bouquet; in the middle incense sends forth its pure and holy aroma and there is water, cool, sweet, and clear;[2] nearby are set golden-brown loaves and a magnificent table laden with cheese and thick honey; in the centre an altar is covered all over with flowers, and song and festivity pervade the room.

For men of good cheer it is meet[3] first to hymn the god[4] with reverent tales and pure words, after pouring libations and praying for the ability to do what is right—for in truth this is a more obvious[5] thing to do, not deeds of violence; it is meet to drink as much as you can hold and come home without an attendant unless you are very old, and to praise that man who after drinking reveals noble thoughts, so that there is a recollection of and striving for excellence; it is not meet to make an array of the wars of

οὔ τι μάχας διέπειν Τιτήνων οὐδὲ Γιγάντων
  οὐδέ ⟨τι⟩ Κενταύρων, πλάσμα⟨τα⟩ τῶν
    προτέρων,
ἢ στάσιας σφεδανὰς—τοῖς οὐδὲν χρηστὸν
    ἔνεστιν—·
  θεῶν ⟨δὲ⟩ προμηθείην αἰὲν ἔχειν ἀγαθήν.

4-22 habet epitome, unde 4-7 Eust. in Hom. *Od.* 1633.3

2 ἀμφιτιθεὶς A, corr. Dindorf   4 κρατὴρ codd., corr.
Hermann   6 ὀζόμενος Hermann, prob. West alii
7 ὀσμὴν epit., Eust.   9 παρκέαται Wackernagel, prob. West
13 ὕμνεν epit., ὑμνεῖν C et edd. plerique, ὑμνὲν A, prob. Gent.-Pr.
19 ἔσθλ᾽ εἰπὼν Fränkel, ἐπιὼν Untersteiner   20 ἡ A, ἡ epit.,
ἦ Ahrens, οἱ Koraes   τὸν ὃς codd., τόνος Koraes   21
διέπει epit., διέπων Fränkel   22 τι add. Meineke, alii alia
πλασμάτων codd., corr. Schweighäuser   23 σφεδανὰς
Osann, φενδόνας A   24 δὲ add. Camerarius   ἀγαθόν
Francke

2 Ath. 10.413c-414c

καὶ οὐδὲν παράδοξον τούτους τοὺς ἄνδρας ἀδηφάγους
γενέσθαι· πάντες γὰρ οἱ ἀθλοῦντες μετὰ τῶν γυμνασ-
μάτων καὶ ἐσθίειν πολλὰ διδάσκονται. διὸ καὶ Εὐριπί-
δης ἐν τῷ πρώτῳ Αὐτολύκῳ λέγει (fr. 282 N.) . . . ταῦτ᾽
εἴληφεν ὁ Εὐριπίδης ἐκ τῶν τοῦ Κολοφωνίου ἐλεγείων
Ξενοφάνους οὕτως εἰρηκότος·

  ἀλλ᾽ εἰ μὲν ταχυτῆτι ποδῶν νίκην τις ἄροιτο
    ἢ πενταθλεύων, ἔνθα Διὸς τέμενος
  πὰρ Πίσαο ῥοῆς ἐν Ὀλυμπίῃ, εἴτε παλαίων

the Titans or Giants or Centaurs, creations of our
predecessors, or violent factions—there is nothing
useful in them; and it is meet always to have a good
regard for the gods.

1 Xenophanes seems to be describing an ideal symposium, not
one actually in progress. The meal presumably formed the subject
of the verses omitted at the beginning.   2 To be mixed with
the wine.   3 I have assumed that χρή (v. 13) governs the
infinitives in vv. 17, 19, 21, and 24, but some explain them as
imperatives and an infinitive may not be the correct text in v. 21.
4 Probably Apollo or Dionysus.   5 Meaning uncertain; liter-
ally "closer at hand."

2 Athenaeus, *Scholars at Dinner*

And it is not surprising that these men became gluttons.
For all athletes are taught to eat large amounts in connec-
tion with their gymnastic exercises. That is why Euripides
says in his first *Autolycus* ... These sentiments have been
taken by Euripides from the elegiac verses of Xenophanes
of Colophon who spoke as follows:

But if someone were to gain a victory by the swift-
ness of his feet or in the pentathlon,1 where there is
the precinct of Zeus by Pisa's stream2 in Olympia, or

ἢ καὶ πυκτοσύνην ἀλγινόεσσαν ἔχων
5   εἴτε τὸ δεινὸν ἄεθλον, ὃ παγκράτιον καλέουσιν,
    ἀστοῖσίν κ' εἴη κυδρότερος προσορᾶν,
    καί κε προεδρίην φανερὴν ἐν ἀγῶσιν ἄροιτο,
    καί κεν σῖτ' εἴη δημοσίων κτεάνων
    ἐκ πόλεως, καὶ δῶρον ὅ οἱ κειμήλιον εἴη—
10   εἴτε καὶ ἵπποισιν, ταῦτά κε πάντα λάχοι
    οὐκ ἐὼν ἄξιος ὥσπερ ἐγώ· ῥώμης γὰρ ἀμείνων
    ἀνδρῶν ἠδ' ἵππων ἡμετέρη σοφίη.
    ἀλλ' εἰκῇ μάλα τοῦτο νομίζεται, οὐδὲ δίκαιον
    προκρίνειν ῥώμην τῆς ἀγαθῆς σοφίης·
15   οὔτε γὰρ εἰ πύκτης ἀγαθὸς λαοῖσι μετείη
    οὔτ' εἰ πενταθλεῖν οὔτε παλαισμοσύνην,
    οὐδὲ μὲν εἰ ταχυτῆτι ποδῶν, τόπερ ἐστὶ
        πρότιμον,
    ῥώμης ὅσσ' ἀνδρῶν ἔργ' ἐν ἀγῶνι πέλει,
    τοὔνεκεν ἂν δὴ μᾶλλον ἐν εὐνομίῃ πόλις εἴη·
20   σμικρὸν δ' ἄν τι πόλει χάρμα γένοιτ' ἐπὶ τῷ,
    εἴ τις ἀεθλεύων νικῷ Πίσαο παρ' ὄχθας·
    οὐ γὰρ πιαίνει ταῦτα μυχοὺς πόλεως.

πολλὰ δὲ καὶ ἄλλα ὁ Ξενοφάνης κατὰ τὴν ἑαυτοῦ
σοφίαν ἐπαγωνίζεται, διαβάλλων ὡς ἄχρηστον καὶ
ἀλυσιτελὲς τὸ τῆς ἀθλήσεως εἶδος.

3 ῥοὰς Schneidewin (cl. v. 21), prob. Gent.-Pr.   5 εἴτε τὸ
Wakefield, εἴτέτι cod.   6 προσεραν cod., corr. Jacobs
10 κ' εἰπάντα cod., corr. Schweighäuser   15 λαοῖσιν ἔτ' εἴη
cod., corr. Stephanus

in wrestling or engaging in painful boxing or in that terrible contest which they call the pankration,[3] he would have greater renown (than others) in the eyes of his townsmen, he would gain a conspicuous front seat at the games, he would have food from the public store granted by the city, and a gift which would be a treasure for him—or if (he were to gain a victory) even with his horses, he would obtain all these things, although he is not as deserving as I. For my expertise[4] is better than the strength of men or horses. But this custom is quite irrational and it is not right to give strength precedence over good expertise. For neither if there were a good boxer among the people nor one good at the pentathlon or in wrestling or again in the swiftness of his feet, the most honoured of the deeds of human strength in the contest, would there for that reason be better law and order in the city. Little would be the city's joy, if one were to win while contending by the banks of Pisa; for this does not fatten the city's treasury.

Xenophanes makes many other contentions with regard to his own wisdom, criticizing the idea of athleticism as useless and unprofitable.

---

[1] The pentathlon involved running, jumping, throwing the discus, throwing the javelin, and wrestling.   [2] Presumably the river Alpheus. Pisa was a town near Olympia.   [3] A combination of wrestling and boxing.   [4] The precise meaning of σοφίη is uncertain. My preference is to see in it both poetic skill and the wise content of his verses.

3 Ath. 12.526a

Κολοφώνιοι δέ, ὥς φησι Φύλαρχος (FGrHist 81 F 66),
τὴν ἀρχὴν ὄντες σκληροὶ ἐν ταῖς ἀγωγαῖς, ἐπεὶ εἰς
τρυφὴν ἐξώκειλαν πρὸς Λυδοὺς φιλίαν καὶ συμμα-
χίαν ποιησάμενοι, προῇεσαν διησκημένοι τὰς κόμας
χρυσῷ κόσμῳ, ὡς καὶ Ξενοφάνης φησίν·

> ἁβροσύνας δὲ μαθόντες ἀνωφελέας παρὰ Λυδῶν,
>   ὄφρα τυραννίης ἦσαν ἄνευ στυγερῆς,
> ᾔεσαν εἰς ἀγορὴν παναλουργέα φάρε' ἔχοντες,
>   οὐ μείους ὥσπερ χείλιοι εἰς ἐπίπαν,
> 5 αὐχαλέοι, χαίτησιν †ἀγαλλομεν εὐπρεπέεσσιν,
>   ἀσκητοῖς ὀδμὴν χρίμασι δευόμενοι.

οὕτω δὲ ἐξελύθησαν διὰ τὴν ἄκαιρον μέθην ὥστε τινὲς
αὐτῶν οὔτε ἀνατέλλοντα τὸν ἥλιον οὔτε δυόμενον
ἑωράκασιν. . . . Θεόπομπος δὲ ἐν πεντεκαιδεκάτῃ
ἱστοριῶν (FGrHist 115 F 117) χιλίους φησὶν ἄνδρας
αὐτῶν ἀλουργεῖς φοροῦντας στολὰς ἀστυπολεῖν, ὃ δὴ
καὶ βασιλεῦσιν σπάνιον τότε ἦν καὶ περισπούδαστον.

1 ἀφροσύνας cod., corr. Schneider   2 ησσαινευ cod.,
corr. Dindorf   4 χίλιοι cod., corr. Hiller   ὡς pro εἰς
Schweighäuser, prob. West   5 χαιτισιν cod., corr. Musurus
ἀγαλλόμεν' Casaubon   6 χρήμασι cod., corr. Musurus

cf. Cic. de rep. 6.2 ut, quemadmodum scribit ille, cotidiano in
forum mille hominum cum pallis conchylio tinctis descenderent.

XENOPHANES

3 Athenaeus, *Scholars at Dinner*

Although the Colophonians, as Phylarchus says, were originally austere in their ways, when they became friends and
allies of the Lydians and drifted into a soft life, they would
go forth with their hair decked out with gold ornaments, as
Xenophanes also says:

> And having learned useless luxury from the Lydians,
> while they were free of hateful tyranny,[1] they used
> to go to the agora[2] wearing robes all of purple, no
> fewer than a thousand[3] as a rule, proud and exult
> ing(?)[4] in the splendour of their hair, drenched with
> the scent of the most refined unguents.

And they were so dissolute because of untimely drinking
that some of them saw neither the rising nor the setting
sun. . . . And Theopompus in the fifteenth book of his *Histories* says that a thousand of them frequented the city
wearing purple robes, a colour which then was rare even
for kings and was much sought after.

[1] Presumably that inflicted by the Medes in the 540s.
[2] It is unclear whether this means place of assembly or marketplace.   [3] Either a ruling aristocracy or simply a large number of rich Colophonians.   [4] Casaubon's reading is syntactically sound, but the elision of -οι is unparalleled, though perhaps
not impossible. Various emendations have been suggested in order to introduce a reference to the gold ornaments mentioned in
the source.

Cicero, *On the State*: "so that, as he (Phylarchus) writes, every
day a thousand men went down into the forum in robes dyed with
purple."

4 Pollux 9.83

. . . εἴτε Φείδων πρῶτος ὁ Ἀργεῖος ἔκοψε νόμισμα . . .
εἴτε Λυδοὶ καθά φησι Ξενοφάνης, εἴτε κτλ.

5 Ath. 11.782a

ἔθος δὲ ἦν πρότερον ἐν τῷ ποτηρίῳ ὕδωρ ἐμβάλ-
λεσθαι, μεθ᾽ ὃ τὸν οἶνον. Ξενοφάνης·

   οὐδέ κεν ἐν κύλικι πρότερον κεράσειέ τις οἶνον
      ἐγχέας, ἀλλ᾽ ὕδωρ καὶ καθύπερθε μέθυ.

2 ἐγχεύας cod., corr. Casaubon

6 Ath. 9.368e

καὶ Ξενοφάνης δὲ ὁ Κολοφώνιος ἐν τοῖς ἐλεγείοις
φησί·

   πέμψας γὰρ κωλῆν ἐρίφου σκέλος ἤραο πῖον
      ταύρου λαρινοῦ, τίμιον ἀνδρὶ λαχεῖν
   τοῦ κλέος Ἑλλάδα πᾶσαν ἀφίξεται, οὐδ᾽
         ἀπολήξει,
      ἔστ᾽ ἂν ἀοιδάων ᾖ γένος Ἑλλαδικόν.

4 Ἑλλαδικῶν C p.c.

7 Diog. Laert. 8.36

περὶ δὲ τοῦ ἄλλοτε ἄλλον αὐτὸν (Πυθαγόραν) γεγε-

XENOPHANES

4 Pollux, *Vocabulary*

... whether Pheidon of Argos was the first to strike coinage
... or the Lydians, as Xenophanes says,[1] or

[1] Some consider the source of this statement to have been an
elegy in view of the reference to Lydians in fr. 3.

5 Athenaeus, *Scholars at Dinner*

It was the custom to put water in the cup first and after that
the wine. Cf. Xenophanes:

> And no one would mix wine by pouring it in the cup
> first, but the water first and on top of it the wine.

6 Athenaeus, *Scholars at Dinner*

And Xenophanes of Colophon also says in his elegiac
verses:

> For although you sent the thigh bone of a kid, you
> won the fat leg of a fatted bull, a thing of honour to
> fall to a man whose[1] fame will spread over the whole
> of Greece and will not die, so long as the Grecian
> form of song exists.

[1] It is unclear whether "whose" refers to the man or to the fat
leg of a bull. Perhaps the poet is satirizing an athlete whose sacri-
fice prior to the games was much inferior to the reward he re-
ceived by his victory, and yet his fame will be celebrated in song
throughout the land. If so, the verses bear a certain resemblance
to fr. 2.

7 Diogenes Laertius, *Lives of the Philosophers*

That Pythagoras had been a different person at different

νῆσθαι Ξενοφάνης ἐν ἐλεγείᾳ προσμαρτυρεῖ, ἧς ἀρχή·

Νῦν αὖτ᾽ ἄλλον ἔπειμι λόγον, δείξω δὲ κέλευθον

νῦν οὖν τ᾽ codd., corr. Stephanus

7a Pergit Diogenes

ὃ δὲ περὶ αὐτοῦ φησιν οὕτως ἔχει·

καί ποτέ μιν στυφελιζομένου σκύλακος παριόντα
    φασὶν ἐποικτῖραι καὶ τόδε φάσθαι ἔπος·
"παῦσαι, μηδὲ ῥάπιζ᾽, ἐπεὶ ἦ φίλου ἀνέρος ἐστὶν
    ψυχή, τὴν ἔγνων φθεγξαμένης ἀϊών."

καὶ ταῦτα μὲν ὁ Ξενοφάνης.

2 ἐποικτεῖραι codd., corr. Fick   4 ἀϊών Diog. cod. B, ἀΐων cet.

8 Diog. Laert. 9.18-19

μακροβιώτατός τε γέγονεν, ὥς που καὶ αὐτός φησιν·

ἤδη δ᾽ ἑπτά τ᾽ ἔασι καὶ ἑξήκοντ᾽ ἐνιαυτοὶ
    βληστρίζοντες ἐμὴν φροντίδ᾽ ἀν᾽ Ἑλλάδα γῆν·
ἐκ γενετῆς δὲ τότ᾽ ἦσαν ἐείκοσι πέντε τε πρὸς τοῖς,
    εἴπερ ἐγὼ περὶ τῶνδ᾽ οἶδα λέγειν ἐτύμως.

---

[1] The precise meaning of ἐμὴν φροντίδα is disputed. Some prefer "my counsel," others "my cares," and the words have also

times is attested by Xenophanes in an elegy whose beginning is:

> Now I will move on to yet another tale and I will show the way

7a Diogenes continues

What he says about Pythagoras is as follows:

> And they say that once, as he was passing by a puppy being beaten, he felt pity and spoke these words: "Stop, don't beat him, since in truth it is the soul of a friend; I recognized it when I heard him yelp."[1]

These are the words of Xenophanes.

[1] It is unclear whether Xenophanes is mocking the Pythagorean belief in the transmigration of souls as such or simply the idea that one could recognize a soul from the yelping of a dog.

8 Diogenes Laertius, *Lives of the Philosophers*

Xenophanes lived a very long life, as he himself states somewhere:

> Three score years and seven have now been tossing my thoughts[1] throughout the land of Greece,[2] and from my birth until then there were five and twenty years[3] in addition to these, if in fact I know how to speak truly about these things.

been explained as a periphrastic equivalent of "myself."
[2] Most of his adult life seems to have been spent in Magna Graecia (see test. 1).   [3] It is usually assumed that he left Colophon at age 25 when the Medes captured the city in the 540s (cf. fr.3.2).

9 *Et. Gen.* (p. 21 Calame) = *Et. Mag.* 230.57, ex Herodiano (ii.266.7 Lentz)

ἔστι δὲ πρώτης καὶ δευτέρας συζυγίας τὸ γηρᾶς, ὥσπερ τὸ πιμπλᾷς, οἷον πιμπλῶ πιμπλᾷς καὶ πιμπλῶ πιμπλεῖς, οἷον "†τὰς Ῥαδάμανθυς πιμπλεῖν βίαν†" (fr. adesp. 969 *PMG*). οὕτως οὖν καὶ γηρῶ γηρᾶς . . . καὶ γηρῶ γηρεῖς . . . ἡ μετοχὴ γηρείς, "γηρεὶς ἐν οἰκίοισι" (fr. adesp. iamb. 4). ἡ γενικὴ γηρέντος ὥσπερ τιθέντος. Ξενοφάνης (Ξενοφῶν codd., corr. Sylburg), οἷον

ἀνδρὸς γηρέντος πολλὸν ἀφαυρότερος

9 *Etymologicum Genuinum* and *Magnum*

The verb γηρῶ (2nd sing. γηρᾷς), 'grow old,' belongs to both the first and the second conjugation, like πιμπλῶ, 'fill,' which has both πιμπλᾷς and πιμπλεῖς, as in (fragment corrupt). Similarly then γηρῶ which has both γηρᾷς . . . and γηρεῖς . . . The participle is γηρείς, "growing old in the house." The genitive is γηρέντος like τιθέντος. Cf. Xenophanes:

much feebler than a man of advanced age

ASIUS

14 Ath. 3.125b-e

"οὐ γὰρ μέλει σοι," ἔφη ὁ Μυρτίλος, "ἱστορίας, ὦ γάστρων. κνισολοιχὸς γάρ τις εἶ <καὶ> (add. Casaubon) κατὰ τὸν Σάμιον ποιητὴν Ἄσιον τὸν παλαιὸν ἐκεῖνον {καὶ} (del. Casaubon) κνισοκόλαξ . . ." πιόντος οὖν αὐτοῦ πάλιν ἐζήτει ὁ Οὐλπιανός· "ποῦ κεῖται ὁ κνισολοιχὸς καὶ τίνα ἐστὶ τὰ τοῦ Ἀσίου ἔπη τὰ περὶ τοῦ κνισοκόλακος;" "τὰ μὲν οὖν τοῦ Ἀσίου," ἔφη ὁ Μυρτίλος, "ἔπη ταῦτ᾽ ἐστι·

χωλός, στιγματίης, πολυγήραος, ἶσος ἀλήτῃ
    ἦλθε κνισοκόλαξ, εὖτε Μέλης ἐγάμει,
ἄκλητος, ζωμοῦ κεχρημένος· ἐν δὲ μέσοισιν
    ἥρως εἱστήκει βορβόρου ἐξαναδύς.

ὁ δὲ κνισολοιχός" κτλ.

4 ἥρωσ᾽ Blaydes

---

[1] See C. P. Jones, "*Stigma*: Tattooing and Branding in Graeco-Roman Antiquity," *JRS* 77 (1987) 139-55. He assumes the tattoo here marks a "slave, or perhaps criminal" (p. 147).   [2] I.e., one who fawns or flatters so as to be fed fat meat, a parasite.
[3] A perplexing fragment. Is Meles the river, who in some sources was said to be Homer's father? Is the hero the fat-flatterer or

ASIUS

Asius of Samos, perhaps to be dated to the 6th century, is primarily known as an epic poet. For the testimonia and epic fragments see A. Bernabé, *Poetae Epici Graeci* i.127-31, or M. Davies, *Epicorum Graecorum Fragmenta* 88-91. The testimonia tell us nothing about the man except that his father was Amphiptolemus (Paus. 2.6.3, 7.4.1).

14 Athenaeus, *Scholars at Dinner*

"That's because you have no interest in history, you glutton," Myrtilus replied. "For you are a fat-licker and, as Asius, that Samian poet of old, puts it, a fat-flatterer. . . ." And so, after Myrtilus had had a drink, Ulpian asked again: "Where is 'fat-licker' found and what are the verses of Asius about the 'fat-flatterer'?" "The verses of Asius," Myrtilus replied, "are as follows:

> Lame, tattooed,[1] aged, like a beggar came the fat-flatterer,[2] uninvited and in need of soup, when Meles was getting married; and in their midst he stood, a hero risen from the mud.[3]

And 'fat-licker'" etc.

Meles or is there a suppressed comparison, "like a hero," or should Blaydes' slight emendation be adopted, "in the midst of the heroes"? See G. L. Huxley, *Greek Epic Poetry* (London 1969) 97, and L. Edmunds, *HSCP* 85 (1981) 230.

DIONYSIUS CHALCUS

TESTIMONIA

1 Plut. *Nic.* 5.2-3

καὶ ὁ μάλιστα ταῦτα συντραγῳδῶν καὶ συμπεριτιθεὶς
ὄγκον αὐτῷ καὶ δόξαν Ἱέρων ἦν, ἀνὴρ τεθραμμένος
ἐπὶ τῆς οἰκίας τοῦ Νικίου περί τε γράμματα καὶ
μουσικὴν ἐξησκημένος ὑπ᾽ αὐτοῦ, προσποιούμενος δ᾽
υἱὸς εἶναι Διονυσίου τοῦ Χαλκοῦ προσαγορευθέντος,
οὗ καὶ ποιήματα σῴζεται, καὶ τῆς εἰς Ἰταλίαν ἀποι-
κίας ἡγεμὼν γενόμενος ἔκτισε Θουρίους.

2 Phot. *lex.* (i.282 Naber)

Θουριομάντεις. τοὺς περὶ Λάμπωνα· τὴν γὰρ εἰς
Σύβαριν ἀποικίαν οἱ μὲν Λάμπωνι ἀνατιθέασιν, οἱ δὲ
Ξενοκρίτῳ, οἱ δὲ Χαλκιδεῖ Διονυσίῳ . . .

DIONYSIUS CHALCUS

TESTIMONIA

1 Plutarch, *Life of Nicias*

And the one who most of all aided him (Nicias) in acting this solemn role and in surrounding him with a cloak of self-important dignity was Hieron, a man who had been reared in the household of Nicias and thoroughly trained by him in letters and the liberal arts. He pretended to be the son of Dionysius called Chalcus (the Bronze), whose poems are in fact extant and who as leader of the colony sent to Italy founded Thurii.[1]

[1]Founded by Athens in 444/3 near the site of Sybaris. See A. Andrewes, *JHS* 98 (1978) 5-8.

2 Photius, *Lexicon*

Thurian seers.[1] Those with Lampon. For some ascribe the colony at Sybaris (i.e., Thurii) to Lampon, others to Xenocritus, others to Dionysius of Chalcis[2] . . .

[1] See Arist. *Clouds* 332 and schol. ad loc. (p. 82 Holwerda).
[2] Χαλκιδεῖ is presumably an error for Χαλκῷ (the Bronze).

429

3 Ath. 13.602b-c

ἔχρησεν δὲ καὶ περὶ τῶν ἀμφὶ τὸν Χαρίτωνα, προ-
τάξας τοῦ ἑξαμέτρου τὸ πεντάμετρον, καθάπερ ὕστε-
ρον καὶ Διονύσιος ὁ Ἀθηναῖος ἐποίησε ὁ ἐπικληθεὶς
Χαλκοῦς ἐν τοῖς ἐλεγείοις.

4 Anon. in Arist. *Rhet.* 3.2.1405a32 (*Comm. in Arist.
Graeca* xxi(2).169.25)

Χαλκοῦν Διονύσιον λέγει τὴν Διονυσίου στήλην·
οὗτος οὖν τοῖς ἐλεγείοις τοῖς ἀναγεγραμμένοις ἐν τῇ
στήλῃ αὐτοῦ τὴν ποίησιν προσαγορεύει καὶ καλεῖ
"κραυγὴν Καλλιόπης."

FRAGMENTS

1-4 Ath. 15.668e-69e

μνημονεύει τῶν λατάγων καὶ τῶν κοττάβων καὶ ὁ
Χαλκοῦς καλούμενος Διονύσιος ἐν τοῖς ἐλεγείοις διὰ
τούτων·

DIONYSIUS CHALCUS

3 Athenaeus, *Scholars at Dinner*

Apollo also gave an oracle concerning Chariton and those about him, placing the pentameter before the hexameter, just as was later done by the Athenian Dionysius, called Chalcus, in his elegies.[1]

[1] Fr. 1 may be an example of this.

4 Anonymous on Aristotle, *Rhetoric*

By Dionysius the Bronze he means the gravestone of Dionysius. In the elegiac verses inscribed on his gravestone Dionysius calls his poetry "the scream of Calliope."[1]

[1] See fr. 7. The commentator's explanation of Chalcus is improbable, although it is perhaps possible that the words were inscribed on his gravestone. Stephanus on the same passage of Aristotle (xxi(2).314.1) erroneously speaks of the gravestone of the tyrant Dionysius. Calliope is one of the nine Muses.

FRAGMENTS

1-4 Athenaeus, *Scholars at Dinner*[1]

Dionysius called Chalcus (Bronze) mentions the wine drops and games of cottabus[2] in his elegies as follows:

[1] The number of poems represented by these fragments is unclear. [2] The cottabus in its various forms involved basically the throwing of wine drops at a target and the player often dedicated his toss to someone with a view to amorous success. For further details see Athenaeus 11.487d-e, 15.665a-69e, and F. Lissarrague, *The Aesthetics of the Greek Banquet* (Princeton 1987) 80-86, and cf. Critias fr. 2.

3

κότταβον ἐνθάδε σοι τρίτον ἑστάναι οἱ δυσέρωτες
ἡμεῖς προστίθεμεν γυμνασίῳ Βρομίου
κώρυκον. οἱ δὲ παρόντες ἐνείρετε χεῖρας ἅπαντες
ἐς σφαίρας κυλίκων· καὶ πρὶν ἐκεῖνον ἰδεῖν,
5   ὄμματι βηματίσασθε τὸν αἰθέρα τὸν κατακλινῆ,
εἰς ὅσον αἱ λάταγες χωρίον ἐκτατέαι.

ἐπὶ τούτοις ὁ Οὐλπιανὸς ᾔτει πιεῖν μεγάλῃ κύλικι,
ἐπιλέγων ἐκ τῶν αὐτῶν ἐλεγείων καὶ τόδε·

3 ἐνείρεται A, corr. Musurus   5 βηματίσαισθε A, corr.
Musurus   κατὰ κλίνην v.l., editores plerique (κλίνης Sartori)
6 ἐκτέταται A., corr. Bücheler, ἐντατέαι Borthwick

4

ὕμνους οἰνοχοεῖν ἐπιδέξια σοί τε καὶ ἡμῖν·
τόν τε σὸν ἀρχαῖον τηλεδαπόν τε φίλον
εἰρεσίῃ γλώσσης ἀποπέμψομεν εἰς μέγαν αἶνον
τοῦδ᾽ ἐπὶ συμποσίου· δεξιότης τε λόγου

3

Thirdly we who are unhappy in love add a cottabus
to take its stand in your honour here in the gymna-
sium of Bromius[3] as a punching-bag. All you who are
present entwine your hands in the thongs[4] of the
cups. And before you look at that,[5] measure with
your eyes the downward-sloping air,[6] to determine
the area over which the wine drops are to extend.[7]

Thereupon Ulpian asked for a drink from a large cup, add-
ing the following from the same elegies:

[3] Bromius = Dionysus and with the phrase "gymnasium of
Bromius" we begin the comparison between symposium and ath-
letics.   [4] Leather thongs entwined round the fingers by box-
ers, so that we have a compendious way of saying: "entwine your
fingers in the handles of the cups as you would in the thongs of
boxing-gloves."   [5] Probably some part of the cottabus appa-
ratus and so, more loosely, the target, but various emendations
have been suggested.   [6] I.e., the trajectory of the tossed
wine drops. Most editors read the variant κατὰ κλίνην, but it is
hard to see how this could mean "down from the couch," unless
Sartori's κλίνης is adopted.   [7] The imagery now seems to
move from boxing to javelin-throwing. On this and the fragment
as a whole see especially E. K. Borthwick, *JHS* 84 (1964) 49-55,
and P. A. Bernardini, *Nikephoros* 3 (1990) 127-32.

4

Pour a draught of songs from left to right for you
and for us. With the oarage of our tongues we shall
send off your longstanding friend from foreign parts
to high praise at this symposium. The dexterity

433

5   Φαίακος Μουσῶν ἐρέτας ἐπὶ σέλματα πέμπει.

. . . πρὸς ὃν ὁ Κύνουλκος, ἀεὶ τῷ Σύρῳ ἀντικορυσ-
σόμενος καὶ οὐδέποτε τῆς φιλονικίας παυόμενος ἧς
εἶχε πρὸς αὐτόν, ἐπεὶ θόρυβος κατεῖχεν τὸ συμ-
πόσιον, ἔφη· "τίς οὗτος ὁ τῶν συρβηνέων χορός; καὶ
αὐτὸς δὲ τούτων τῶν ἐπῶν μεμνημένος τινῶν ἐρῶ, ἵνα
μὴ ὁ Οὐλπιανὸς βρενθύηται ὡς ἐκ τῶν ἀποθέτων τοῖς
Ὁμηρίδαις μόνος ἀνασπάσας τὰ κοττάβεια,

2 τηλεπαδον A, corr. Casaubon   4 ἀπὸ Emperius
5 Φαίακας Casaubon

2

ἀγγελίας ἀγαθῆς δεῦρ' ἴτε πευσόμενοι,
καὶ κυλίκων ἔριδας διαλύσατε, καὶ κατάθεσθε
    τὴν ξύνεσιν παρ' ἐμοί, καὶ τάδε μανθάνετε,

εἰς τὴν παροῦσαν ζήτησιν ἐπιτήδεια ὄντα. . . ." καὶ ὁ
Δημόκριτος "ἀλλ' ἵνα κἀγώ," φησίν, "μνημονεύσω
τῶν τοῦ Χαλκοῦ ποιητοῦ καὶ ῥήτορος Διονυσίου—
Χαλκοῦς δὲ προσηγορεύθη διὰ τὸ συμβουλεῦσαι
Ἀθηναίοις χαλκῷ νομίσματι χρήσασθαι, καὶ τὸν
λόγον τοῦτον ἀνέγραψε Καλλίμαχος ἐν τῇ τῶν Ῥητο-
ρικῶν Ἀναγραφῇ (fr. 430 Pf.)—λέξω τι καὶ αὐτὸς ἐκ
τῶν ἐλεγείων· σὺ δέ, ὦ Θεόδωρε (τοῦτο γάρ σου τὸ
κύριον ὄνομα),

1 πεσσόμενοι A, corr. Casaubon

434

of Phaeax's[8] words is sending the oarsmen of the
Muses to the benches.

. . . In response to him Cynulcus, who was always taking up
arms against the Syrian (i.e., Ulpian) and never stopped
quarreling with him, said, when an uproar was spreading
throughout the symposium, "What is this band of rowdies?
I too will recall and recite some of these verses, so that
Ulpian may not plume himself for being the only one to
draw cottabus material from the stores of the Homeridae,[9]

[8] For Phaeax from the deme Acharnae see J. K. Davies, *Athenian Propertied Families 600-300 B.C.* (Oxford 1971) 521-24, and
J. D. Smart, *JHS* 92 (1972) 141-43. What follows seems to be nothing more than an ornate way of describing poetry.   [9] Text
and translation uncertain.

2

Come hither to hear the good news, put an end to
the quarreling caused by the cups, think as I do,[10]
and learn the following,

since these verses are relevant to our present enquiry." . . .
And Democritus said: "But so that I too may recall the
verses of the poet and politician Dionysius Chalcus—he
was called Chalcus (Bronze) because he advised the Athenians to use bronze currency,[11] and Callimachus recorded
this speech(?) in his *Register of Oratory*—I too will recite
something from his elegies. And do you, Theodorus[12] (for
this is your proper name),

[10] Literally, "deposit your understanding with me."
[11] In 406 silver-plated bronze coins were minted in Athens because of the scarcity of silver. One year later these are mentioned

1

> δέχου τήνδε προπινομένην
> τὴν ἀπ᾽ ἐμοῦ ποίησιν· ἐγὼ δ᾽ ἐπιδέξια πέμπω
> σοὶ πρώτῳ, Χαρίτων ἐγκεράσας χάριτας.
> καὶ σὺ λαβὼν τόδε δῶρον ἀοιδὰς ἀντιπρόπιθι,
5 > συμπόσιον κοσμῶν καὶ τὸ σὸν εὖ θέμενος.

5 Ath. 10.443d

ὁ Ποντιανὸς ἔφη πάντων τούτων εἶναι τῶν δεινῶν
μητρόπολιν τὸν οἶνον, δι᾽ ὃν καὶ τὰς μέθας καὶ τὰς
μανίας, ἔτι δὲ καὶ τὰς παροινίας γίνεσθαι· οὐ τοὺς
ἐκπαθῶς μεταλαμβάνοντας οὐ κακῶς ὁ Χαλκοῦς ἐπι-
καλούμενος Διονύσιος ἐν τοῖς ἐλεγείοις "κυλίκων
ἐρέτας" ἔφη·

> καί τινες οἶνον ἄγοντες ἐν εἰρεσίᾳ Διονύσου,
> συμποσίου ναῦται καὶ κυλίκων ἐρέται,

DIONYSIUS CHALCUS

disparagingly by Aristophanes in *Frogs* 725 (τούτοις τοῖς
πονηροῖς χαλκίοις). For a different explanation of why he was
called Bronze see test. 4.   [12] Most assume that ὦ Θεόδωρε
should be inserted at the beginning of v. 1 and that this was v. 1
of the poem. The latter assumption would result in the poem's
opening with a pentameter, but this can be defended by test. 3.
Theodorus is usually identified as the Theodorus who was impli-
cated with Alcibiades in profaning the Eleusinian mysteries (Plut.
Alc. 19), but it is a very common name. It may even be the real
name of Cynulcus mentioned after fr. 4 in view of Ath. 15.692b (ὦ
Κύνουλκε Θεόδωρε), in which case it should not be inserted in
v. 1.

1

> receive this poem pledged as a toast from me. I am
> sending it from left to right for you first, having
> mixed in the graces of the Graces.[13] Do you take this
> gift and pledge me songs as a toast in return, adorn-
> ing our symposium and enhancing your own reputa-
> tion(?).

[13] See B. MacLachlan, *The Age of Grace* (Princeton 1993) 83-
84.

5 Athenaeus, *Scholars at Dinner*

Pontianus said that wine is the source of all these horrors
and that as a result of it intoxication, acts of madness, and
in addition drunken violence occur. Those who partake of
wine with a passion are not ineptly described by Dionysius,
called the Bronze, in his elegies as "oarsmen of cups":

> And some carrying wine in the oarage of Dionysus,
> sailors of the symposium and oarsmen of the cups,[1]

437

⟨　　　　⟩ περὶ τοῦδε· τὸ γὰρ φίλον οὐκ
ἀπόλωλε.

3 ⟨μάρνανται⟩ et ὦκ' Hermann, ⟨σπεύδουσιν⟩ Ebert

6 Ath. 15.702b-c

ταῦτα, φίλτατε Τιμόκρατες, κατὰ τὸν Πλάτωνα (Epist.
2.314c) οὐ "Σωκράτους νέου καὶ καλοῦ" παίγνια, ἀλλὰ
τῶν δειπνοσοφιστῶν σπουδάσματα. κατὰ γὰρ τὸν
Χαλκοῦν Διονύσιον

τί κάλλιον ἀρχομένοισιν
ἢ καταπαυομένοις ἢ τὸ ποθεινότατον;

1 ἀρχομένοις codd., corr. Casaubon

7 Arist. Rhet. 3.2.1405a31

ἔστιν δὲ καὶ ἐν ταῖς συλλαβαῖς ἁμαρτία, ἐὰν μὴ
ἡδείας ᾖ σημεῖα φωνῆς, οἷον Διονύσιος προσαγορεύει
ὁ Χαλκοῦς ἐν τοῖς ἐλεγείοις "κραυγὴν Καλλιόπης"
τὴν ποίησιν, ὅτι ἄμφω φωναί, φαύλη δὲ ἡ μεταφορὰ
†ταῖς ἀσήμοις φωναῖς.†

(fight?) over this; for that which is dear does not die away.[2]

[1] For nautical imagery and the symposium see Lissarrague (n. 2 above) 107-22.   [2] This seems to mean that desire for wine never dies.

6 Athenaeus, *Scholars at Dinner*

These things, dearest Timocrates, are not in Plato's words the light jests "of a young and handsome Socrates," but the serious pursuits of the scholars at dinner. For according to Dionysius Chalcus

> At the beginning or the end what is better than that which is most desired?[1]

[1] With this citation Athenaeus concludes his work. The first six words of the citation appear in Arist. *Knights* 1264-66, where the scholiast gives Pindar (fr. 89a) as the source. Eustathius on *Il.* 18.570 (iv.260.23 V.d.Valk) also quotes Dionysius' fragment (without naming the author) and calls it "proverbial."

7 Aristotle, *Rhetoric*

A fault also lies in the combination of letters if it does not represent a pleasing sound, as for instance in Dionysius Chalcus who in his elegies calls poetry

> the scream of Calliope,

since although both words represent sounds,[1] the metaphor is in bad taste because . . .

[1] Calliope, one of the Muses, is literally 'the beautiful-voiced.' See test. 4.

EUENUS

TESTIMONIA

1 Harpocr. s.v. Εὔηνος (p. 116 Keaney)

Ὑπερείδης ἐν τῷ κατ᾽ Αὐτοκλέους (fr. 58 Blass). δύο ἀναγράφουσιν Εὐήνους ἐλεγείων ποιητὰς ὁμωνύμους ἀλλήλοις, καθάπερ Ἐρατοσθένης ἐν τῷ περὶ χρονογραφιῶν (*FGrHist* 241 F 3), ἀμφοτέρους λέγων Παρίους εἶναι, γνωρίζεσθαι δέ φησι τὸν νεώτερον μόνον. μέμνηται δὲ θατέρου αὐτῶν καὶ Πλάτων.

2 Artem. *onir.* 1.4

τὸ ζῷον τὸ καλούμενον κάμηλος μέσους κάμπτει τοὺς μηροὺς ὑποτεμνόμενον τοῖν σκελοῖν τὸ ὕψος, ἐτύμως

440

EUENUS

TESTIMONIA

1 Harpocration, *Lexicon of the Ten Attic Orators*

Euenus. Hyperides in the speech *Against Autocles* (c. 360). Two elegiac poets named Euenus are recorded, according to Eratosthenes in his work *On Annals* who says that they were both from Paros, but that only the younger was well-known. One of them is mentioned by Plato (see testt. 5-7).[1]

[1] This is the only explicit reference to two poets named Euenus, apart from the *Suda* (ii.449.4 Adler) which simply repeats Harpocration. Jerome (p. 111.12 Helm) gives 460 as the floruit of an Euenus and if this is the same Euenus as Plato makes a contemporary of Socrates, he must have lived a very long life. The *Suda* (iv.726.26 Adler) states that the historian Philistus was a pupil of the elegiac poet Euenus and Philistus was born c. 430. There were also two or more poets named Euenus included in the *Greek Anthology* (see Gow-Page, *The Garland of Philip* ii.289) and one of the poems ascribed to Euenus is usually assigned to the 5th-cent. poet (see fr. 2).

2 Artemidorus, *Interpretation of Dreams*

The animal called camel (κάμηλος) bends its thighs in the middle, thereby reducing the height of its legs. The

κεκλημένον κάμηλος οἱονεὶ *κάμμηρος, ὥς φησιν Εὔ-
ηνος ἐν τοῖς εἰς Εὔνομον ἐρωτικοῖς.

3 Epict. *diatr.* 4.9.6

καὶ τί, φησίν, ἀπολλύω;—Ἄνθρωπε, ὑπῆρχες αἰδή-
μων καὶ νῦν οὐκέτι εἶ· οὐδὲν ἀπολώλεκας; ἀντὶ Χρυ-
σίππου καὶ Ζήνωνος Ἀριστείδην ἀναγιγνώσκεις καὶ
Εὔηνον· οὐδὲν ἀπολώλεκας;

4 Auson. *cento nupt.* 10 (p. 168 Prete)

"lasciva est nobis pagina, vita proba," ut Martialis dicit
(1.4.8) . . . nam quid Anniani Fescenninos, quid antiquissi-
mi poetae Laevii Erotopaegnion libros loquar? quid Eue-
num, quem Menander sapientem vocavit (fr. 439 K.-A.)?
quid ipsum Menandrum? quid comicos omnes? quibus se-
vera vita est et laeta materia.

5 Pl. *Apol.* 20a-b

ἐπεὶ καὶ ἄλλος ἀνήρ ἐστι Πάριος ἐνθάδε σοφός, ὃν
ἐγὼ ᾐσθόμην ἐπιδημοῦντα· . . . "τίς τῆς τοιαύτης
ἀρετῆς, τῆς ἀνθρωπίνης τε καὶ πολιτικῆς, ἐπιστήμων
ἐστίν; . . . ἔστιν τις," ἔφην ἐγώ, "ἢ οὔ;" "πάνυ γε," ἦ δ'

camel derives its name from *κάμμηρος ('bent-thigh'), as
Euenus says in his *Erotica* addressed to Eunomus.[1]

[1] The etymology is nonsense, but there is evidence for the
erotic writings of an Euenus. See the next two testimonia.

3 Epictetus, *Discourses*

And what, someone says, do I lose?—Fellow, you used to
be modest and now you are no longer. Have you lost noth-
ing? Instead of Chrysippus and Zeno you read Aristides
and Euenus.[1] Have you lost nothing?

[1] Since the Aristides named is presumably the author (1st cent.
B.C.) of the erotic *Milesian Tales*, Epictetus is referring to Euenus'
erotic works. Wilamowitz, however, emended Εὔηνον to Εὔβιον:
Eubius is mentioned along with Aristides in Ovid, *Tristia* 2.413-
16. Chrysippus and Zeno were Stoic philosophers.

4 Ausonius, *Nuptial Cento*

"My page is wanton, but my life virtuous," as Martial says.
. . . For what shall I say of the Fescennine verses of
Annianus, what of the volumes of *Love Jests* by Laevius,
that most ancient poet? What of Euenus, whom Menander
called wise? What of Menander himself? What of the
comic poets? They combined an austere life with humor-
ous subject matter.

5 Plato, *Apology*

For there is also another wise man here, a Parian, who I
learned was in town. . . . "Who is knowledgeable in such ex-
cellence, both the human and political kind? . . . Is there
anyone," I said, "or not?" "Certainly," he said. "Who is he,"

ὅς. "τίς," ἦν δ᾽ ἐγώ. "καὶ ποδαπός, καὶ πόσου
διδάσκει;" "Εὔηνος," ἔφη (scil. ὁ Καλλίας), "ὦ Σώκρα-
τες, Πάριος, πέντε μνῶν." καὶ ἐγὼ τὸν Εὔηνον ἐμα-
κάρισα, εἰ ὡς ἀληθῶς ἔχοι ταύτην τὴν τέχνην καὶ
οὕτως ἐμμελῶς διδάσκει.

6 Pl. *Phaed.* 60d

περὶ γάρ τοι τῶν ποιημάτων ὧν πεποίηκας ἐντείνας
τοὺς τοῦ Αἰσώπου λόγους καὶ τὸ εἰς τὸν Ἀπόλλω
προοίμιον καὶ ἄλλοι τινές με ἤδη ἤροντο, ἀτὰρ καὶ
Εὔηνος πρῴην, ὅ τι ποτὲ διανοηθείς, ἐπειδὴ δεῦρο
ἦλθες, ἐποίησας αὐτά, πρότερον οὐδὲν πώποτε
ποιήσας. εἰ οὖν τί σοι μέλει τοῦ ἔχειν ἐμὲ Εὐήνῳ
ἀποκρίνασθαι ὅταν με αὖθις ἐρωτᾷ—εὖ οἶδα γὰρ ὅτι
ἐρήσεται—εἰπὲ τί χρὴ λέγειν. "λέγε τοίνυν," ἔφη,
"αὐτῷ, ὦ Κέβης, τἀληθῆ, ὅτι οὐκ ἐκείνῳ βουλόμενος
οὐδὲ τοῖς ποιήμασιν αὐτοῦ ἀντίτεχνος εἶναι ἐποίησα
ταῦτα—ᾔδειν γὰρ ὡς οὐ ῥᾴδιον εἴη—ἀλλ᾽ . . .

7 Pl. *Phaedr.* 267a

τὸν δὲ κάλλιστον Πάριον Εὔηνον ἐς μέσον οὐκ ἄγο-
μεν; ὃς ὑποδήλωσίν τε πρῶτος ηὗρεν καὶ παρεπαί-
νους—οἱ δ᾽ αὐτὸν καὶ παραψόγους φασὶν ἐν μέτρῳ
λέγειν, μνήμης χάριν— σοφὸς γὰρ ἀνήρ.

I said, "from what country does he come, and how much does he charge for teaching?" "He is Euenus, Socrates," Callias said, "he is from Paros, and he charges five minae." And I deemed Euenus blessed, if he should really have this skill and teaches so reasonably.

6 Plato, *Phaedo*

For some others have already asked about the poems which you composed, putting into verse the fables of Aesop and the prelude to Apollo, and just the other day Euenus asked what your purpose was in composing them after you came here (i.e., to prison), when you had never done so before. If then you care about my being able to answer Euenus when he asks me again—for I am sure that he will—say what I am to tell him. "Very well, Cebes," he said, "tell him the truth, that I did not compose these poems because I wanted to compete with him or his poems—for I know that it would not be easy—but . . ."[1]

[1]Euenus is also mentioned several times in what immediately follows, but no new information about him is provided.

7 Plato, *Phaedrus*

Shall we not introduce the distinguished Parian, Euenus? He was the first to invent insinuation and incidental praise—and some say that he also put into verse, as an aid to memory, incidental censure; for he is a clever man.[1]

[1] These inventions indicate that Euenus employed an indirect method of praise and censure.

8 Max. Tyr. 38.4 (p. 449.73 Koniaris)

καὶ οὐδὲ αὐτή σοι (scil. ἡ Ἀσπασία τῷ Σωκράτει)
ἀρκεῖ διδάσκαλος, ἀλλ᾽ ἐρανίζῃ παρὰ μὲν Διοτίμας τὰ
ἐρωτικά, παρὰ δὲ Κόννου τὰ μουσικά, παρὰ δὲ Εὐήνου
τὰ ποιητικά, παρὰ δὲ Ἰσχομάχου τὰ γεωργικά, παρά
τε Θεοδώρου τὰ γεωμετρικά.

9 Quint. 1.10.17

transeamus igitur id quoque, quod grammatice quondam
ac musice iunctae fuerunt, si quidem Archytas atque Eue-
nus etiam subiectam grammaticen musicae putaverunt, et
eosdem utriusque rei praeceptores fuisse cum Sophron (fr.
155 Kaibel) ostendit ... tum Eupolis (frr. 17, 208 K.-A.) ...

FRAGMENTS

1-8c. Elegi

1 Ath. 9.367d-e

σιωπῶντος οὖν τοῦ Οὐλπιανοῦ "ἀλλ᾽ ἐγώ," φησιν ὁ
Λεωνίδης, "εἰπεῖν εἰμι δίκαιος, πολλὰ ἤδη σιωπήσας."

πολλοῖς δ᾽ ἀντιλέγειν μέν,

"κατὰ τὸν Πάριον Εὔηνον,"

ἔθος περὶ παντὸς ὁμοίως,
ὀρθῶς δ᾽ ἀντιλέγειν, οὐκέτι τοῦτ᾽ ἐν ἔθει.
καὶ πρὸς μὲν τούτους ἀρκεῖ λόγος εἷς ὁ παλαιός·
"σοὶ μὲν ταῦτα δοκοῦντ᾽ ἔστω, ἐμοὶ δὲ τάδε."

8 Maximus of Tyre, *Discourses*

And not even she (Aspasia) is a sufficient teacher for you (Socrates), but you receive as a contribution the erotic from Diotima, music from Connus, poetry from Euenus, agriculture from Ischomachus, and geometry from Theodorus.

9 Quintilian, *Principles of Oratory*

Let us therefore pass over this point too, that philology and music were once united, although in fact Archytas and also Euenus considered the former subordinate to the latter, and that the same were teachers of both is shown not only by Sophron . . . but also by Eupolis . . .

FRAGMENTS

1-8c. Elegies

1 Athenaeus, *Scholars at Dinner*

Since Ulpian had nothing to say, Leonides spoke up: "Having been silent for a long time now, I have a right to speak. As Euenus of Paros says":

Many are in the habit of contradicting on every point alike, but not in the habit of doing so in the right way. And as for them, one ancient saying is sufficient: "Let that be your opinion and this mine."

5   τοὺς ξυνετοὺς δ' ἄν τις πείσειε τάχιστα λέγων εὖ,
      οἵπερ καὶ ῥήστης εἰσὶ διδασκαλίης.

Stob. 2.2.10 (vv. 1-4)
Ath. 10.429f (v. 4)

1 δ' om. Stob.   μὲν om. Ath.   2 τοῦτο ἐθέλει Ath.
3 τούτοις Ath.   ὡς pro εἷς Stob.   4 μέντοι αὐτὰ Ath. 367
ἐστὶν Stob., ἐστ' Ath. 429   6 ῥάστης cod., corr. West
διδασκαλίας cod., corr. Jacobs

2 *Anth. Pal.* 11.49 Εὐήνου (Εὐίνου codd., corr. Jacobs)

    Βάκχου μέτρον ἄριστον ὃ μὴ πολὺ μηδ'
      ἐλάχιστον·
    ἔστι γὰρ ἢ λύπης αἴτιος ἢ μανίης.
    χαίρει κιρνάμενος δὲ τρισὶν Νύμφαισι τέταρτος·
      τῆμος καὶ θαλάμοις ἐστὶν ἑτοιμότατος.
5   εἰ δὲ πολὺς πνεύσειεν, ἀπέστραπται μὲν ἔρωτας,
      βαπτίζει δ' ὕπνῳ, γείτονι τοῦ θανάτου.

Anth. Plan. (sine poetae nomine)

3 κιρνάμενος τρισὶ νύμφαις τέτρατος αὐτός Plan.
5 ἀπέστραι Pal.   6 τοῦ Plan., τῷ Pal.

3 Stob. 2.15.4 Ζήνου (Εὐήνου Bach, Ζηνοδότου Gais-
ford)

    ἡγοῦμαι σοφίης εἶναι μέρος οὐκ ἐλάχιστον
      ὀρθῶς γινώσκειν οἷος ἕκαστος ἀνήρ.

1 σοφίας cod., corr. Usener

One can very quickly persuade men of sense by words well spoken, for they are the easiest to teach.

2 *Palatine Anthology*

From Euenus:

> The best measure of Bacchus is that which is neither large, nor very small, for he is the cause either of grief or of madness.[1] He delights in being mixed as the fourth with three Nymphs;[2] then he's most ready for the bedroom.[3] But if he should blow with gale force, he turns his back on love and plunges one into sleep, the neighbour of death.

[1] The meaning seems to be that a very small amount of wine is inadequate to dispel grief, while a large amount brings on madness. I have attempted to explain the imagery and language in *Mnemosyne* 41 (1988) 39-45.   [2] I.e., one part of wine to three of water.   [3] I.e., for sexual activity.

3 Stobaeus, *Anthology*

From Euenus(?):

> I consider that a correct understanding of each man's character is not the least part of wisdom.

4 Stob. 4.10.5 Εὐήνου

πρὸς σοφίῃ μὲν ἔχειν τόλμαν μάλα σύμφορόν
  ἐστιν,
χωρὶς δὲ βλαβερή, καὶ κακότητα φέρει.

1 σοφίᾳ cod. M, corr. West: σοφίαν SA

5 Stob. 3.20.2 Εὐήνου

πολλάκις ἀνθρώπων ὀργὴ νόον ἐξεκάλυψεν
κρυπτόμενον· μανίης πουλὺ χερειότερον.

2 μανίας codd., corr. West   πολὺ χειρότερον codd., corr.
Turnebus: <ἢ> πολὺ χειρ. dub. West

6 Plut. *de amore prolis* 4.497a

ὥστε ἐπαινεῖσθαι καὶ μνημονεύεσθαι τοῦ Εὐήνου
τοῦτο μόνον, ὡς ἐπέγραψεν·

ἢ δέος ἢ λύπη παῖς πατρὶ πάντα χρόνον.

Artem. *onir.* 1.15; Hermias in Pl. *Phaedr.* 267a (p. 238.7
Couvreur); Macar. 4.38 (*Paroem. Gr.* ii.170.14)

φόβος et πάντα βίον Hermias

7 Ps.-Arist. π. ἀρετῶν καὶ κακιῶν 7.1251a30 (= Stob.
  3.1.194)

ἀδικίας δέ ἐστιν εἴδη τρία, ἀσέβεια πλεονεξία ὕβρις.
. . . ὕβρις δέ, καθ᾽ ἣν τὰς ἡδονὰς αὑτοῖς παρα-

4 Stobaeus, *Anthology*

From Euenus:

> It is a great advantage to have daring combined with wisdom, but daring apart from wisdom is harmful and brings misery.

5 Stobaeus, *Anthology*

From Euenus:

> Often men's anger uncovers their hidden mind; that is much worse than madness.

6 Plutarch, *On Affection for Offspring*

As a result this alone of Euenus is praised and remembered, when he wrote:

> For the father a child is a constant source either of fear or of grief.

7 Pseudo-Aristotle, *On Virtues and Vices*

There are three kinds of wrongdoing: impiety, greed, and outrage. . . . Outrage is the wrongdoing whereby men pro-

σκευάζουσιν εἰς ὄνειδος ἄγοντες ἑτέρους· ὅθεν καὶ
Εὔηνος περὶ αὐτῆς λέγει·

ἥτις κερδαίνουσ᾿ οὐδὲν ὅμως ἀδικεῖ.

8 Arist. *Metaph.* 4.5.1015a28

τὸ γὰρ βίαιον ἀναγκαῖον λέγεται, διὸ καὶ λυπηρόν,
ὥσπερ καὶ Εὔηνός φησι·

πᾶν γὰρ ἀναγκαῖον πρῆγμ᾿ ἀνιηρὸν ἔφυ.

Plut. *non posse suav. viv. sec. Epic.* 21.1102c; Theogn. 472

πρᾶγμ᾿ Arist., Plut., corr. Winterton: χρῆμ᾿ Theogn.
ἀνιηρὸν Plut. v.l., Theogn.: ἀνιαρὸν Arist.: ὀδυνηρὸν Plut. v.l.

8a = Theogn. 467-96

8b = Theogn. 667-82

8c = Theogn. 1341-50

9. Hexametri

9 Arist. *Eth. Nic.* 7.10.1152a30

διὰ γὰρ τοῦτο καὶ τὸ ἔθος χαλεπόν, ὅτι τῇ φύσει
ἔοικεν, ὥσπερ καὶ Εὔηνος λέγει·

φημὶ πολυχρόνιον μελέτην ἔμεναι, φίλε, καὶ δὴ
ταύτην ἀνθρώποισι τελευτῶσαν φύσιν εἶναι.

cure pleasures for themselves while leading others into disgrace. Consequently Euenus says about it:

> (outrage) which brings no profit and nevertheless does wrong

8 Aristotle, *Metaphysics*

For that which is forced is said to be constraining, and therefore painful, as Euenus states:

> For every act of constraint is painful.[1]

[1] See n. 1 on Theognis 467-96. Plutarch also assigns the verse to Euenus, while other sources cite it without naming the author.

9. Dactylic Hexameters

9 Aristotle, *Nicomachean Ethics*

For this reason habit is difficult (to change), because it resembles nature, as Euenus states:

> My friend, I say that it is a long-standing practice and that this is in the end men's nature.

ELEGIAC POETRY

9a. Trimeter

9a Simpl. in Arist. *Phys.* 4.221a31 (*Comm. in Arist. Gr.* ix.741.1)

ὁ δὲ Σιμωνίδης (fr. 645 *PMG*) τὸ σοφώτατον τῷ χρόνῳ
περιῆψε, τούτῳ γὰρ ἔφη πάντας εὑρίσκειν καὶ μαν-
θάνειν, ⟨Πάρων δὲ ὁ Πυθαγόρειος τὸ ἀμαθέστατον,
ὅτι ἐπιλανθάνονται ὑπὸ χρόνου⟩ (suppl. Diels e Sim-
plicio infra citato)· Εὔηνος δὲ ἐξ ἀμφοῖν πεποίηκε τὸ

σοφώτατόν τοι κἀμαθέστατον χρόνος.

χρόνον codd., corr. Diels

10. Incerti Metri

10 Plut. *quaest. Plat.* 10.3.1010c

"τί οὖν;" φήσαι τις ἄν, "οὐδὲν ταῦτα συμβάλλεται
πρὸς λόγον;" ἔγωγε φήσαιμ᾿ ἄν, ὥσπερ ἅλας συμ-
βάλλεσθαι πρὸς ὄψον, ὕδωρ δὲ πρὸς μᾶζαν· Εὔηνος δὲ
καὶ τὸ πῦρ ἔφασκεν ἡδυσμάτων εἶναι κράτιστον· ἀλλ᾿
οὔθ᾿ ὕδωρ μάζης ἢ ἄρτου μέρος εἶναι λέγομεν, οὔτε
πῦρ οὔθ᾿ ἅλας ἑψήματος ἢ βρώματος.

9a. Iambic Trimeter

9a Simplicius on Aristotle, *Physics*

Simonides made time the wisest thing, since he said that by means of this everyone discovers and learns, ‹but Paron the Pythagorean said it was the most stupid, since people forget because of this›. And Euenus combined the two to make:

> The wisest and most stupid thing is time.

10. Uncertain Meter

10 Plutarch, *Platonic Questions*

"Well, then," one might say, "do these things contribute nothing to speech?" I for my part should say that they do, just as salt contributes to a dish and water to barley bread. And Euenus even claimed that fire was the best of seasonings.[1] But we do not say that water is a part of barley bread or wheat bread or that fire or salt is a part of vegetables or meat.

[1] This same saying is attributed to Euenus in Plut. *quomodo adulator internosc.* 2.50a and *quaest. conv.* 7 praef. 697c-d, but in *de tuenda san.* 8.126c-d it is attributed to Prodicus (84 B 10 D.-K.).

CRITIAS

TESTIMONIA

1 Diog. Laert. 3.1

Πλάτων Ἀρίστωνος καὶ Περικτιόνης—ἢ Πωτώνης—
ἥτις τὸ γένος ἀνέφερεν εἰς Σόλωνα, Ἀθηναῖος. τούτου
γὰρ ἦν ἀδελφὸς Δρωπίδης, οὗ Κριτίας, οὗ Κάλ-
λαισχρος, οὗ Κριτίας ὁ τῶν τριάκοντα καὶ Γλαύκων,
οὗ Χαρμίδης καὶ Περικτιόνη, ἧς καὶ Ἀρίστωνος
Πλάτων, ἕκτος ἀπὸ Σόλωνος.

2 Io. Philop. in Arist. *de anima* 1.405b5 (*Comm. in Arist.
Gr.* xv.89.8)

Κριτίαν εἴτε τὸν ἕνα τῶν τριάκοντα, ὃς καὶ Σωκράτους
ἠκροάσατο, ἢ καὶ ἄλλον τινὰ λέγει, οὐδὲν διαφερό-
μεθα. φασὶ δὲ καὶ ἄλλον Κριτίαν γεγονέναι σο-

CRITIAS

TESTIMONIA

Most of the testimonia on Critias pertain to his political career, association with Socrates, prose style, or moral character and are therefore omitted here. All the testimonia are printed in *Die Fragmente der Vorsokratiker* (as well as in Gentili-Prato) and are translated by D. N. Levin in R. K. Sprague (ed.), *The Older Sophists* (Columbia, S.C. 1972) 242-49. See also Archilochus test. 33 and Solon fr. 22a.

1 Diogenes Laertius, *Lives of the Philosophers*

Plato, the Athenian, was the son of Ariston and Perictione (or Potone), who traced her family back to Solon. For Solon's brother Dropides was the father of Critias who was the father of Callaeschrus. His sons were Critias, a member of the thirty (tyrants), and Glaucon, the father of Charmides and Perictione. Plato, the son of Perictione and Ariston, was in the sixth generation after Solon.

2 John Philoponus on Aristotle, *On the Soul*

It makes no difference to us whether Aristotle means Critias, one of the thirty (tyrants), who also listened to Socrates, or someone else. They say that there was also

φιστήν, οὗ καὶ τὰ φερόμενα συγγράμματα εἶναι, ὡς
Ἀλέξανδρος λέγει· τὸν γὰρ τῶν τριάκοντα μηδὲ
γεγραφέναι ἄλλο τι πλὴν Πολιτείας ἐμμέτρους.

3 Ath. 4.184d

ἔμελεν δὲ τοῖς πάλαι πᾶσιν Ἕλλησι μουσικῆς· διόπερ
καὶ ἡ αὐλητικὴ περισπούδαστος ἦν. Χαμαιλέων γοῦν
ὁ Ἡρακλεώτης ἐν τῷ ἐπιγραφομένῳ Προτρεπτικῷ (fr.
3 Wehrli) Λακεδαιμονίους φησὶ καὶ Θηβαίους πάντας
αὐλεῖν μανθάνειν, Ἡρακλεώτας τε τοὺς ἐν τῷ Πόντῳ
καθ᾽ ἑαυτὸν ἔτι, Ἀθηναίων τε τοὺς ἐπιφανεστάτους
Καλλίαν τε τὸν Ἱππονίκου καὶ Κριτίαν τὸν Καλ-
λαίσχρου.

4 Mall. Theod. de metris (Gramm. Lat. vi.589.20 Keil)

metrum dactylicum hexametrum inventum primitus ab
Orpheo Critias asserit, Democritus (68 B 16 D.-K.) a
Musaeo.

another Critias, a sophist and author of the writings in question, as Alexander states. For the member of the thirty has not written anything except the *Well-balanced Constitutions*.[1]

[1] Or possibly *"Constitutions* in verse." Critias was the author of a *Constitution of the Thessalians* (88 B 31 D.-K.) and *of the Spartans* (B 32-37), but these were in prose. There is no evidence to support the claim of a second Critias.

3 Athenaeus, *Scholars at Dinner*

All the Greeks of old cared about music and hence they showed much zeal for pipe-playing. At any rate Chamaeleon of Heraclea in his *Hortatory Treatise*, as it is called, states that the Spartans and Thebans all learned to play the pipe and that the inhabitants of Heraclea on the Pontus still do individually, while among the Athenians the most conspicuous were Callias, the son of Hipponicus, and Critias, the son of Callaeschrus.

4 Mallius Theodorus, *On Meters*

Critias asserts that the dactylic hexameter was invented originally by Orpheus,[1] Democritus by Musaeus.

[1] Diels-Kranz printed this as fr. 3, but there is no reason to assume that the statement occurred in an elegy.

FRAGMENTS

1. Hexametri

1 Ath. 13.600d-e

ὃν (sc. Ἔρωτα) ὁ σοφὸς ὑμνῶν αἰεί ποτε Ἀνακρέων
πᾶσίν ἐστιν διὰ στόματος. λέγει οὖν περὶ αὐτοῦ καὶ ὁ
κράτιστος Κριτίας τάδε·

> τὸν δὲ γυναικείων μελέων πλέξαντά ποτ᾽ ᾠδὰς
> ἡδὺν Ἀνακρείοντα Τέως εἰς Ἑλλάδ᾽ ἀνῆγεν,
> συμποσίων ἐρέθισμα, γυναικῶν ἠπερόπευμα,
> αὐλῶν ἀντίπαλον, φιλοβάρβιτον, ἡδύν, ἄλυπον.
> 5 οὔ ποτέ σου φιλότης γηράσεται οὐδὲ θανεῖται,
> ἔστ᾽ ἂν ὕδωρ οἴνῳ συμμειγνύμενον κυλίκεσσιν
> παῖς διαπομπεύῃ, προπόσεις ἐπιδέξια νωμῶν,
> παννυχίδας θ᾽ ἱερὰς θήλεις χοροὶ ἀμφιέπωσιν,
> πλάστιγξ θ᾽ ἡ χαλκοῦ θυγάτηρ ἐπ᾽ ἄκραισι
>   καθίζῃ
> 10 κοττάβου ὑψηλαῖς κορυφαῖς Βρομίου
>   ψακάδεσσιν;

5 ποτε τοῦ Hermann   7 πρόποσιν E, -σις A, corr.
Musurus   10 ὑψηλὴ Wilamowitz

CRITIAS

FRAGMENTS

1. Dactylic Hexameters

1 Athenaeus, *Scholars at Dinner*

Skilled Anacreon who is on the lips of everyone once constantly sang of Eros. Hence mighty Critias says the following about him:

> Teos brought to Greece the one who once wove songs with strains celebrating women, sweet Anacreon,[1] stimulus for symposia, seducer of women, opponent of the pipes, lover of the lyre, sweet, banisher of pain. Never will love of you grow old or perish, so long as a slave boy carries round water mixed with wine for the cups, dispensing toasts to the right, and female choruses conduct sacred allnight festivities, and the scale-pan, daughter of bronze, sits on the high and lofty top of the cottabus[2] for the drops of Bromius.[3]

[1] For the poetry of Anacreon see Campbell's Loeb edition, *Greek Lyric* ii.22 ff. According to the scholiast on Aesch. *PV* 128a (p. 93 Herington) Anacreon spent time in Athens "out of love for Critias" (Κριτίου ἐρῶν), i.e., the grandfather of our Critias.
[2] For the cottabus and its apparatus see n. 2 on Dion. Chal. fr. 3.
[3] Another name for Dionysus and standing here for wine.

ELEGIAC POETRY

2-9. *Elegi*

2 Ath. 1.28b-c

Κριτίας δὲ οὕτως·

κότταβος ἐκ Σικελῆς ἐστι χθονός, ἐκπρεπὲς ἔργον,
ὃν σκοπὸν ἐς λατάγων τόξα καθιστάμεθα.
εἶτα δ᾽ ὄχος Σικελὸς κάλλει δαπάνῃ τε κράτιστος
. . . .
Θεσσαλικὸς δὲ θρόνος γυίων τρυφερωτάτη ἕδρα.
5   εὐναίου δὲ λέχους †κάλλος† ἔχει
Μίλητός τε Χίος τ᾽ ἔναλος πόλις Οἰνοπίωνος.
Τυρσηνὴ δὲ κρατεῖ χρυσότυπος φιάλη,
καὶ πᾶς χαλκὸς ὅτις κοσμεῖ δόμον ἔν τινι χρείᾳ.
Φοίνικες δ᾽ ηὗρον γράμματ᾽ ἀλεξίλογα.
10   Θήβη δ᾽ ἁρματόεντα δίφρον συνεπήξατο πρώτη,
φορτηγοὺς δ᾽ ἀκάτους Κᾶρες ἁλὸς ταμίαι.
τὸν δὲ τροχοῦ γαίας τε καμίνου τ᾽ ἔκγονον ηὗρεν
κλεινότατον κέραμον, χρήσιμον οἰκονόμον,
ἡ τὸ καλὸν Μαραθῶνι καταστήσασα τρόπαιον.

καὶ ἐπαινεῖται ὄντως ὁ Ἀττικὸς κέραμος.

Ath. 15.666b (vv. 1-2)
Eust. in Hom. *Od.* 1771.45 (vv. 9 + 11)

3 σικελικὸς καλλι codd., corr. Musurus, Casaubon
4 γυω codd., corr. Musurus   5 ⟨ἔξοχα⟩ κάλλος Musurus,
κάλλ⟨εἴ κῦδ⟩ος Kalinka, alii alia   8 ὅστις codd., corr.
Musurus   12 τροχὸν codd. (rec. West), corr. Casaubon
τὲ γόνον codd., corr. Musurus   14 μαραθῶν(ος) codd., corr.
Musurus

2-9. Elegies

2 Athenaeus, *Scholars at Dinner*

And Critias speaks as follows:[1]

From the land of Sicily comes the cottabus,[2] a remarkable achievement; we set it up as a target for shafts of wine drops. Next, a Sicilian wagon is the most beautiful and expensive . . .[3] A Thessalian chair is the most comfortable seat for the limbs. Miletus and Chios, Oenopian's[4] city by the sea, are famed(?) for the beauty of the marriage bed.[5] The Etruscan bowl of beaten gold prevails, and all the bronze that adorns a house for any use. Phoenicians invented letters as a means of preserving discourse. Thebes was the first to construct the carriage for a chariot, and Carians, stewards of the sea, cargo vessels.[6] And she that set up the beautiful trophy at Marathon[7] invented the offspring of wheel, earth, and oven, pottery of highest fame, a useful housekeeper.

And Attic pottery is truly praised.

[1] Athenaeus 1.27d-28d includes this passage among several which list the chief products of a particular place.   [2] See n. 2 on Dion. Chal. fr. 3.   [3] Perhaps only a pentameter is missing.

[4] In 1.26b-c Athenaeus, on the authority of Theopompus, states that Oenopian was a son of Dionysus, founded the island-state, and was the first to teach viticulture. See Ion fr. 29 (*Greek Lyric* iv.365).   [5] Or perhaps simply "bed for sleeping."

[6] For the Carians as seafarers see Gomme on Thuc. 1.8.

[7] I.e., Athens.

3 = test. **4**

4 Hephaest. *Ench.* 2.3

ἢ δύο βραχεῖαι εἰς μίαν βραχεῖαν, ὅπερ ἐν τοῖς
ἄλλοις εὑρίσκεται μέτροις . . . ἐν δὲ τοῖς ἔπεσι
σπανίως· ὥστε Κριτίας ἐν τῇ εἰς Ἀλκιβιάδην ἐλεγείᾳ
οὐκ ᾤετο ἐγχωρεῖν τοῦ Ἀλκιβιάδου τὸ ὄνομα· φησὶ
γάρ·

καὶ νῦν Κλεινίου υἱὸν Ἀθηναῖον στεφανώσω
Ἀλκιβιάδην νέοισιν ὑμνήσας τρόποις·
οὐ γάρ πως ἦν τοὔνομ' ἐφαρμόζειν ἐλεγείῳ,
νῦν δ' ἐν ἰαμβείῳ κείσεται οὐκ ἀμέτρως.

1 Ἀθηναίου v.l.

5 Plut. *Alcib.* 33.1

τὸ μὲν οὖν ψήφισμα τῆς καθόδου πρότερον ἐκεκύρωτο
Κριτίου τοῦ Καλλαίσχρου γράψαντος, ὡς αὐτὸς ἐν
ταῖς ἐλεγείαις πεποίηκεν, ὑπομιμνῄσκων τὸν Ἀλκι-
βιάδην τῆς χάριτος ἐν τούτοις·

γνώμην δ' ἥ σε κατήγαγ', ἐγὼ ταύτην ἐν ἅπασιν
εἶπον, καὶ γράψας τοὖργον ἔδρασα τόδε,
σφραγὶς δ' ἡμετέρης γλώσσης ἐπὶ τοίσδεσι
κεῖται.

1 γνώμη cod. Y (ret. Gent.-Pr.)   ἥστε Y   2 εἰπὼν
Ziegler   3 ἡμετέρας Cobet   γλώττης Y

4 Hephaestion, *Handbook of Meters*

. . . or two short syllables (are used) for one short, which is
found in the other meters . . . but rarely in hexameters. As a
result Critias in his elegy on Alcibiades did not think that
Alcibiades' name was allowable, for he says:

> And now I shall crown the Athenian son of Cleinias,
> Alcibiades, with a song in a new manner. For it was
> not possible in any way to fit the name into elegiac
> verse; now it will lie, not unmetrically, in an iambic
> line.[1]

[1] Iambic trimeters are occasionally found as a substitute for
the pentameter, as here in v. 2, or for the hexameter.

5 Plutarch, *Life of Alcibiades*

Now the decree for his recall had been ratified earlier (411
B.C.), on the motion of Critias the son of Callaeschrus, as
Critias himself has written in his elegiac verses, reminding
Alcibiades of the favour as follows:

> As for the proposal which restored you, I was the
> one who delivered it among all the people, and by
> my motion I accomplished this deed. The seal of my
> tongue is set on these (words?, verses?).[1]

[1] Meaning uncertain (see n. 2 on Theognis 19-38), but proba-
bly Critias is referring either to the official copy of the decree
which would contain the name of the mover and would be depos-
ited in the state archives, so that "tongue" is in effect Critias'
name, or to a purely metaphorical seal which consists of Critias'
poetic style.

6 Ath. 10.432d-33b

προπόσεις δὲ τὰς γινομένας ἐν τοῖς συμποσίοις
Λακεδαιμονίοις οὐκ ἦν ἔθος ποιεῖν, οὐδὲ φιλοτησίας
διὰ τούτων πρὸς ἀλλήλους ποιεῖσθαι. δηλοῖ δὲ ταῦτα
Κριτίας ἐν τοῖς ἐλεγείοις·

> καὶ τόδ᾽ ἔθος Σπάρτῃ μελέτημά τε κείμενόν ἐστι·
> πίνειν τὴν αὐτὴν οἰνοφόρον κύλικα,
> μηδ᾽ ἀποδωρεῖσθαι προπόσεις ὀνομαστὶ λέγοντα,
> μηδ᾽ ἐπὶ δεξιτερὰν χεῖρα κύκλῳ θιάσου
> . . . .
> 5   ἄγγεα Λυδὴ χεὶρ ηὖρ᾽ Ἀσιατογενής,
> καὶ προπόσεις ὀρέγειν ἐπιδέξια, καὶ προκαλεῖσθαι
> ἐξονομακλήδην ᾧ προπιεῖν ἐθέλει.
> εἶτ᾽ ἀπὸ τοιούτων πόσεων γλώσσας τε λύουσιν
> εἰς αἰσχροὺς μύθους σῶμά τ᾽ ἀμαυρότερον
> 10   τεύχουσιν· πρὸς δ᾽ ὄμμ᾽ ἀχλὺς ἀμβλωπὸς ἐφίζει
> λῆστις δ᾽ ἐκτήκει μνημοσύνην πραπίδων,
> νοῦς δὲ παρέσφαλται· δμῶες δ᾽ ἀκόλαστον ἔχουσιν
> ἦθος· ἐπεισπίπτει δ᾽ οἰκοτριβὴς δαπάνη.
> οἱ Λακεδαιμονίων δὲ κόροι πίνουσι τοσοῦτον
> 15   ὥστε φρέν᾽ εἰς ἱλαρὰν †ἀσπίδα πάντ᾽ ἀπάγειν†
> εἴς τε φιλοφροσύνην γλῶσσαν μέτριόν τε γέλωτα.
> τοιαύτη δὲ πόσις σώματί τ᾽ ὠφέλιμος
> γνώμῃ τε κτήσει τε· καλῶς δ᾽ εἰς ἔργ᾽ Ἀφροδίτης
> πρός θ᾽ ὕπνον ἥρμοσται, τὸν καμάτων λιμένα,
> 20   πρὸς τὴν τερπνοτάτην τε θεῶν θνητοῖς Ὑγίειαν
> καὶ τὴν Εὐσεβίης γείτονα Σωφροσύνην.

6 Athenaeus, *Scholars at Dinner*

It was not the custom of the Spartans to propose toasts at drinking parties or to offer loving-cups by these means to one another. Critias makes this clear in his elegiac verses:[1]

This too is the custom and established practice at Sparta: to drink from the same[2] wine-bearing cup, and not to give toasts while proposing them (to someone) by name, and not (to pass the cup?) to the right in the circle of company . . .[3] A Lydian hand, born in Asia, invented (wine) vessels,[4] extending of toasts to the right, and challenging by name the person to whom one wishes to drink a toast. Then, as a result of such drinking their tongues are loosened into disgraceful words and their bodies are made weaker.[5] Upon their eyes a dark mist settles, oblivion melts away memory from their minds, and reason is tripped up. The servants have an undisciplined manner and house-ruining extravagance bursts in. But Spartan youths drink only enough (to turn?) their mind to cheerful . . .,[6] their tongue to friendliness and moderate laughter. Such drinking is beneficial for body, mind, and property. It is well suited to the deeds of Aphrodite and to sleep, a haven from toils, and to Health, most pleasing of the gods to mortals, and to Discretion, the neighbour of Piety.

ἑξῆς τε πάλιν φησίν·

αἱ γὰρ ὑπὲρ τὸ μέτρον κυλίκων προπόσεις
    παραχρῆμα
τέρψασαι λυποῦσ᾽ εἰς τὸν ἅπαντα χρόνον·
ἡ Λακεδαιμονίων δὲ δίαιθ᾽ ὁμαλῶς διάκειται,
25   ἔσθειν καὶ πίνειν σύμμετρα πρὸς τὸ φρονεῖν
καὶ τὸ πονεῖν εἶναι δυνάτους· οὐκ ἔστ᾽ ἀπότακτος
ἡμέρα οἰνῶσαι σῶμ᾽ ἀμέτροισι πότοις.

2 αὑτῷ Bach, αὑτοῦ Diehl, αὐτῶν Kalinka   8 τελέουσιν
codd., corr. Musurus   9 ἀφαυρότερον malit West
15 ἐλπίδα Emperius   πάντας ἄγειν Bergk   20 ὑγείαν
codd., corr. Musurus   21 Εὐσεβίας Wilamowitz
25 ἐσθίειν A, corr. Musurus   τὸ φανέν A, corr. Bach
26 "possis κεῖναι vel δυνατούς τ᾽" West   26-27 ἀπότακτος
ἡμέρα CE, ἀπότακτον ἡμέρᾳ A

7 Schol. Eur. *Hipp.* 264 (ii.39.3 Schwartz), "οὕτω τὸ λίαν
ἧσσον ἐπαινῶ τοῦ μηδὲν ἄγαν· καὶ ξυμφήσουσι
σοφοί μοι"

τὸ "μηδὲν ἄγαν" οἱ μὲν Χίλωνι τῷ Λακεδαιμονίῳ
ἀνατιθέασιν, ὡς Κριτίας, οἱ δὲ Σωδάμῳ, ὡς τὸ ἐν
Τεγέᾳ ἐπίγραμμα δηλοῖ· "ταῦτ᾽ ἔλεγεν Σώδαμος
Ἐπηράτου, ὅς μ᾽ ἀνέθηκεν· / μηδὲν ἄγαν, καιρῷ πάντα
πρόσεστι καλά."

Diog. Laert. 1.41

διαφωνοῦνται δὲ καὶ αἱ ἀποφάσεις αὐτῶν (sc. τῶν ἑπτὰ
σοφῶν), καὶ ἄλλου ἄλλο φασίν, ὡς ἐκεῖνο·

He goes on to say again:

> For toasts from cups that go beyond due measure,
> though they give momentary pleasure, bring grief
> for all time. But the Spartan way of life is evenly or-
> dered: to eat and drink moderately so as to be able to
> think and work. There is no day set apart[7] to intoxi-
> cate the body with immoderate drinking.

[1] Possibly from the work mentioned in test. 2.   [2] I.e.,
one's own cup, without exchanging it for someone else's.
[3] It is unclear whether the genitive depends on the preceding da-
tive or on something in the following lacuna. The lacuna may in-
volve more than one verse, since we expect to be told that vv. 3-4
refer to the drinking practice in Athens.   [4] Probably nothing
more than the common attribution of soft living to the Lydians.
[5] I.e., unsteadiness caused by excessive drinking.   [6] On the
text see West, *Studies* 170, and A. Meriani, *QUCC* n.s. 56 (1997)
81–86.   [7] As occurred in Athens for festivals of Dionysus.
Cf. Plato, *Laws* 1.637b.

7 Scholiast on Euripides, *Hippolytus* ("And so I praise
excess less than nothing in excess, and the wise will
agree with me.")

Some attribute "nothing in excess" to the Spartan Chilon,
as does Critias, others to Sodamus, as the epigram in Tegea
makes clear: "Sodamus, son of Eperatus, who set me up,
said these words: nothing in excess, to due measure be-
longs everything that is good."[1]

Diogenes Laertius, *Lives of the Philosophers*

The utterances of the Seven Sages are variously attributed,
now to one, now to another, such as the following:

ἦν Λακεδαιμόνιος Χίλων σοφός, ὃς τάδ᾽ ἔλεξε·
"μηδὲν ἄγαν, καιρῷ πάντα πρόσεστι καλά."

8 Plut. *Cimon* 10.5

ἔτι τοίνυν Γοργίας μὲν ὁ Λεοντῖνός (82 B 20 D.-K.)
φησι τὸν Κίμωνα τὰ χρήματα κτᾶσθαι μὲν ὡς χρῷτο,
χρῆσθαι δ᾽ ὡς τιμῷτο· Κριτίας δὲ τῶν τριάκοντα
γενόμενος ἐν ταῖς ἐλεγείαις εὔχεται

πλοῦτον μὲν Σκοπαδῶν, μεγαλοφροσύνην δὲ
    Κίμωνος,
νίκας δ᾽ Ἀρκεσίλα τοῦ Λακεδαιμονίου.

2 ἀγησίλα codd., corr. Westermann

9 Stob. 3.29.11 Κριτίου·

ἐκ μελέτης πλείους ἢ φύσεως ἀγαθοί.

ἢ ᾽κ Bergk

470

It was Chilon,[2] the Spartan sage, who said this: "Nothing in excess, to due measure belongs everything that is good."[3]

[1] See D. L. Page, *Further Greek Epigrams* 492-93. The disputed authorship is recorded also by Clem. *Strom.* 1.61.1 and schol. Pind. *Pyth.* 2.63 (ii.42.20 Dr.). [2] A 6th-cent. Spartan statesman (see G. L. Huxley, *Early Sparta* [London 1962] 69-71) and one of the Seven Sages. For a list of apophthegms attributed to him see *Vorsokr.* i.63 D.-K. from Stobaeus 3.1.172.

[3] Dietrich inserted the couplet after v. 21 of fr. 6. For v. 2 cf. Theognis 401.

8 Plutarch, *Life of Cimon*

Furthermore, Gorgias of Leontini says that Cimon acquired money so that he might use it and used it so that he might be honoured. And Critias who became one of the thirty (tyrants) prays in his elegies for

the wealth of the Scopadae,[1] the magnanimity of Cimon, and the victories of the Spartan Arcesilaus.[2]

[1] A ruling family in Thessaly celebrated by Simonides (cf. Theocr. 16.42-47). [2] Winner in the chariot race at Olympia in 448 and 444.

9 Stobaeus, *Anthology*

From Critias:

More men excel from practice than from nature.

ADESPOTA ELEGIACA

1 Pl. *Resp.* 2.368a

οὐ κακῶς εἰς ὑμᾶς, ὦ παῖδες ἐκείνου τοῦ ἀνδρός, τὴν
ἀρχὴν τῶν ἐλεγείων ἐποίησεν ὁ Γλαύκωνος ἐραστής,
εὐδοκιμήσαντας περὶ τὴν Μεγαροῖ μάχην, εἰπών·

> παῖδες Ἀρίστωνος, κλεινοῦ θεῖον γένος ἀνδρός.

2 Pl. *Prot.* 344d

τῷ μὲν γὰρ ἐσθλῷ ἐγχωρεῖ κακῷ γενέσθαι, ὥσπερ καὶ
παρ᾽ ἄλλου ποιητοῦ μαρτυρεῖται τοῦ εἰπόντος·

> αὐτὰρ ἀνὴρ ἀγαθὸς τοτὲ μὲν κακός, ἄλλοτε δ᾽
> ἐσθλός.

cf. Xen. *mem.* 1.2.20, Stob. 3.29.95

ὁτὲ Xen. cod. unus, ποτὲ Stob. cod. A

472

ANONYMOUS ELEGIACS

1 Plato, *Republic*

When you had distinguished yourselves in the battle at Megara,[1] Glaucon's lover[2] composed an excellent beginning to his elegiac verses[3] on you, sons of that well-known man,[4] saying:

> Sons of Ariston,[5] god-like offspring of a famous man

1 Diod. Sic. 13.65 records a victory of the Athenians against a superior force of Megarians in 409.   2 Thought by some to be Critias.   3 Aristides *or.* 45 (ii.98 Dindorf) and the scholia ad loc. (iii.420.1) cite the verse and call it an epigram (ἐπίγραμμα).   4 It is unclear whether this is Ariston.
5 Father of Glaucon, Adeimantus, and Plato.

2 Plato, *Protagoras*

It is possible for a good man to become bad, as is attested by another poet[1] who said:

> but a good man is at one time bad, at another good[2]

1 I.e., other than Simonides whose poem (fr. 542 *PMG*) on this topic is examined at some length in the dialogue.   2 No distinction, I think, is intended between ἀγαθός and ἐσθλός. By 'good' is meant one who is held in esteem through birth, conduct, circumstances etc. and by 'bad' is meant the opposite. Perhaps 'worthy' and 'wretched' would be more accurate translations.

ELEGIAC POETRY

2a Pl. *Phaedr.* 241d

ταὐτά τε οὖν χρή, ὦ παῖ, ξυννοεῖν, καὶ εἰδέναι τὴν
ἐραστοῦ φιλίαν, ὅτι οὐ μετ᾽ εὐνοίας γίγνεται, ἀλλὰ
σιτίου τρόπον, χάριν πλησμονῆς,

> ὡς λύκοι ἄρν᾽ ἀγαπῶσ᾽, ὡς παῖδα φιλοῦσιν
> ἐρασταί.

cf. schol. ad loc. (p. 78 Greene), schol. Hom. *Il.* 22.263b
(v.319.64 Erbse), Diogen. 8.76 (*Paroem. Gr.* i.320.9), Aristaen.
2.20 etc.

ἄρνας codd. Plat., ἄρνα φιλοῦσι λύκοι νέον ὡς φιλέουσιν
ἐρασταί schol. Hom.

3 Arist. *Eth. Nic.* 2.6.1106b28

ἔτι τὸ μὲν ἁμαρτάνειν πολλαχῶς ἔστιν . . . τὸ δὲ
κατορθοῦν μοναχῶς . . . καὶ διὰ ταῦτ᾽ οὖν τῆς μὲν
κακίας ἡ ὑπερβολὴ καὶ ἡ ἔλλειψις, τῆς δὲ ἀρετῆς ἡ
μεσότης·

> ἐσθλοὶ μὲν γὰρ ἁπλῶς, παντοδαπῶς δὲ κακοί.

4 Arist. *Eth. Nic.* 8.5.1157b11

ἐὰν δὲ χρόνιος ἡ ἀπουσία γίνηται, καὶ τῆς φιλίας
δοκεῖ λήθην ποιεῖν· ὅθεν εἴρηται·

> πολλὰς δὴ φιλίας ἀπροσηγορία διέλυσεν.

2a Plato, *Phaedrus*

These things, lad, you should bear in mind, and you should know that a lover's friendship is not based on good will, but, like food, it is to get one's fill:

As wolves love a lamb, so lovers love a boy.

3 Aristotle, *Nicomachean Ethics*

Furthermore, error is multiform ... but success is possible in one way only ... And so because of this excess and deficiency are a mark of vice, whereas the mean is a mark of virtue:

The good are good in one way only, the bad are bad in all sorts of ways.

4 Aristotle, *Nicomachean Ethics*

But if absence is prolonged, it seems to bring forgetfulness of friendship. Hence the statement:

Lack of discourse dissolves many a friendship.

5 Arist. *Eth. Eud.* 7.2.1236a34

διὰ γὰρ τὸ χρήσιμοι εἶναι φιλοῦσιν ἀλλήλους, καὶ
μέχρι τούτου, ὥσπερ ἡ παροιμία· (Arch. fr. 15) . . ., καί·

οὐκέτι γιγνώσκουσιν Ἀθηναῖοι Μεγαρῆας.

6 Arist. *Ath. Pol.* 20.5

ἔτι δὲ πρότερον τῶν Ἀλκμεωνιδῶν Κήδων ἐπέθετο τοῖς
τυράννοις, διὸ καὶ ἦδον καὶ εἰς τοῦτον ἐν τοῖς σκο-
λίοις·

ἔγχει καὶ Κήδωνι, διάκονε, μηδ᾽ ἐπιλήθου,
εἰ χρὴ τοῖς ἀγαθοῖς ἀνδράσιν οἰνοχοεῖν.

7 Theophrast. *de ventis* 51 (p. 50 Coutant-Eichenlaub)

ἐπεὶ δὲ πρὸς τὰς χώρας ἑκάστοις καὶ τοὺς τόπους
ἐπινεφῆ καὶ αἰθρίαι, διὰ τοῦτο καὶ τῶν ἐν παροιμίᾳ
λεγομένων πρός τινας τόπους ἔνια, ὡς περὶ τοῦ Ἀρ-
γέστου καὶ Λιβός. ἰσχυρὸς δὲ μάλιστα περὶ Κνίδον
καὶ Ῥόδον·

Λὶψ ἄνεμος ταχὺ μὲν νεφέλας, ταχὺ δ᾽ αἴθρια
ποιεῖ·
Ἀργέστῃ δ᾽ ἀνέμῳ πᾶσ᾽ ἔπεται νεφέλη.

5 Aristotle, *Eudemian Ethics*

For they are friends of one another only as long as they are useful, as the proverb goes: (Archilochus fr. 15), and:

> Athenians no longer recognize Megarians.[1]

[1] The verse is repeated in 1242b22.

6 Aristotle, *Constitution of the Athenians*

At a still earlier time than that of the Alcmaeonidae Cedon attacked the tyrants,[1] and hence they sang of him too in their scolia:

> Pour a cup for Cedon[2] too, waiter, and don't forget him, if you are to pour wine for men of worth.[3]

[1] Hippias and Hipparchus, sons of Peisistratus. [2] Otherwise unknown. [3] The couplet is also quoted by Athenaeus 15.695e among his examples of Attic scolia. For some ancient explanations of the term 'scolia,' see the Loeb *Greek Lyric* v.274-79, and for a commentary on the couplet see E. Fabbro, *I carmi conviviali attici* (Rome 1995) 182-85.

7 Theophrastus, *On Winds*

Since cloudy and clear skies are associated with each wind according to districts and places, for this reason some of the things said in proverbs are associated with certain places, as for example concerning the Northwest and the Southwest winds. The latter is especially strong round about Cnidus and Rhodes:

> The Southwest wind quickly brings clouds and quickly a clear sky, but all the clouds accompany the Northwest wind.

8 Chrysipp. π. ἀποφατικῶν (ii.54.23 von Arnim)

εἰ ποιητής τις οὕτως ἀπεφήνατο,

οὔ μοι ἔτ᾽ εὐκελάδων ὕμνων μέλει οὐδ᾽ ἔτι μολπῆς,

φάσις ἐστὶν ὅπερ οὕτω λεχθείη ἄν· "μοὶ—μολπῆς" κτλ.

9 Polyb. 4.18.7

οἱ δὲ Αἰτωλοὶ διὰ ταύτας τὰς αἰτίας ταχέως ἐγκρατεῖς γενόμενοι τῆς πόλεως τῶν ἀδίκων ἔργων ἐν τοῦτο ἔπραξαν δικαιότατον.

Id. 15.26a.1

Δείνωνα τὸν Δείνωνος ἐπανείλετο Ἀγαθοκλῆς, καὶ τοῦτο ἔπραξε τῶν ἀδίκων ἔργων, ὡς ἡ παροιμία φησί, δικαιότατον.

Suda (iv.577.12 Adler)

τοῦτο ποιήσας ἓν κατὰ τὴν παροιμίαν τῶν ἀδίκων ἔργων δικαιότατον.

10 Polyb. 15.16.6

ἔστι μὲν γὰρ ὅτε καὶ ταὐτόματον ἀντέπραξε ταῖς ἐπιβολαῖς τῶν ἀγαθῶν ἀνδρῶν, ἔστι δ᾽ ὅτε πάλιν κατὰ τὴν παροιμίαν

ANONYMOUS ELEGIACS

8 Chrysippus, *On Negatives*

If a poet expressed himself thus,

> No longer do I care for melodious songs, no longer
> for song and dance,

it is a statement which could be made as follows: "I care for
. . . song and dance" etc.

9 Polybius, *Histories*

For these reasons the Aetolians quickly became masters of
the city, and among their unjust deeds they did this one
that was most just.

The same

Agathocles killed Deinon, the son of Deinon, and among
his unjust deeds he did this that was most just, as the prov-
erb goes.

Suda

Having done among his unjust deeds this one that was
most just, as the proverb goes.[1]

[1]The proverb is probably best represented either by Cobet's
pentameter τῶν ἀδίκων ἔργων τοῦτο δικαιότατον or by Bergk's
τῶν ἀδίκων ἔργων ἐν τὸ δικαιότατον.

10 Polybius, *Histories*

Sometimes chance counteracts the designs of good men,
and sometimes according to the proverb

ELEGIAC POETRY

ἐσθλὸς ἐὼν ἄλλου κρείττονος ἀντέτυχεν.

11 Dion. Hal. *de comp. verb.* 200-201

. . . πεντάμετρον ἐλεγειακὸν ἔσται συντετελεσμένον τουτί (Demosth. 23.1), "μήτ᾽ ἰδίας ἔχθρας μηδεμιᾶς ἕνεκα," ὅμοιον τούτοις·

κοῦραι ἐλαφρὰ ποδῶν ἴχνι᾽ ἀειράμεναι.

12 Plut. *Alex.* 53.5 (= Hermippus fr. 50 Wehrli)

οὕτω δὴ τὸν ἄνδρα πρὸς τὴν παλινῳδίαν τραπόμενον πολλὰ παρρησιάσασθαι κατὰ τῶν Μακεδόνων, καὶ τὴν Ἑλληνικὴν στάσιν αἰτίαν ἀποφήναντα τῆς γενομένης περὶ Φίλιππον αὐξήσεως καὶ δυνάμεως εἰπεῖν·

ἐν δὲ διχοστασίῃ καὶ ὁ πάγκακος ἔλλαχε τιμῆς.

cf. Plut. *Nic.* 11.3, *Sull.* 39.3 (*comp. Lys. et Sull.* 1.3), *de frat. amore* 2.479a; *Paroem. Gr.* i.76.2

ἔμμορε *frat. am., Nic.* cod. unus, *Paroem. Gr.*

although a good man, he met another who was better[1]

[1] The *Suda* (ii.350.6 Adler) cites the passage and explains the fragment as referring to Hyllus, son of Heracles, killed by Echemus of Tegea (reading Ἐχέμου τοῦ Τεγεάτου for εὐχέμου τοῦ αἰγεάτου of the MSS). For the combat see Herodotus 9.26.

11 Dionysius of Halicarnassus, *On Literary Composition*

. . . it will be a complete elegiac pentameter as follows, "and not because of any private hostility,"[1] similar to these words:

girls who lifted up their light footsteps (in the dance)

[1] The passage in Demosthenes is: μήτ' ἰδίας ἔχθρας ἐμὲ μηδεμιᾶς ἕνεχ' ἥκειν.

12 Plutarch, *Life of Alexander*

And so the man (Callisthenes), resorting to a palinode, spoke openly and loudly against the Macedonians, and after showing that faction among the Greeks was responsible for the increase of Philip's power, said:

in times of discord even the utterly base man wins honour

13 Plut. *Them.* 18.3

πρὸς δέ τινα τῶν καλῶν γεγονότων Ἀντιφάτην ὑπερηφάνως αὐτῷ κεχρημένον πρότερον, ὕστερον δὲ θεραπεύοντα διὰ τὴν δόξαν, "ὦ μειράκιον," εἶπεν, "ὀψὲ μέν, ἀμφότεροι δ᾽ ἅμα νοῦν ἐσχήκαμεν."

> ὀψὲ μέν, ἀμφότεροι δ᾽ ἅμα νοῦν ἐσχήκαμεν, ‹ὦ
> παῖ›

ὦ παῖ add. West

14a Schol. Aesch. *Cho.* 344a (p. 24.1 Smith), "νεοκρᾶτα" κρατῆρα. ‹   ›

> νεοκρήτου τ᾽ εἰσεπιλειβομένας.

-μένας / ‹σπονδάς› Weil -μένης Wilamowitz

16 Ps.-Herodian. *Philet.* 167 (p. 59 Dain) = excerpta 72 (p. 80 Dain)

> ‹– ‿‿ –› ὀλίγης ἐστὶ διδασκαλίας,

ἀντὶ τοῦ "ὀλίγων δεῖται πρὸς μάθησιν."

διδασκαλίης? West

17 Paus. 4.16.6

Ἀριστομένει δὲ ὡς ἀνέστρεψεν ἐς τὴν Ἀνδανίαν ταινίας αἱ γυναῖκες καὶ τὰ ὡραῖα ἐπιβάλλουσαι τῶν

13 Plutarch, *Life of Themistocles*

And to one of those who had been handsome, Antiphates, and who had earlier treated him with disdain but later courted him because of his fame, Themistocles said, "Young man, it's late, but we have both come to our senses."

It's late, (boy), but we have both come to our senses.[1]

[1] The same story of Themistocles and Antiphates is reported in Plut. *reg. et imp. apophth.* 185c, but with ἀλλά in place of δ' ἅμα.

14a Scholiast on Aeschylus, *Choephori* ("newly mixed")

Mixing bowl . . .

(libations?) poured of newly mixed (wine)

16 Pseudo-Herodian, *Philetairos*

it requires little instruction,

instead of "there is need of little to effect learning."

17 Pausanias, *Description of Greece*

When Aristomenes returned to Andania, the women threw ribbons and flower blossoms over him and all the

ἀνθῶν ἐπέλεγον ᾆσμα τὸ καὶ ἐς ἡμᾶς ἔτι ἀδόμενον·

ἔς τε μέσον πεδίον Στενυκλήριον ἔς τ' ὄρος ἄκρον
εἶπετ' Ἀριστομένης τοῖς Λακεδαιμονίοις.

18 Paus. 8.28.3

Ἄλεντος δὲ τοῦ ἐν Κολοφῶνι καὶ ἐλεγείων ποιηταὶ τὴν
ψυχρότητα ᾄδουσι.

19 Ath. 8.337e

. . . οὐκ ἀνοήτως γε τοῦτο φήσας ὁ αὐλητής· λόγος
γὰρ παλαιὸς ὡς ὅτι

ἀνδρὶ μὲν αὐλητῆρι θεοὶ νόον οὐκ ἐνέφυσαν,
ἀλλ' ἅμα τῷ φυσῆν χὼ νόος ἐκπέταται.

20 Aphthonius (*Gramm. Lat.* vi.112.20 Keil)

hoc quoque notandum in enuntiatione pentametri elegia-
ci; nam plerumque aurem fallit, ut in illo Graeco versu:

ἡμεῖς δ' εἰς Ἕλλης πόντον ἀπεπλέομεν.

nam si coniunctim Ἑλλήσποντον enuntiarimus, effugerit
aurium sensum, ut nequaquam versus esse credatur; at si
per hemistichium pronuntiemus, ipsa subdistinctione ge-
nus metri declarabimus, ita, ἡμεῖς δ' εἰς Ἕλλης, dehinc
πόντον ἀπεπλέομεν.

while sang a song which is still sung even to our day:

> To the middle of the Stenyclerian plain and to the
> mountain top Aristomenes[1] pursued the Spartans.

[1] A Messenian who distinguished himself in the second war
against the Spartans, fought during Tyrtaeus' lifetime.

18 Pausanias, *Description of Greece*

Even elegiac poets sing of the coldness of the Ales (river)[1]
in Colophon.

[1] See n. 2 on Mimn. fr. 9.

19 Athenaeus, *Scholars at Dinner*

... this was no foolish comment by the piper, for there is an
ancient saying that

> The gods did not implant sense in a piper, but with
> his blowing his sense flies out as well.

20 Aphthonius, *On meters*

This too should be noted in the delivery of the elegiac pen-
tameter. Frequently the ear is deceived, as in the Greek
verse,

> We were sailing away to Helle's sea.

For if we pronounce Helle's sea as one word (Hellespont),
it escapes the perception of the ear, with the result that it
is not thought to be a verse at all. But if we pronounce it as
a hemistich, we will show the type of meter by the very
separation, namely, "to Helle's," then "sea we were sailing
away."

21 Stob. 1.1.6

Ζεὺς πάντων αὐτὸς φάρμακα μοῦνος ἔχει.

πάντως codd., corr. Grotius

22 Stob. 1.8.15

οὐκ ἔστιν μείζων βάσανος χρόνου οὐδενὸς ἔργου,
    ὃς καὶ ὑπὸ στέρνοις ἀνδρὸς ἔδειξε νόον.

1 ἔστι codd., corr. Canter

23 Stob. 1.8.16

ὤφελεν ὡς ἀφανὴς οὕτω φανερώτατος εἶναι
    καιρός· ὃς αὐξάνεται πλεῖστον ἀπ' εὐλαβίης.

1 ὤφελον codd., corr. Grotius

24 Stob. 4.10.10 Εὐριπίδου ἐκ Τηλέφου (= fr. 702 N.²)

†τόλμ' ἀεὶ† κἄν τι τρηχὺ νέμωσι θεοί.

τόλμης ἀεὶ cod. A, unde δεῖ Meineke   τόλμα δή Bergk
τραχὺ νείμωσιν Bothe νέμωσιν S¹M

25 Schol. Eur. *Andr.* 184 (ii.265.15 Schwartz), "κακόν γε
θνητοῖς τὸ νέον"

διὰ τὴν προπέτειαν κακὸν τὸ νέον.

21 Stobaeus, *Anthology*

Zeus alone has cures for everything.

22 Stobaeus, *Anthology*

There is no better test for any action than time, which reveals a man's thoughts even when hidden in his breast.

23 Stobaeus, *Anthology*

Would that a hidden opportunity might thus be perfectly clear; it is enhanced most by caution.

24 Stobaeus, *Anthology* (from Euripides, *Telephus*[1])

Endure, even if the gods deal you a hard lot.

[1] If the passage is a pentameter, as it appears to be, the attribution to Euripides is improbable.

25 Scholiast on Euripides, *Andromache* ("youth is indeed a curse to mankind")

Youth is a curse because of its rashness.

ἡ νεότης ἀσύφηλος ἀεὶ θνητοῖσι τέτυκται·
εἰ δὲ δίκην βλάπτοι, πουλὺ χερειοτέρη.

2 εἰ δὲ δίκαιον οὐ δύναται ἔχειν χερειοτέρα cod. O   πολὺ
M, corr. Matthiae

26 Macar. 8.39 (*Paroem. Gr.* ii.219.10)

τὸν φρουρὸν φρουρεῖν χρή, τὸν ἐρῶντα δ' ἐρᾶν.

χρὴ φρουρεῖν codd., transp. Bergk

27 P. Berol. 13270, ed. Schubart-Wilamowitz, *BKT*
v(2).62

χαίρετε, συμπόται ἄνδρες ὁμ[......· ἐ]ξ ἀγαθοῦ
    γὰρ
ἀρξάμενος τελέω τὸν λόγον [ε]ἰς ἀγα[θό]ν.
χρὴ δ', ὅταν εἰς τοιοῦτο συνέλθωμεν φίλοι
    ἄνδρες
πρᾶγμα, γελᾶν παίζειν χρησαμένους ἀρετῆι,
5   ἥδεσθαί τε συνόντας, ἐς ἀλλήλους τε φ[λ]υαρεῖν
καὶ σκώπτειν τοιαῦθ' οἷα γέλωτα φέρειν.
ἡ δὲ σπουδὴ ἐπέσθω, ἀκούωμέν [τε λ]εγόντων
ἐν μέρει· ἥδ' ἀρετὴ συμποσίου πέλεται.
τοῦ δὲ ποταρχοῦντος πειθώμεθα· ταῦτα γάρ ἐστιν
10   ἔργ' ἀνδρῶν ἀγαθῶν εὐλογίαν τε φέρει.

1 ὁμ[ήλικες Schubart, ὁμ[όφρονες Pellizer   6 φέρει
Wilamowitz   7 [τε λ]εγόντων Wilamowitz, [δὲ λ]εγόντων
Ferrari   10 φέρειν pap., corr. Wilamowitz

Youth is ever headstrong among mortals; but if it should harm justice, it is far worse.

26 Macarius, *Proverbs*

The guard should guard, the lover love.

27 Berlin papyrus (c. 300 B.C.)

Hail, fellow drinkers, (age-mates?). Fine was my beginning and fine will be the end of my discourse. Whenever we friends gather for such an activity, we ought to laugh and joke, behaving properly, take pleasure in being together, engage in foolish talk with one another, and utter jests such as to arouse laughter. But let seriousness follow and let us listen to the speakers in their turn: this is the best form of symposium. And let us obey the symposiarch: this is the conduct of good men and it wins praise.[1]

[1] Or possibly "produces good discourse." For a commentary on the poem see F. Ferrari, *SCO* 38 (1988) 219-27.

61 P. Oxy. xxx.2507, ed. Lobel

]νοσ[

]λος ατε[

].η πολυω[νυμ-

]μιν πῆμ' ἐφυτ[ευ-

5   ο]ὐκ ἂν ἔγωγε μ[

]των φάσγανον[

]ην μοι κεχαρισμ[έν-

]νεην Θεσσαλ[

]στος Ἀθηναίησ[

10   ]ν δῶρον ἐπιστ[αμεν-

ἀ]λκὴν ἐρρύσατο .[

]δακρυόεντα β[έλεα

]η πυρὶ μὲν πολυ[

]γος λάμπετο και[ομεν-

4 ἐφυτ[ευ- Lobel, ἐφύτ[ευσε βροτοῖς West   8 κυ]νέην dub. West   θεσσαμ[εν- Tarditi   12 suppl. West   cetera Lobel

62 P. Oxy. xxx.2508, ed. Lobel

]ην τετράφαλον[

]τοῖσιν ἔβη ταχύ[

]ὲν γὰρ τοῦτ' ἔπος α[

]ισιν ἕνα πρόμον[

5   ].ας ἀσπίδας ἀντ[

].τείνηισι Καρύσ[τι-

]ον χῶρον Ἐρετρ[ιέων

ANONYMOUS ELEGIACS

61 Oxyrhynchus papyrus (2nd c. A.D.)[1]

... of many names[2] ... brought about bane ... I
would not ... sword ... pleasing to me ... Thessalian
(helmet?) ... Athena ... knowledgeable in the gift[3]
... valour, saved (checked?) ... woeful (missiles) ...
with fire ... gleamed burning ...

[1] The fragment begins with an hexameter.   [2] Probably an
epithet of a deity.   [3] A phrase found in Archil. fr. 1.2. Lobel
hesitantly assigns both fr. 61 and fr. 62 to Archilochus.

62 Oxyrhynchus papyrus (1st c. A.D.)

... (helmet?) with four ridges(?)[1] ... came swiftly ...
for this speech[2] ... one champion ... shields ...
stretches Carystian[3] ... land of the Eretrians ... de-

]ν ἔργον ἐμήσατ[ο
]πάλων βουσὶν ἐσ[
10]ης ἐς ἀνάκτορ[ον
]δυσμενέων ἑ[
]υσα μένει δ.[
]ωνδ᾽ εἶπε τάδ[
ἐ]νοπήν θωρή[
15]ν ἄνδρα Διὶ ξυ[ν
]ς ἐχέτω δόμο[
]ἀνέρα· τὼσφ.[
]λος ἔβη[
]τως ἔφε[
20]ἁδων .[
]ης ἀντ[
]εμουτ[
]άληι σὺν[
]ἔπαυσε[
25]λης ἁιτ[

1 κυνέ]ην e.g. West   3 ἐν Lobel propter accentum
5 ἀμφ[sscr. ντ   9 ἀντι]πάλων Lobel   10 ἐπ sscr. ς
14 θωρή[κων Lobel

492

vised a deed . . . cattle (of the adversaries?) . . . to the temple . . . enemies . . . stands fast(?) . . . said this . . . sound . . . man with the aid of(?) Zeus . . . let him hold . . . man . . . went . . . ceased . . .

[1] The compound occurs twice in Homer (*Il.* 12.384, 22.315) as a description of a helmet, but the meaning of φάλος is unknown.

[2] It is unclear whether this marks the beginning of a speech, with v. 13 its end, or whether this concludes a speech and v. 13 begins a second one. [3] Carystus was at the southern end of Euboea and Eretria (v. 7) on the west coast of the island. Fighting in Euboea is mentioned in Archil. fr. 3. For the verb Lobel remarks: "The subjunctive may imply a clause of the form 'as far as stretches', say, the Carystian plain, ridge."

*Composed in ZephGreek and ZephText by
Technologies 'N Typography, Merrimac, Massachusetts.
Printed in Great Britain by St. Edmundsbury Press Ltd,
Bury St. Edmunds, Suffolk, on acid-free paper.
Bound by Hunter & Foulis Ltd, Edinburgh, Scotland.*